OUT OF PICTURE

ART FROM THE OUTSIDE LOOKING IN

OUT OF PICTURE

ART FROM THE OUTSIDE LOOKING IN

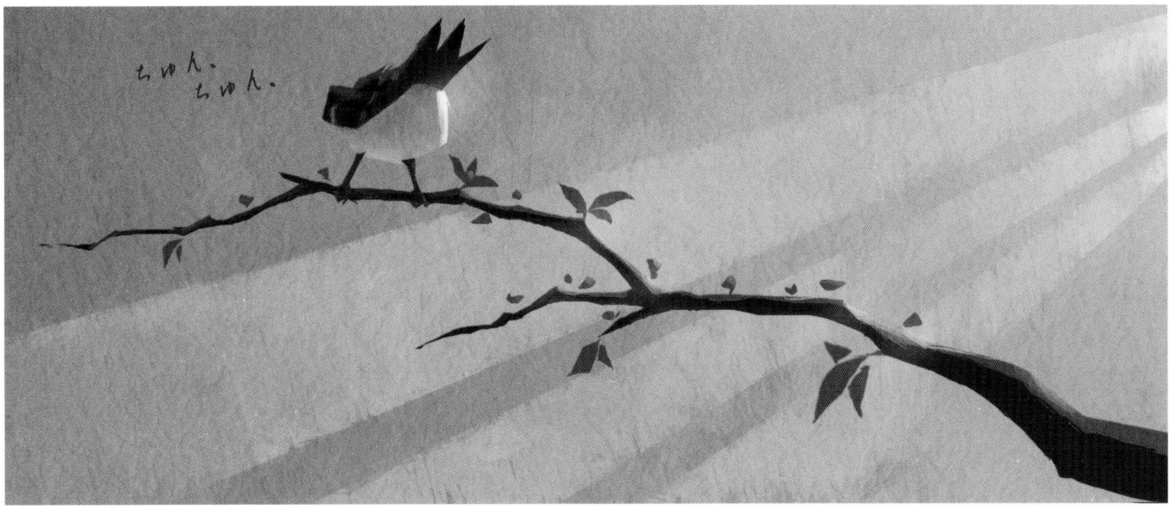
ちゅん。
ちゅん。

VOLUME TWO

VILLARD · NEW YORK

Villard Books Trade Paperback Edition

Published in the United States by Villard Books, an imprint of The Random House Publishing Group, a division of Random House, Inc., New York.

VILLARD and "V" CIRCLED Design are registered trademarks of Random House, Inc.

ISBN 978-0-345-49873-1

This edition published by arrangement with Out of Picture Press LLC.

Printed in China

www.villardbooks.com

9 8 7 6 5 4 3 2 1

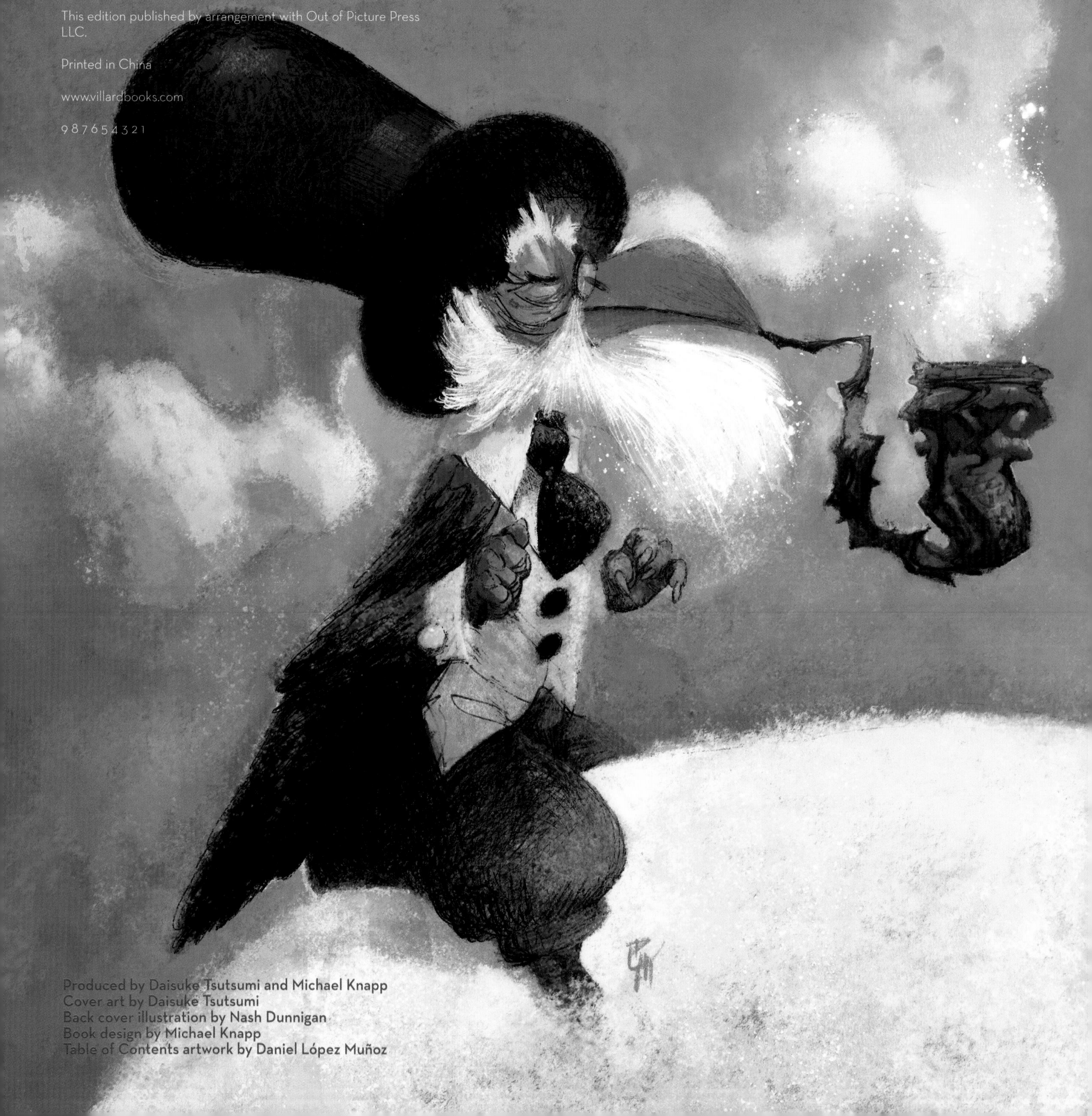

Produced by Daisuke Tsutsumi and Michael Knapp
Cover art by Daisuke Tsutsumi
Back cover illustration by Nash Dunnigan
Book design by Michael Knapp
Table of Contents artwork by Daniel López Muñoz

TABLE OF
(MAL)
CONTENTS

FOREWORD by William Joyce   9

PREFACE by Daisuke Tsutsumi   11

THE STORIES

1. "Sub Plotter" by Jason Sadler   14

2. "The Youth of Jimmy" by Benoit le Pennec   22

3. "Part 1" by Kyle MacNaughton   32

4. "The Antler Boy" by Jake Parker   42

5. "Are You the Right Color?" by Andrea Blasich   54

6. "Crawdaddyo" by Lizette Vega   64

7. "A Dream of Kyosuke" by Daisuke Tsutsumi   74

8. "The Carnivore" by Vincent Nguyen   94

9. "Plane Food" by Willie Real   102

10. "The Rupture" by David Gordon   118

11. "Why Bother? A Tale of Urban Relocation" by Nash Dunnigan   132

12. "The Fun Trip" by Sang Jun Lee   148

13. "Under Pressure: A Breakerboy Chronicle" by Michael Knapp   156

14. "The Missive" by Peter Nguyen   176

DEVELOPMENT GALLERY   191

Artist Biographies   234

Acknowledgments   236

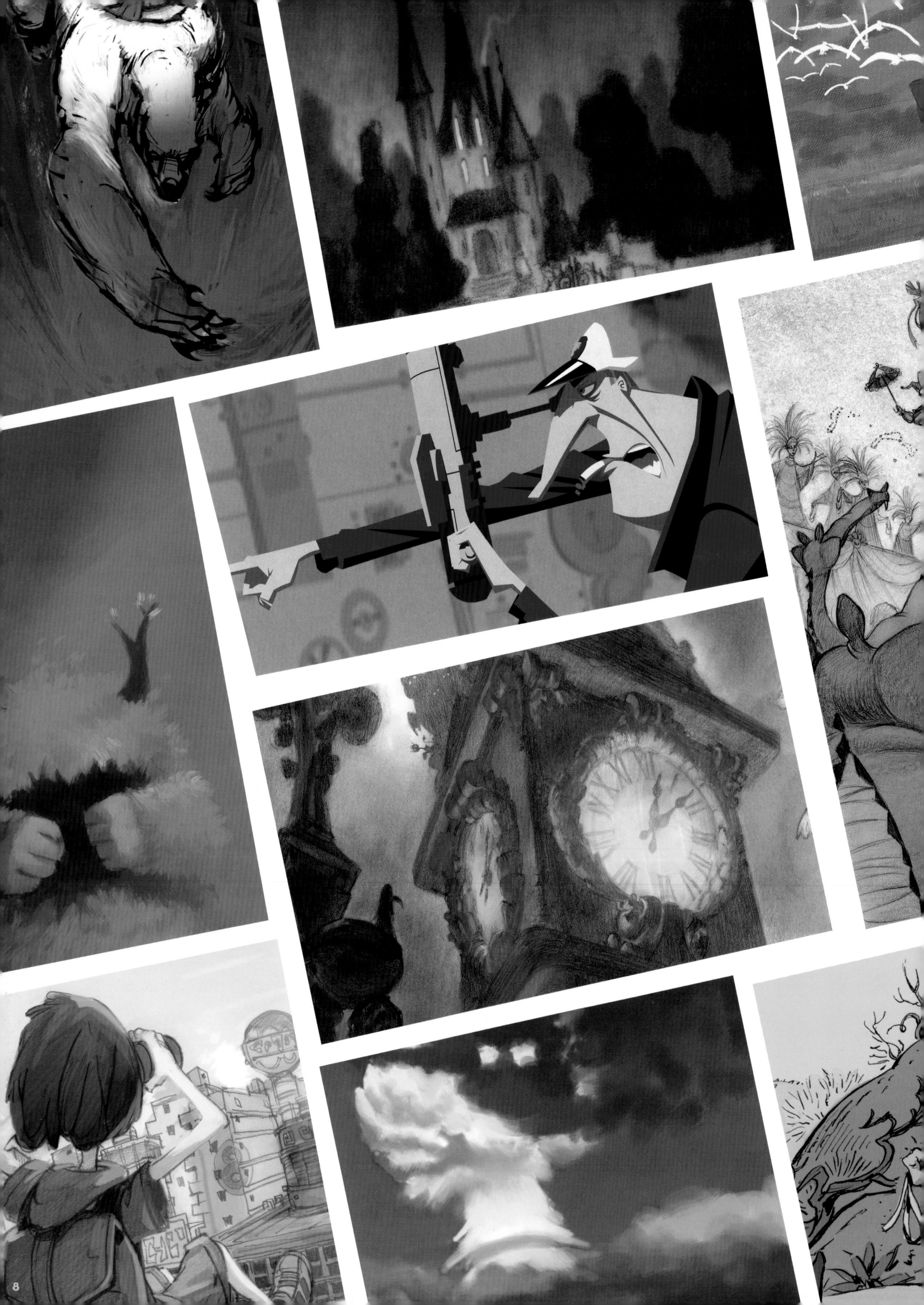

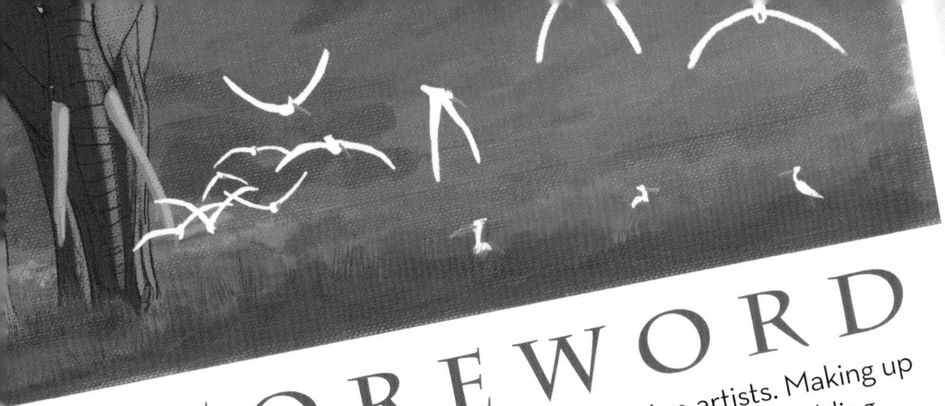

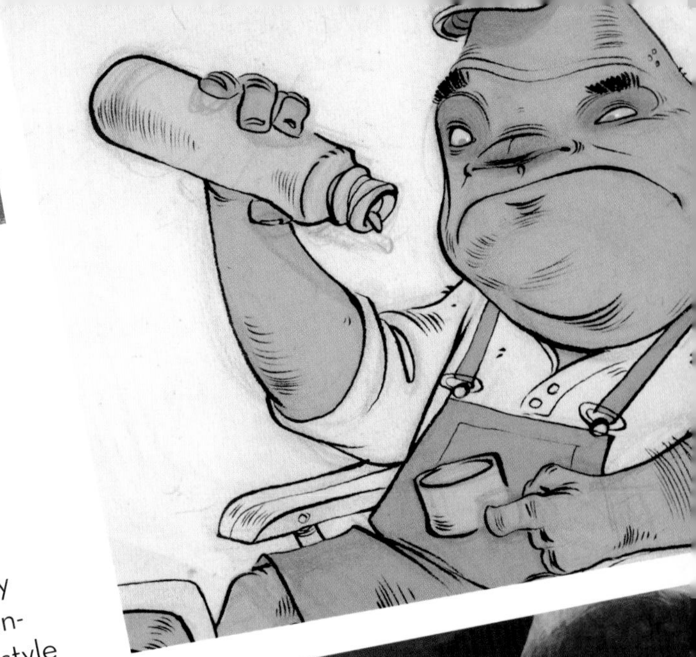

FOREWORD

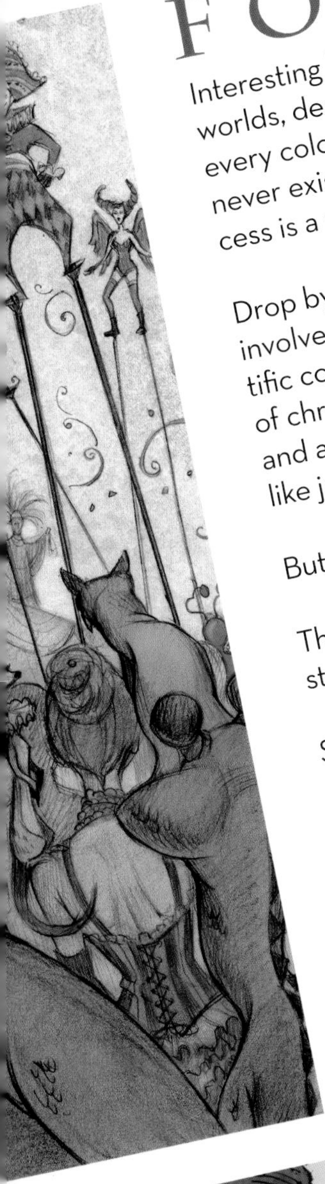

Interesting lot, the animation production artists. Making up worlds, designing the equivalent of movie stars. Adding every color, texture, and shape to lands and peoples that never existed. The diligence and care that go into the process is a wonder to watch.

Drop by the art department and you'll see people happily involved in the obsessive study of Slinky physics. Or scientific conjectures on mammoth fur. Or the most pleasing style of chrome trim to put on a flying car. It's a daydream of a job, and a real smile to walk among these artists at work: riffing like jazzmen on whatever tune they've been given.

But it's always somebody else's song.

The pieces in *Out of Picture* are all theirs. Their worlds, stories, people.

So, gentle reader, hang on tight. These cats can swing.

William Joyce
December 2007

Children's book author/illustrator, producer, and production designer of animated films

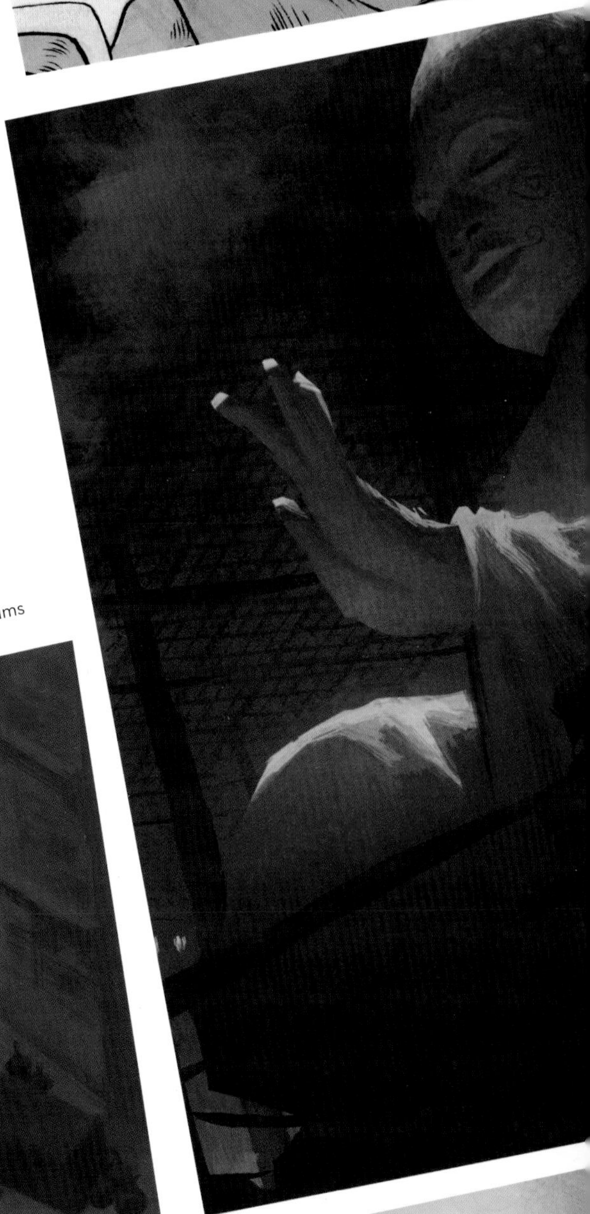

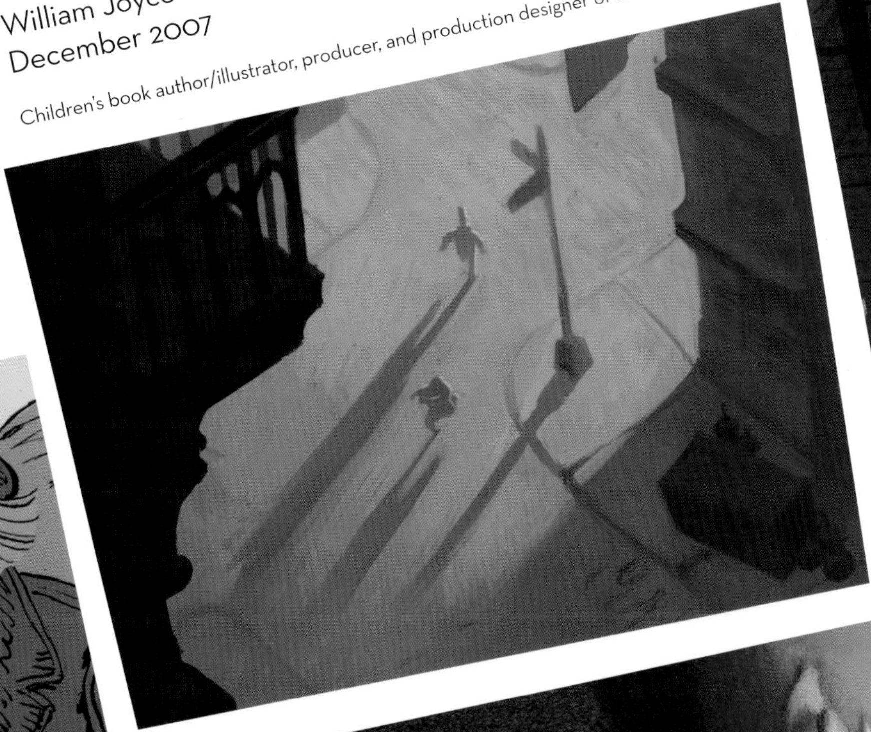

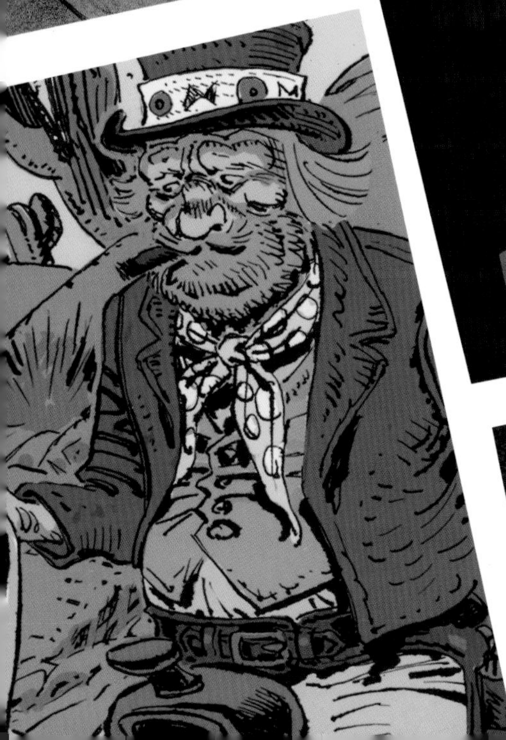

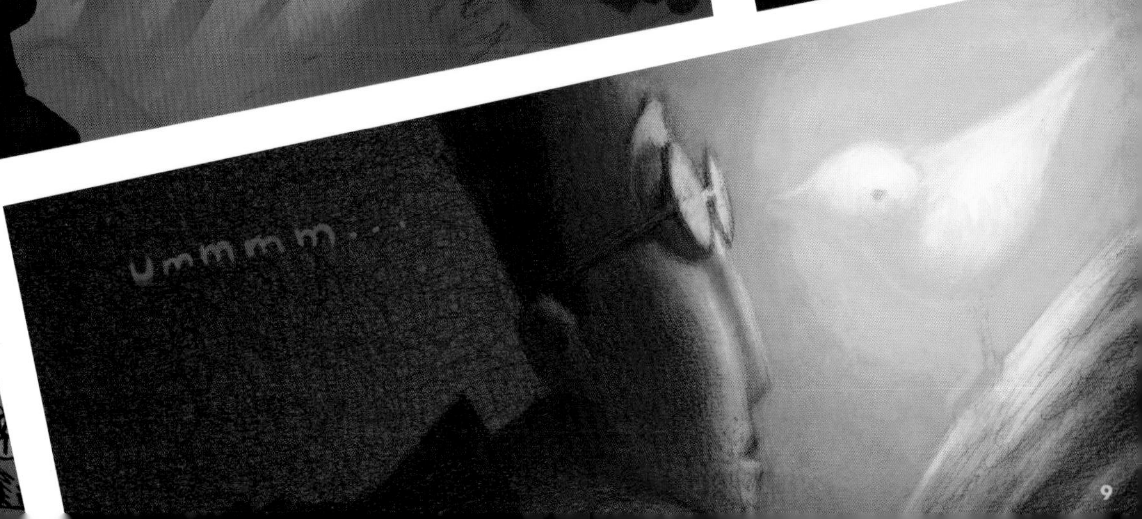
Ummmm...

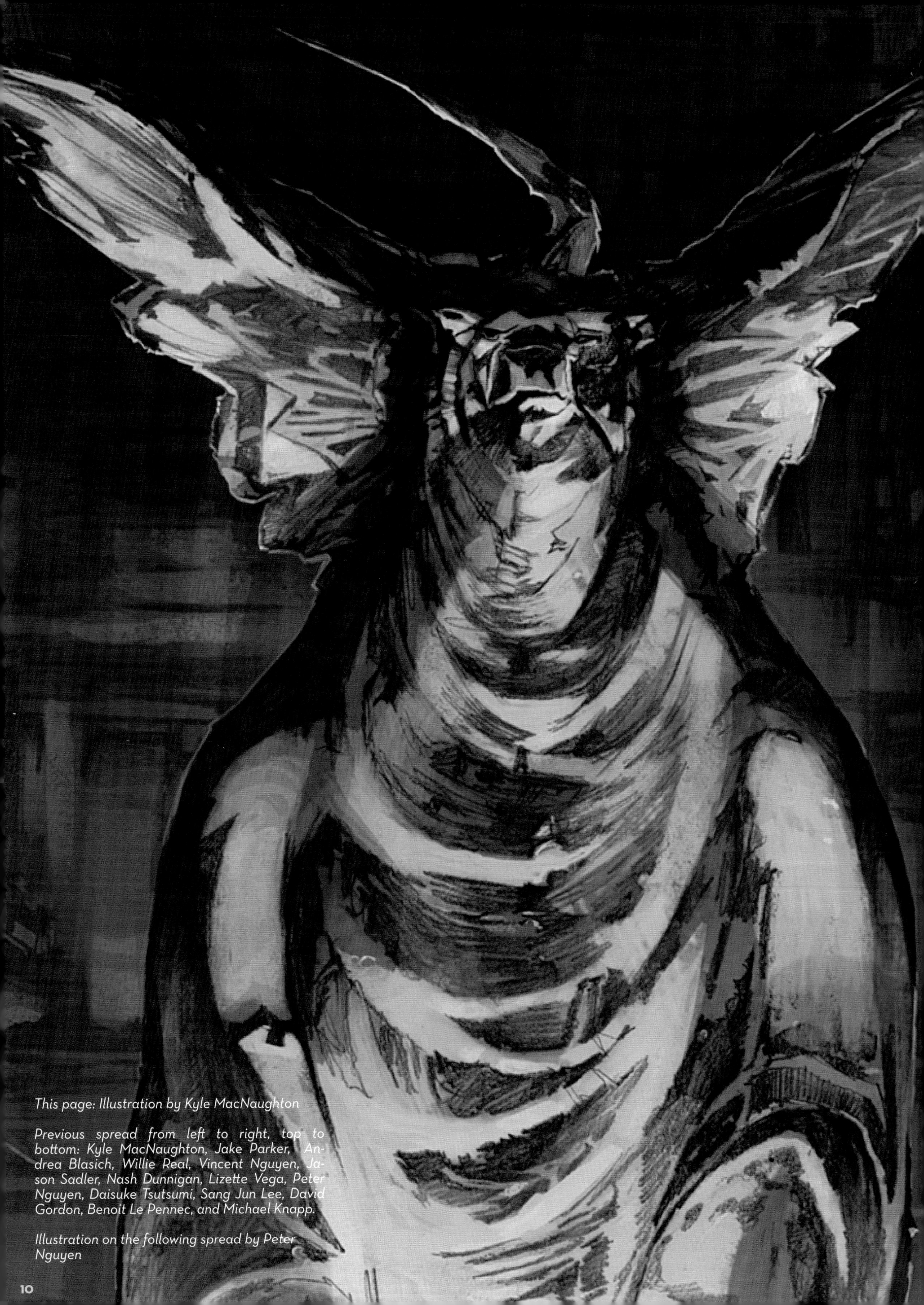

This page: Illustration by Kyle MacNaughton

Previous spread from left to right, top to bottom: Kyle MacNaughton, Jake Parker, Andrea Blasich, Willie Real, Vincent Nguyen, Jason Sadler, Nash Dunnigan, Lizette Vega, Peter Nguyen, Daisuke Tsutsumi, Sang Jun Lee, David Gordon, Benoit Le Pennec, and Michael Knapp.

Illustration on the following spread by Peter Nguyen

PREFACE

There was a period of time during which incredible artists gathered in the art department of Blue Sky Studios. The team chemistry was amazing. The work ethic was tremendous. It was like the '98 Yankees, where the concentration of talents in the lineup was too good to be true.

"We must document this." That is how Vincent and I started talking about this project in the car on our way home from work three years ago: a book to document this rare period in time.

This ambitious project was no easy business. OOP 1 and 2 each took us approximately twelve months to complete. We worked nights and weekends in addition to our already demanding day jobs. Of course, this process occasionally required brutal honesty, which caused some friction here and there, but it could not have been done without encouragement, support, and trust from one another.

Now some of us have left Blue Sky Studios and live far away from where it all began, but the Out of Picture project is the connecting link for our continuing friendship.

This book is a collection of our leftover "OOPed" imagination and inspiration, given with the heart and spirit that have been nurtured through our camaraderie over the years.

—Dice Tsutsumi

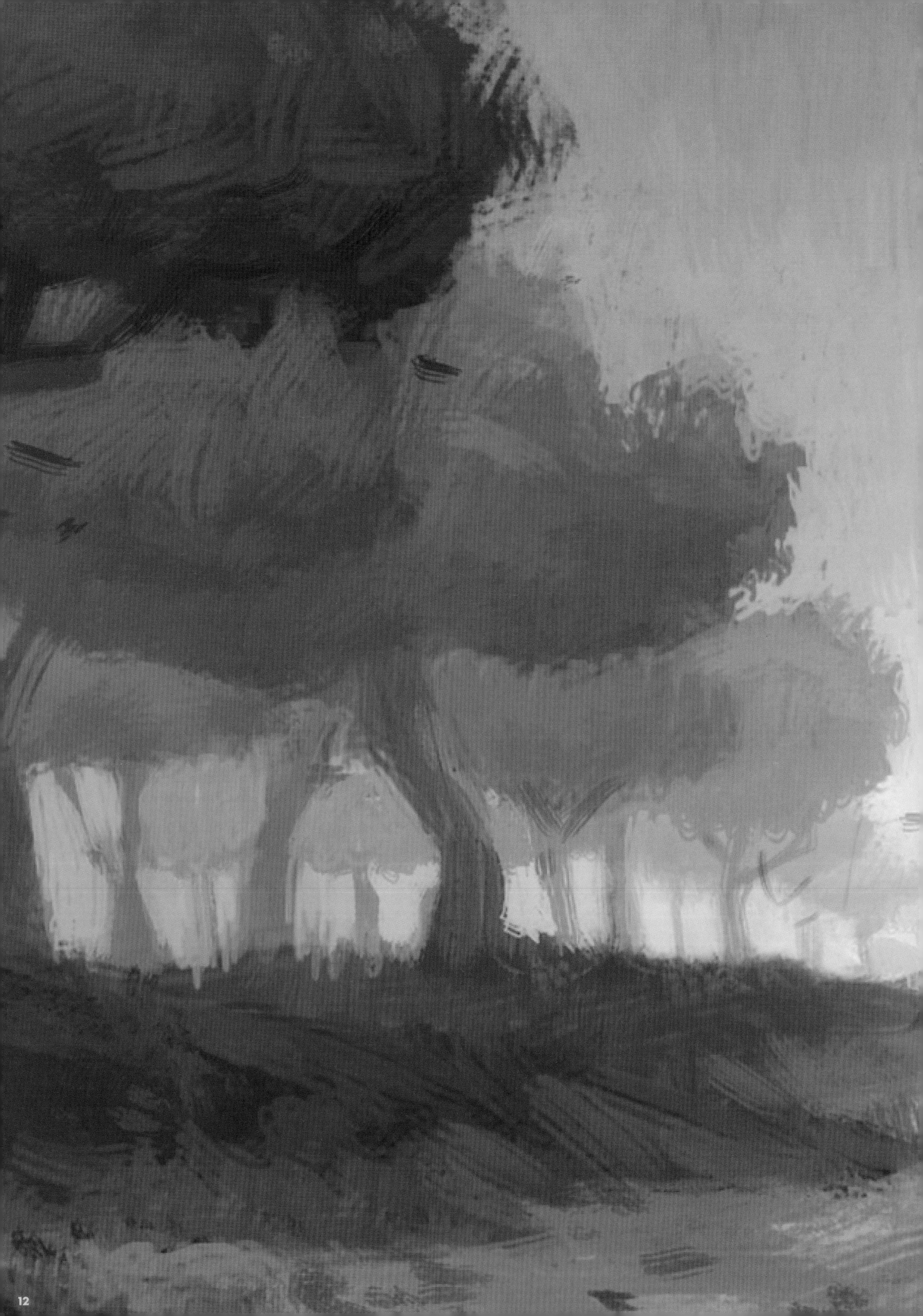

THE STORIES

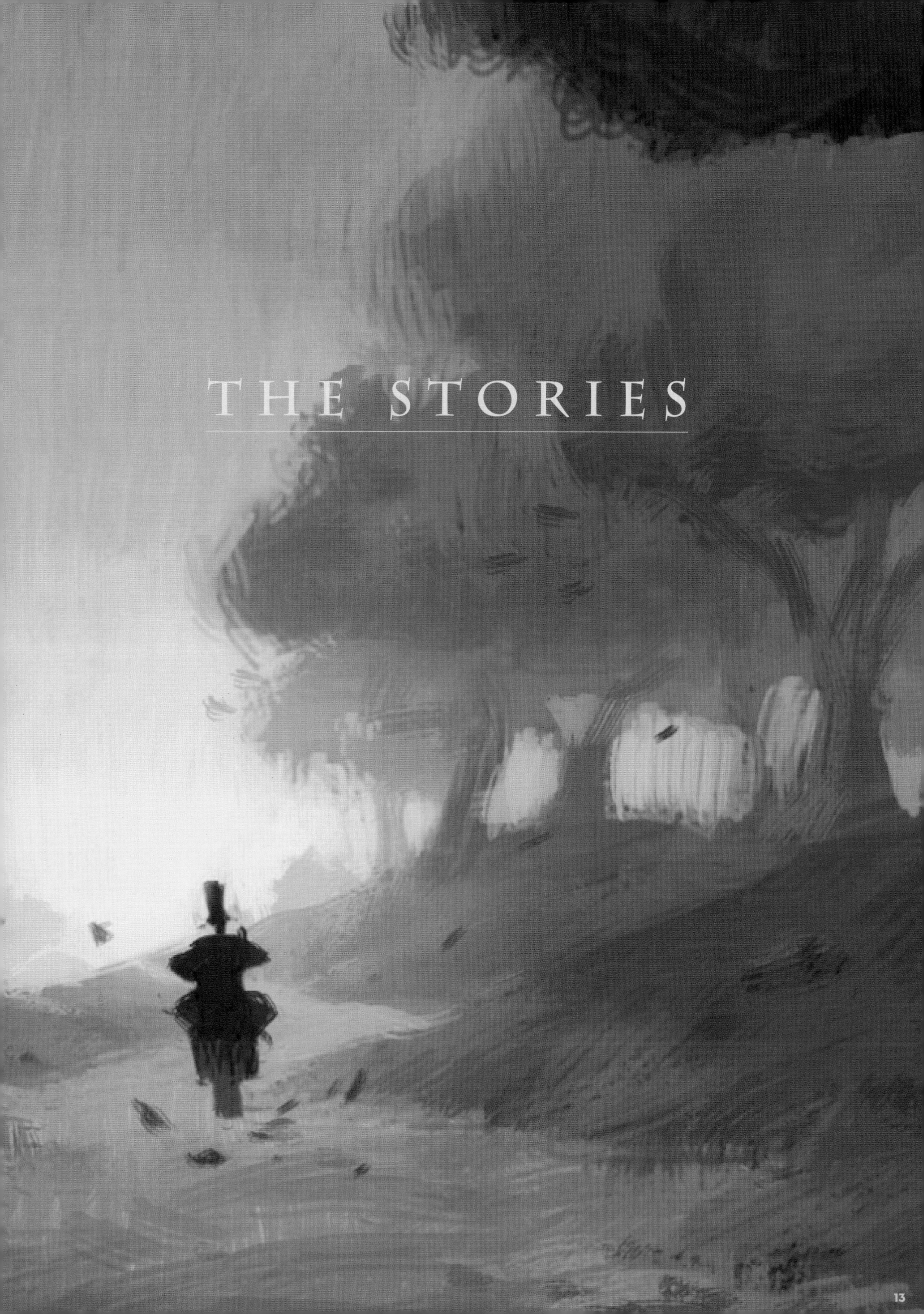

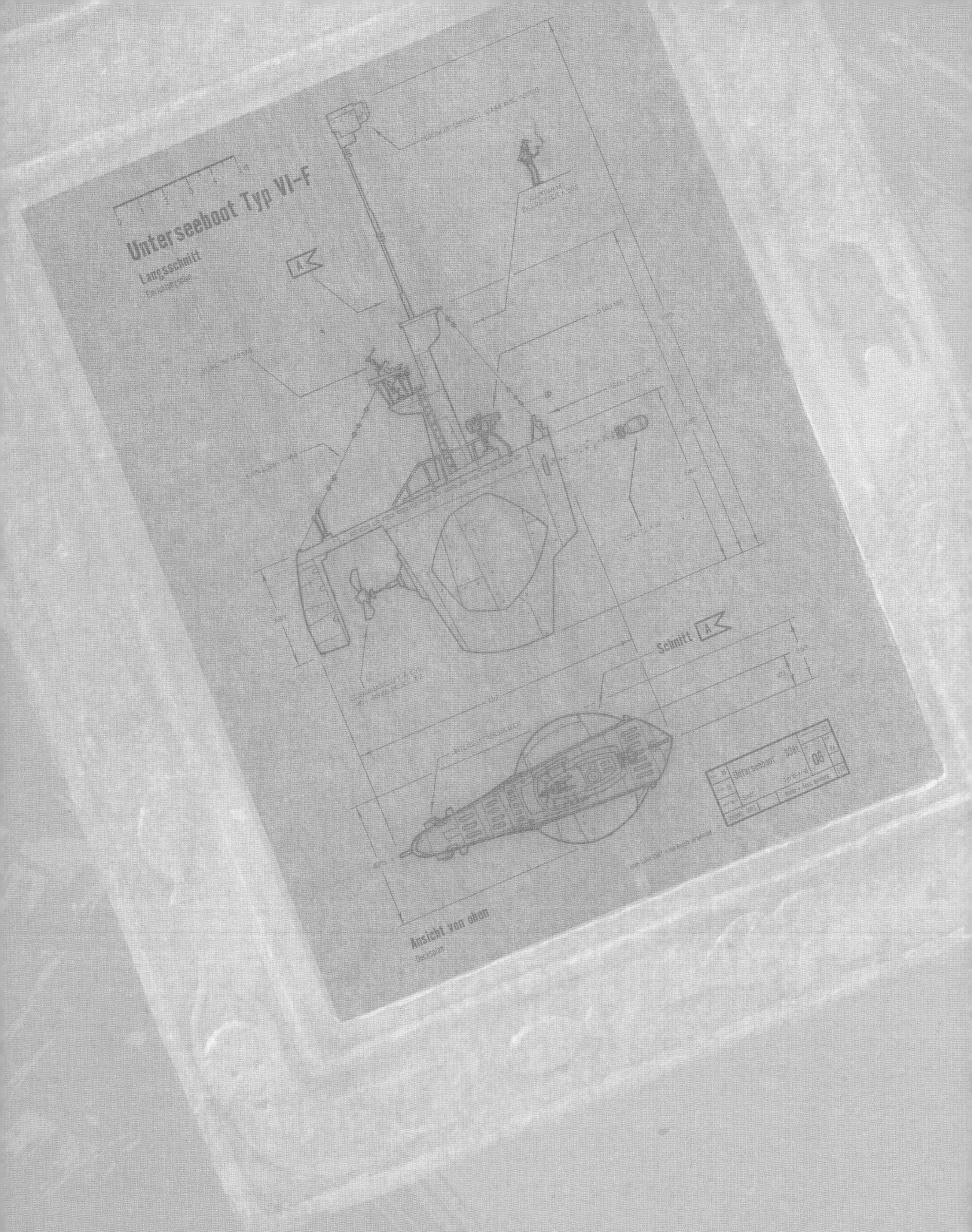
Unterseeboot Typ VI-F
Langsschnitt
Schnitt A
Ansicht von oben
Decksplan
Unterseeboot

JASON SADLER

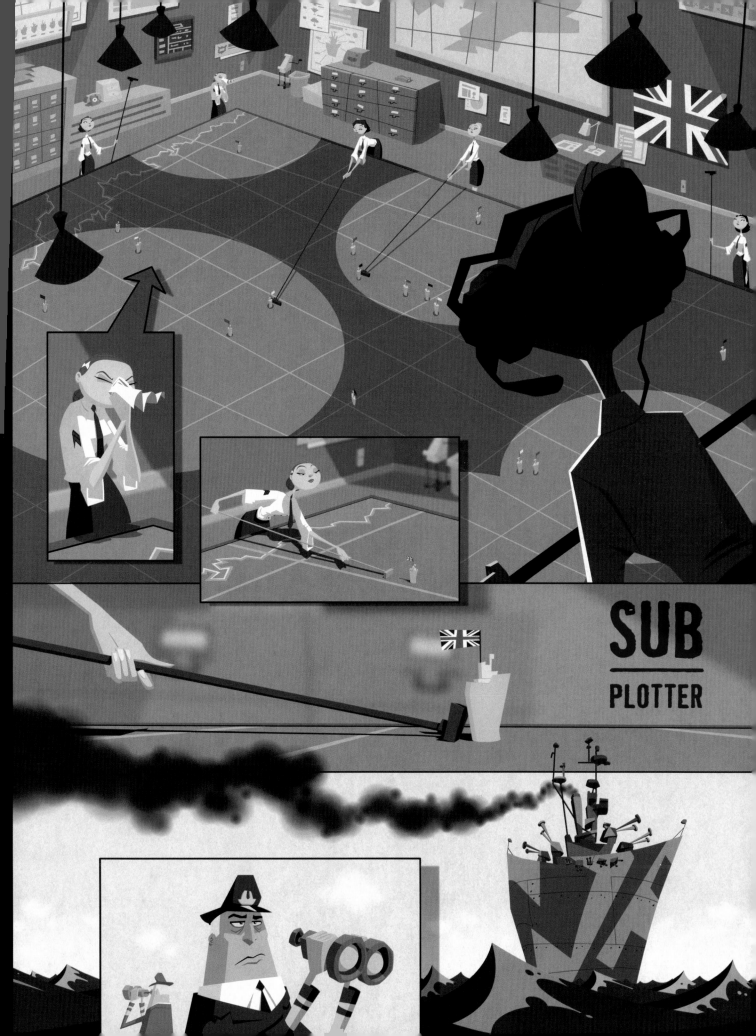

SUB
PLOTTER

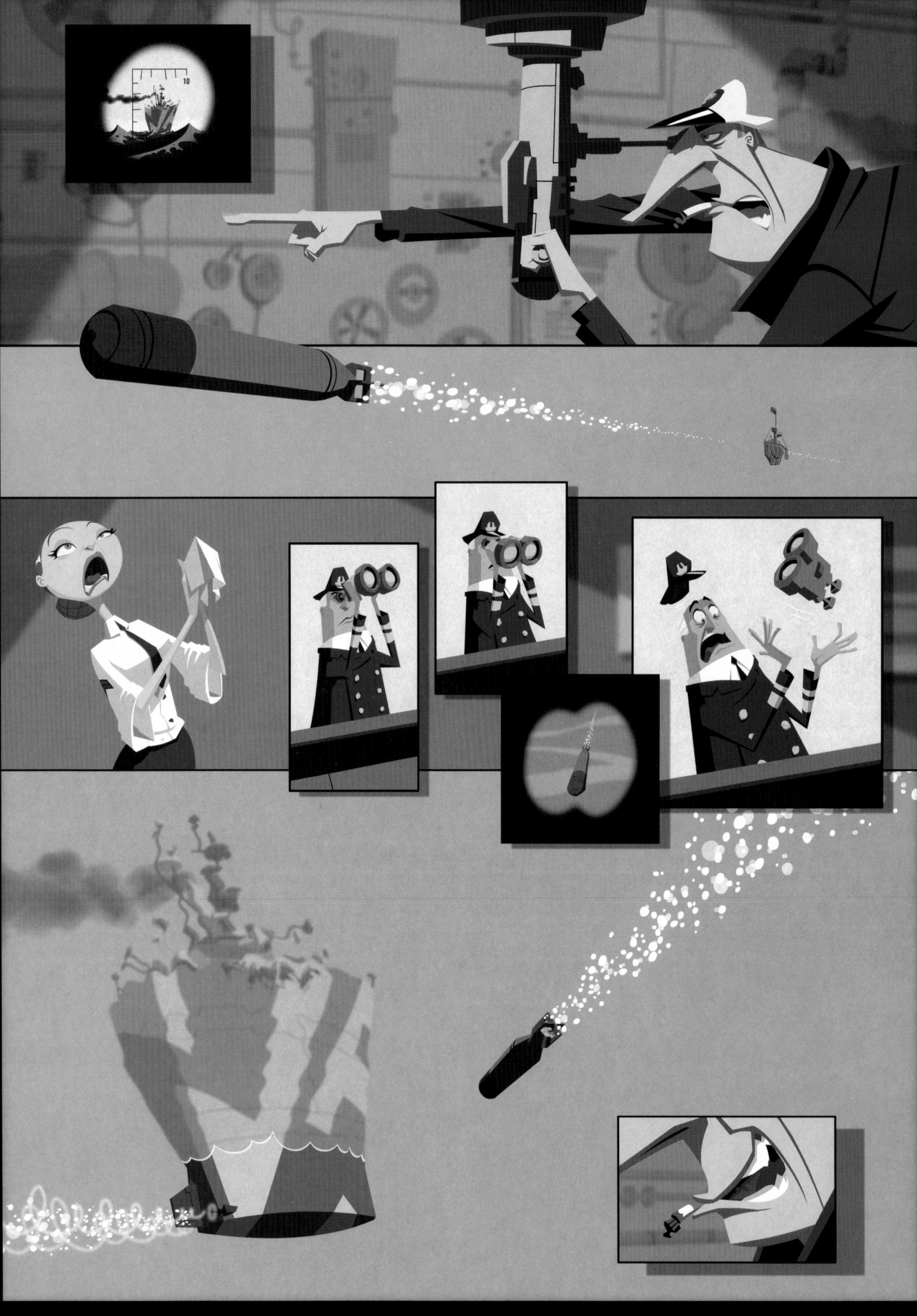
10

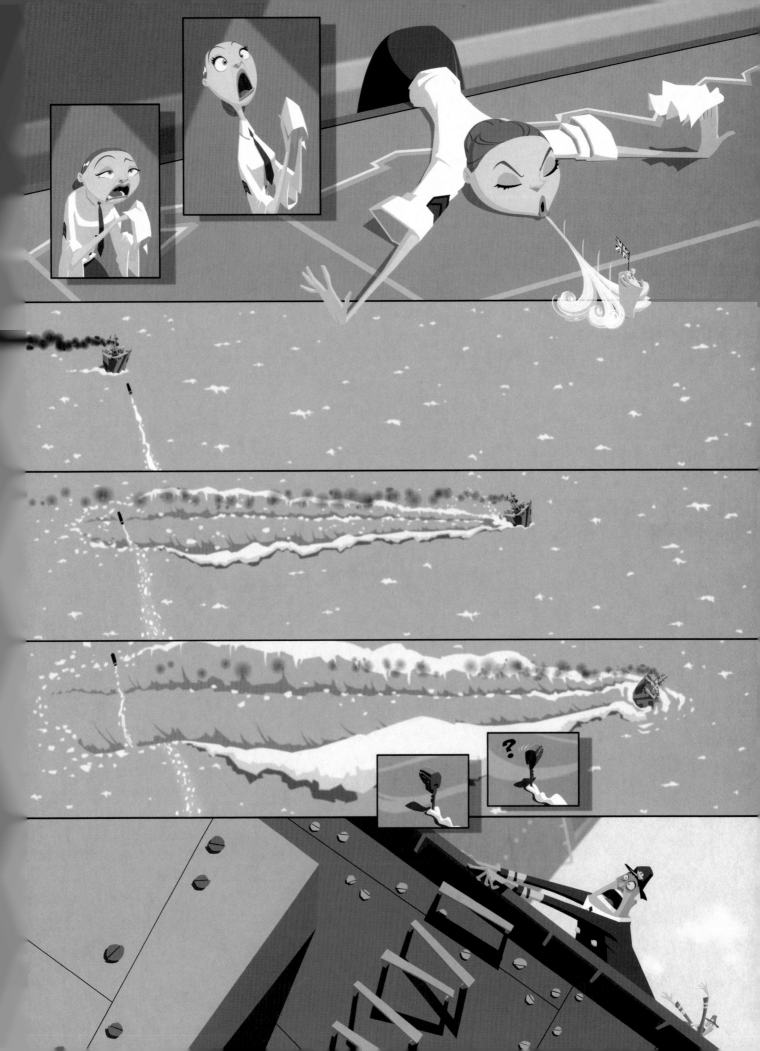

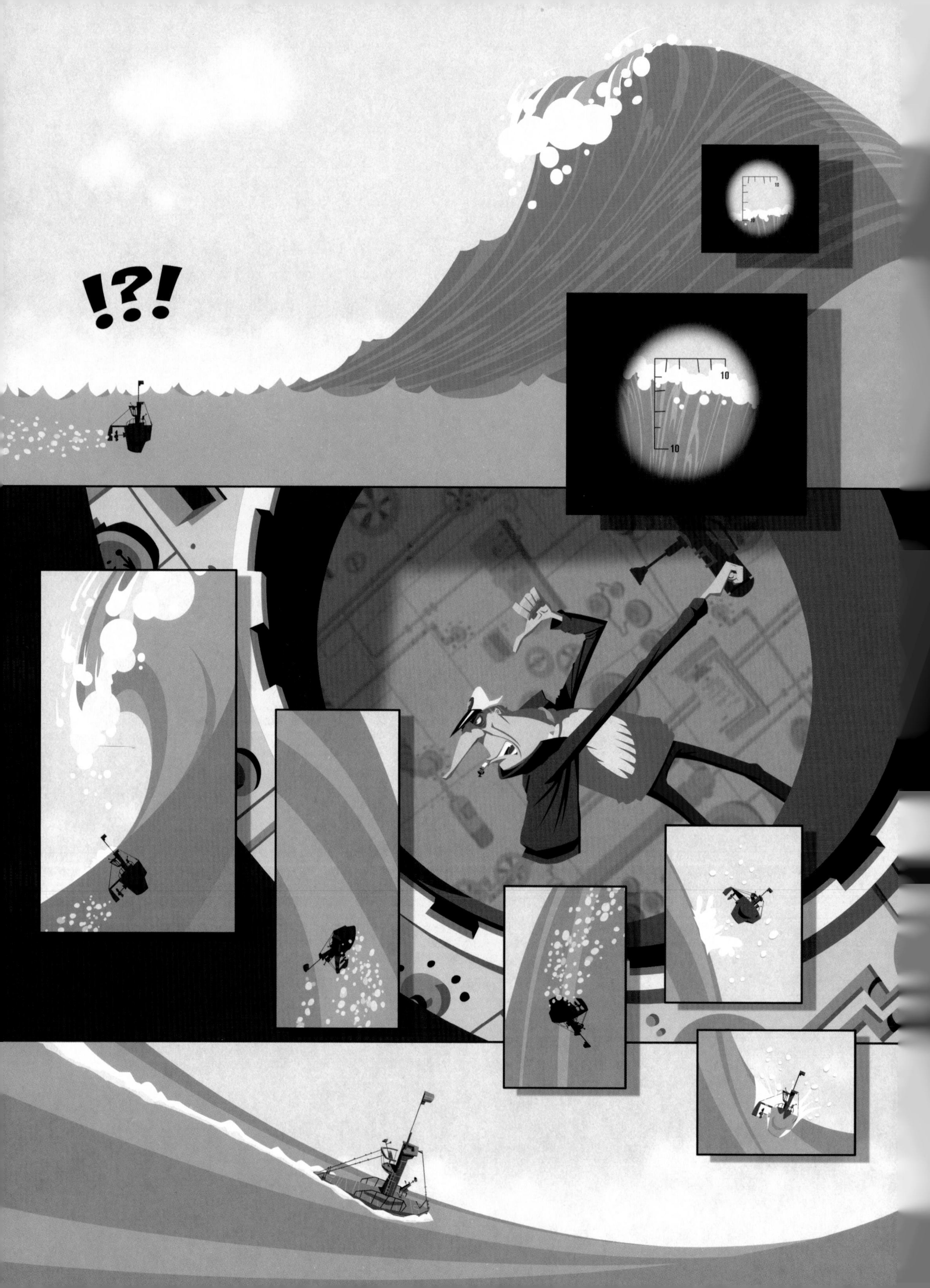
!?!

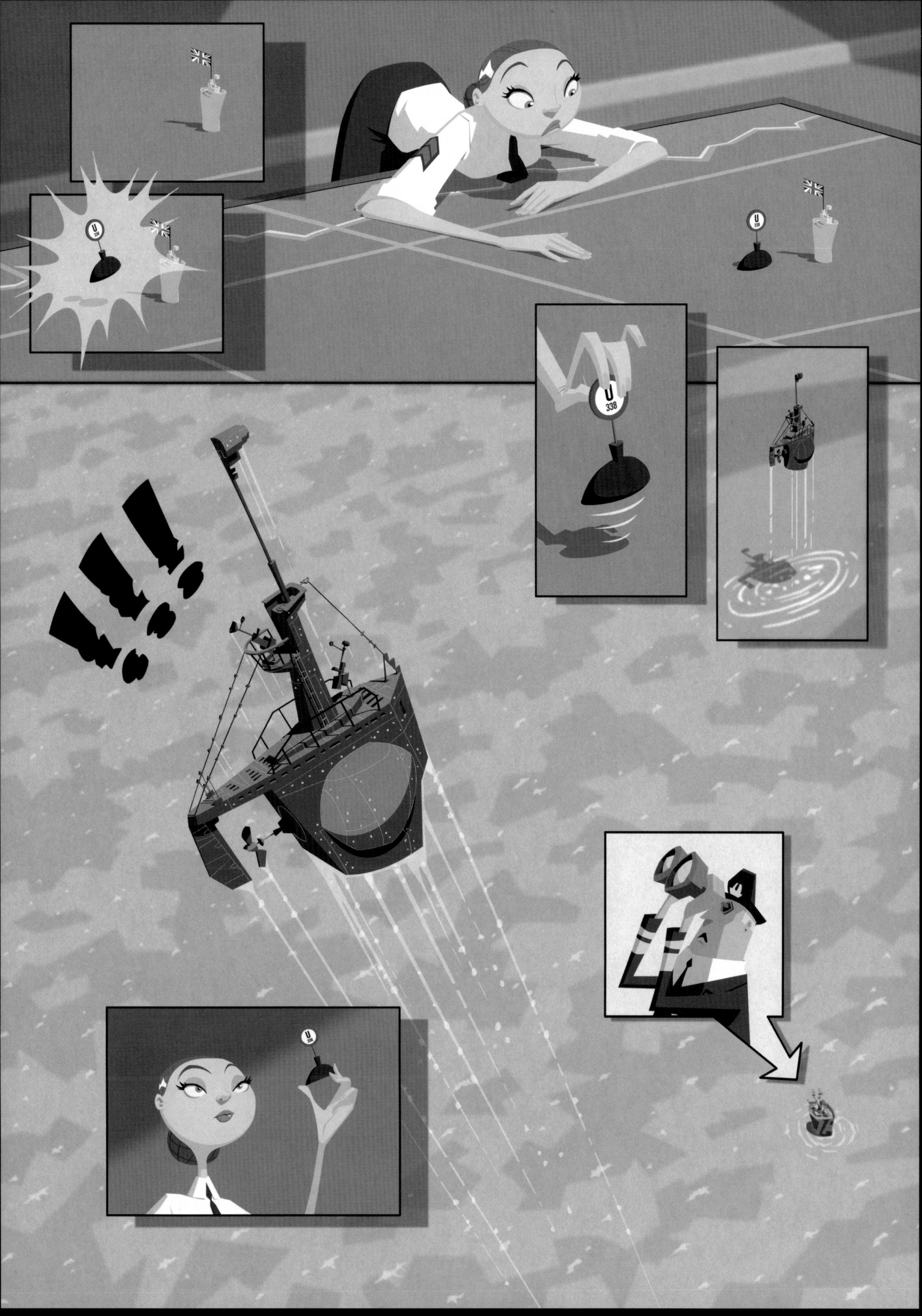
U
338

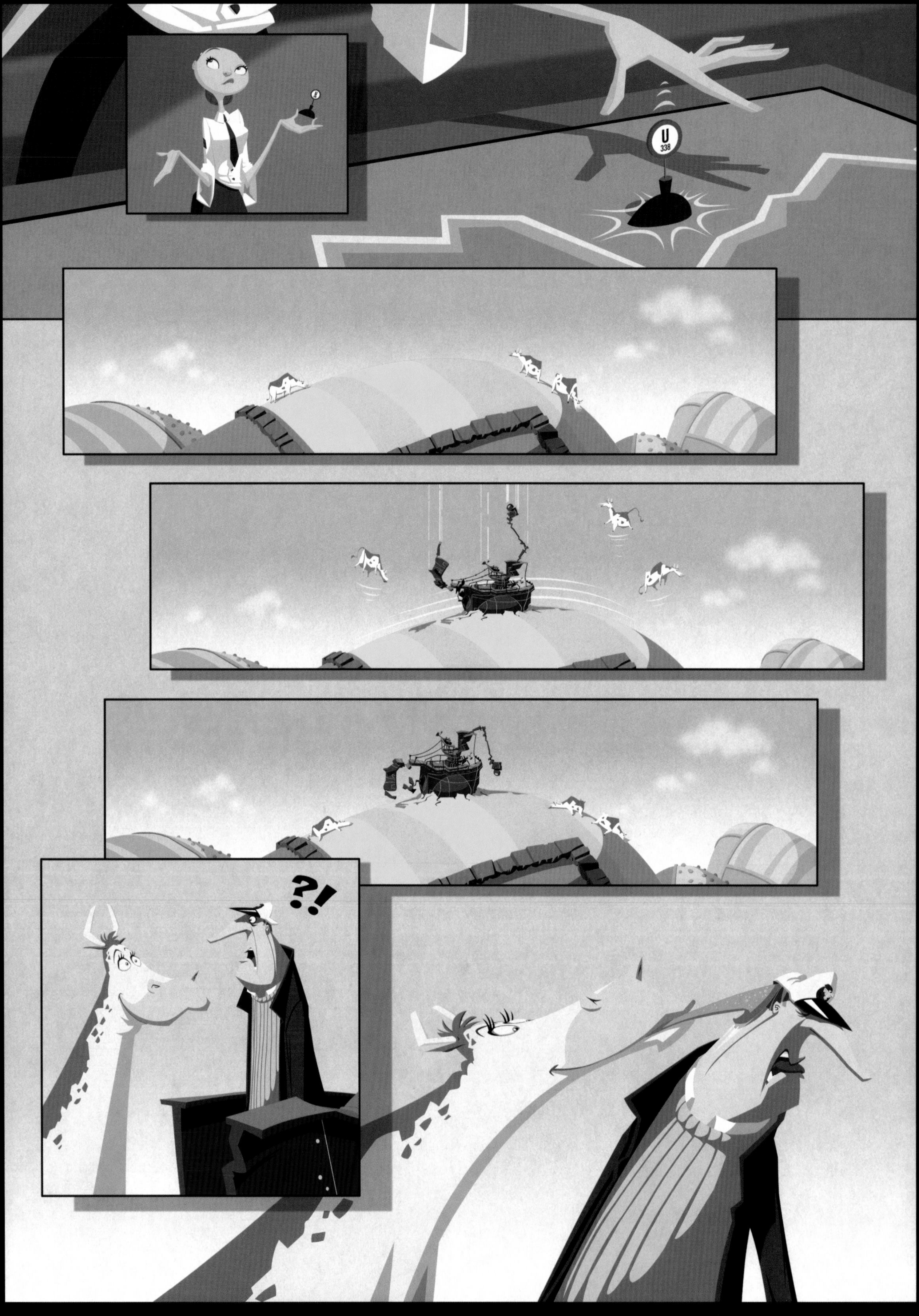
U
338
?!

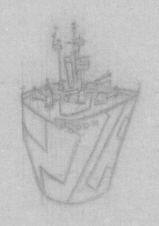

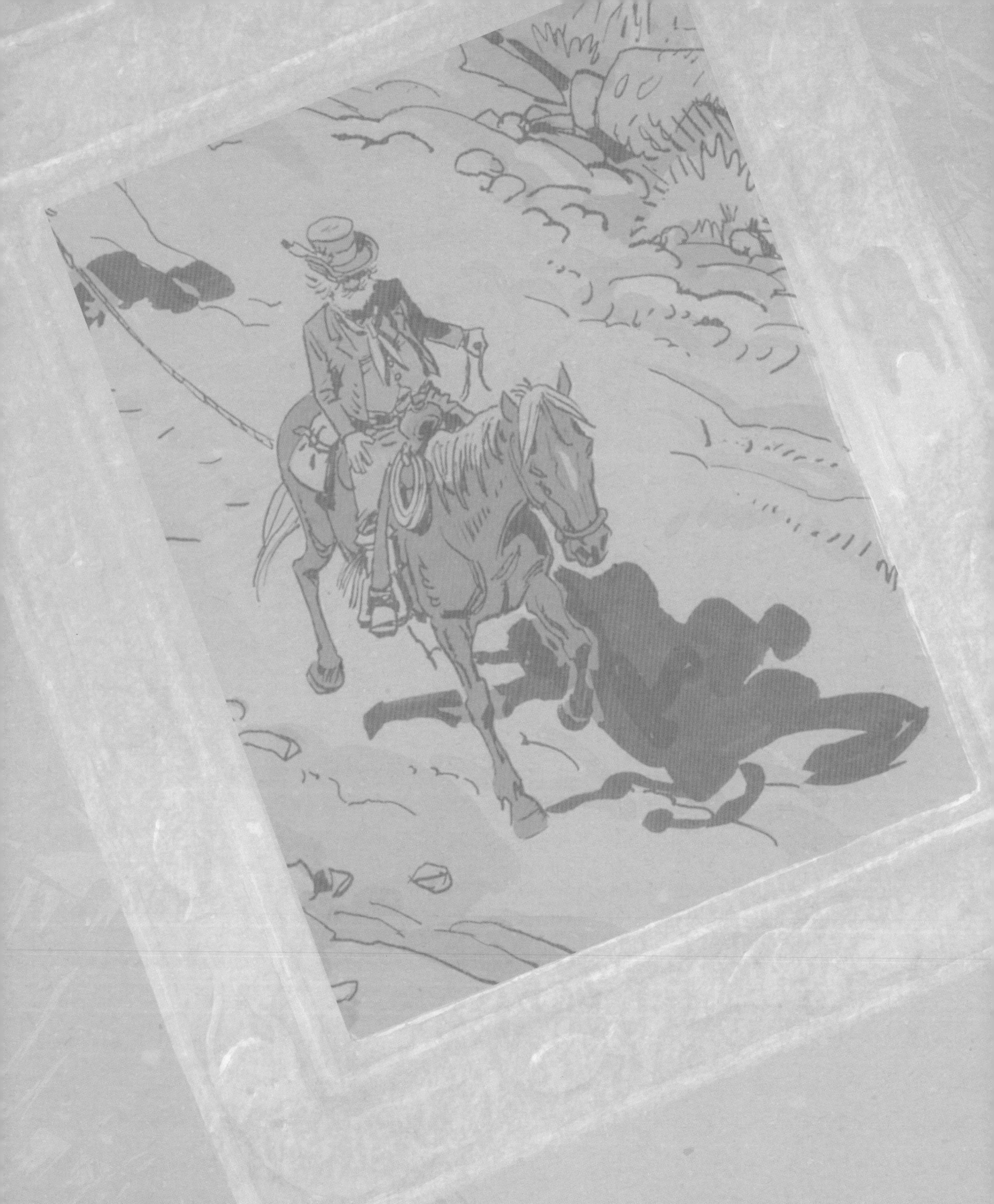

BENOIT LE PENNEC

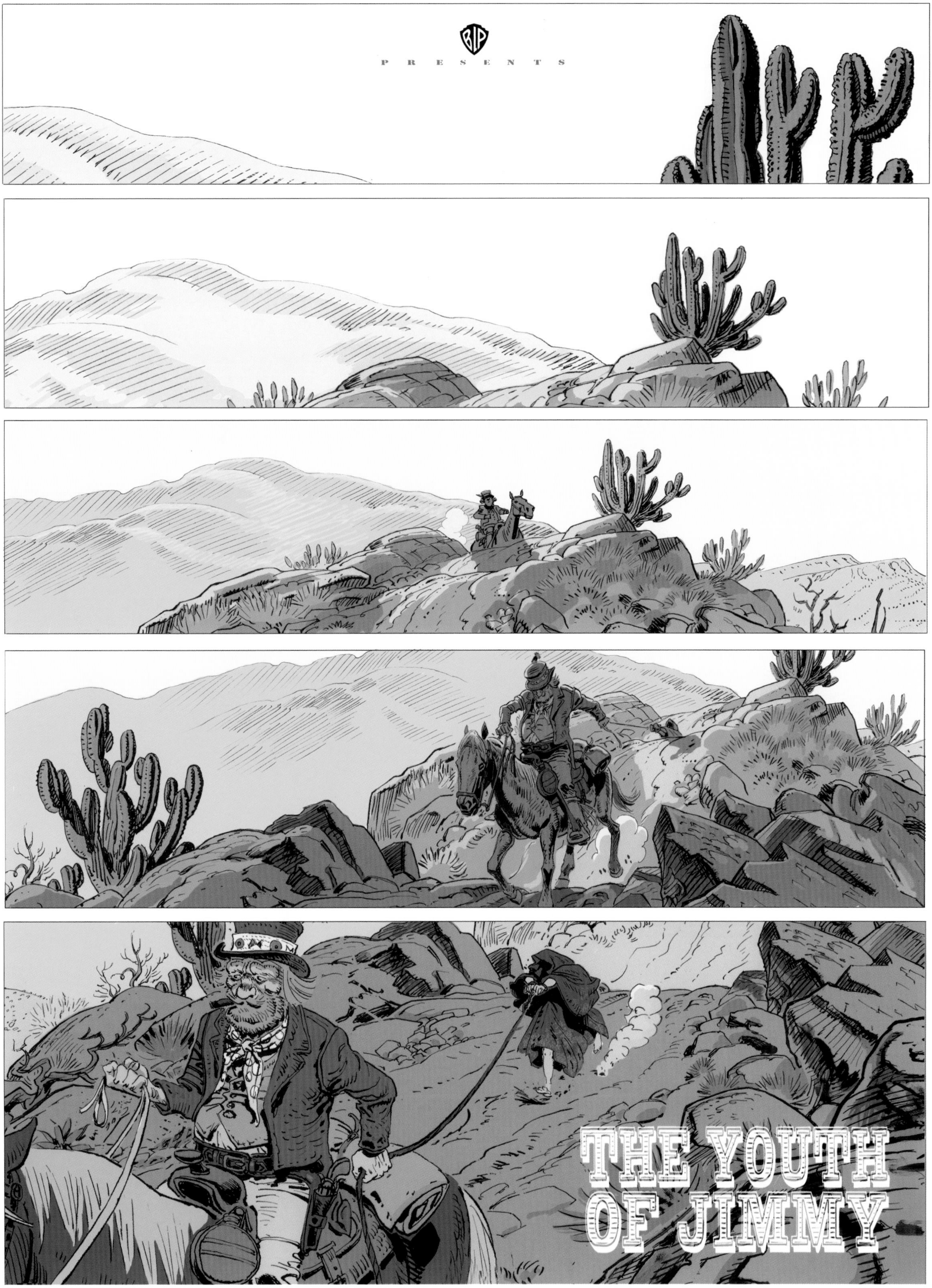
P R E S E N T S
THE YOUTH OF JIMMY

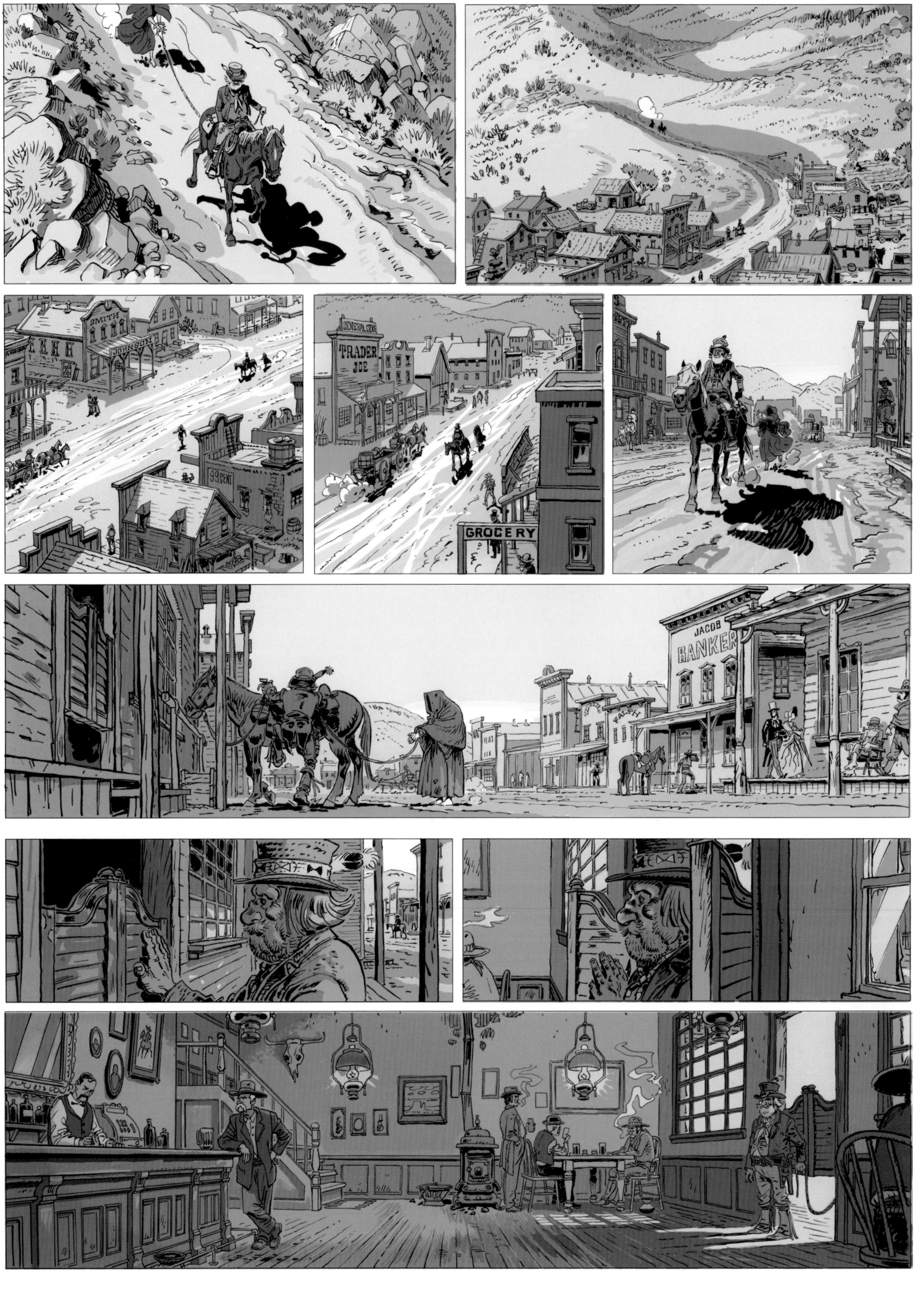
SMITH
JOHNSON
99 CENT
GENERAL STORE
TRADER JOE
GROCERY
JACOB
BANKER

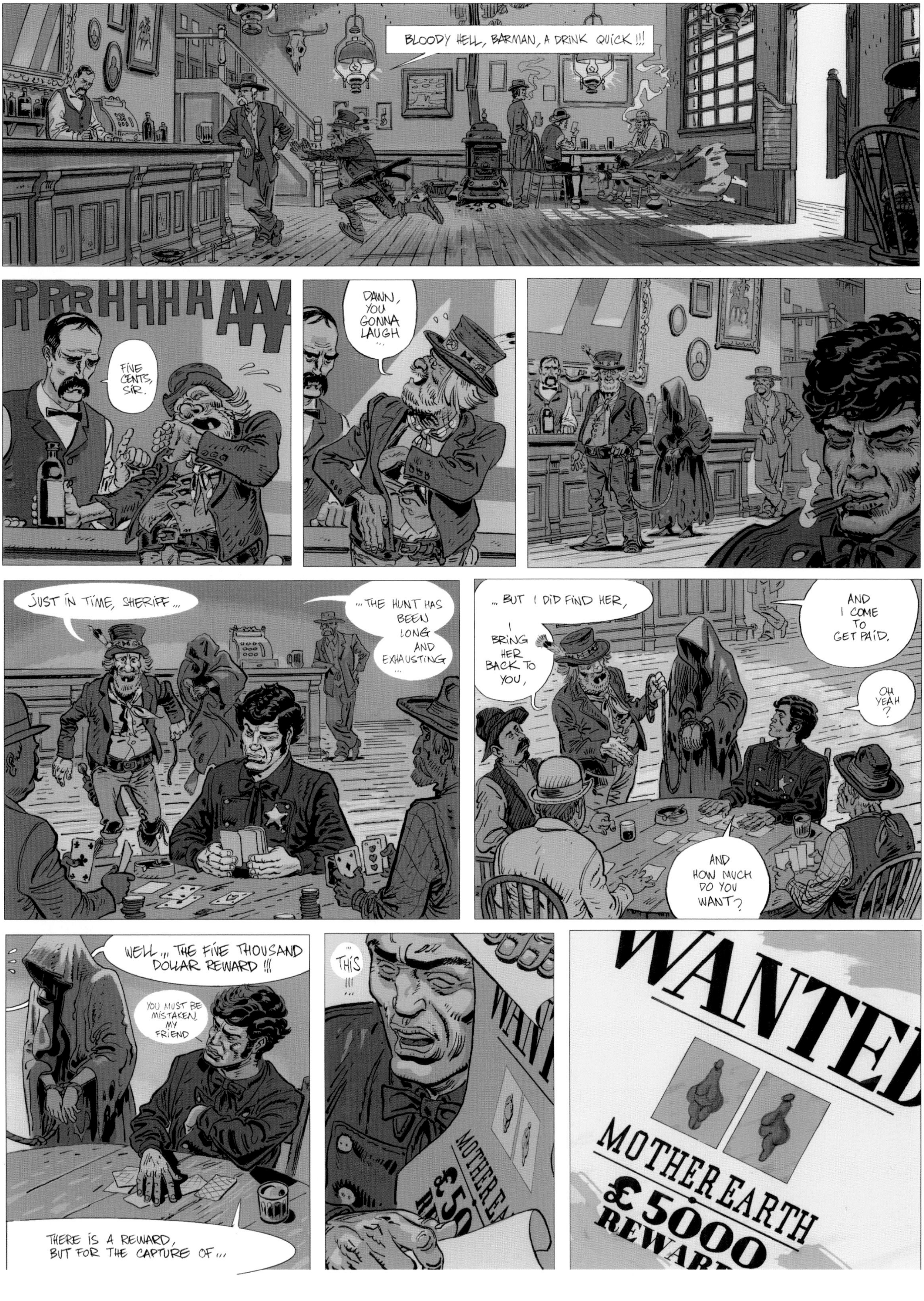
BLOODY HELL, BARMAN, A DRINK QUICK !!!
RRRHHHHAAAA
FIVE CENTS, SIR.
DAMN, YOU GONNA LAUGH ...
JUST IN TIME, SHERIFF...
...THE HUNT HAS BEEN LONG AND EXHAUSTING ...
... BUT I DID FIND HER,
I BRING HER BACK TO YOU,
AND I COME TO GET PAID.
OH YEAH ?
AND HOW MUCH DO YOU WANT?
WELL... THE FIVE THOUSAND DOLLAR REWARD !!!
YOU MUST BE MISTAKEN, MY FRIEND
THERE IS A REWARD, BUT FOR THE CAPTURE OF...
"THIS" !!!
WANTED
MOTHER EARTH
£5000
REWARD

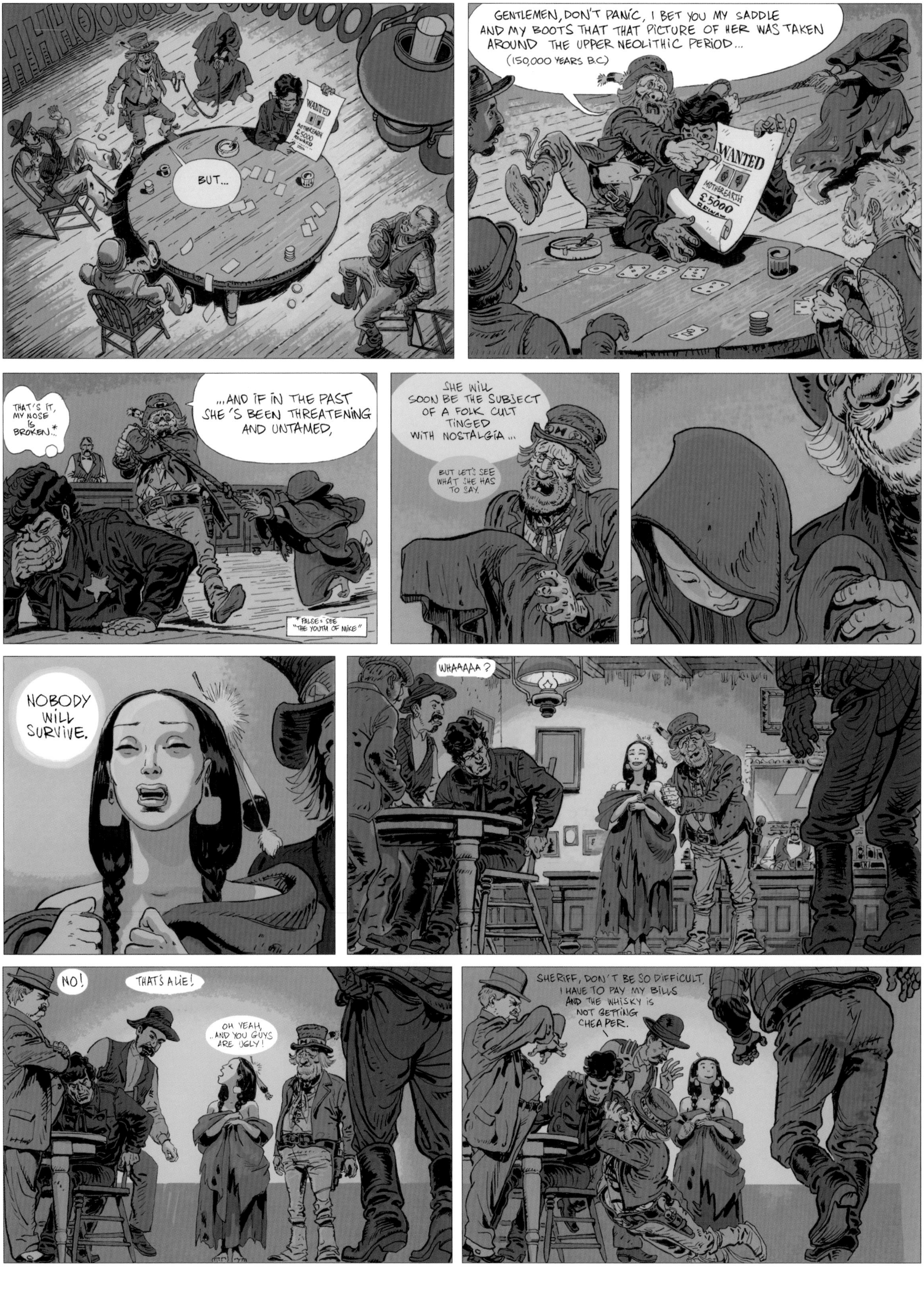

BUT...
GENTLEMEN, DON'T PANIC, I BET YOU MY SADDLE AND MY BOOTS THAT THAT PICTURE OF HER WAS TAKEN AROUND THE UPPER NEOLITHIC PERIOD...
(150,000 YEARS B.C)
WANTED
THAT'S IT, MY NOSE IS BROKEN...*
...AND IF IN THE PAST SHE'S BEEN THREATENING AND UNTAMED,
* FALSE: SEE "THE YOUTH OF MIKE"
SHE WILL SOON BE THE SUBJECT OF A FOLK CULT TINGED WITH NOSTALGIA...
BUT LET'S SEE WHAT SHE HAS TO SAY.
NOBODY WILL SURVIVE.
WHAAAAA?
NO!
THAT'S A LIE!
OH YEAH, ..AND YOU GUYS ARE UGLY!
SHERIFF, DON'T BE SO DIFFICULT, I HAVE TO PAY MY BILLS AND THE WHISKY IS NOT GETTING CHEAPER.

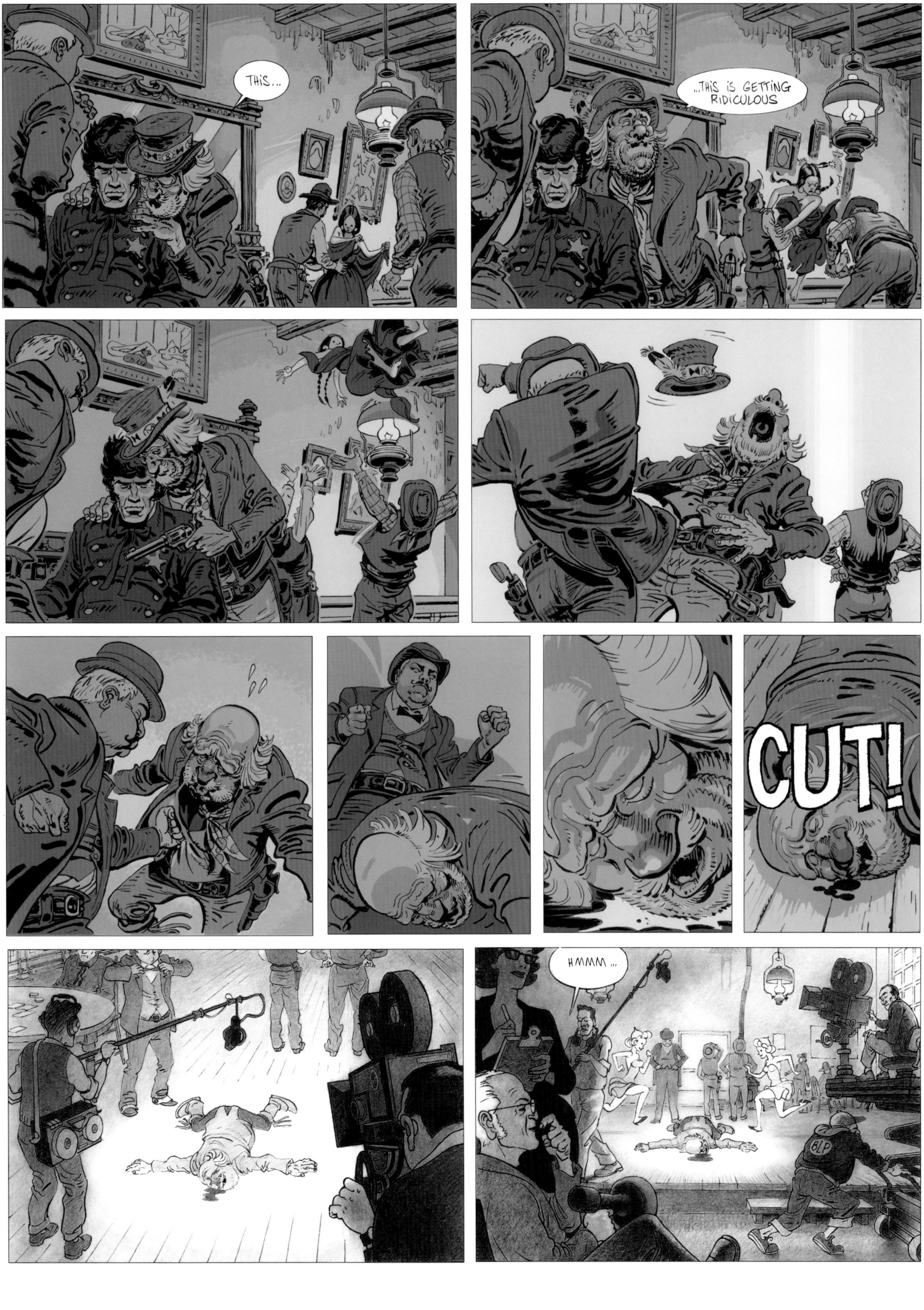
THIS...
...THIS IS GETTING RIDICULOUS
CUT!
HMMM...
BLP

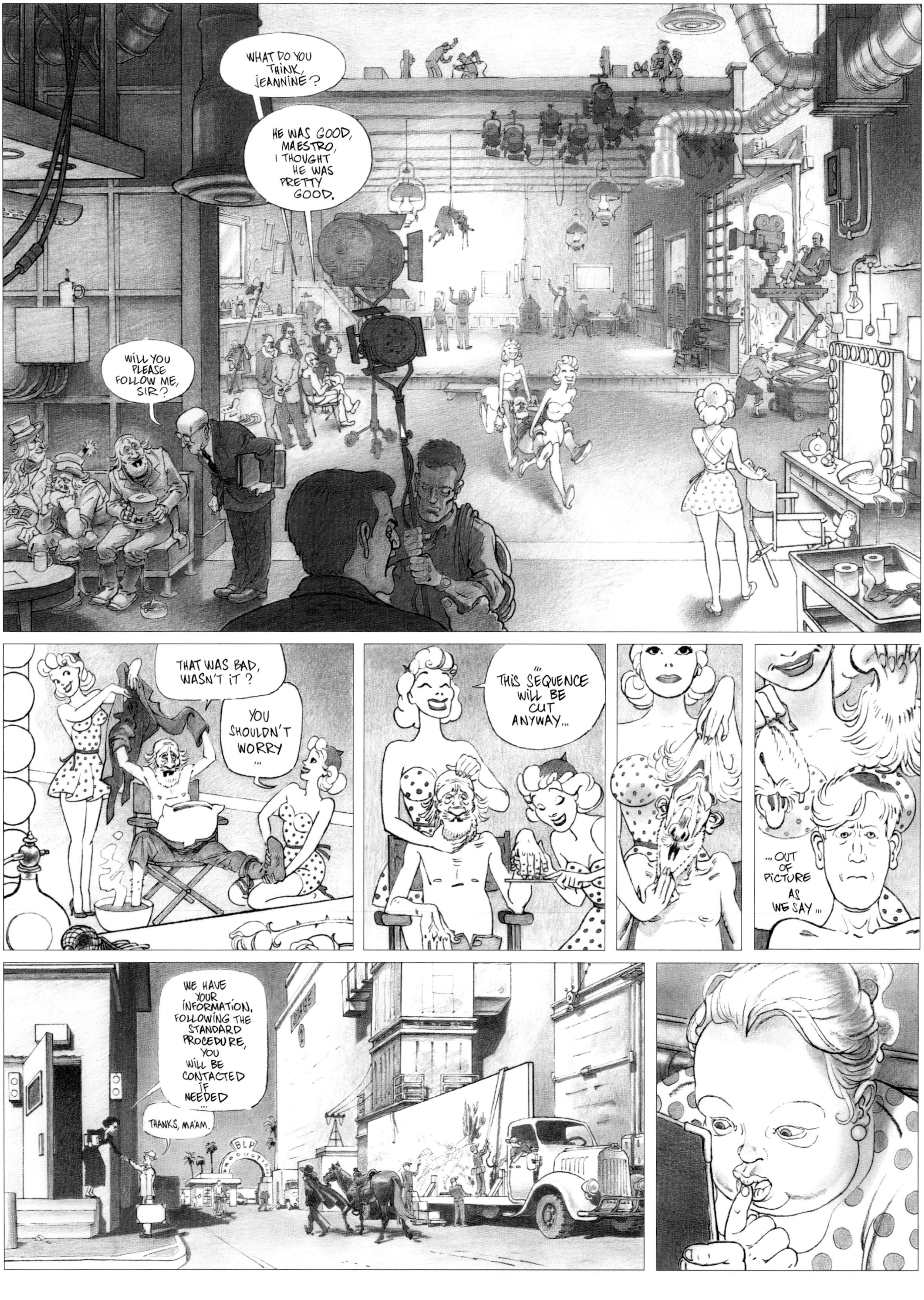
WHAT DO YOU THINK, JEANNINE?
HE WAS GOOD, MAESTRO, I THOUGHT HE WAS PRETTY GOOD.
WILL YOU PLEASE FOLLOW ME, SIR?
THAT WAS BAD, WASN'T IT?
YOU SHOULDN'T WORRY ...
... THIS SEQUENCE WILL BE CUT ANYWAY...
... OUT OF PICTURE AS WE SAY ...
WE HAVE YOUR INFORMATION, FOLLOWING THE STANDARD PROCEDURE, YOU WILL BE CONTACTED IF NEEDED ...
THANKS, MA'AM.

I'LL TAKE YOUR ALL-YOU-CAN-EAT SPAGHETTI WITH A VANILLA MILK SHAKE AND COUNTRY BISCUITS FOR A STARTER ...

WONDERFUL, I WILL BRING ALL THIS OUT IN JUST A SECOND !

...NOT THE LEAD ROLE, MA, BUT THE SIDEKICK OF THE HERO, A SPICY CHARACTER WITH A WEAKNESS FOR THE BOTTLE BUT ALWAYS READY TO HELP HIS FRIEND GET OUT OF BREATHTAKING ADVENTURES ...

ALL-YOU-CAN-EAT SPAGHETTI !!!

...NO TOMATO...

THE CLIMAX.

I AM COMIING !!

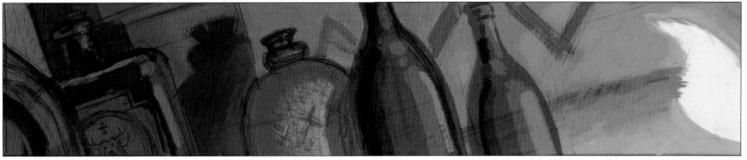

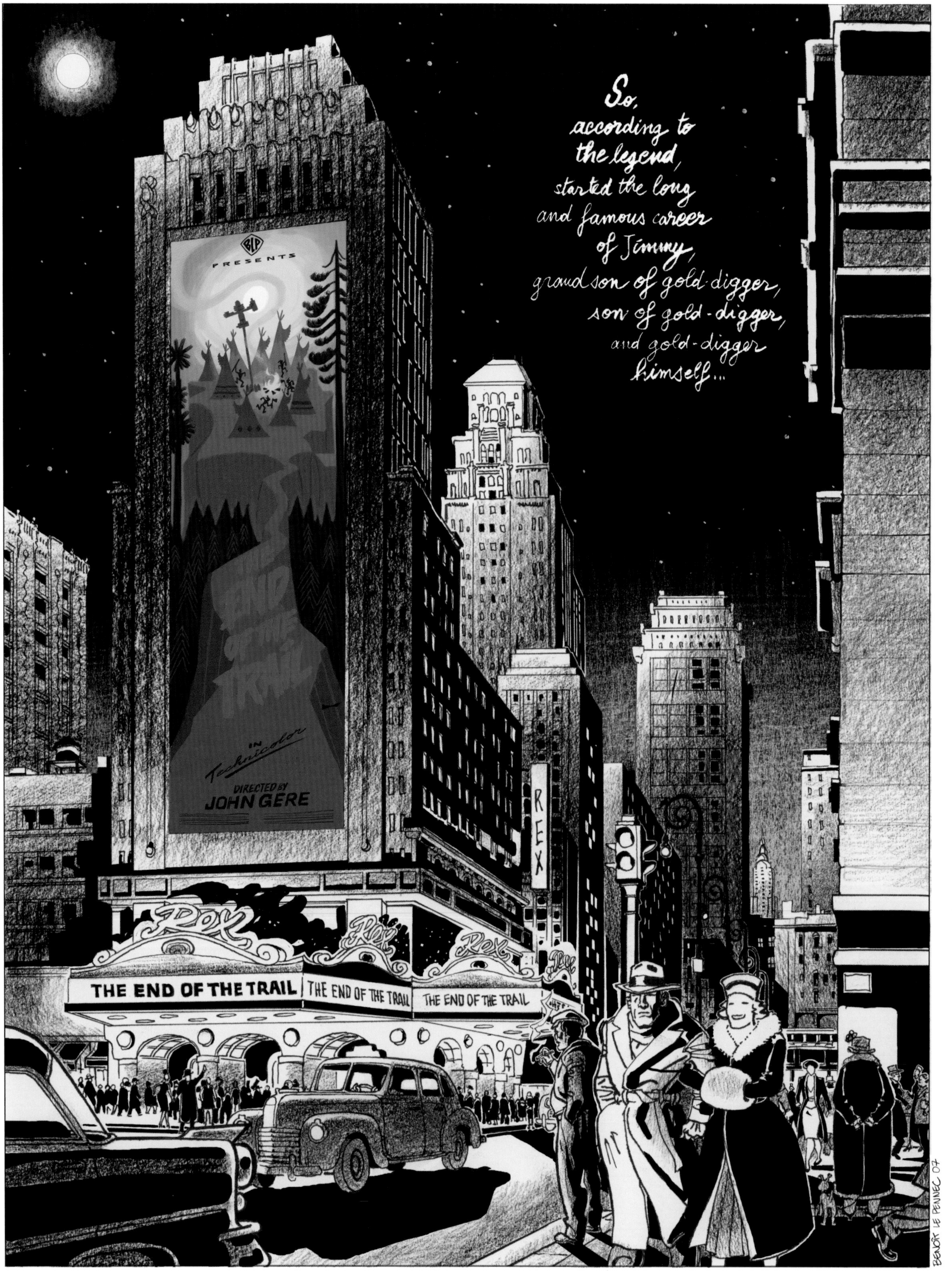
So,
according to
the legend,
started the long
and famous career
of Jimmy,
grandson of gold-digger,
son of gold-digger,
and gold-digger
himself...
PRESENTS
THE END OF THE TRAIL
IN Technicolor
DIRECTED BY
JOHN GERE
REX
Rex
THE END OF THE TRAIL
THE END OF THE TRAIL
THE END OF THE TRAIL
BENOÎT LE PENNEC 07

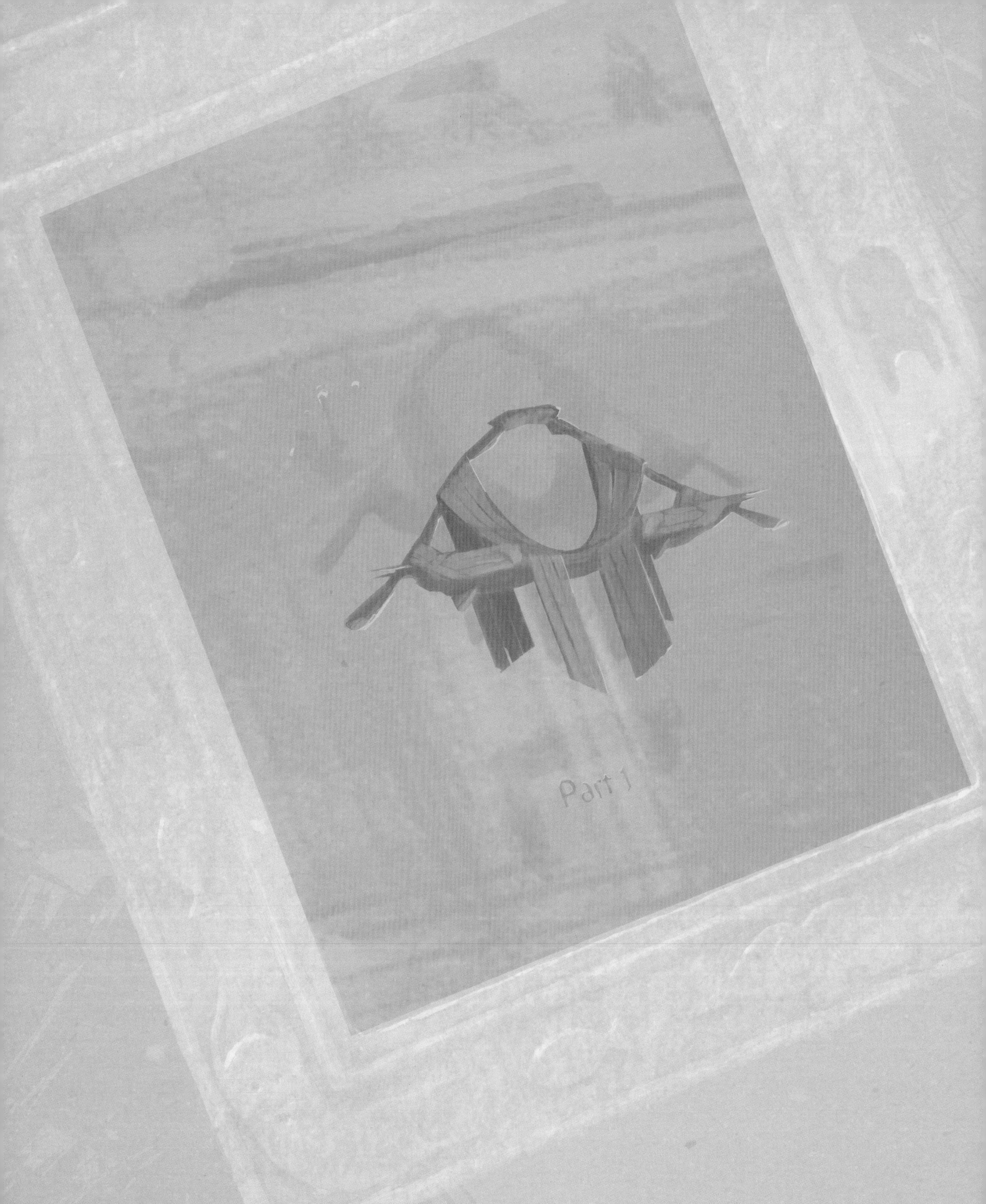
Part 1

KYLE MACNAUGHTON

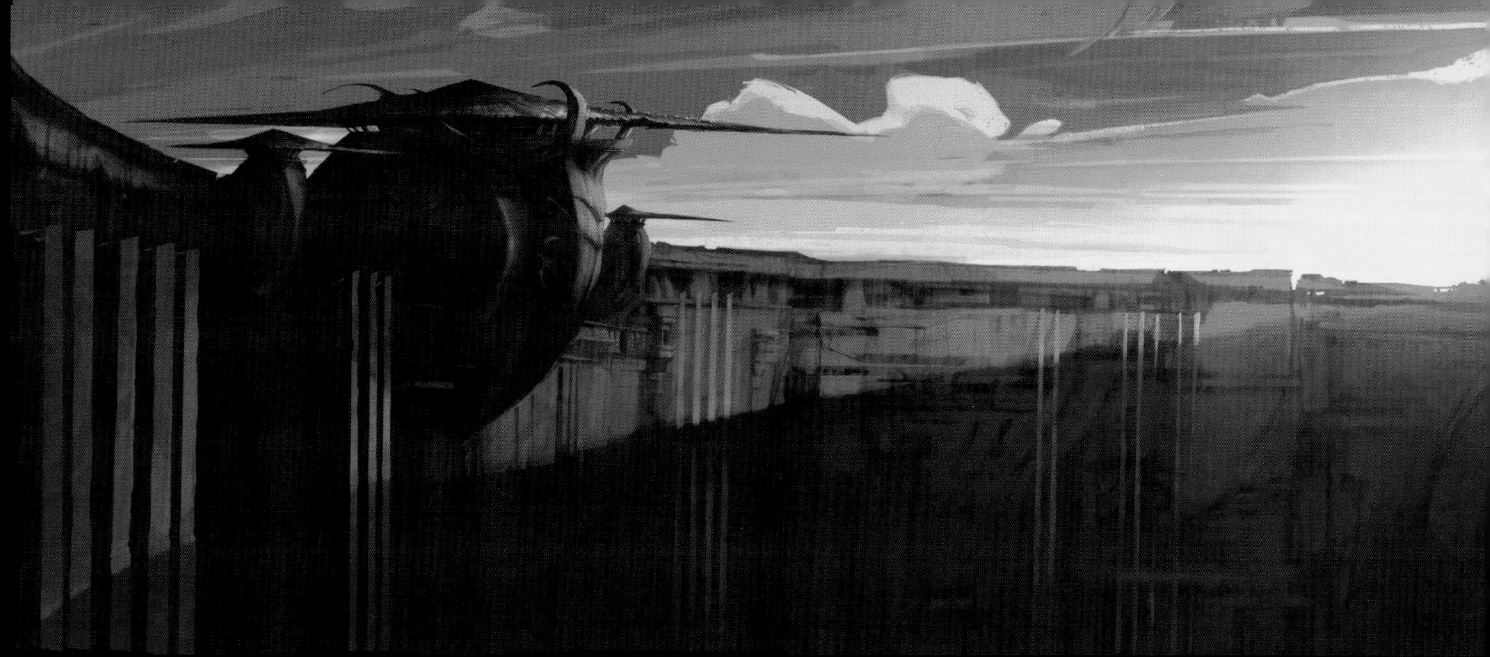

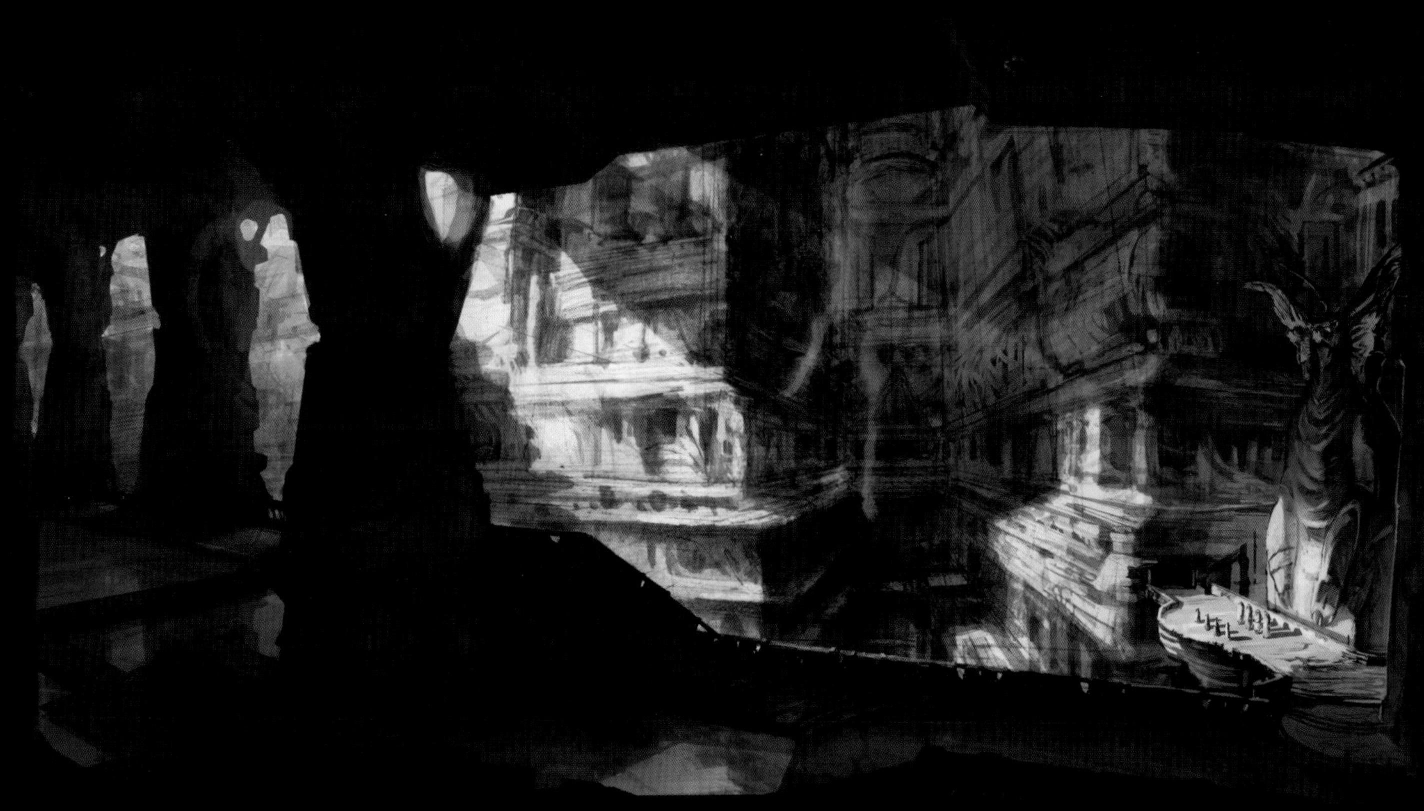

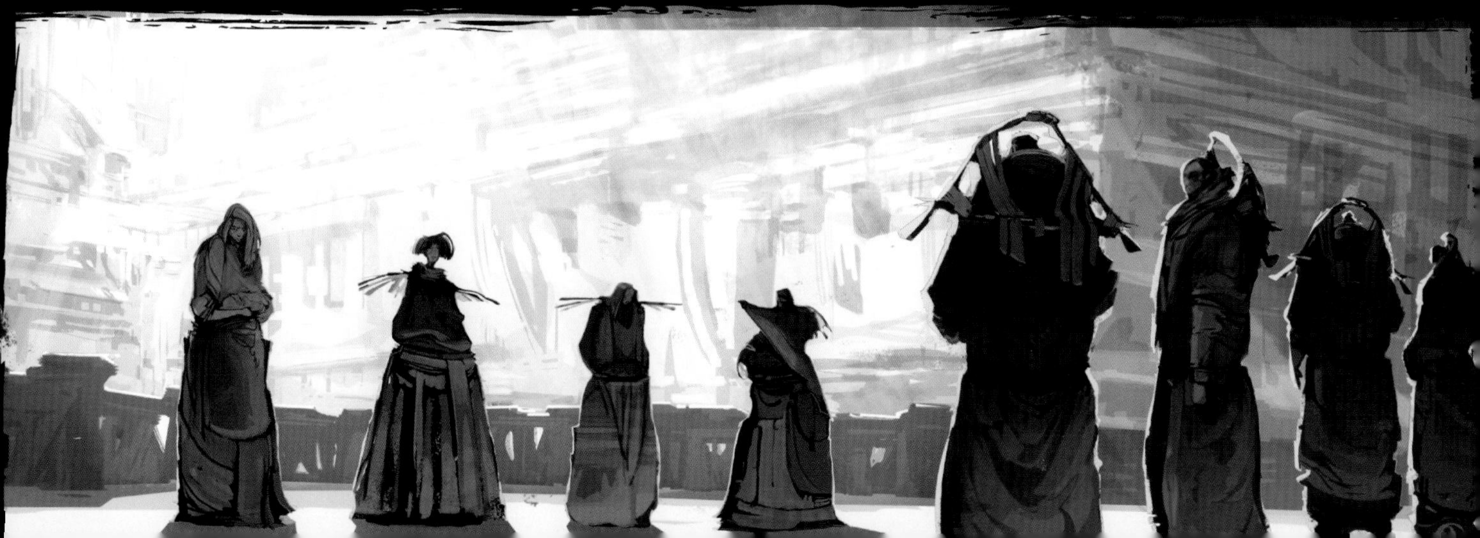

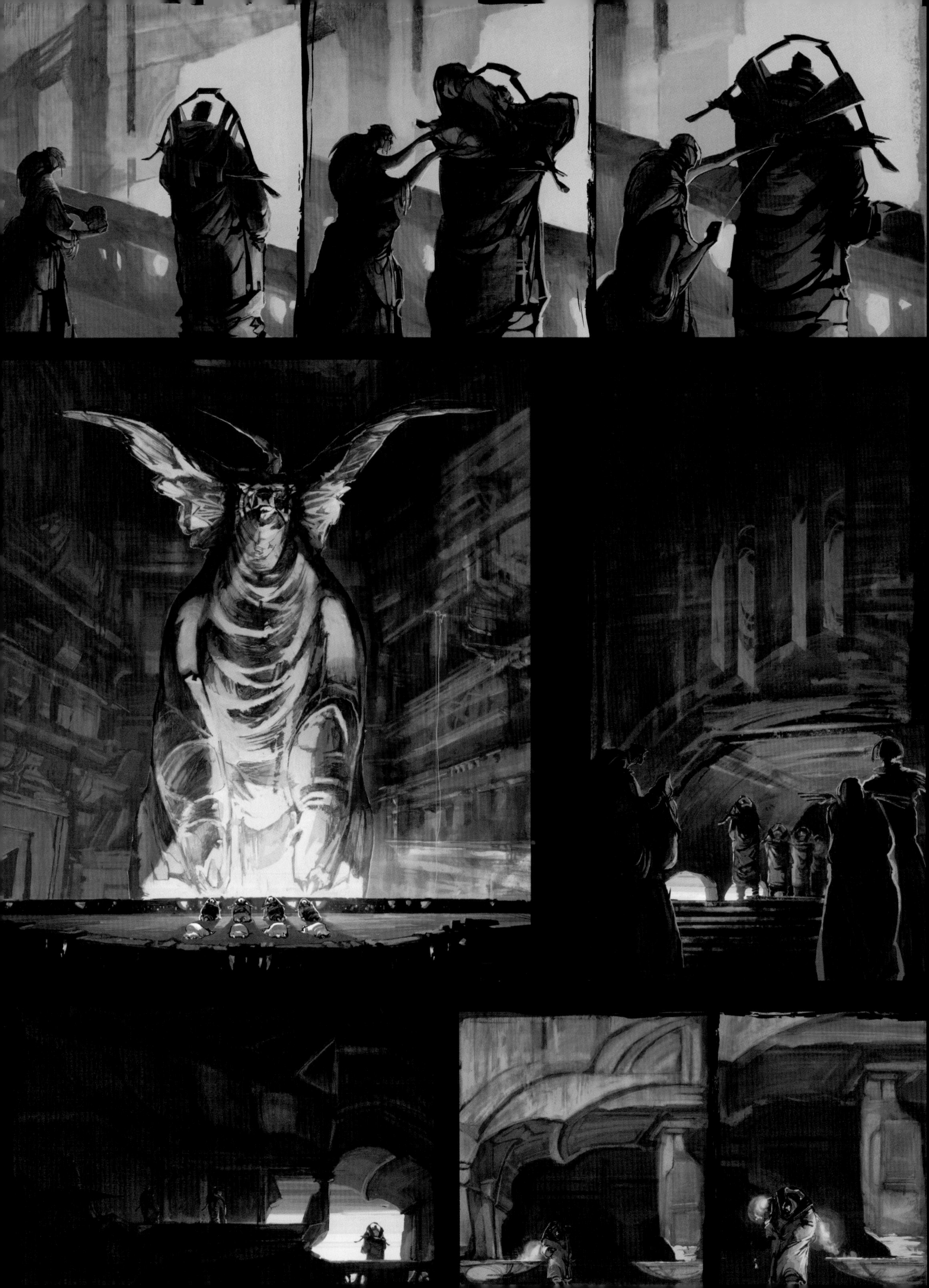

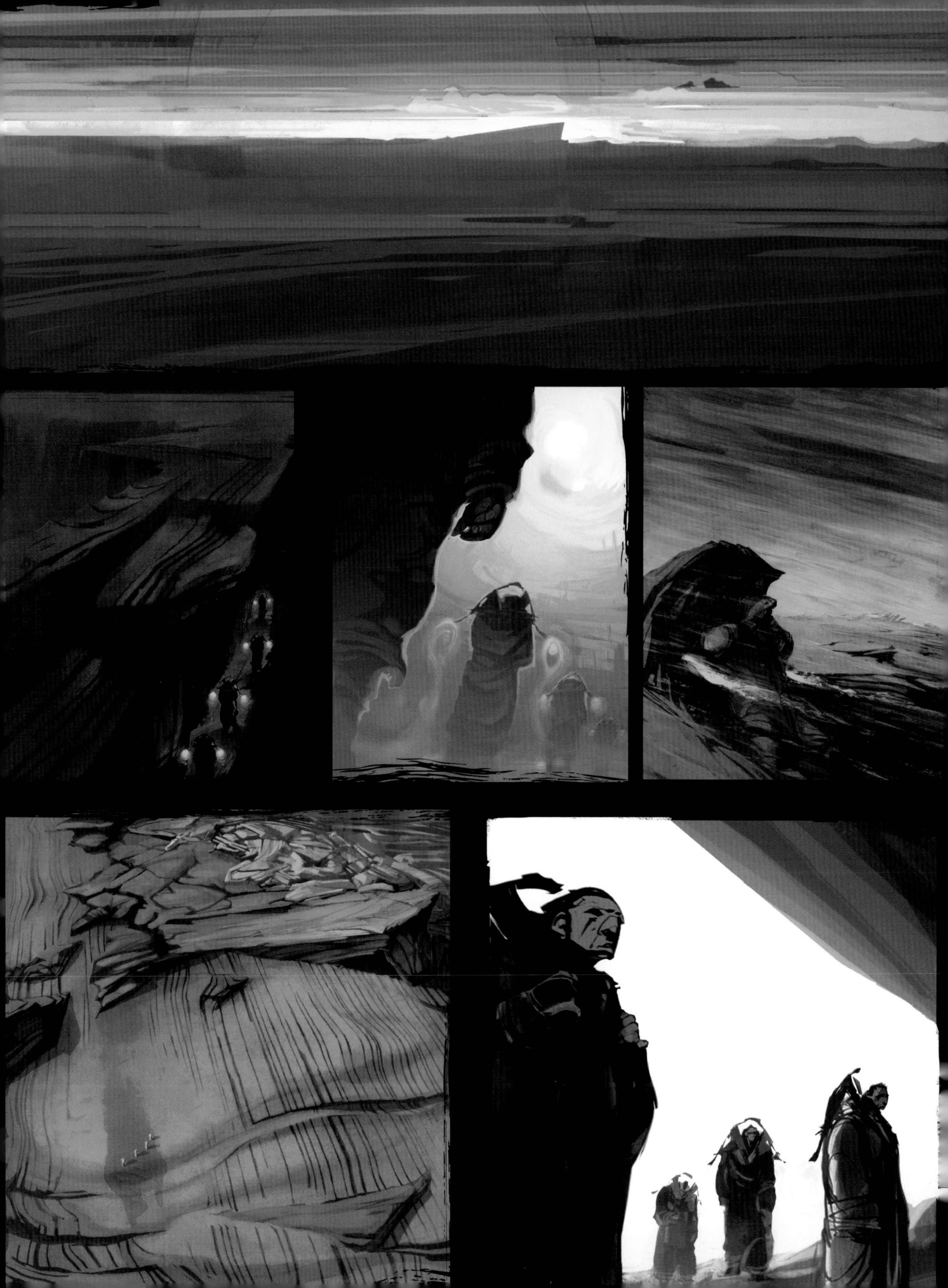

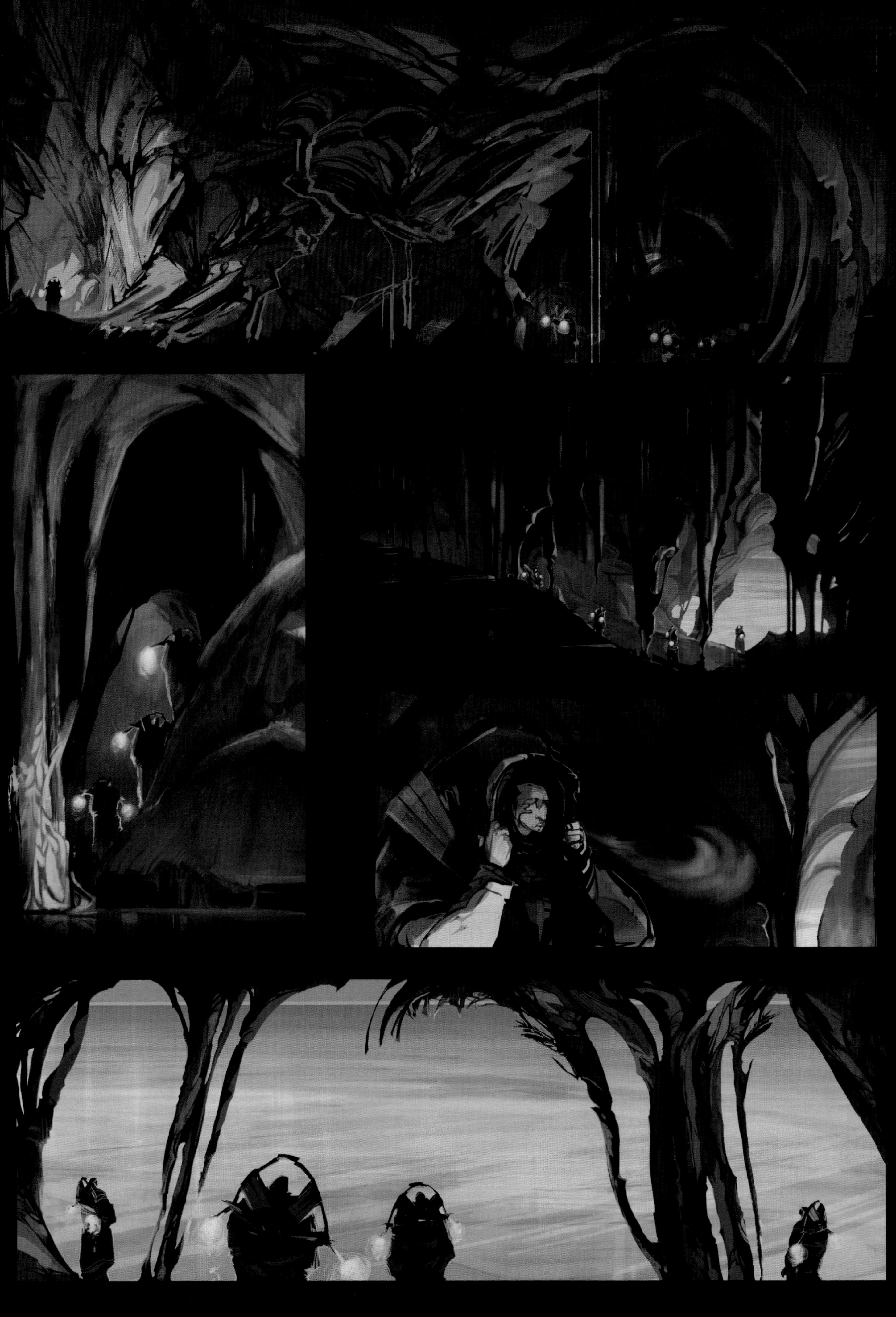

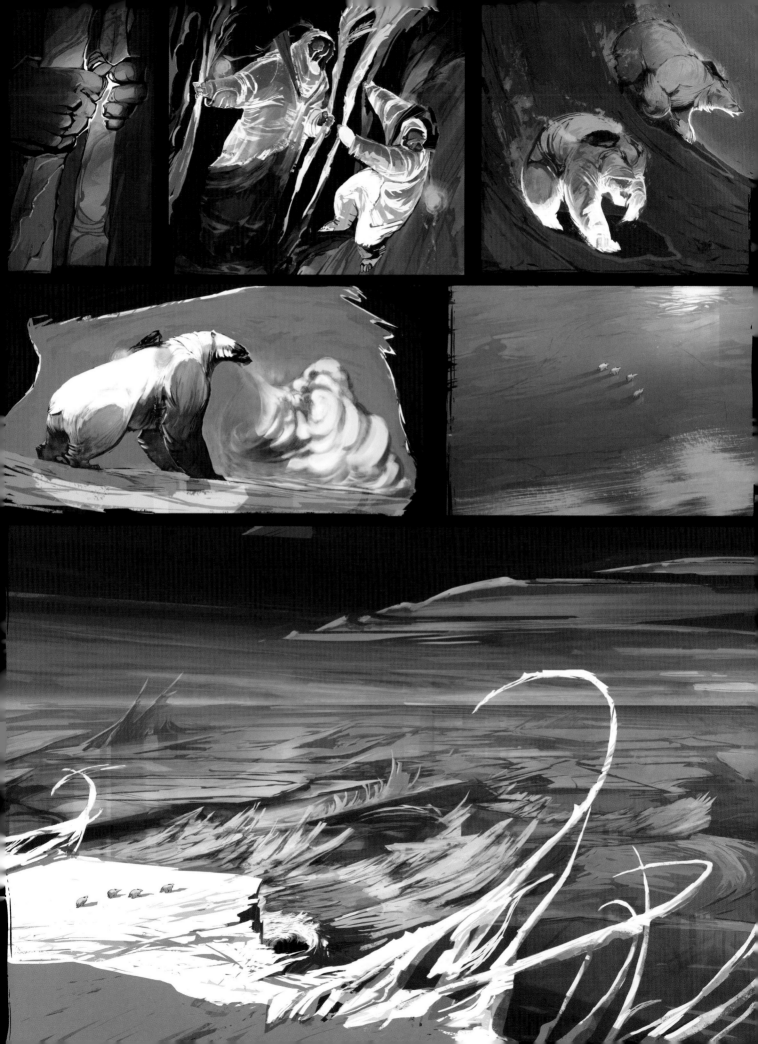

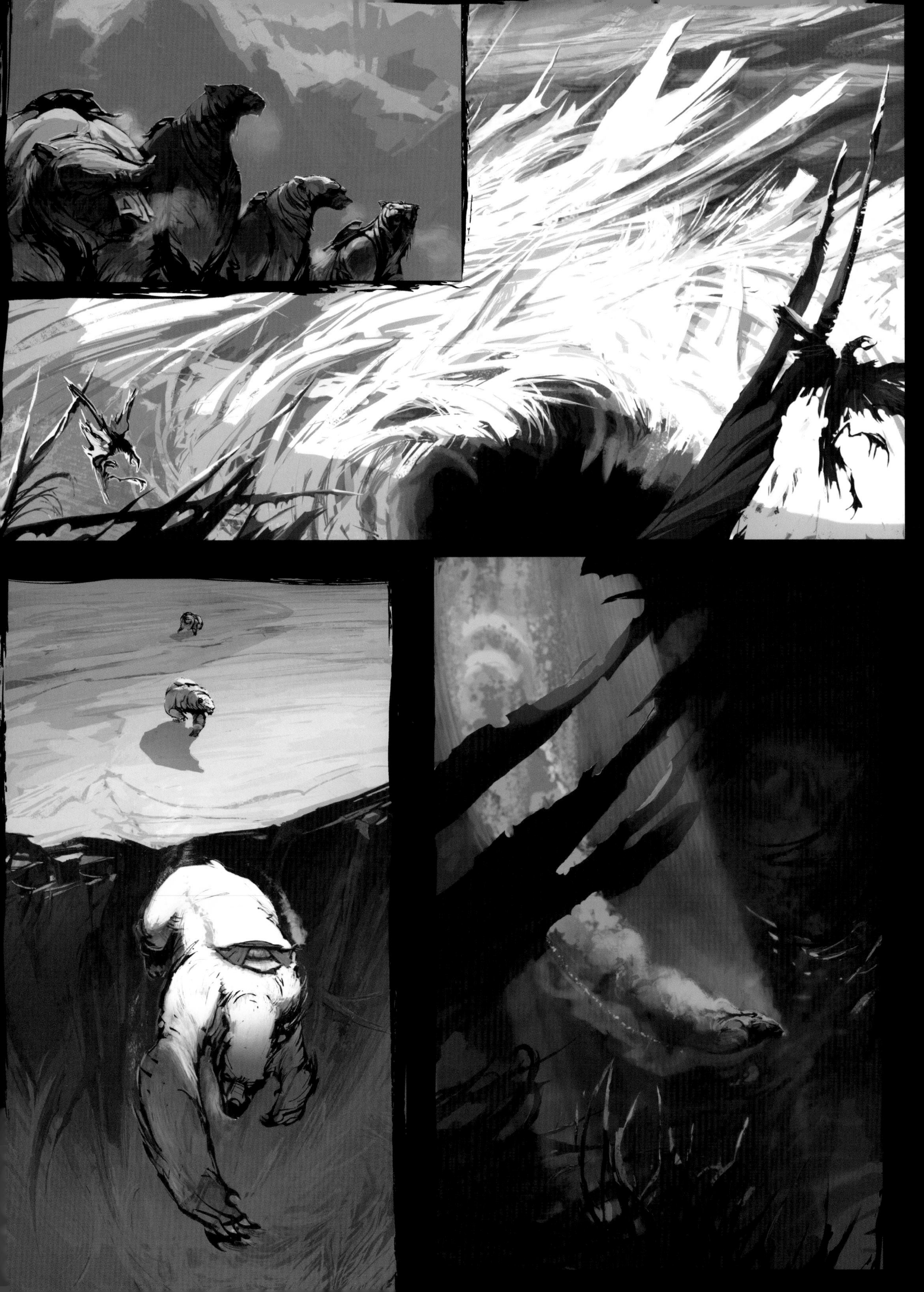

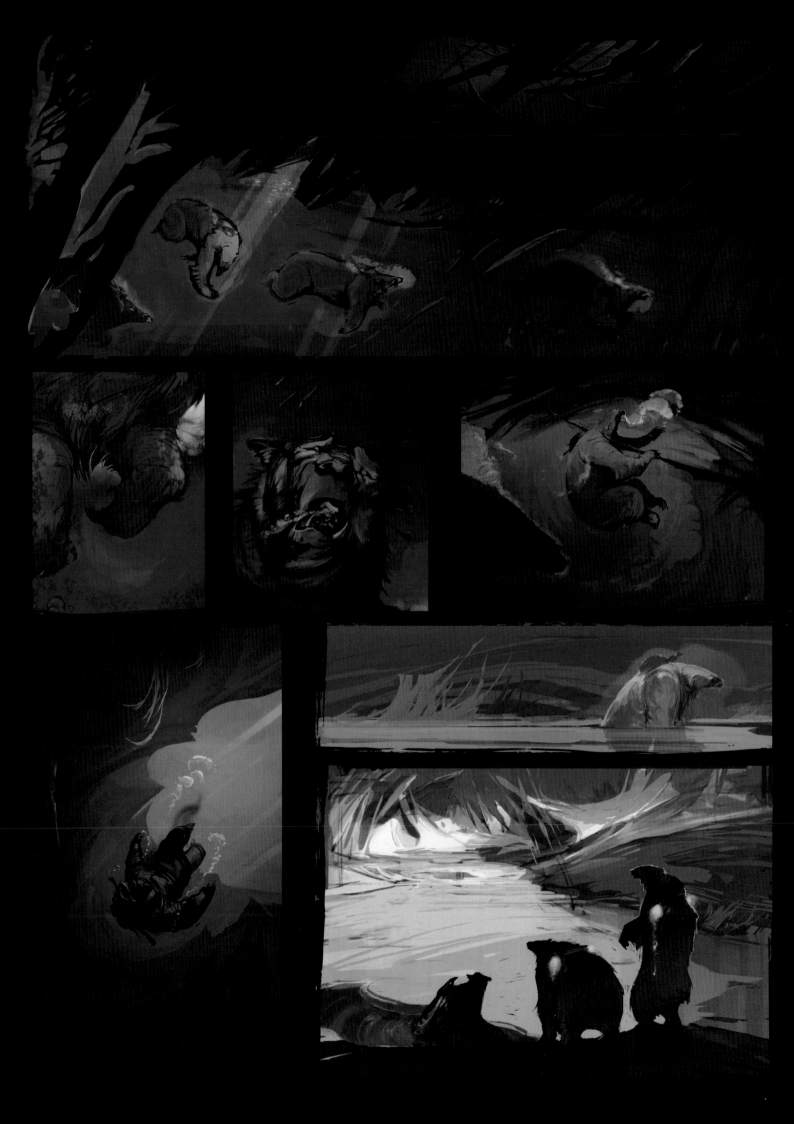

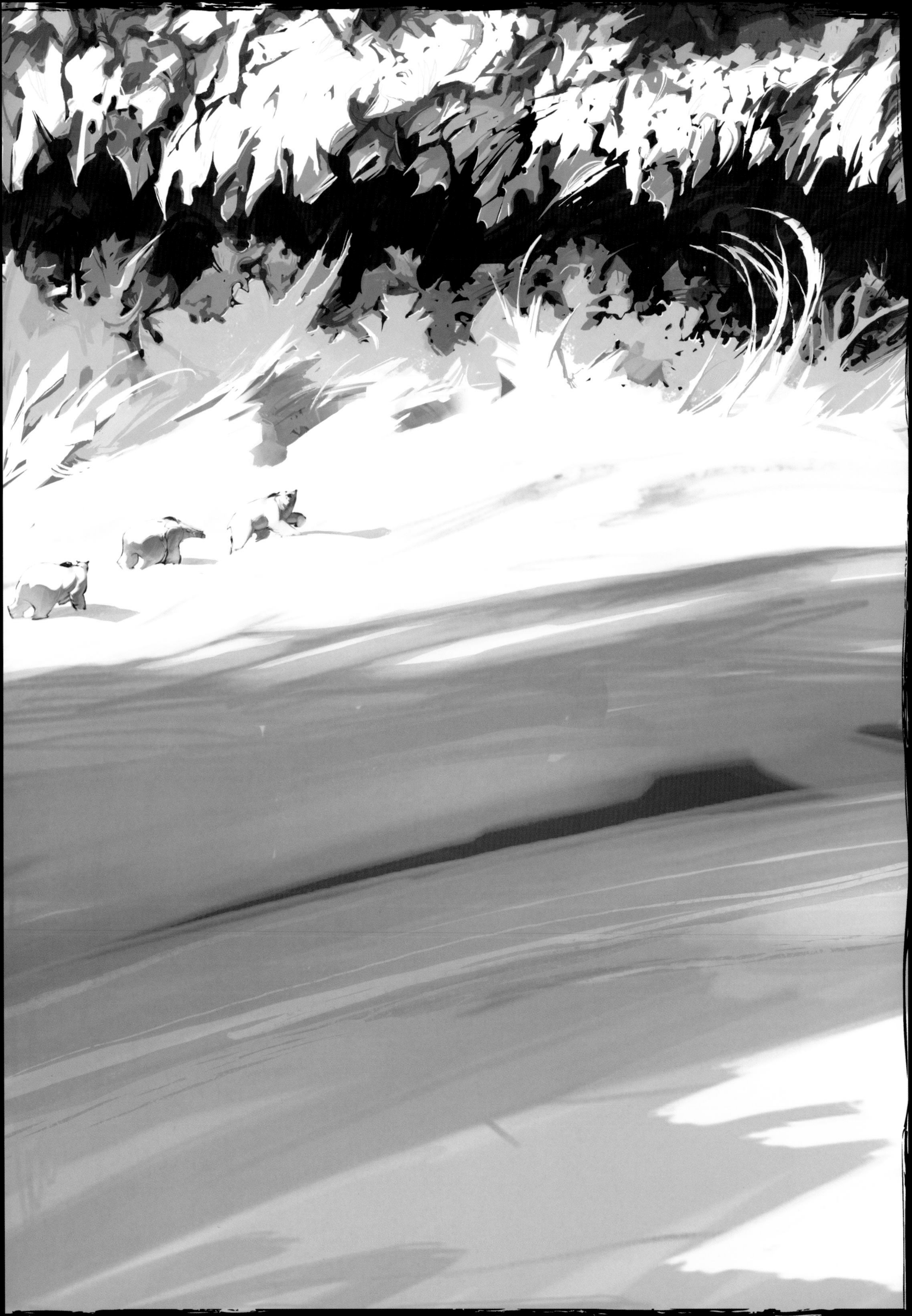

OUT OF PICTURE

JAKE PARKER

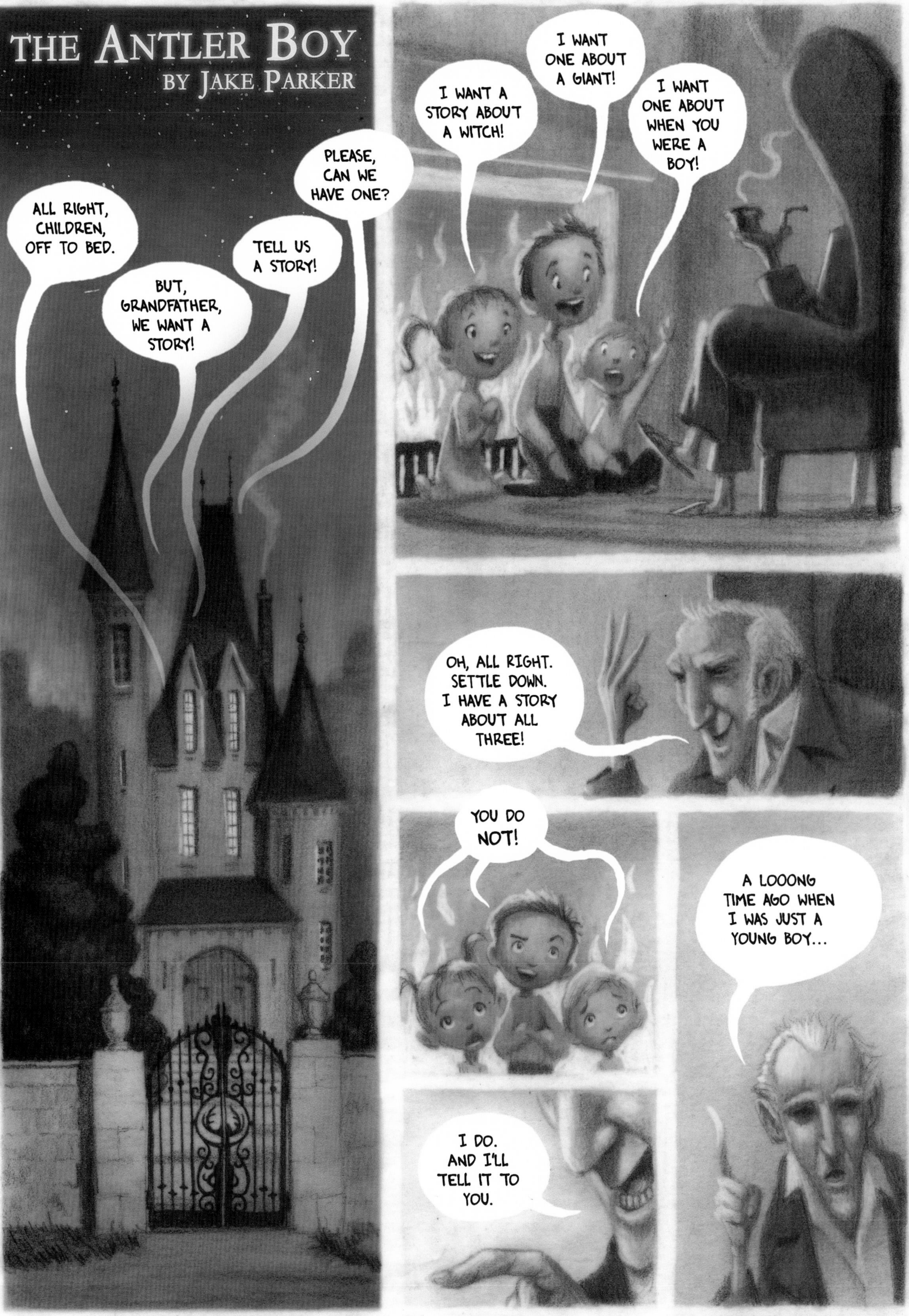
THE ANTLER BOY
BY JAKE PARKER
ALL RIGHT, CHILDREN, OFF TO BED.
BUT, GRANDFATHER, WE WANT A STORY!
TELL US A STORY!
PLEASE, CAN WE HAVE ONE?
I WANT A STORY ABOUT A WITCH!
I WANT ONE ABOUT A GIANT!
I WANT ONE ABOUT WHEN YOU WERE A BOY!
OH, ALL RIGHT. SETTLE DOWN. I HAVE A STORY ABOUT ALL THREE!
YOU DO NOT!
I DO. AND I'LL TELL IT TO YOU.
A LOOONG TIME AGO WHEN I WAS JUST A YOUNG BOY...

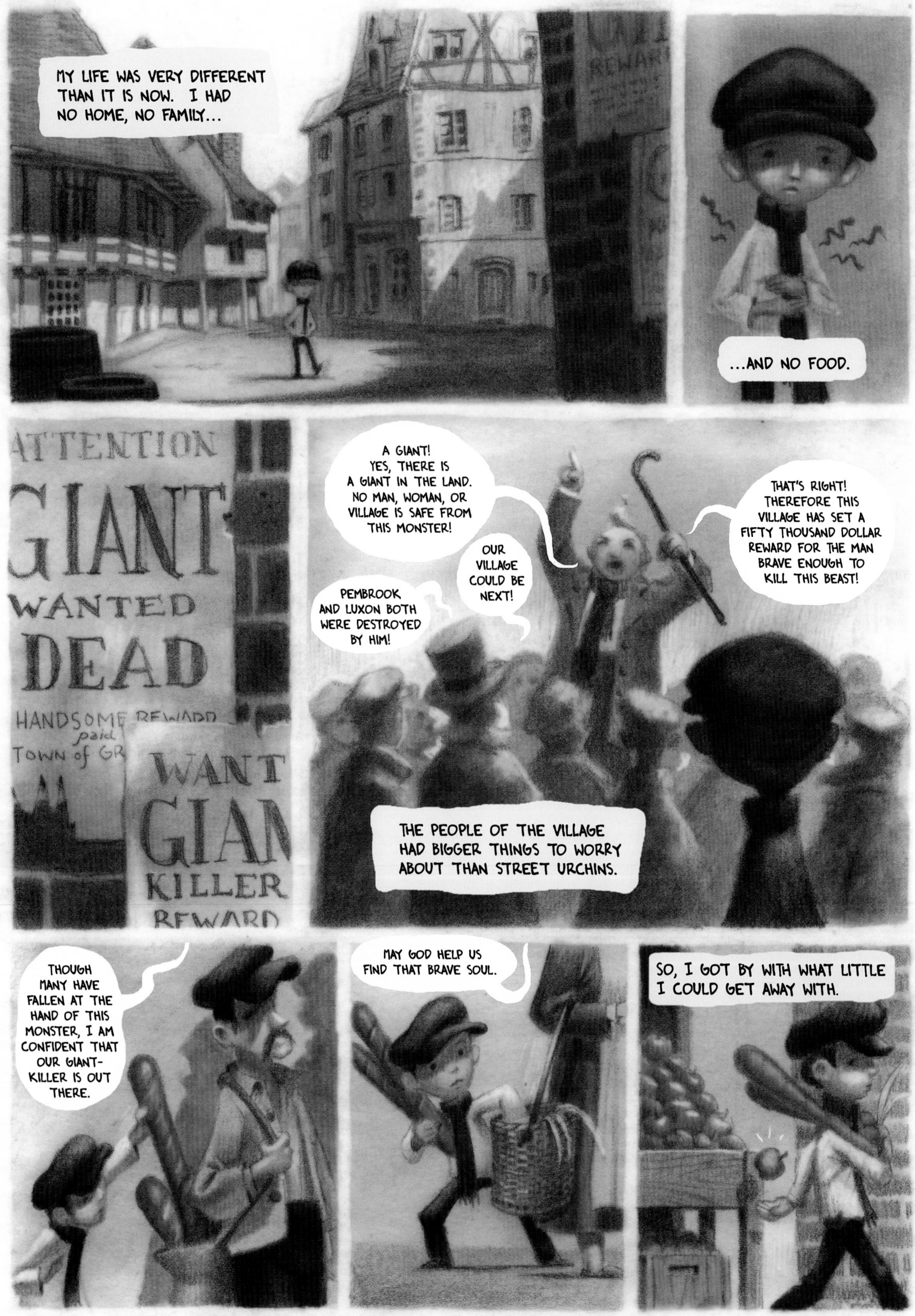
MY LIFE WAS VERY DIFFERENT THAN IT IS NOW. I HAD NO HOME, NO FAMILY...
...AND NO FOOD.
ATTENTION
GIANT
WANTED
DEAD
HANDSOME REWARD paid
TOWN of GR
WANT
GIAN
KILLER
REWARD
A GIANT! YES, THERE IS A GIANT IN THE LAND. NO MAN, WOMAN, OR VILLAGE IS SAFE FROM THIS MONSTER!
OUR VILLAGE COULD BE NEXT!
PEMBROOK AND LUXON BOTH WERE DESTROYED BY HIM!
THAT'S RIGHT! THEREFORE THIS VILLAGE HAS SET A FIFTY THOUSAND DOLLAR REWARD FOR THE MAN BRAVE ENOUGH TO KILL THIS BEAST!
THE PEOPLE OF THE VILLAGE HAD BIGGER THINGS TO WORRY ABOUT THAN STREET URCHINS.
THOUGH MANY HAVE FALLEN AT THE HAND OF THIS MONSTER, I AM CONFIDENT THAT OUR GIANT-KILLER IS OUT THERE.
MAY GOD HELP US FIND THAT BRAVE SOUL.
SO, I GOT BY WITH WHAT LITTLE I COULD GET AWAY WITH.

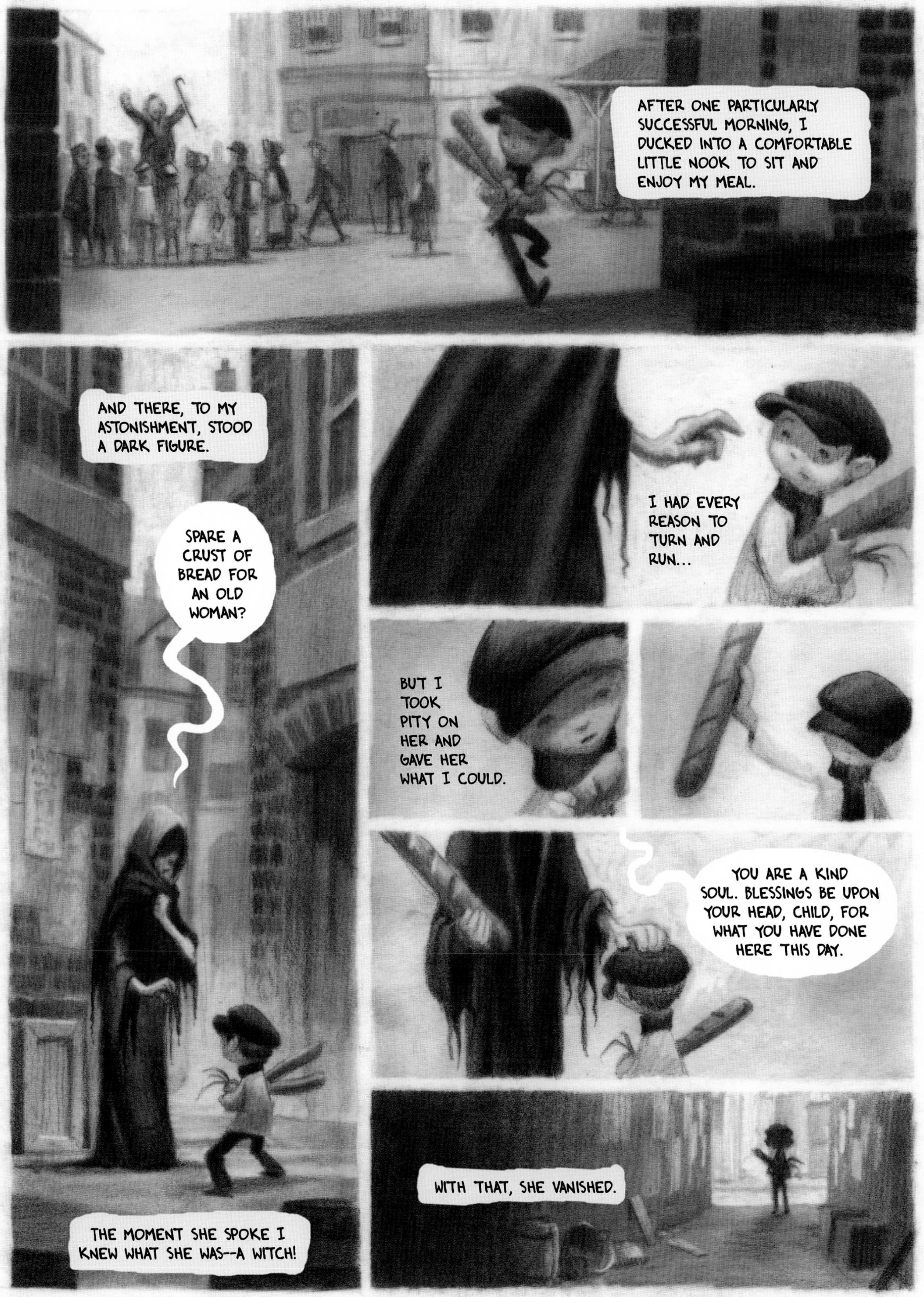
AFTER ONE PARTICULARLY SUCCESSFUL MORNING, I DUCKED INTO A COMFORTABLE LITTLE NOOK TO SIT AND ENJOY MY MEAL.
AND THERE, TO MY ASTONISHMENT, STOOD A DARK FIGURE.
SPARE A CRUST OF BREAD FOR AN OLD WOMAN?
THE MOMENT SHE SPOKE I KNEW WHAT SHE WAS--A WITCH!
I HAD EVERY REASON TO TURN AND RUN...
BUT I TOOK PITY ON HER AND GAVE HER WHAT I COULD.
YOU ARE A KIND SOUL. BLESSINGS BE UPON YOUR HEAD, CHILD, FOR WHAT YOU HAVE DONE HERE THIS DAY.
WITH THAT, SHE VANISHED.

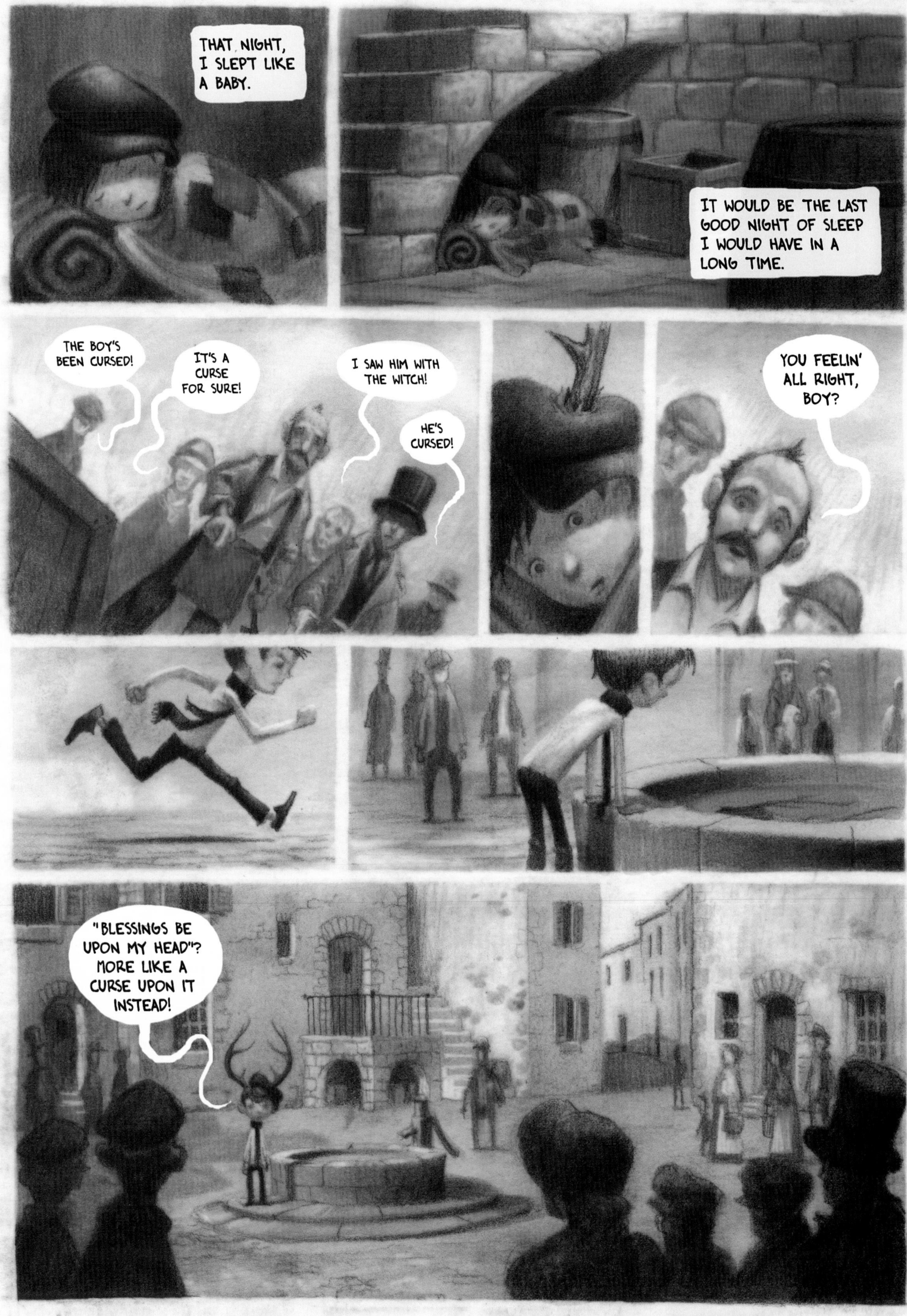
THAT NIGHT, I SLEPT LIKE A BABY.
IT WOULD BE THE LAST GOOD NIGHT OF SLEEP I WOULD HAVE IN A LONG TIME.
THE BOY'S BEEN CURSED!
IT'S A CURSE FOR SURE!
I SAW HIM WITH THE WITCH!
HE'S CURSED!
YOU FEELIN' ALL RIGHT, BOY?
"BLESSINGS BE UPON MY HEAD"? MORE LIKE A CURSE UPON IT INSTEAD!

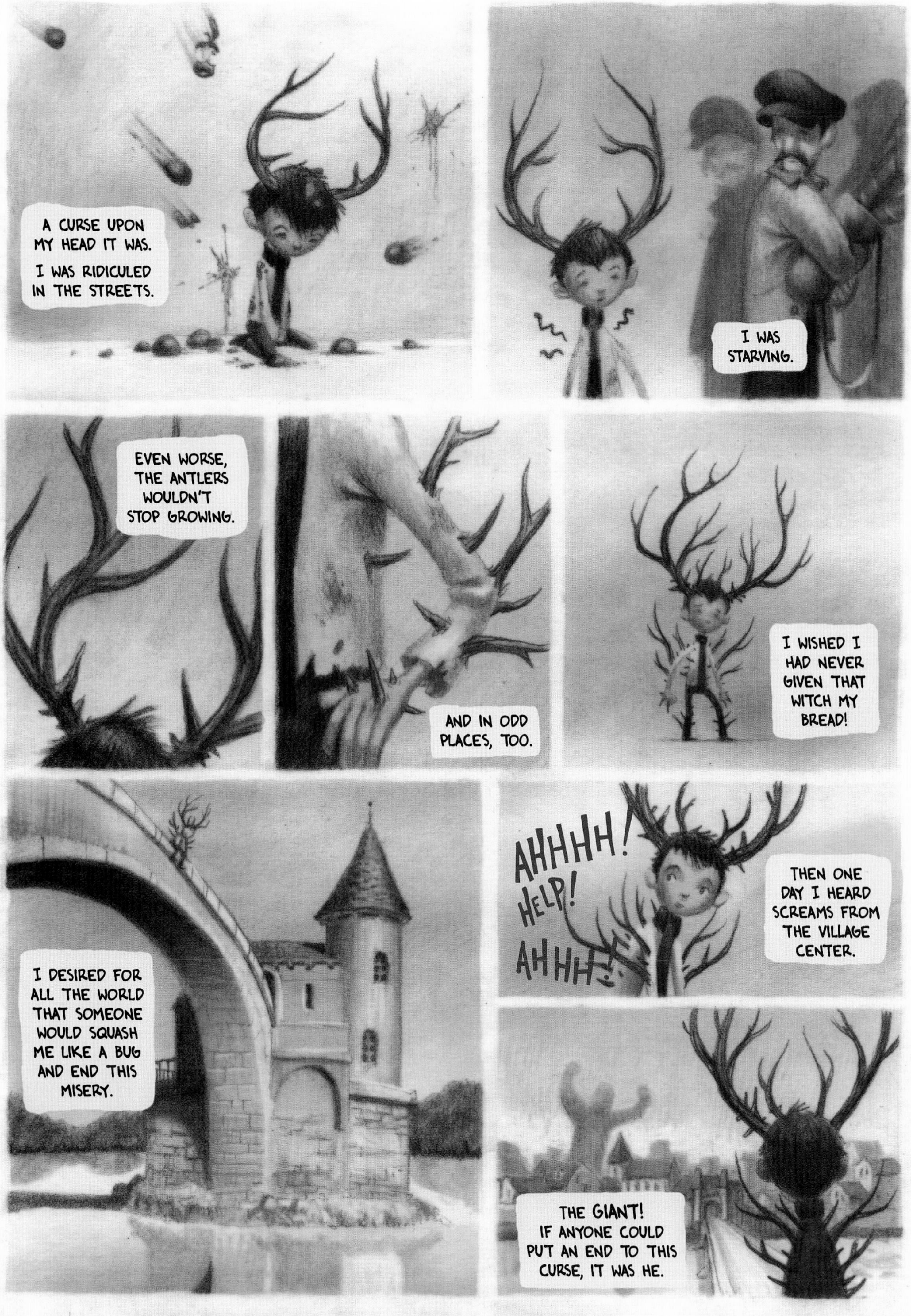
A CURSE UPON MY HEAD IT WAS.
I WAS RIDICULED IN THE STREETS.
I WAS STARVING.
EVEN WORSE, THE ANTLERS WOULDN'T STOP GROWING.
AND IN ODD PLACES, TOO.
I WISHED I HAD NEVER GIVEN THAT WITCH MY BREAD!
I DESIRED FOR ALL THE WORLD THAT SOMEONE WOULD SQUASH ME LIKE A BUG AND END THIS MISERY.
AHHHH!
HELP!
AHHH!
THEN ONE DAY I HEARD SCREAMS FROM THE VILLAGE CENTER.
THE GIANT! IF ANYONE COULD PUT AN END TO THIS CURSE, IT WAS HE.

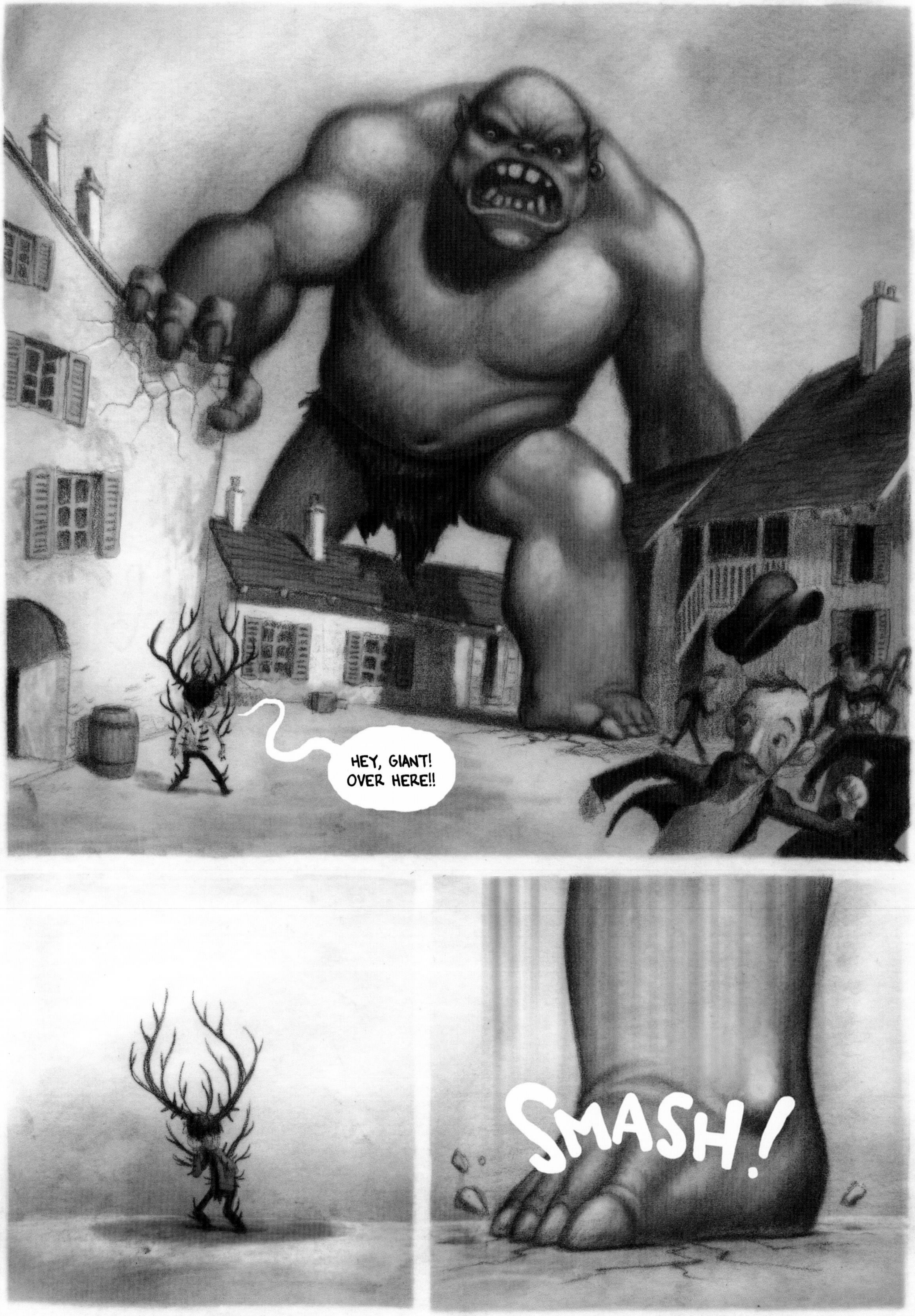
HEY, GIANT!
OVER HERE!!
SMASH!

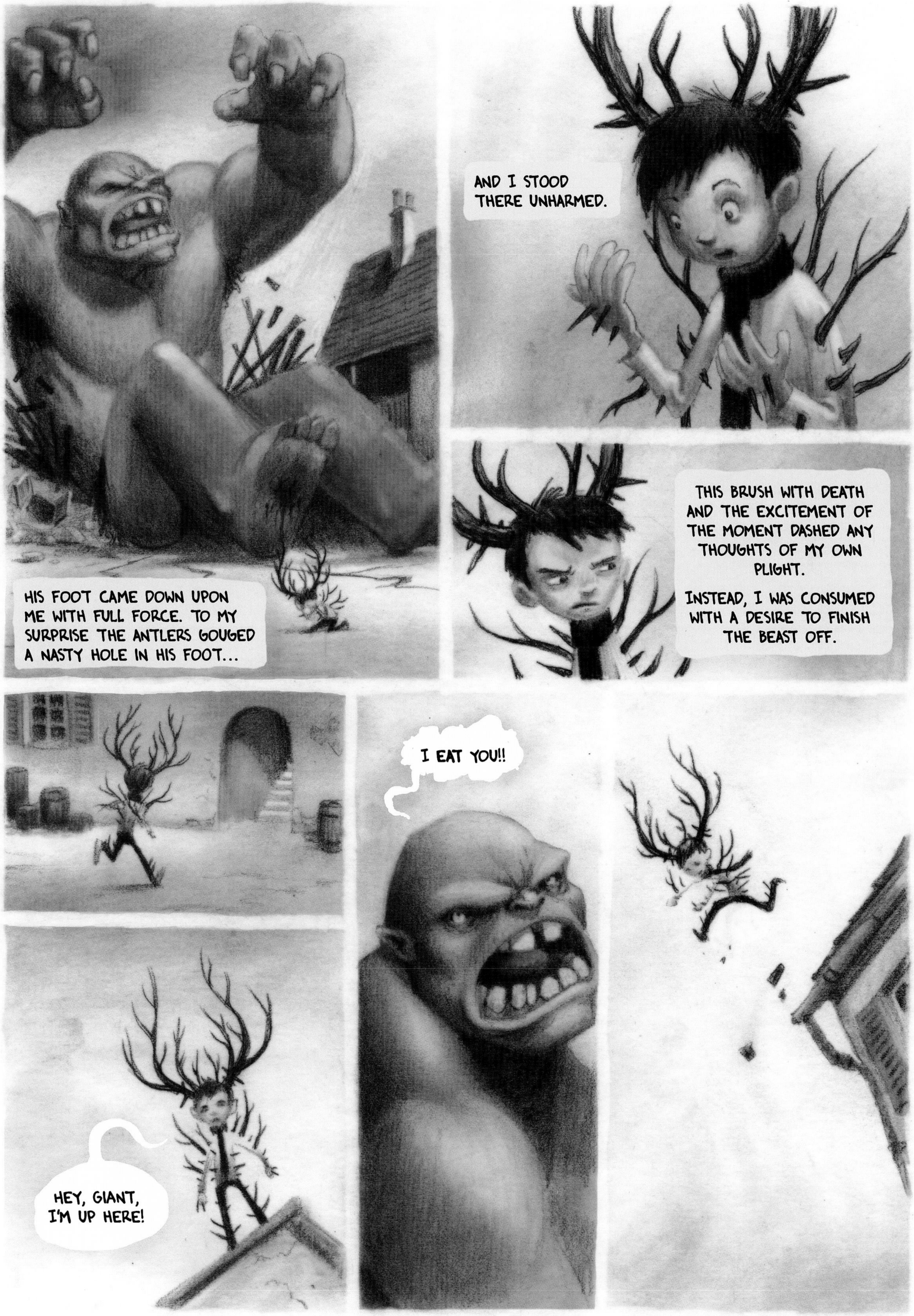
HIS FOOT CAME DOWN UPON ME WITH FULL FORCE. TO MY SURPRISE THE ANTLERS GOUGED A NASTY HOLE IN HIS FOOT...
AND I STOOD THERE UNHARMED.
THIS BRUSH WITH DEATH AND THE EXCITEMENT OF THE MOMENT DASHED ANY THOUGHTS OF MY OWN PLIGHT.
INSTEAD, I WAS CONSUMED WITH A DESIRE TO FINISH THE BEAST OFF.
HEY, GIANT, I'M UP HERE!
I EAT YOU!!

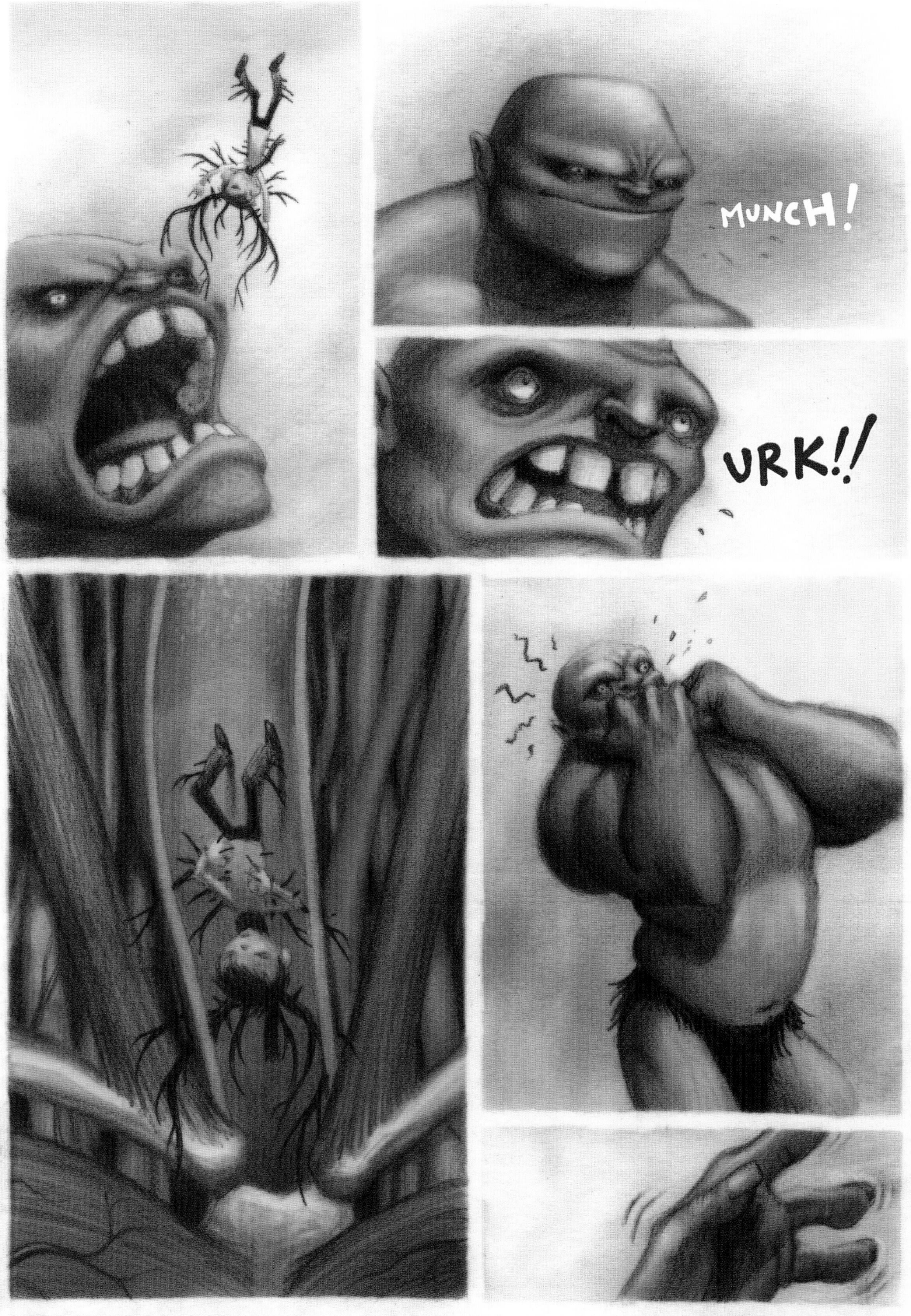
MUNCH!
URK!!

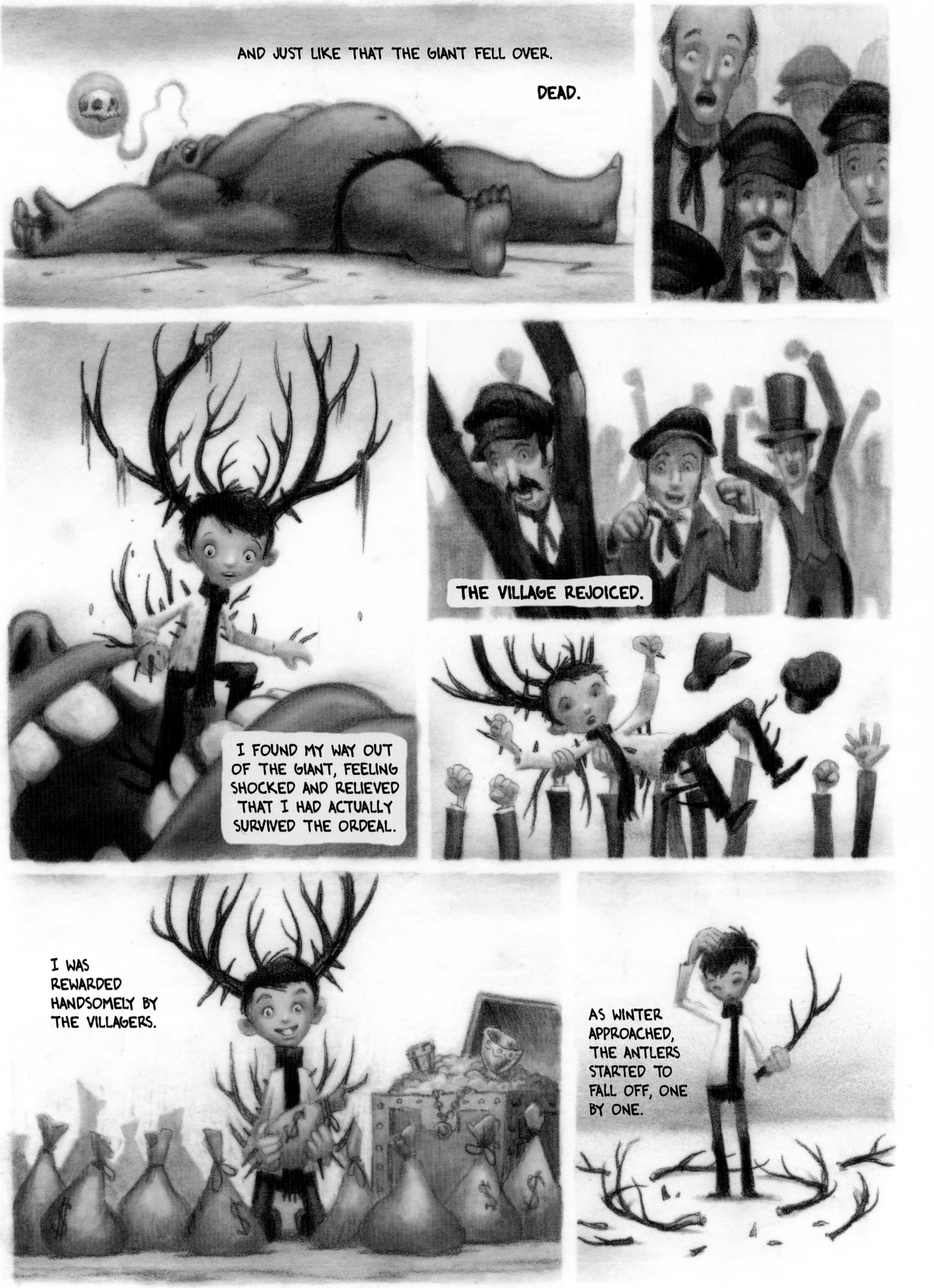
AND JUST LIKE THAT THE GIANT FELL OVER.
DEAD.
I FOUND MY WAY OUT OF THE GIANT, FEELING SHOCKED AND RELIEVED THAT I HAD ACTUALLY SURVIVED THE ORDEAL.
THE VILLAGE REJOICED.
I WAS REWARDED HANDSOMELY BY THE VILLAGERS.
AS WINTER APPROACHED, THE ANTLERS STARTED TO FALL OFF, ONE BY ONE.

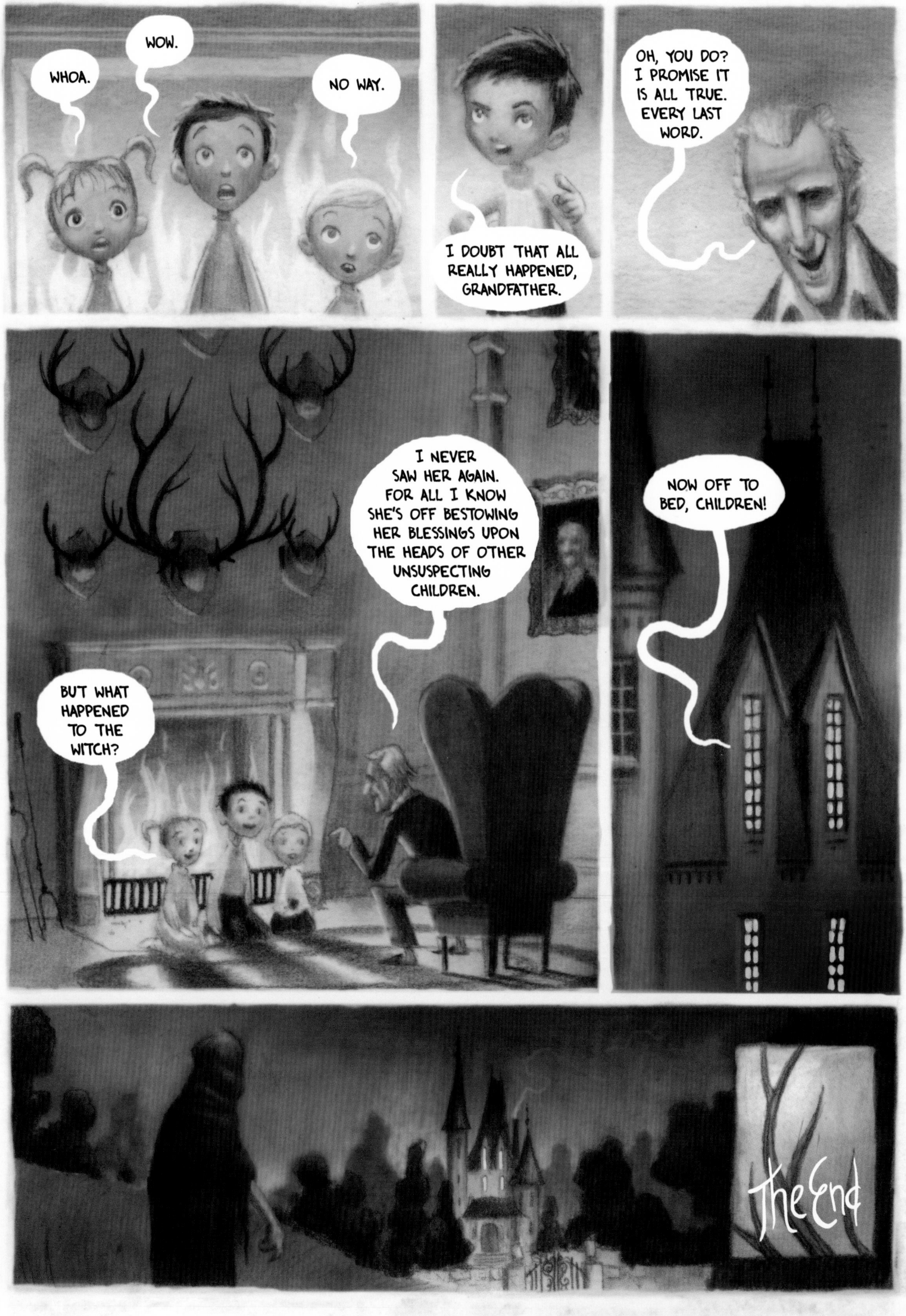
WHOA.
WOW.
NO WAY.
I DOUBT THAT ALL REALLY HAPPENED, GRANDFATHER.
OH, YOU DO? I PROMISE IT IS ALL TRUE. EVERY LAST WORD.
BUT WHAT HAPPENED TO THE WITCH?
I NEVER SAW HER AGAIN. FOR ALL I KNOW SHE'S OFF BESTOWING HER BLESSINGS UPON THE HEADS OF OTHER UNSUSPECTING CHILDREN.
NOW OFF TO BED, CHILDREN!
The End

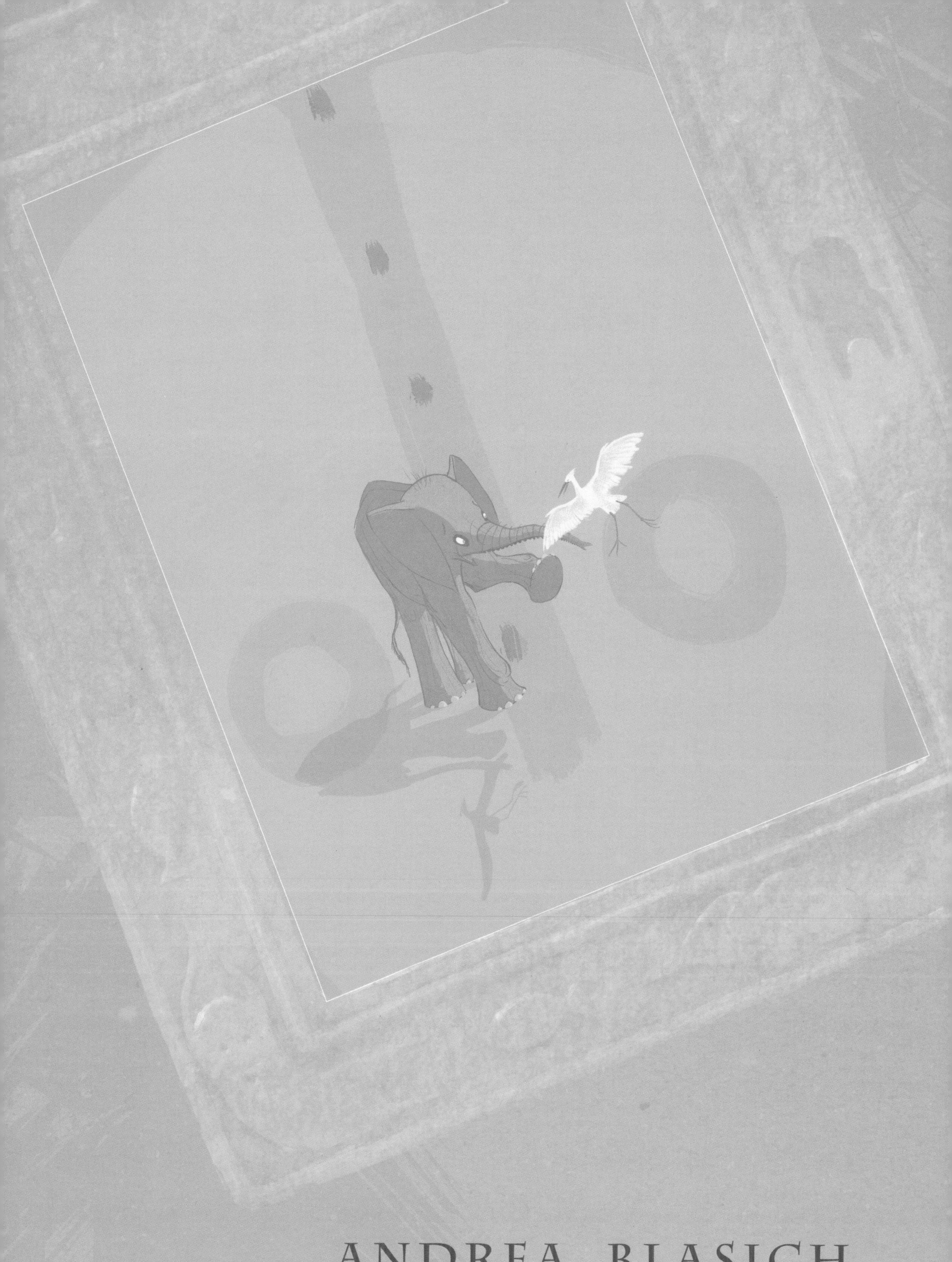

ANDREA BLASICH

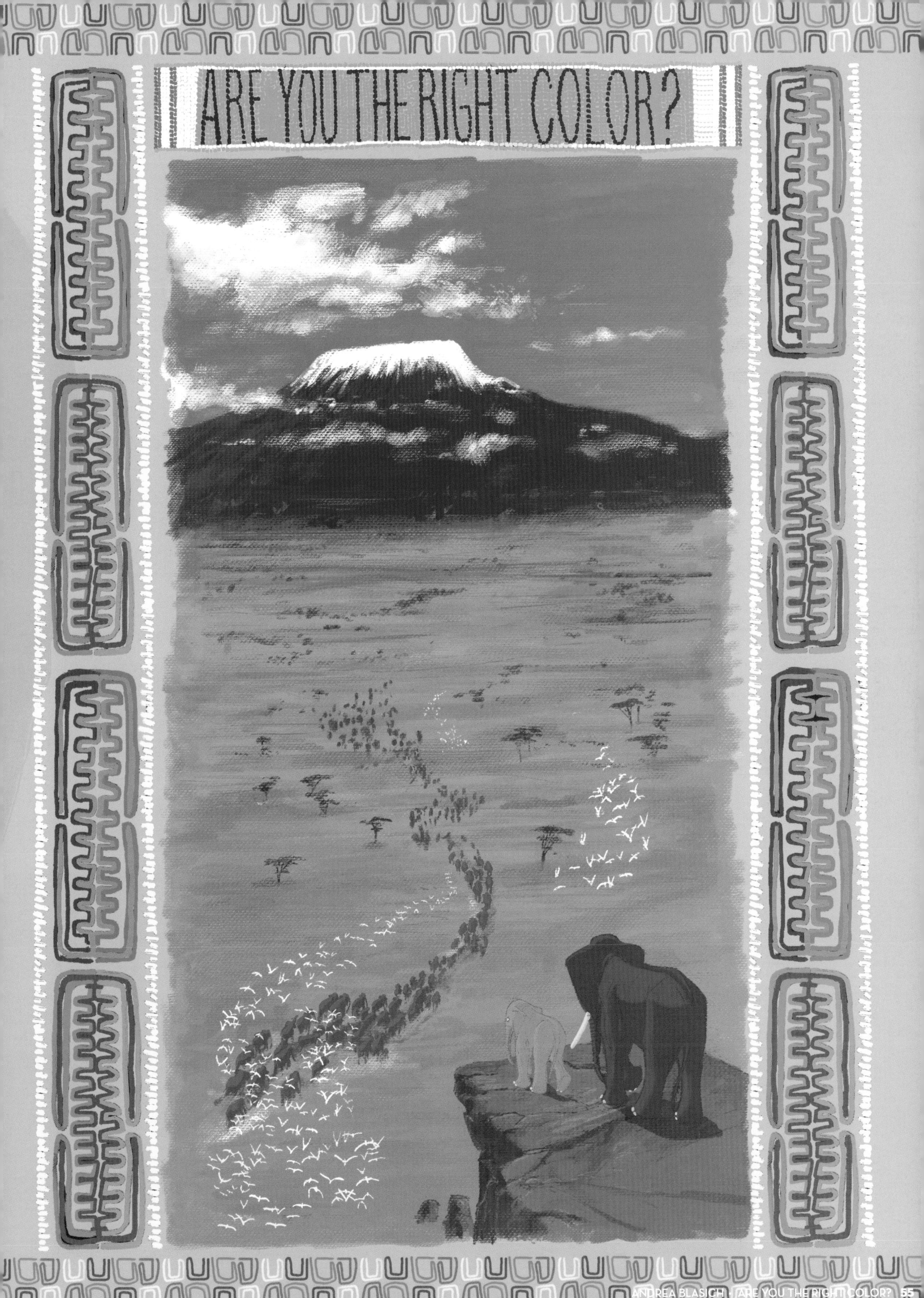
ARE YOU THE RIGHT COLOR?

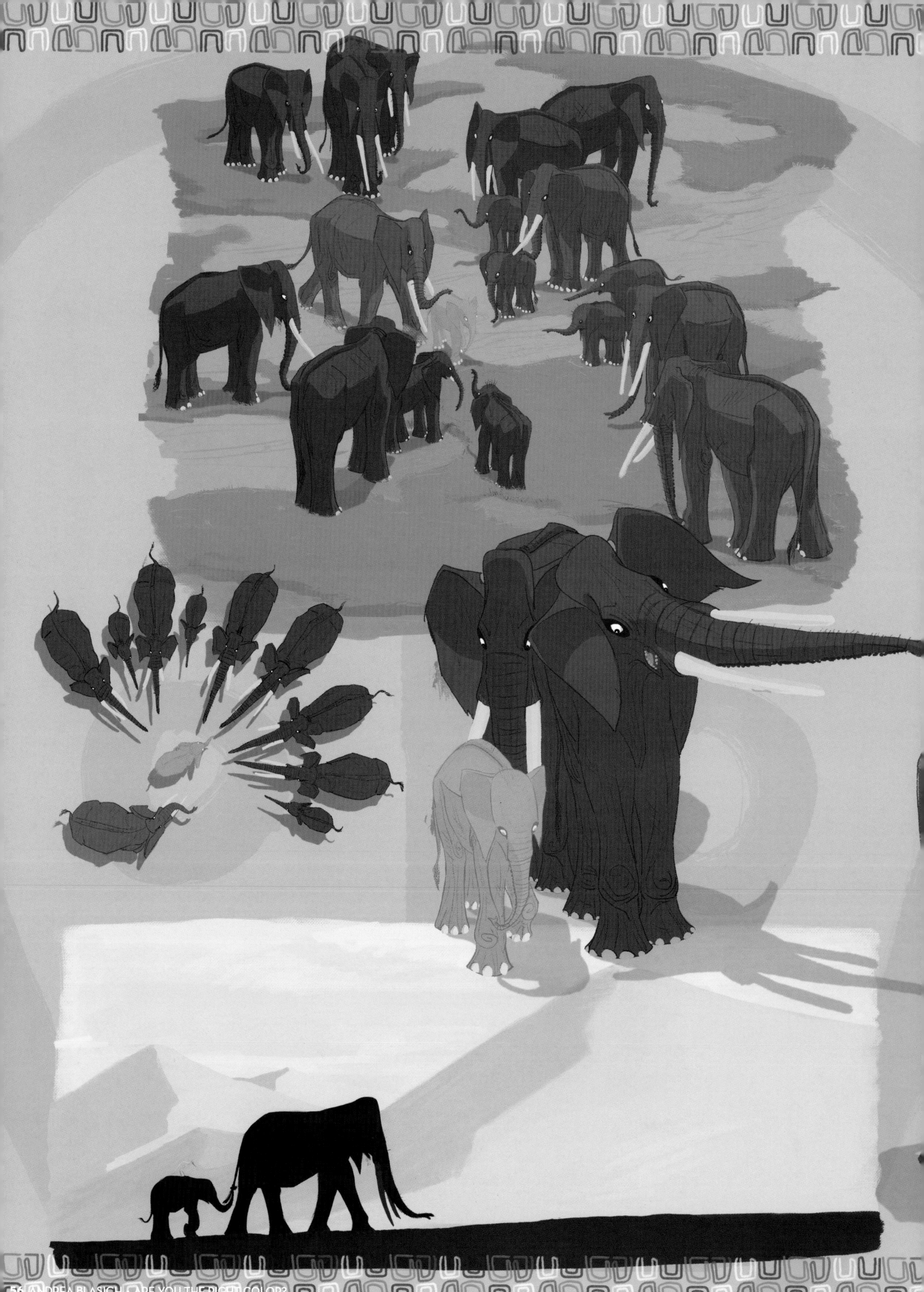

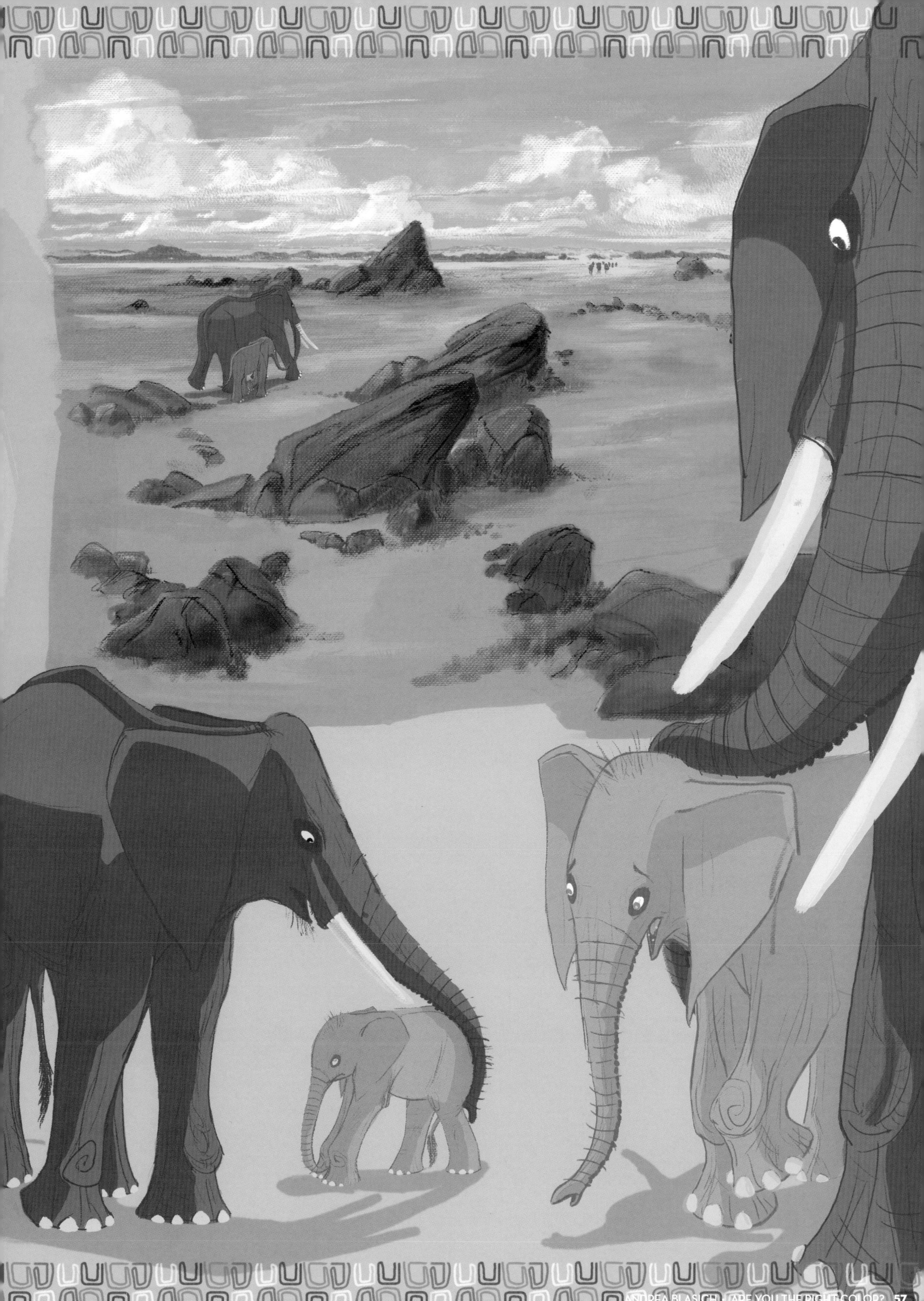

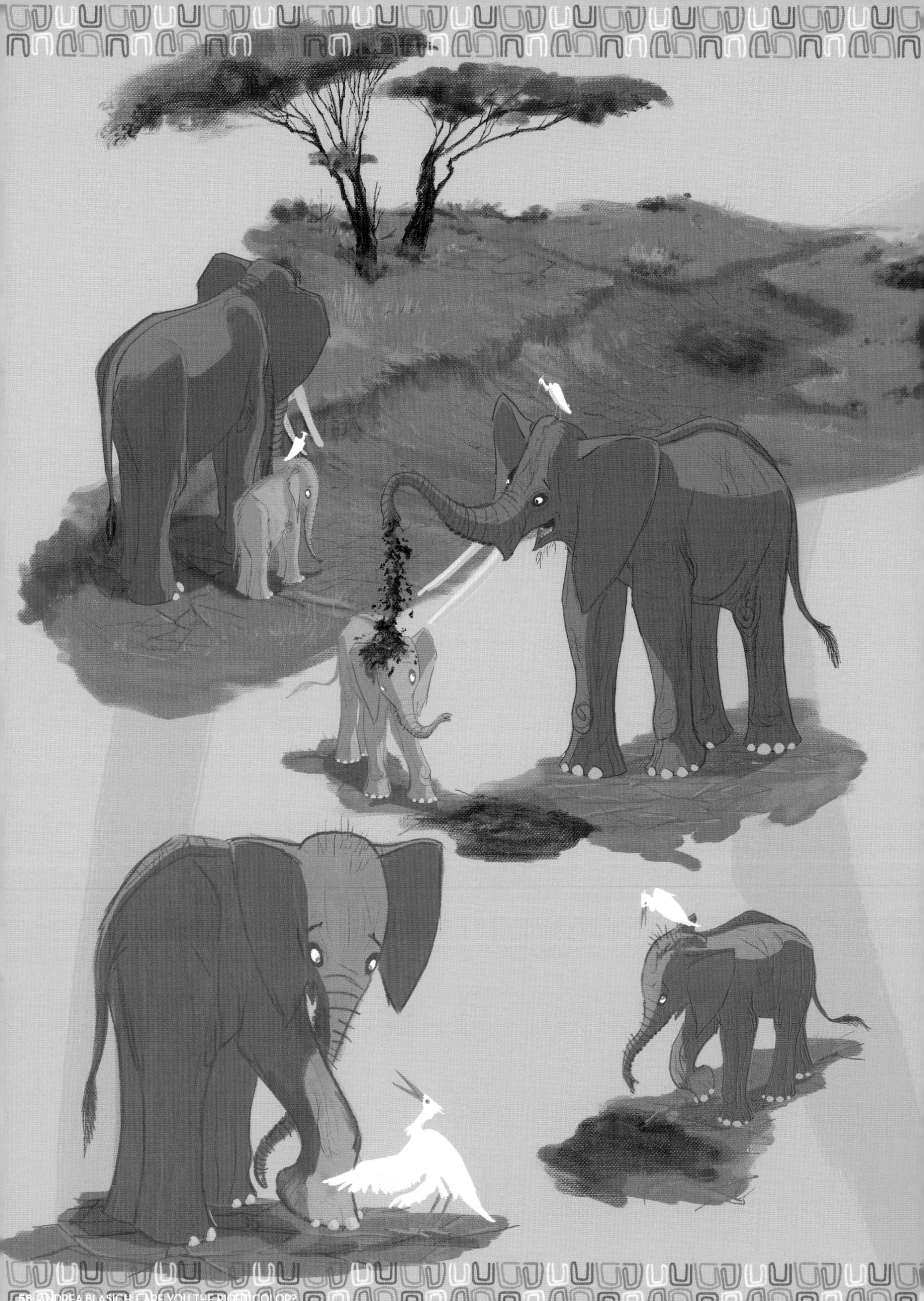

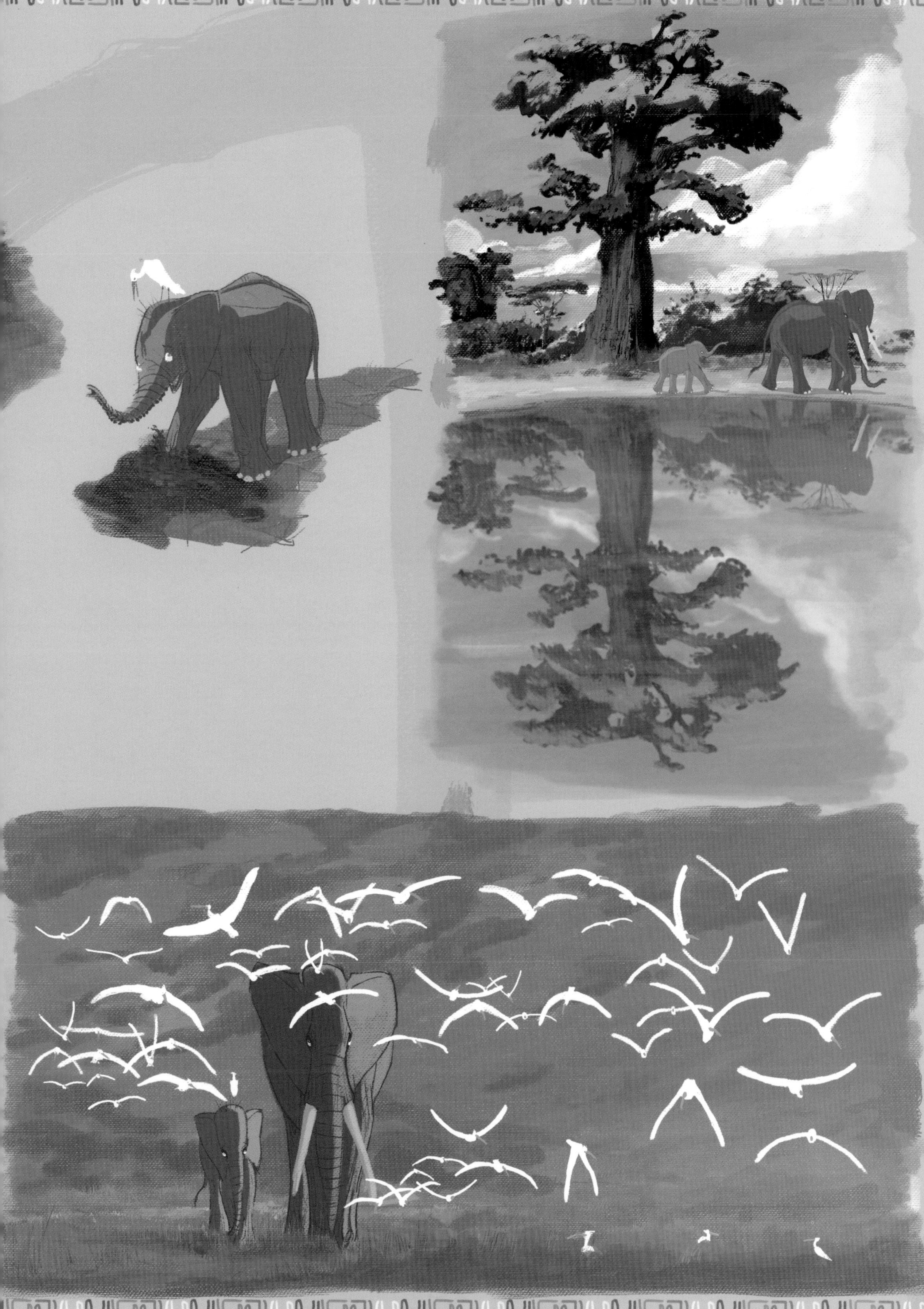

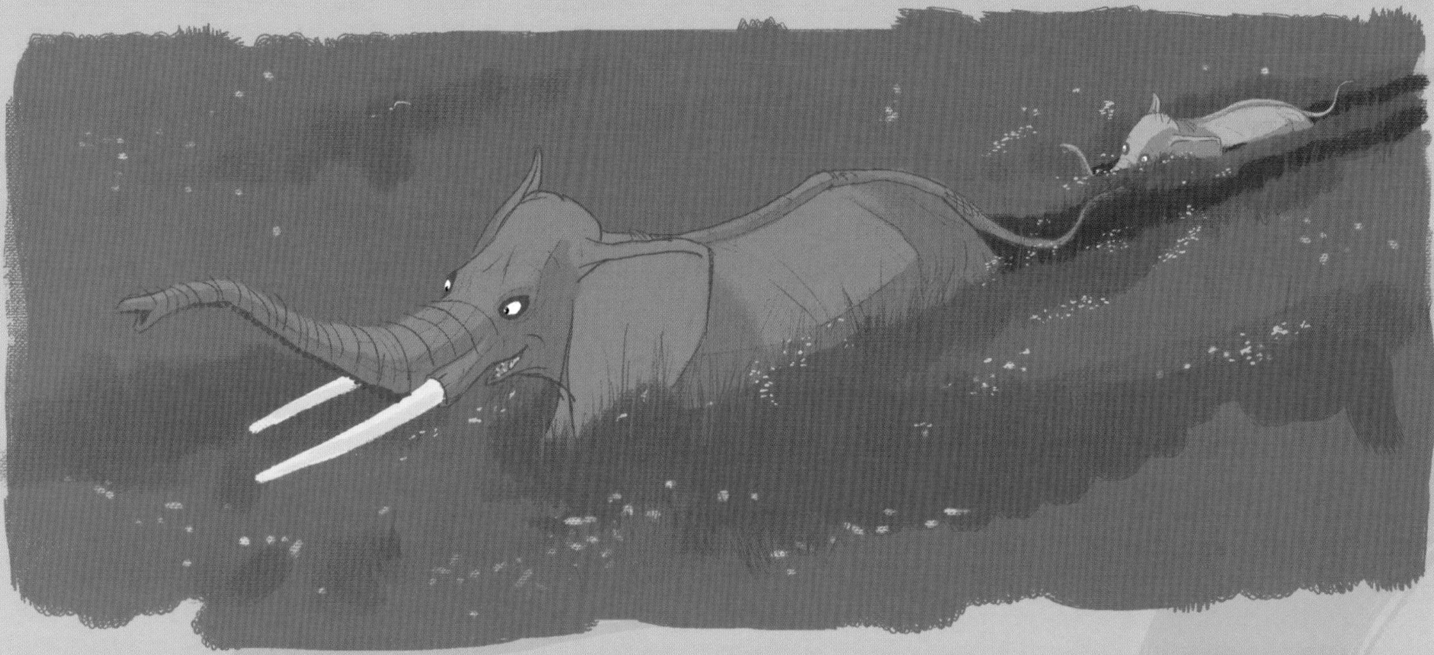

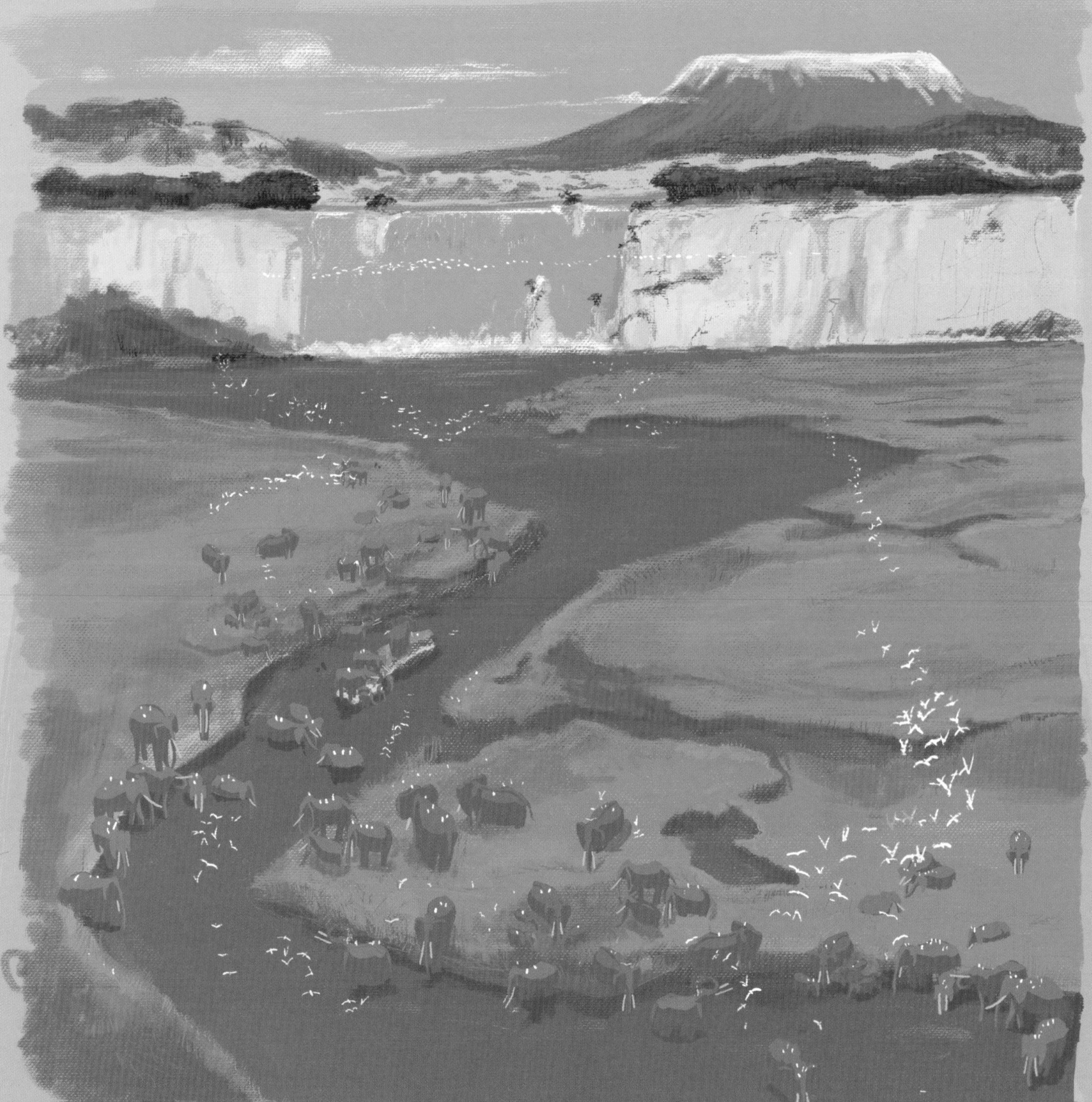

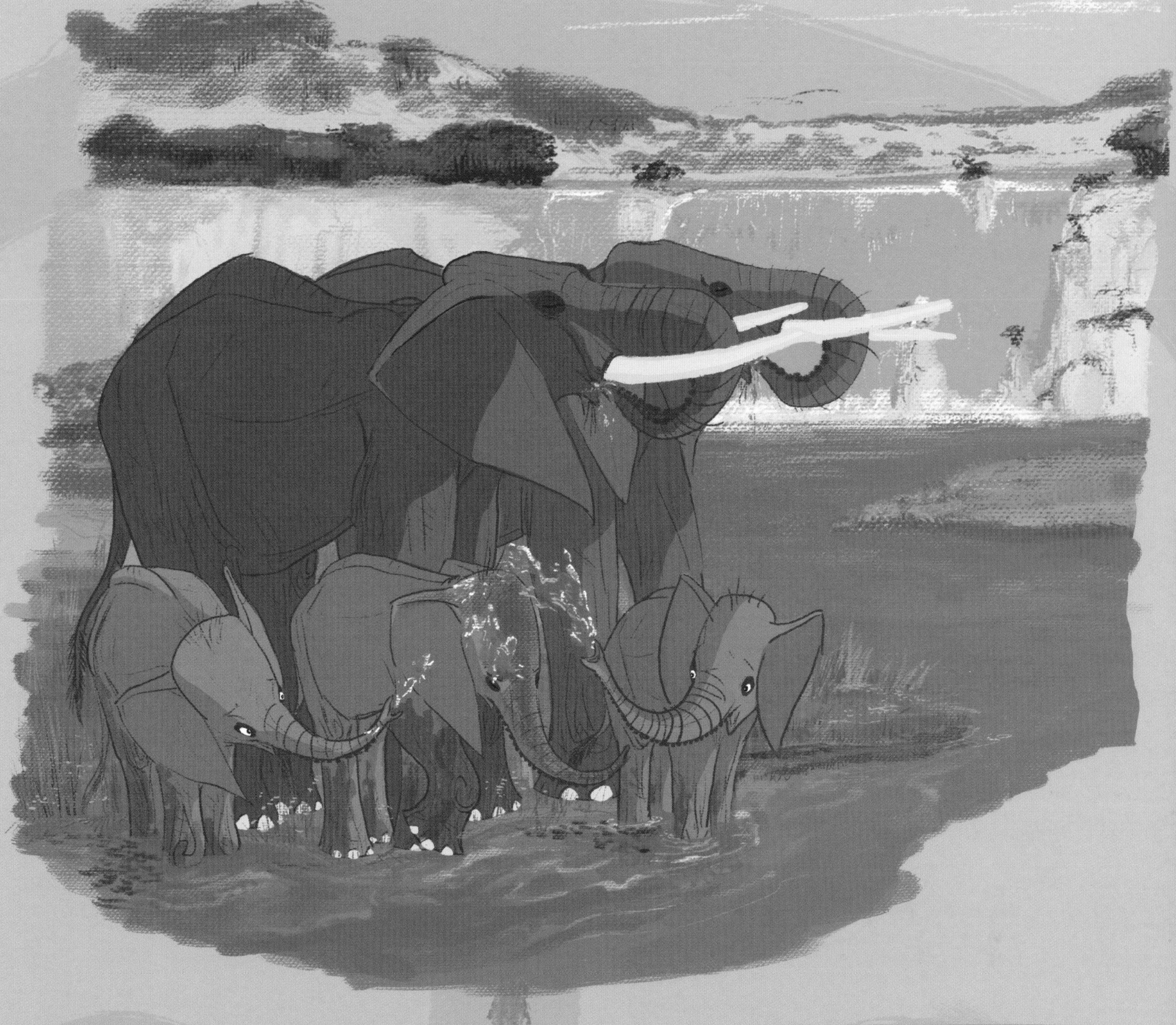

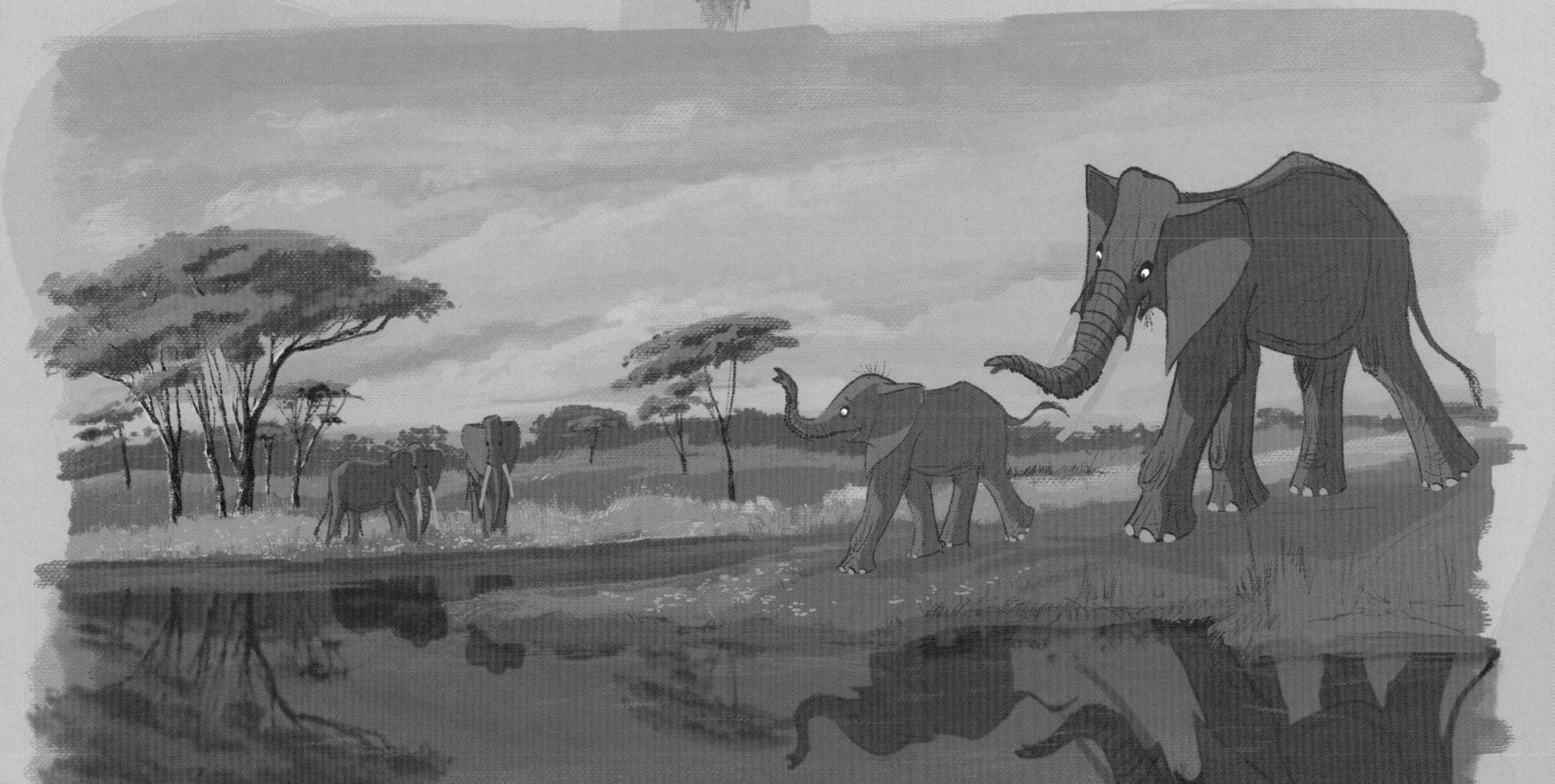

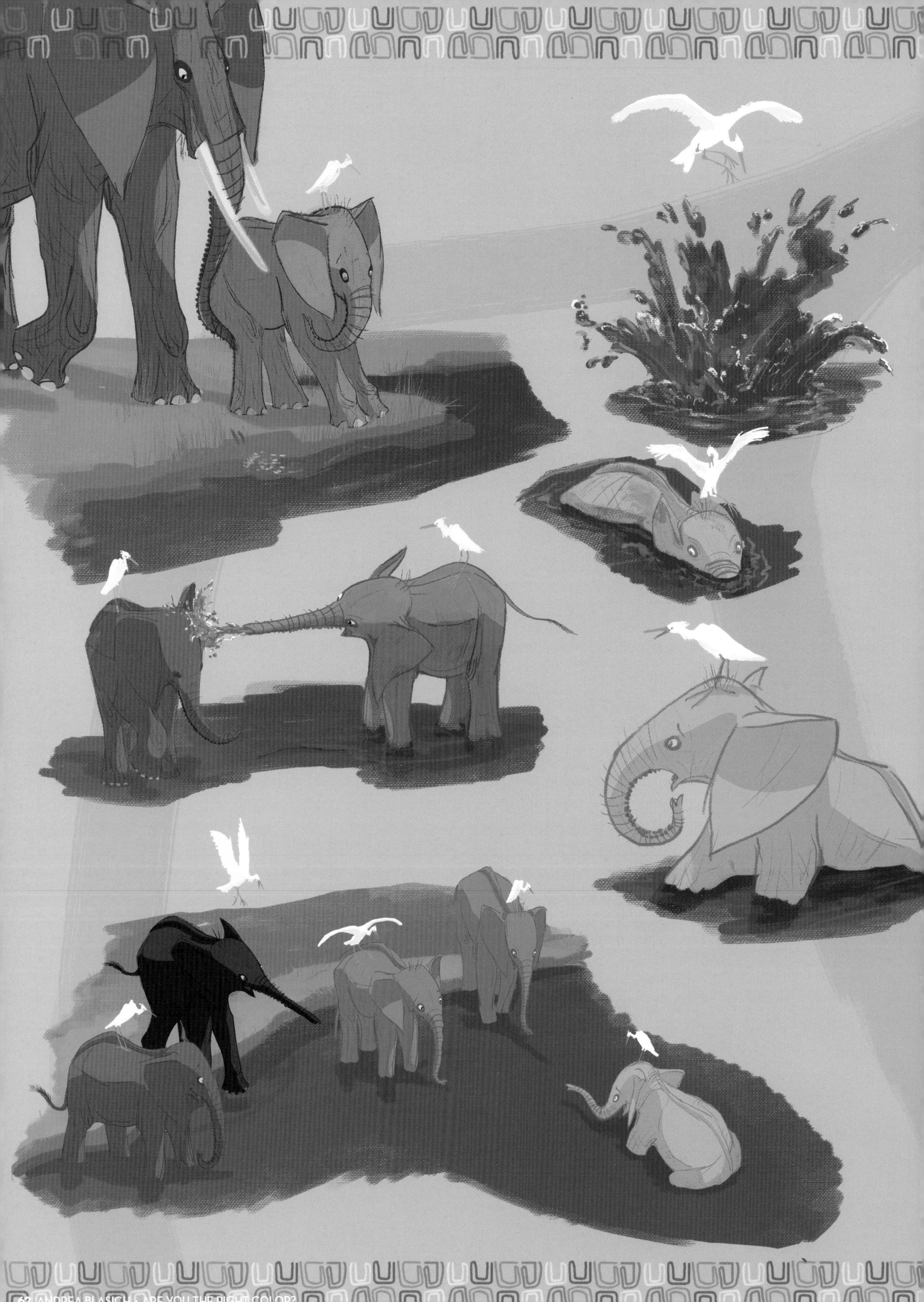

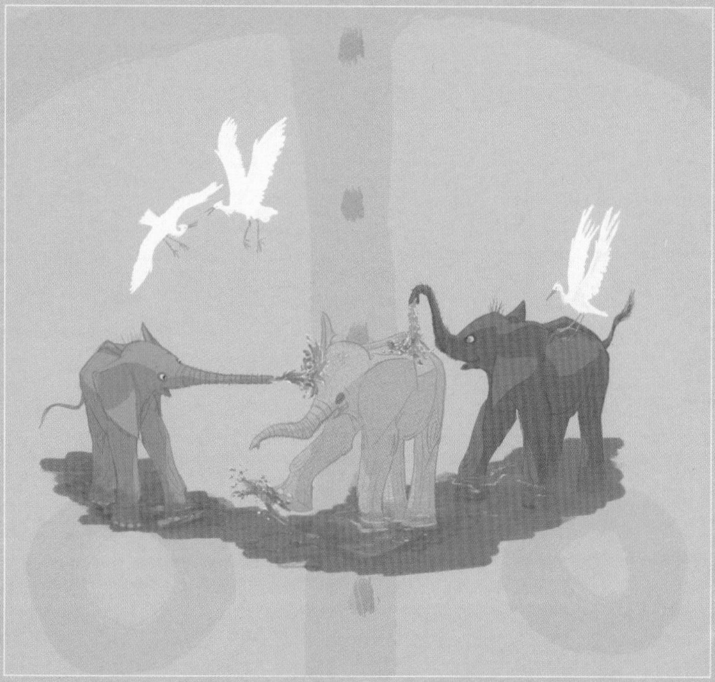

OUT OF PICTURE

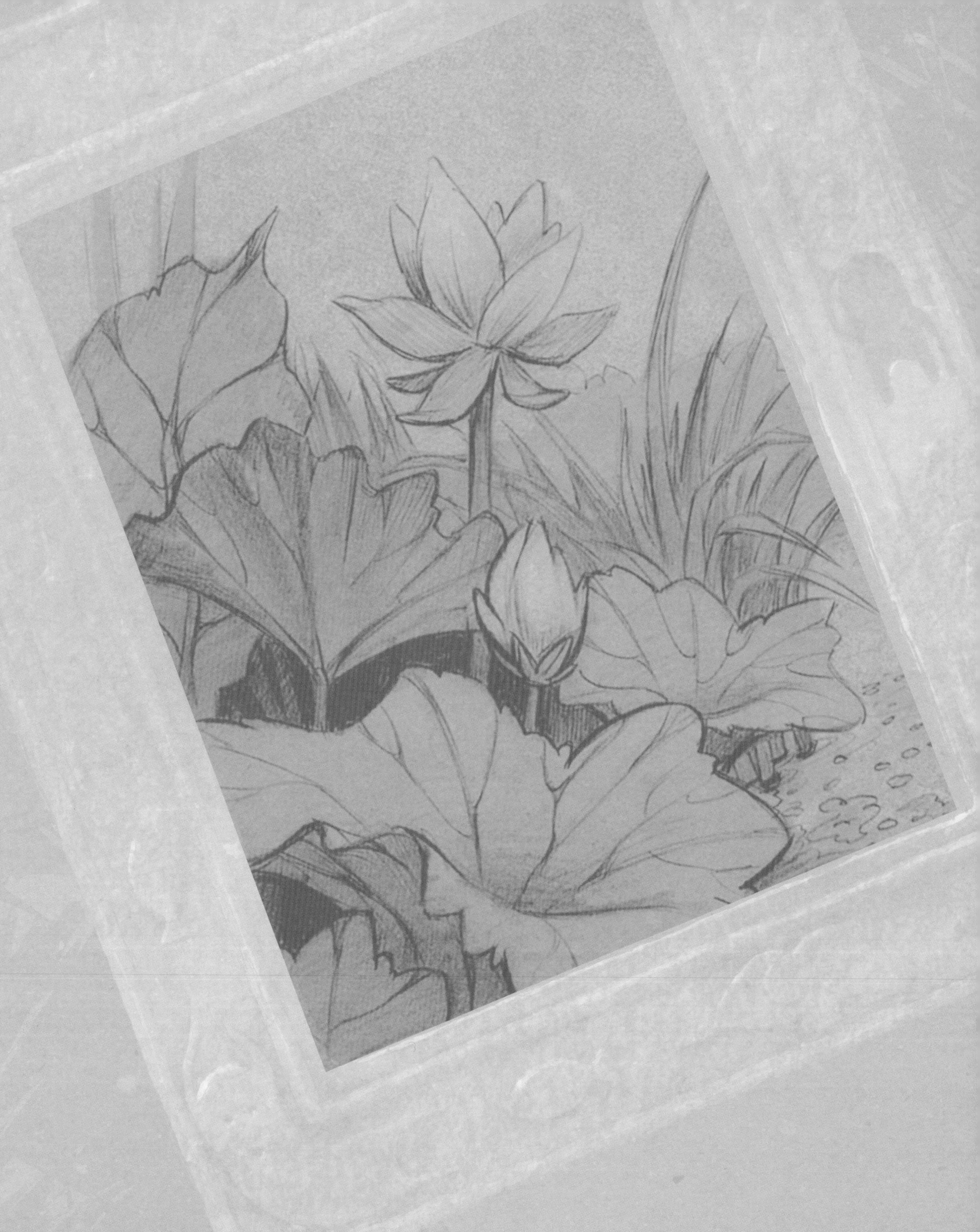

LIZETTE VEGA

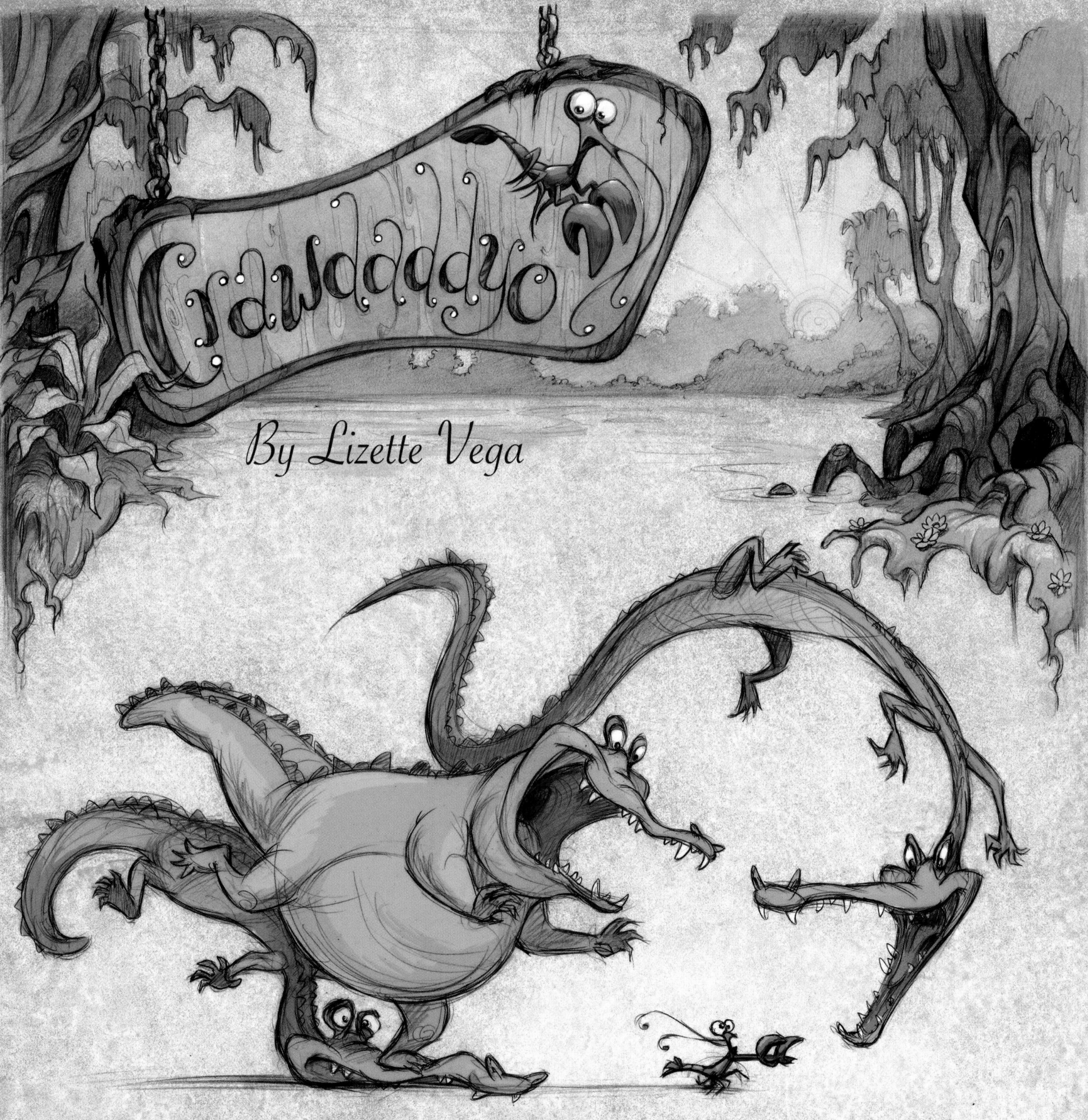
Crawdaddyo
By Lizette Vega

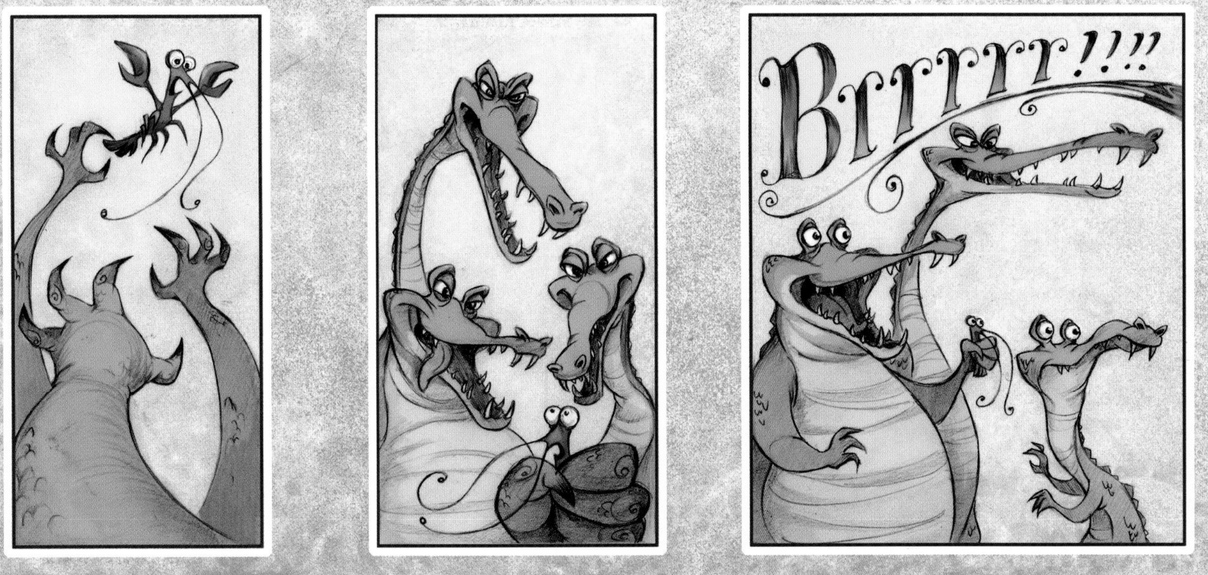
Brrrrr!!!!

Git 'em!!!

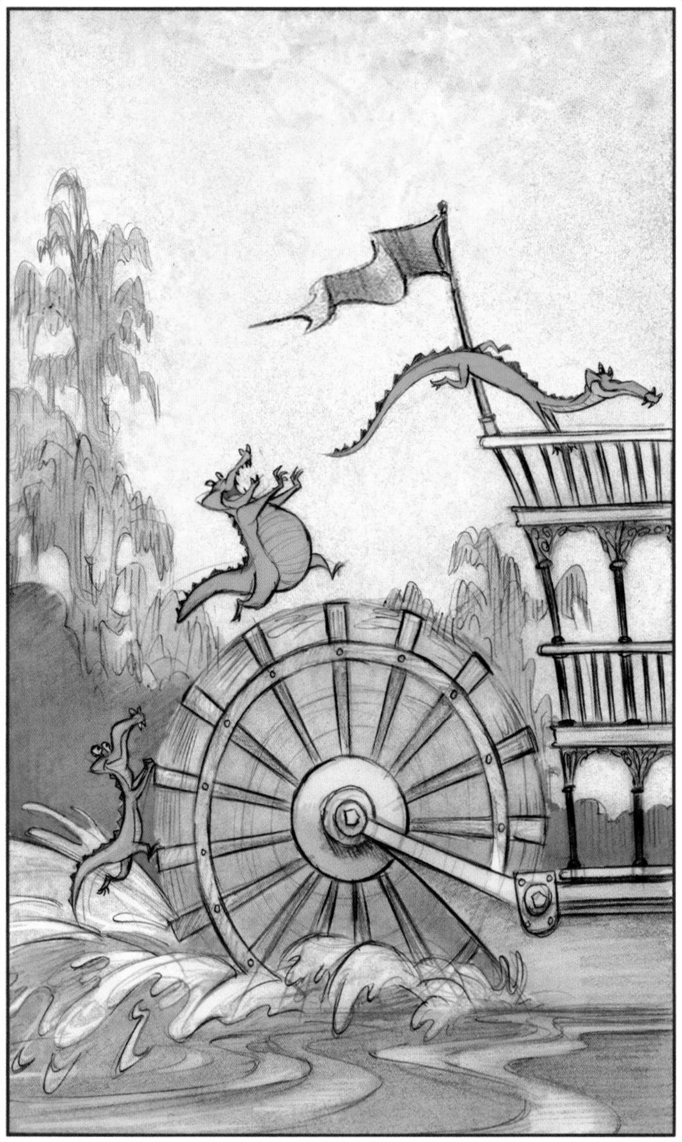

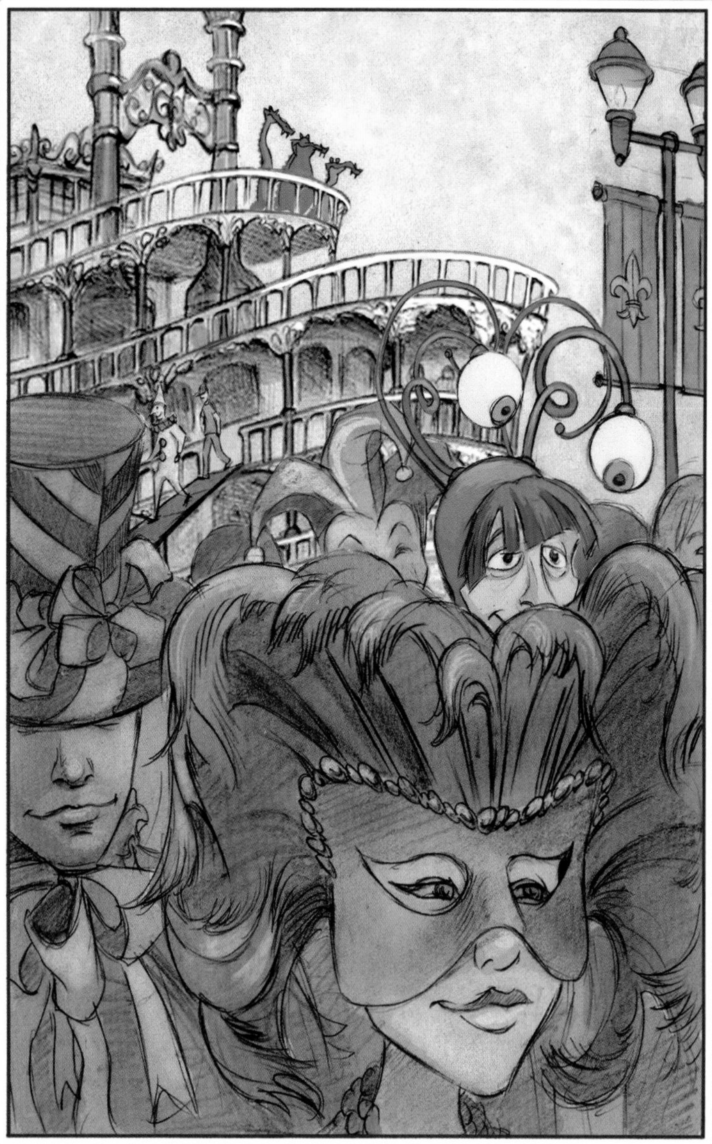

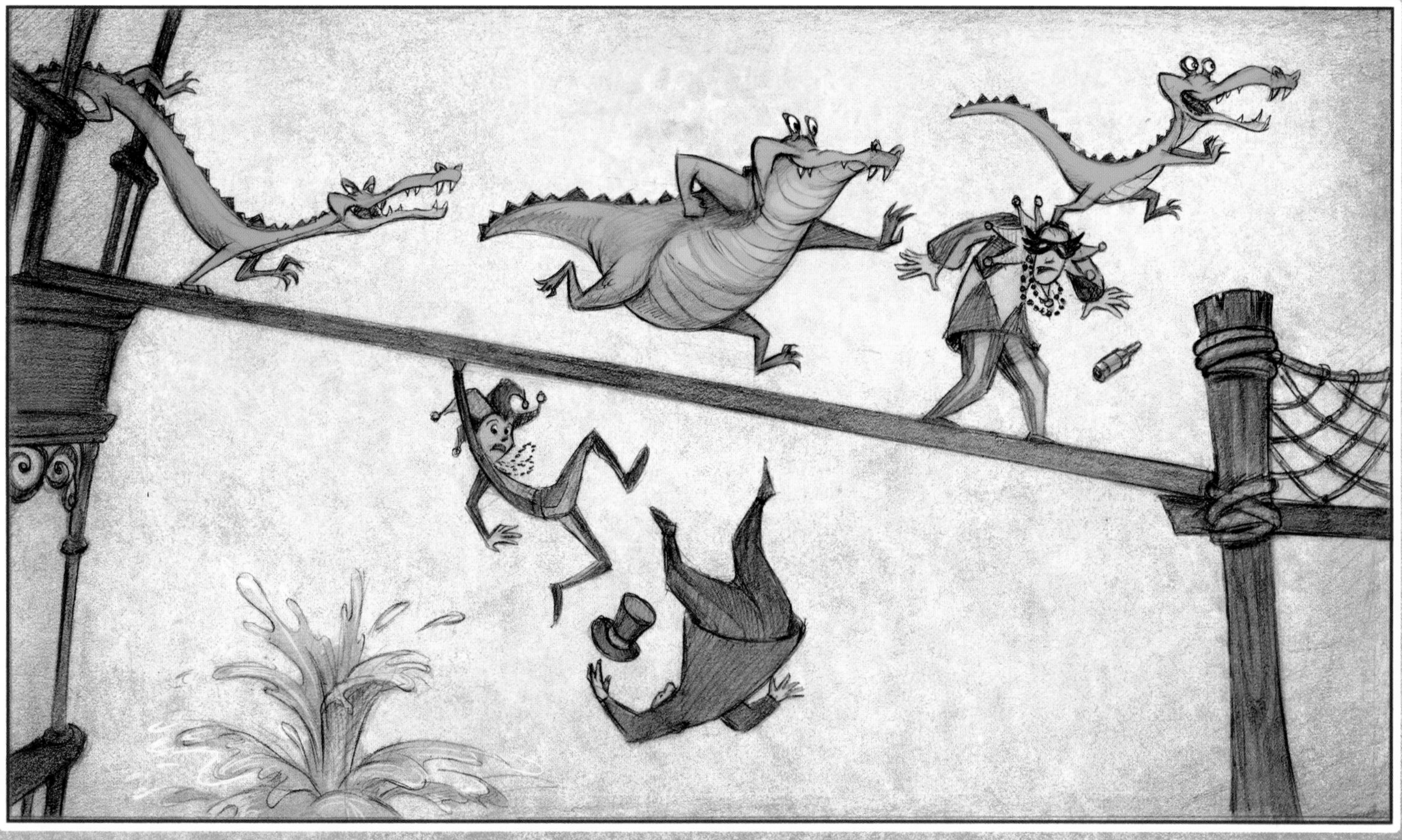

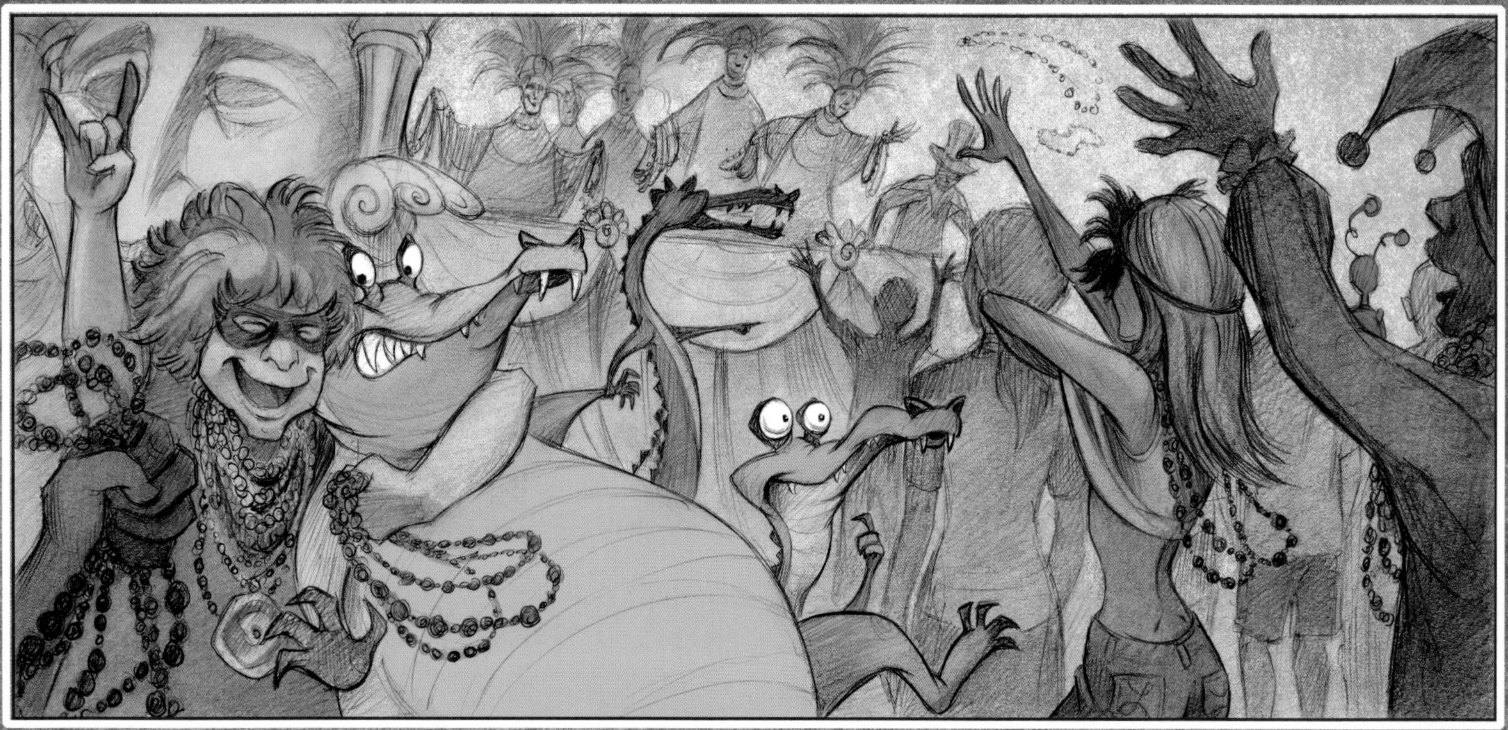

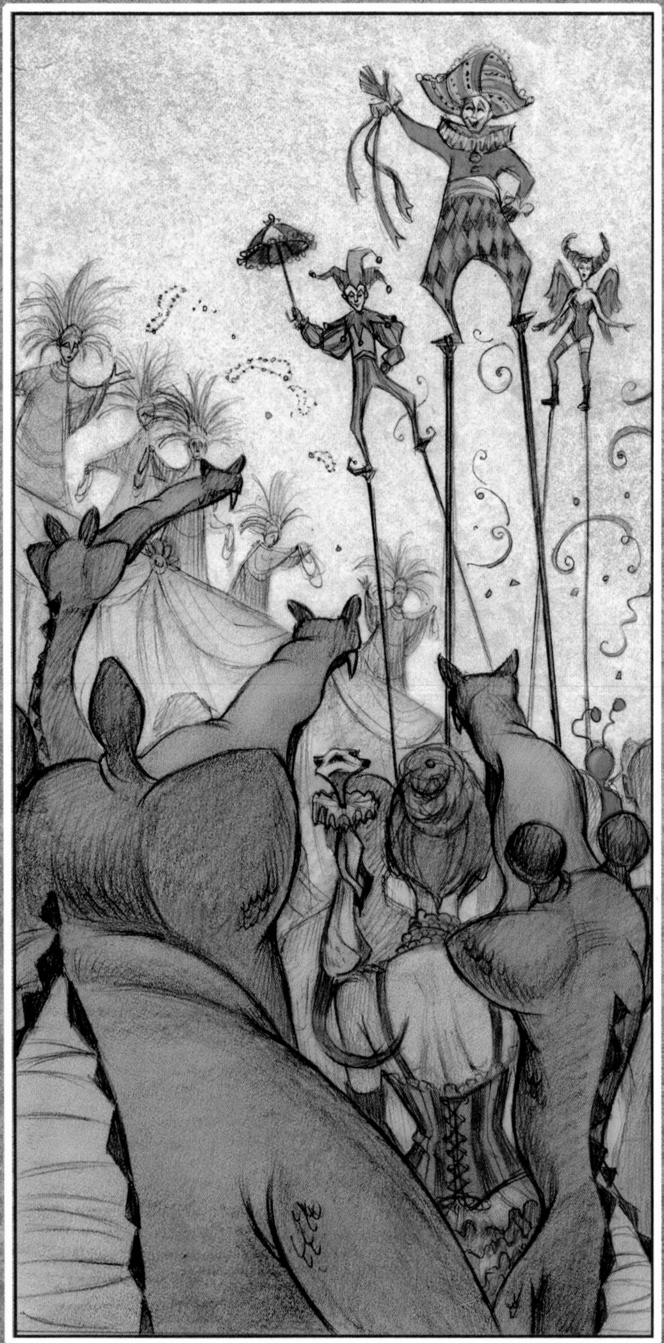

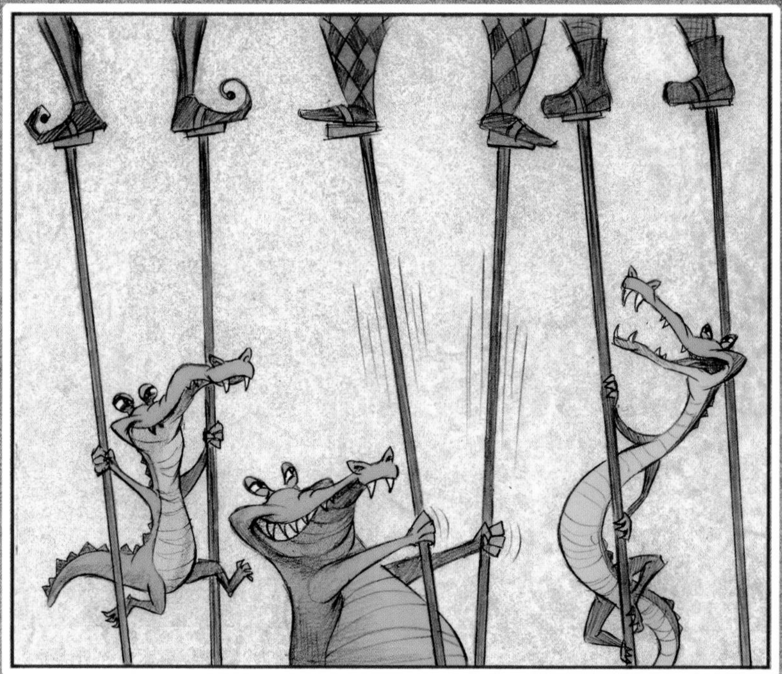

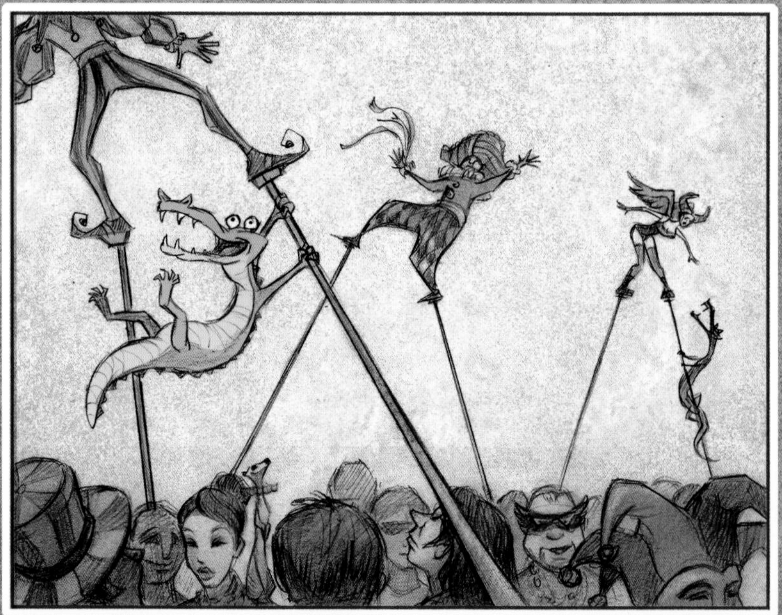

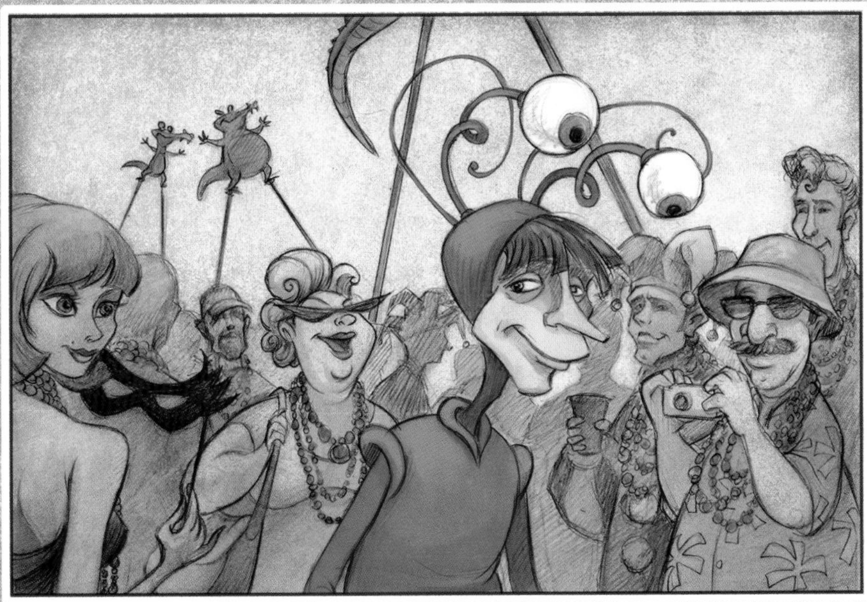

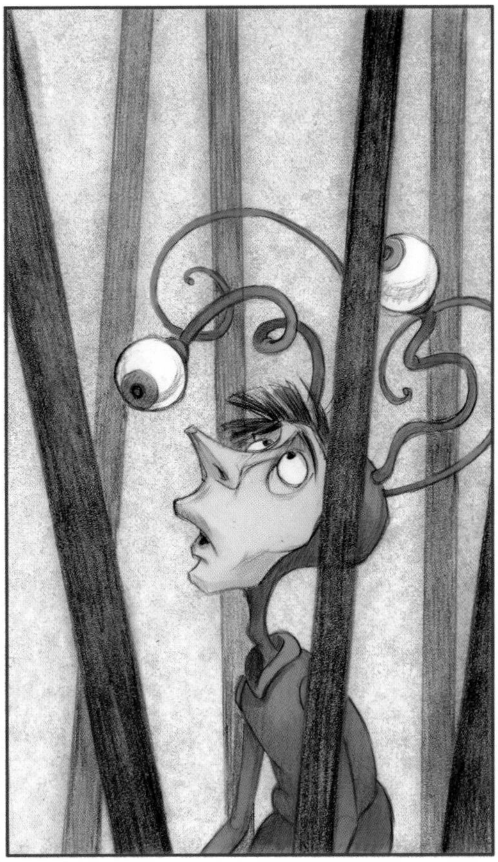

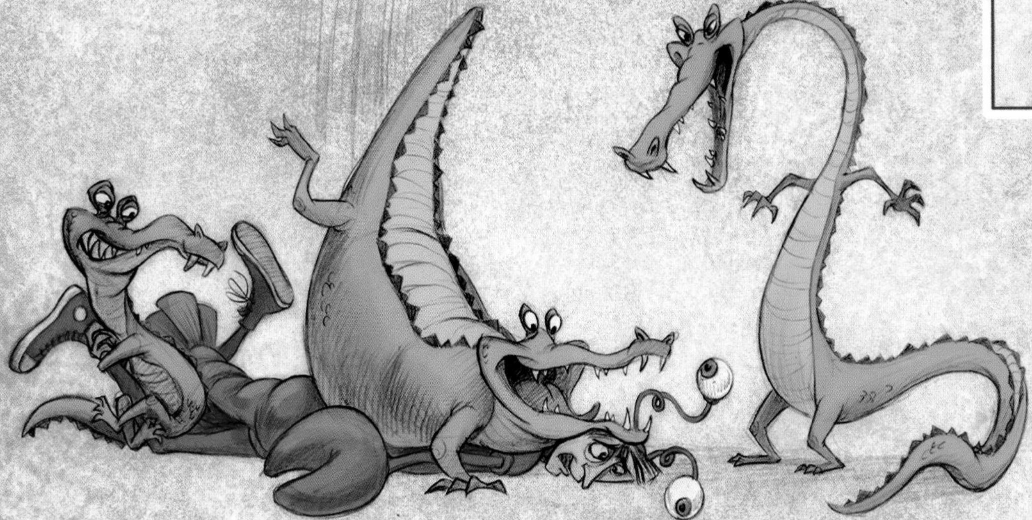

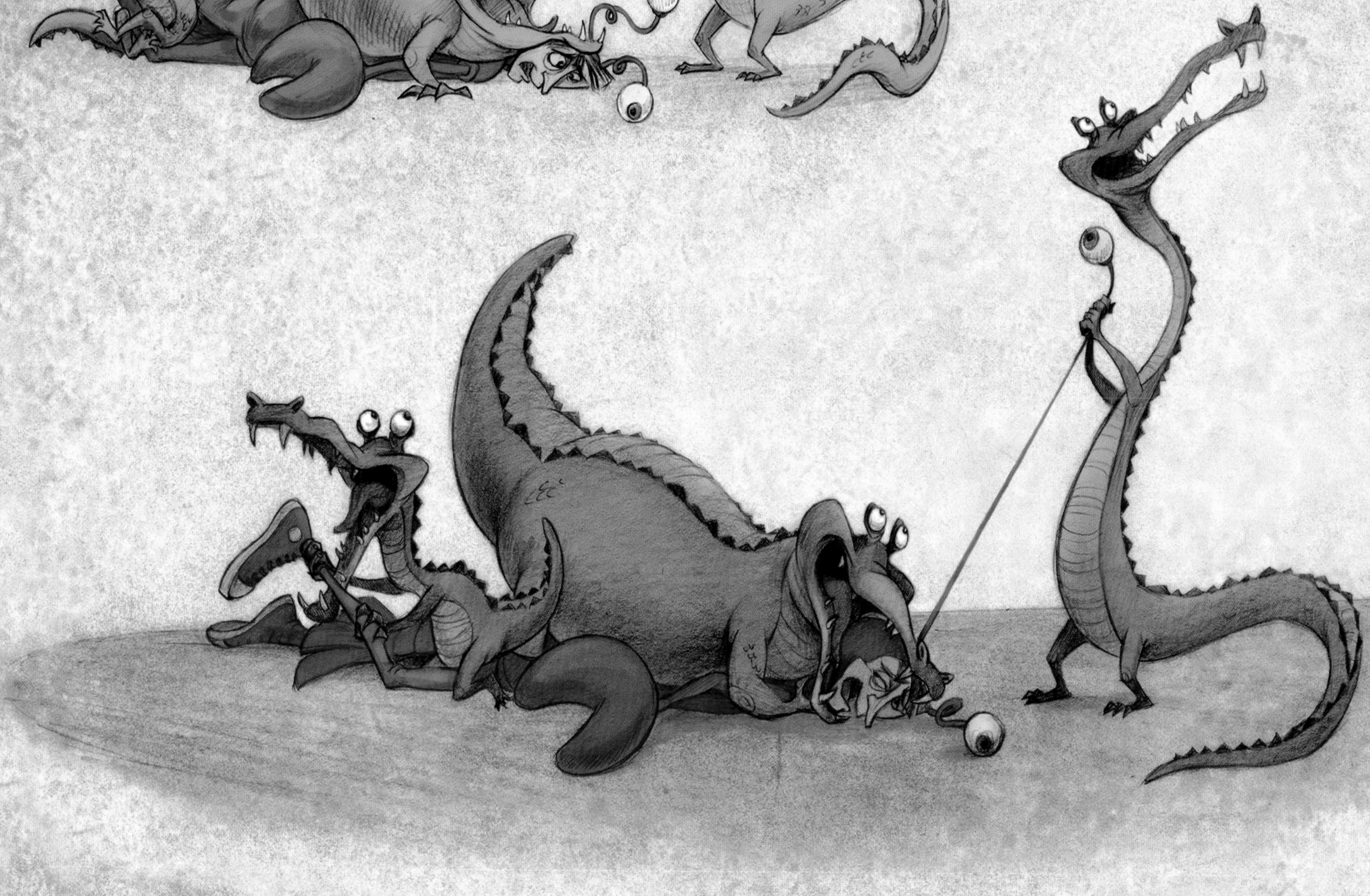

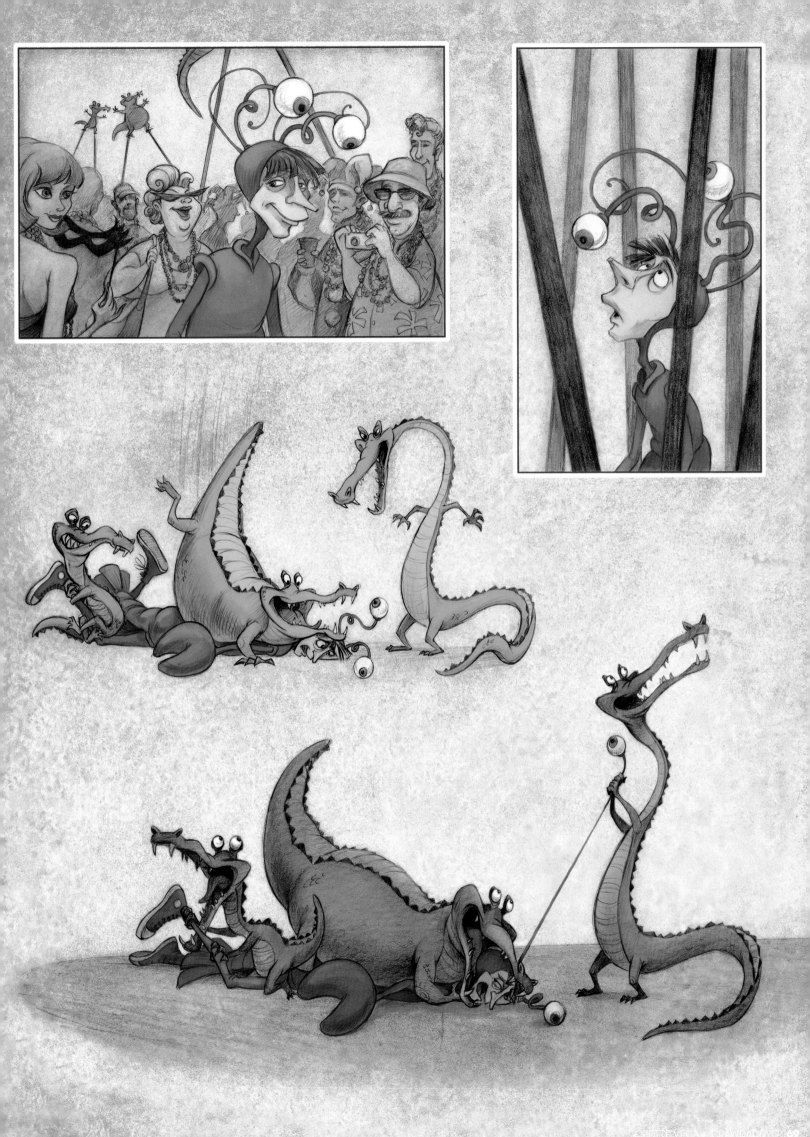

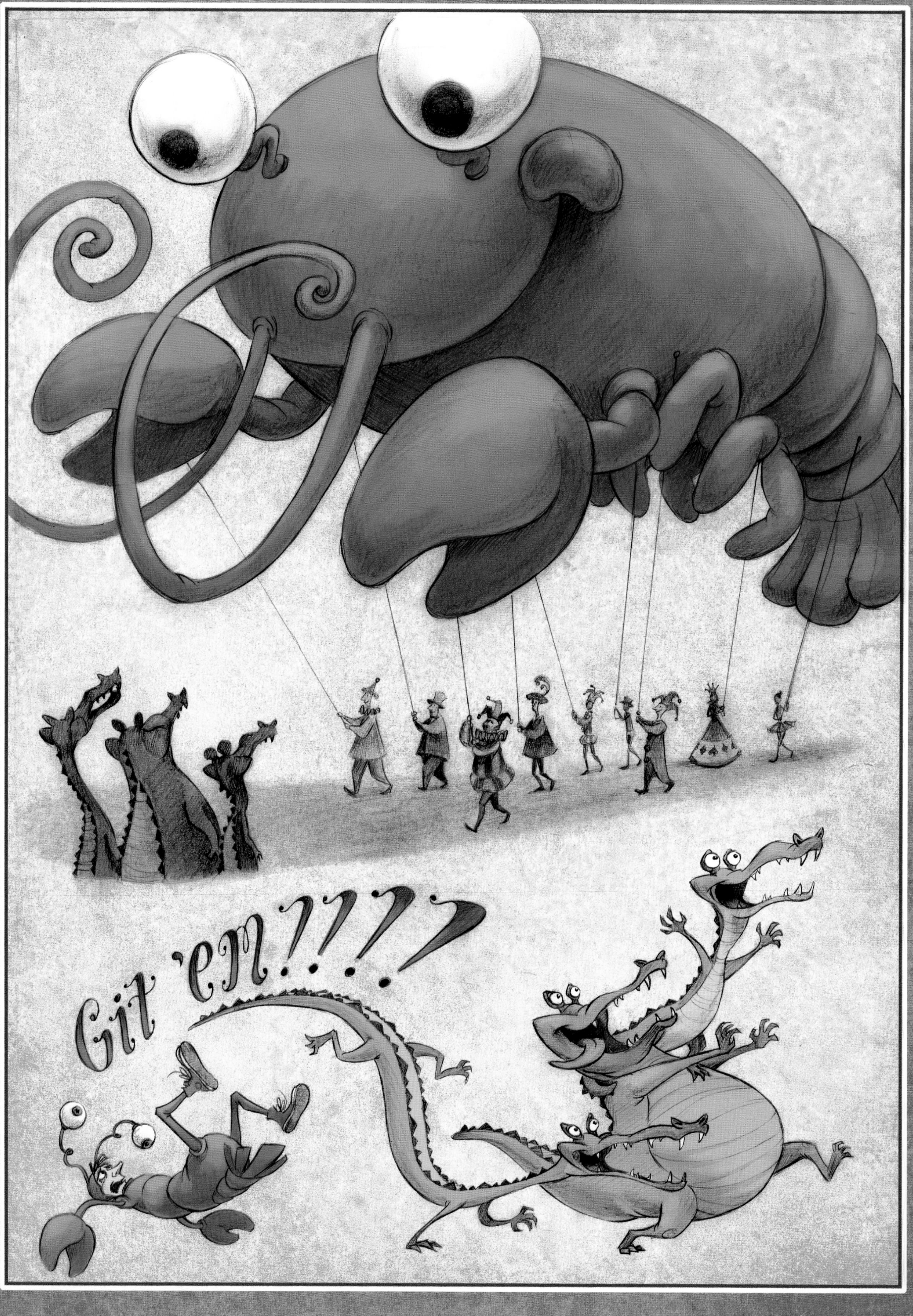
Git 'em!!!!

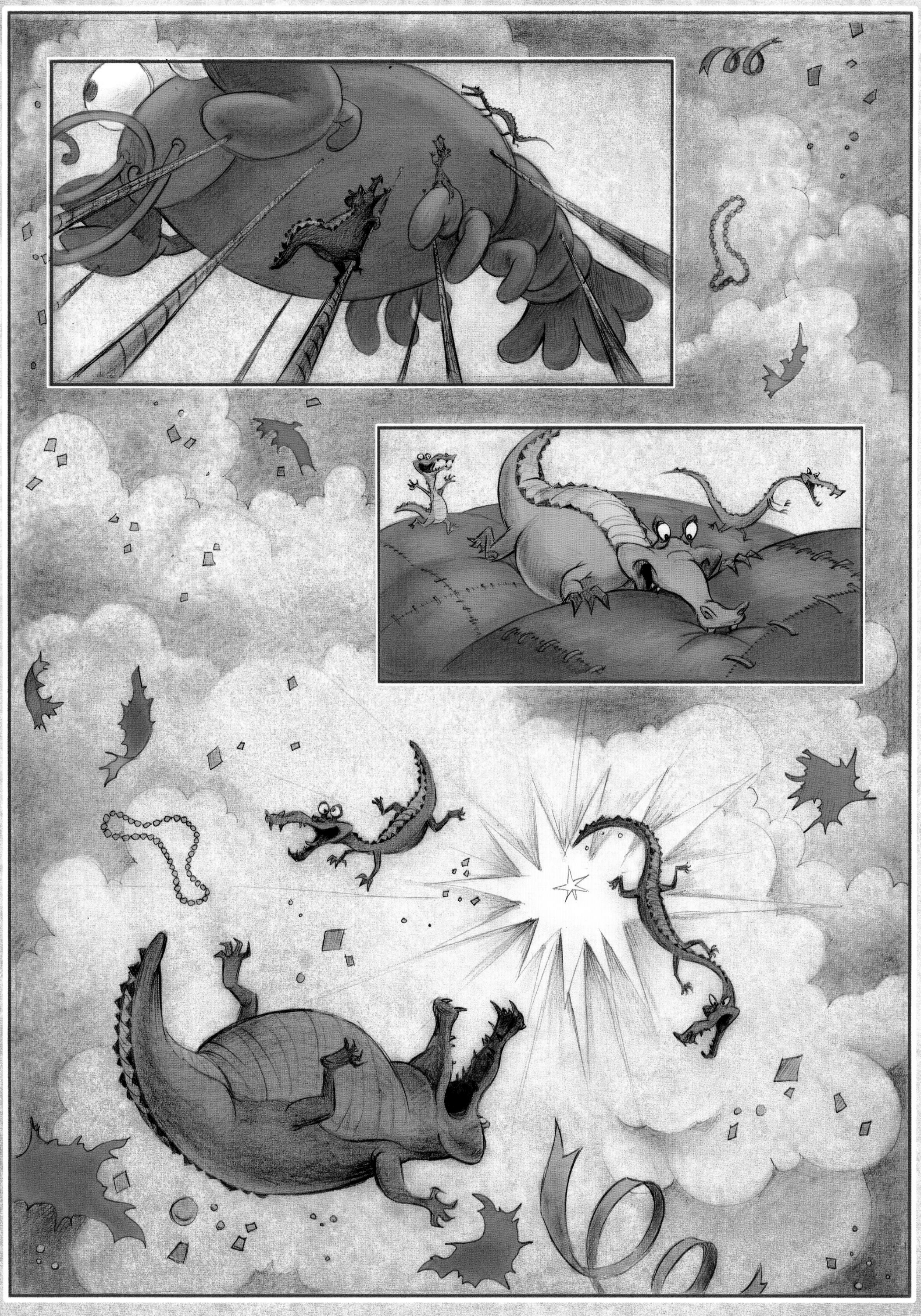

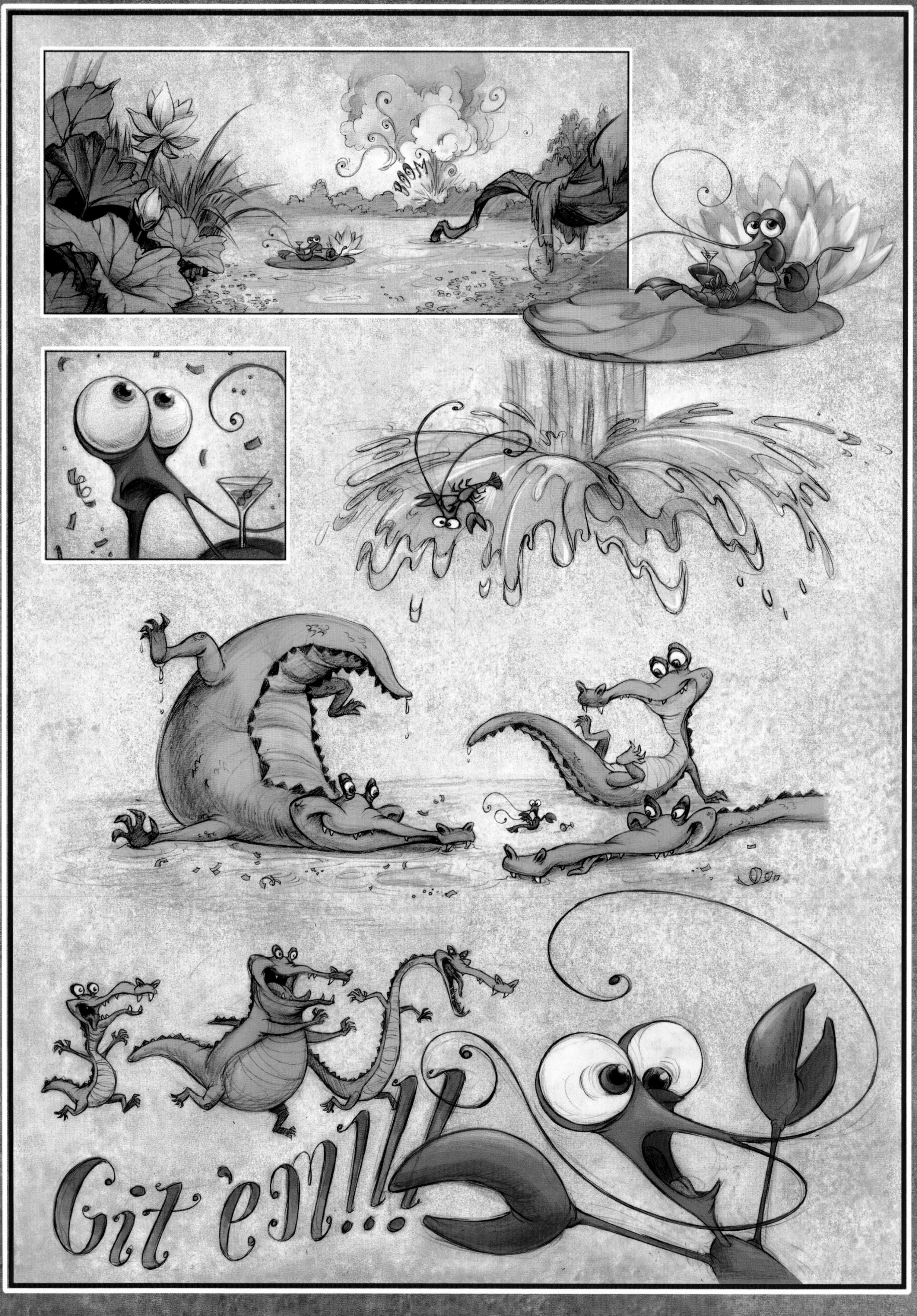
BOOM
Git 'em!!!

DAISUKE TSUTSUMI

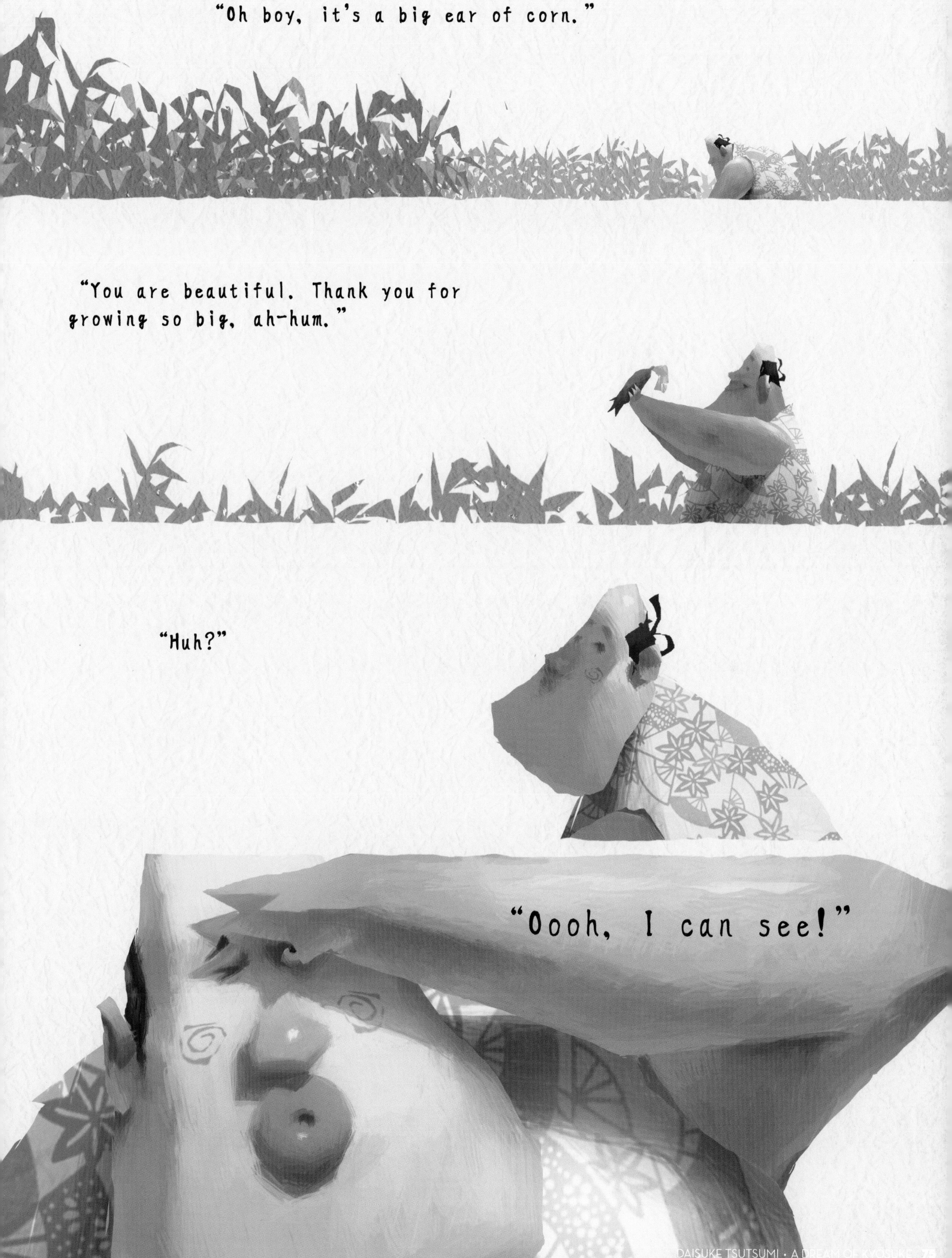
"Oh boy, it's a big ear of corn."
"You are beautiful. Thank you for growing so big, ah-hum."
"Huh?"
"Oooh, I can see!"

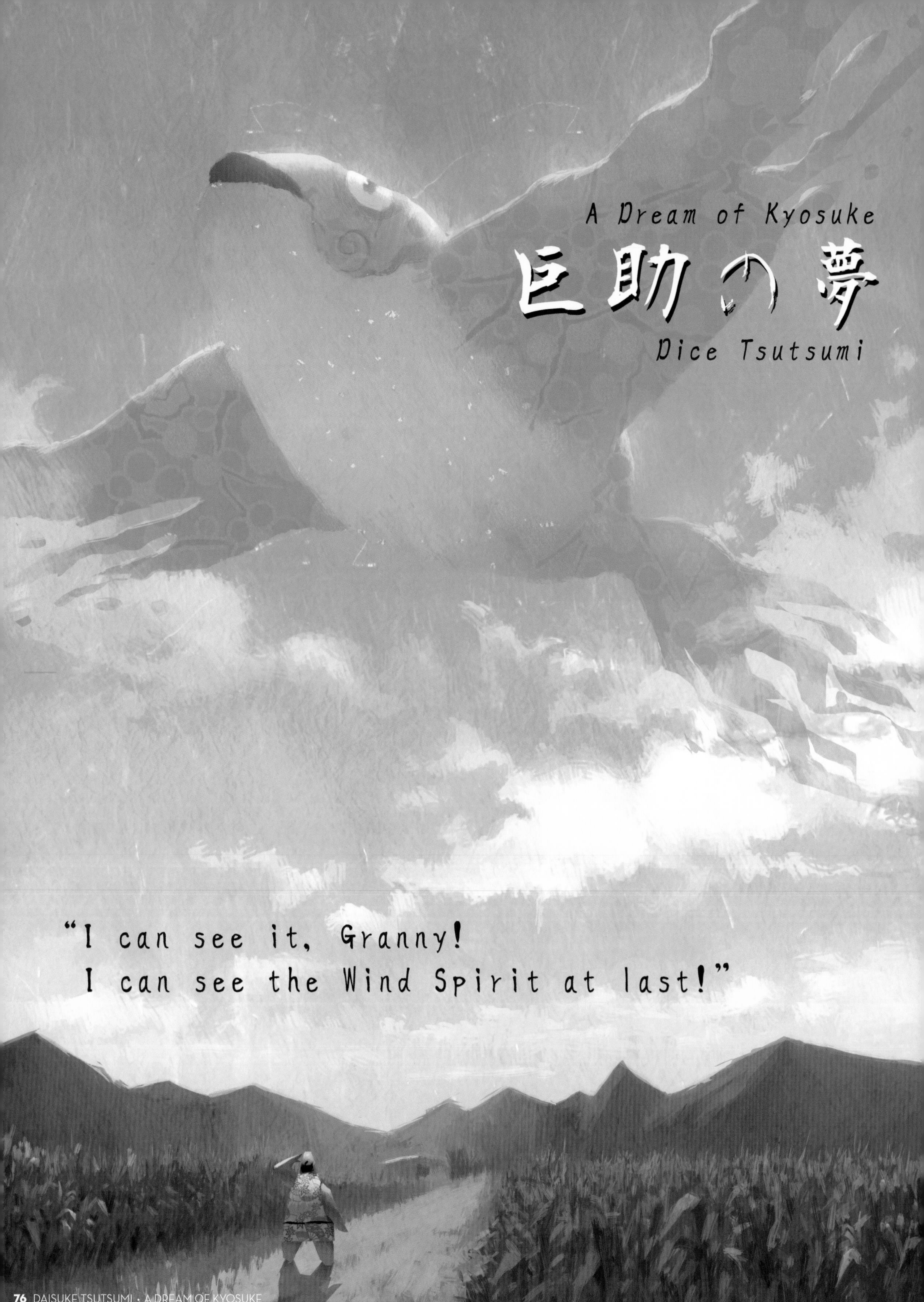
A Dream of Kyosuke
巨助の夢
Dice Tsutsumi
"I can see it, Granny!
I can see the Wind Spirit at last!"

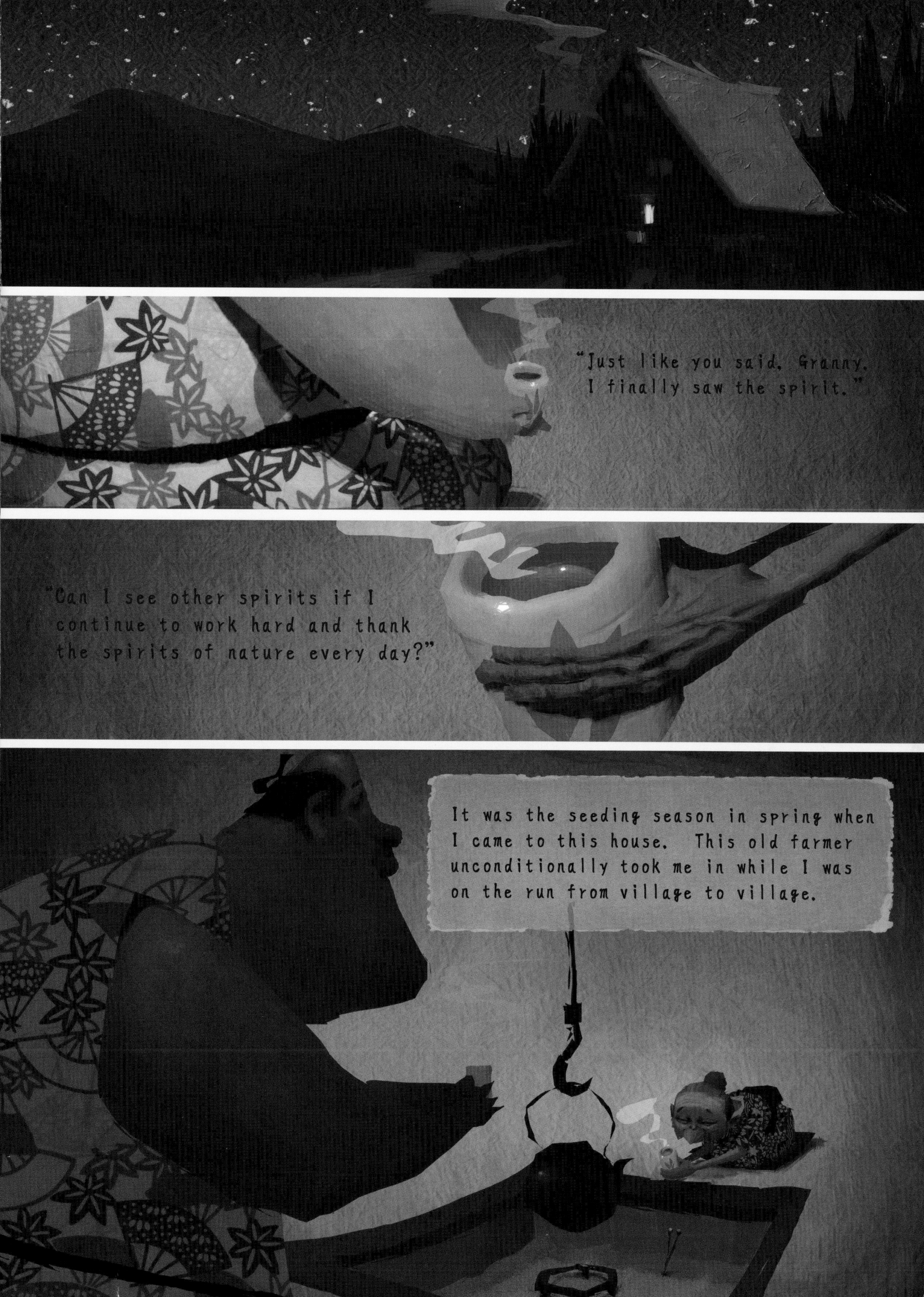
"Just like you said, Granny. I finally saw the spirit."
"Can I see other spirits if I continue to work hard and thank the spirits of nature every day?"
It was the seeding season in spring when I came to this house. This old farmer unconditionally took me in while I was on the run from village to village.

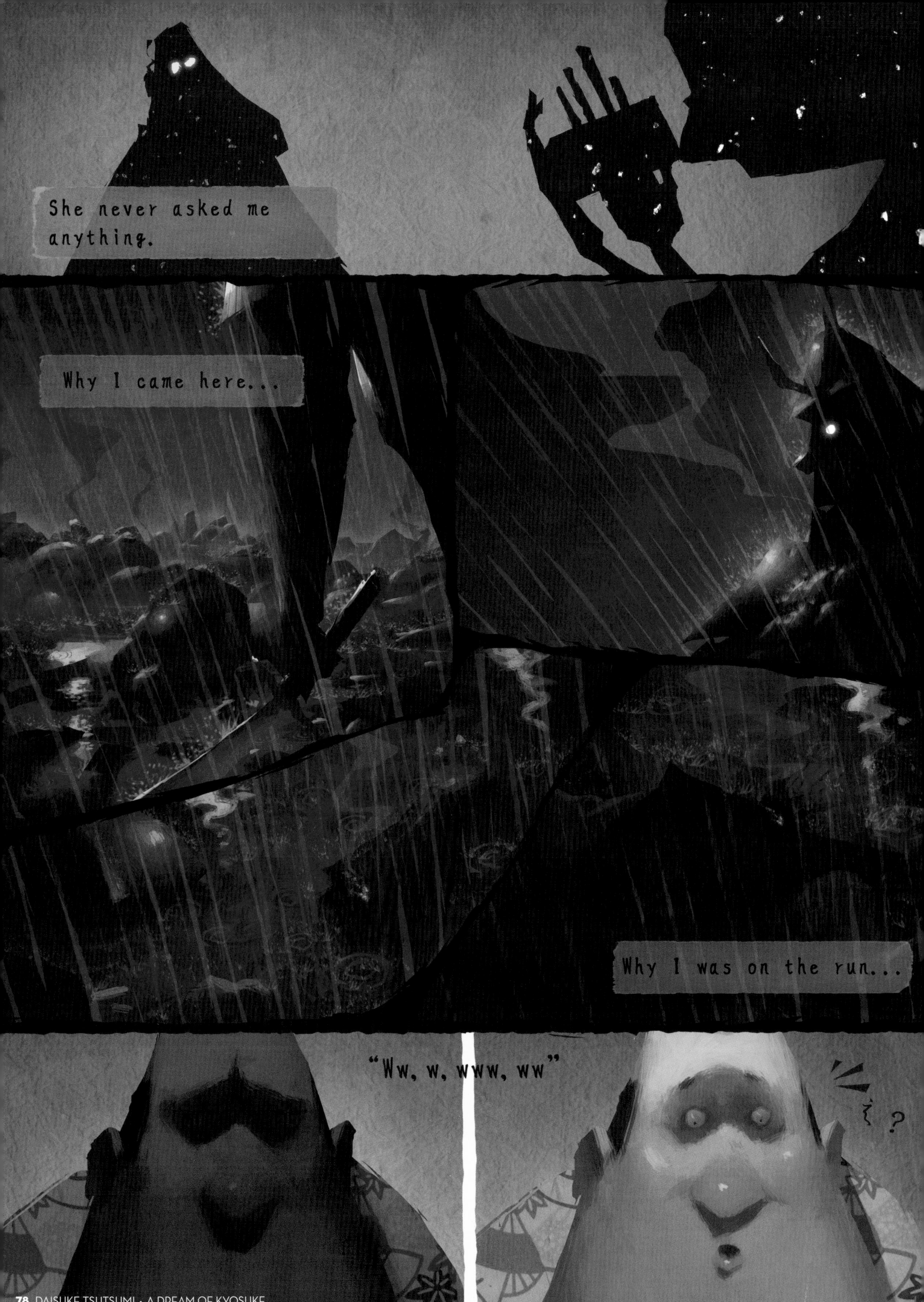
She never asked me anything.
Why I came here...
Why I was on the run...
"Ww, w, www, ww"
?

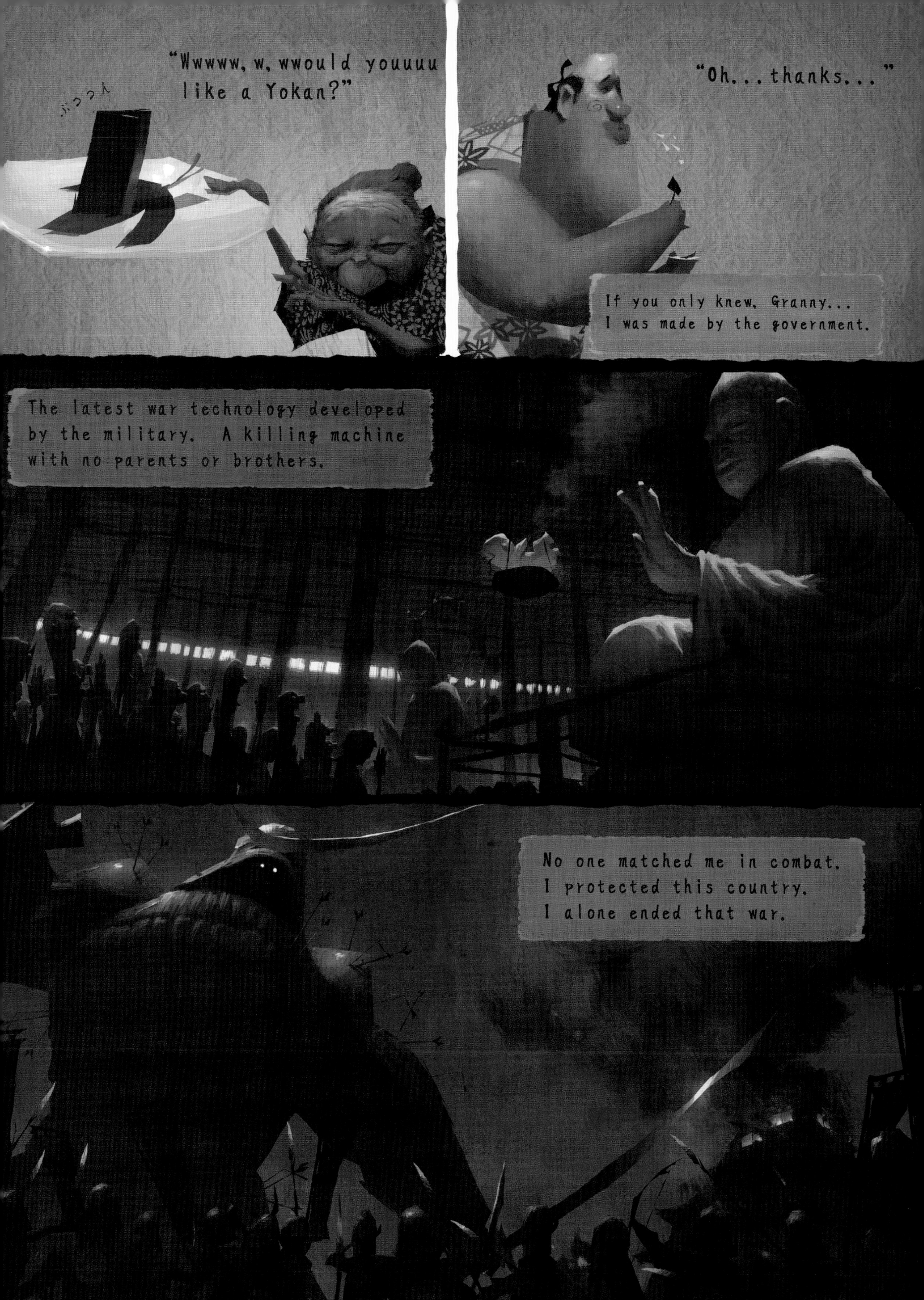
"Wwwww, w, wwould youuuu like a Yokan?"
ぶっっん
"Oh... thanks..."
If you only knew, Granny... I was made by the government.
The latest war technology developed by the military. A killing machine with no parents or brothers.
No one matched me in combat. I protected this country. I alone ended that war.

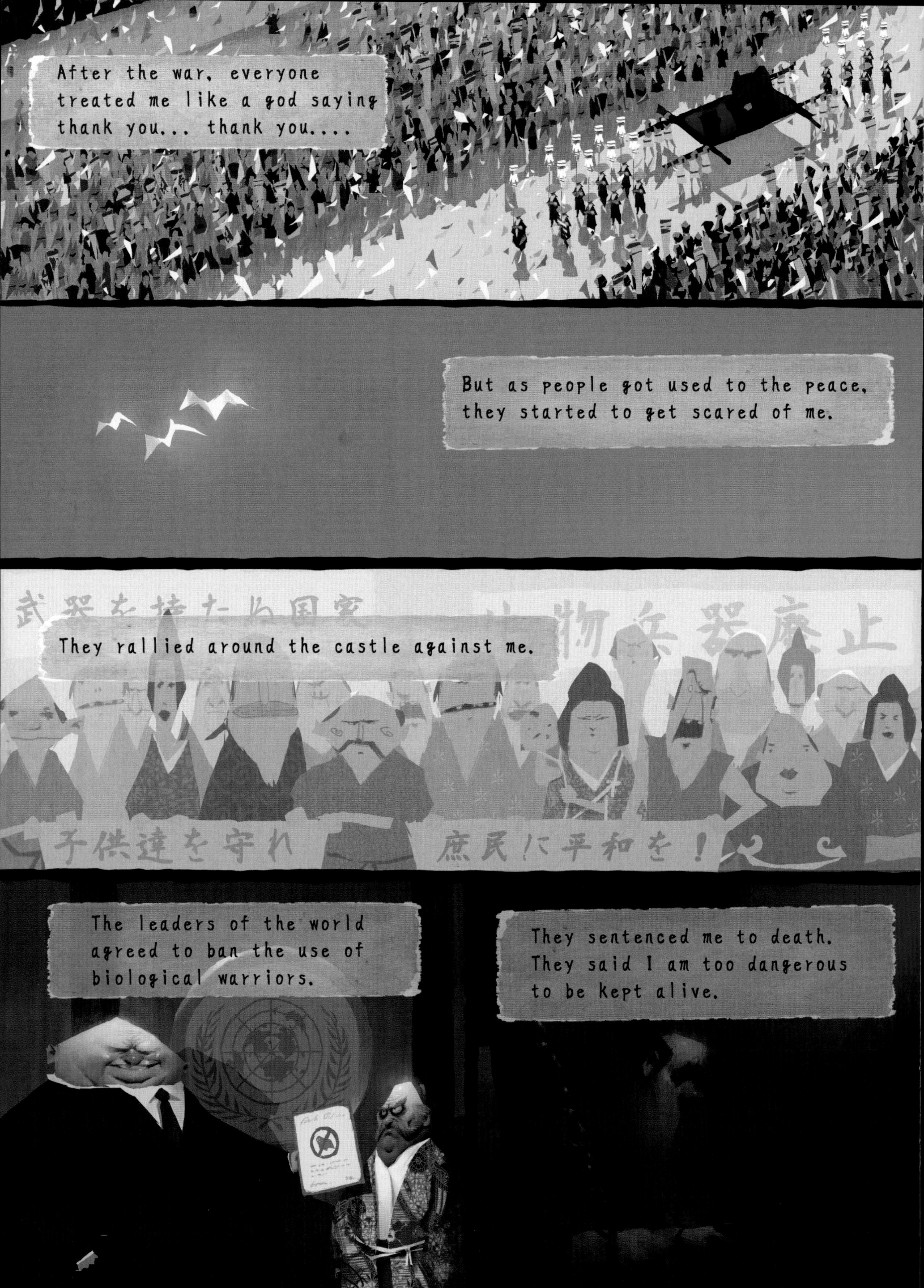

After the war, everyone treated me like a god saying thank you... thank you....
But as people got used to the peace, they started to get scared of me.
They rallied around the castle against me.
子供達を守れ
庶民に平和を！
The leaders of the world agreed to ban the use of biological warriors.
They sentenced me to death. They said I am too dangerous to be kept alive.

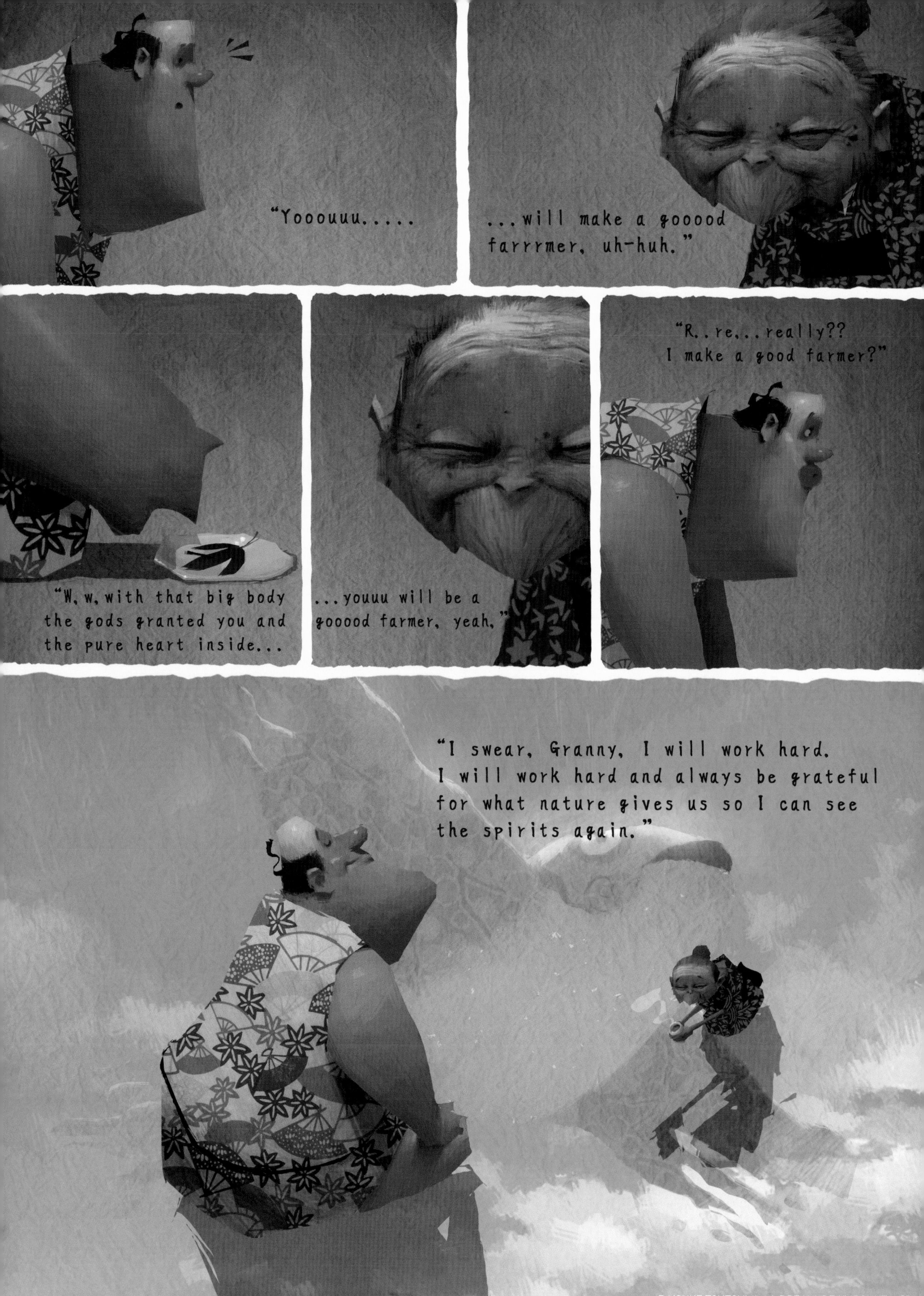

"Yooouuu.....
...will make a gooood farrrmer, uh-huh."
"W, w, with that big body the gods granted you and the pure heart inside...
...youuu will be a gooood farmer, yeah."
"R..re,...really?? I make a good farmer?"
"I swear, Granny, I will work hard. I will work hard and always be grateful for what nature gives us so I can see the spirits again."

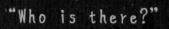

"I'm going outside for
some fresh air.
You stay here, Granny."

"Who is there?"

"So this is where you've
been hiding..."

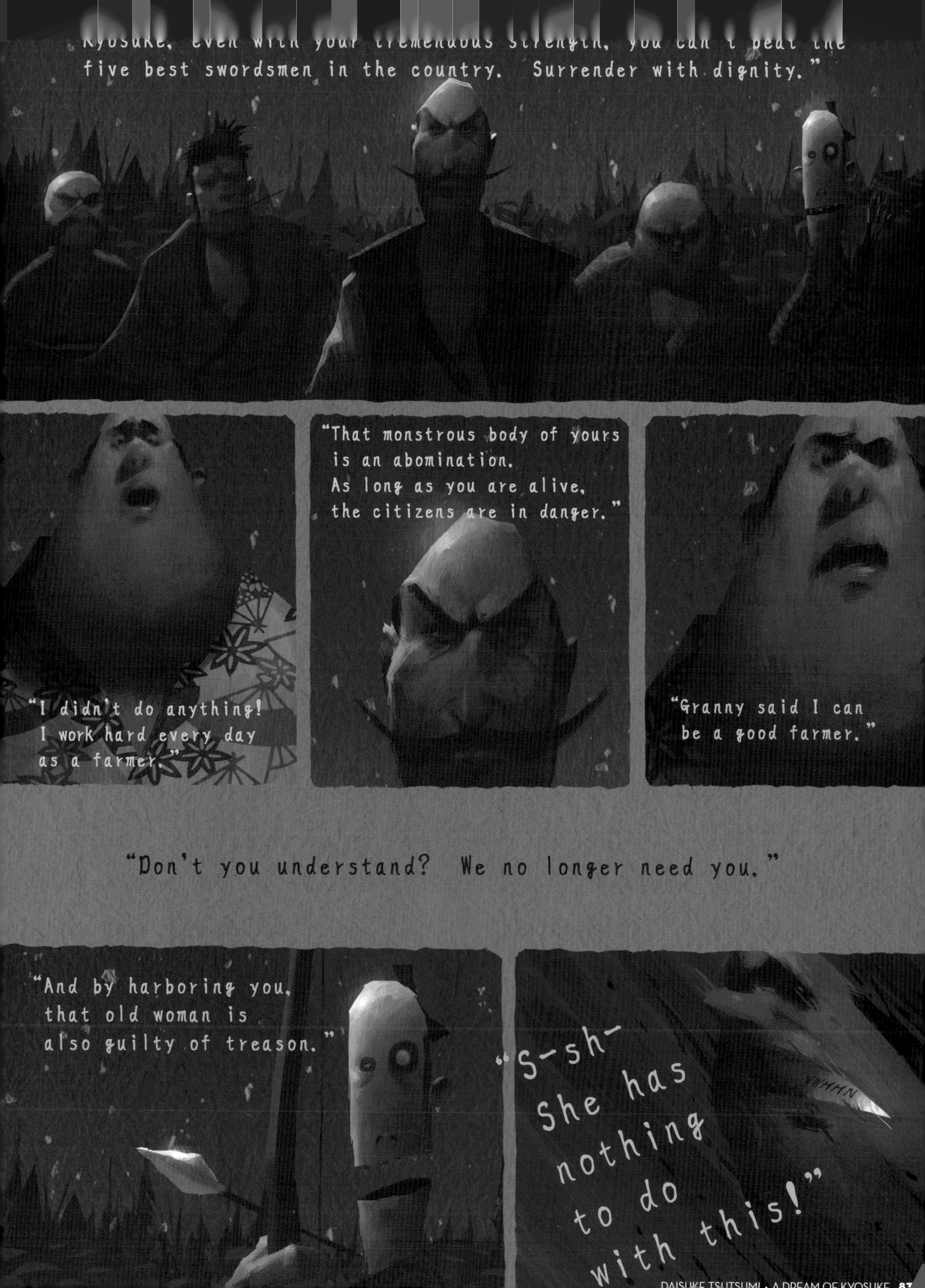
"Kyosuke, even with your tremendous strength, you can't beat the five best swordsmen in the country. Surrender with dignity."
"I didn't do anything! I work hard every day as a farmer."
"That monstrous body of yours is an abomination. As long as you are alive, the citizens are in danger."
"Granny said I can be a good farmer."
"Don't you understand? We no longer need you."
"And by harboring you, that old woman is also guilty of treason."
"S-sh- She has nothing to do with this!"
WHHN

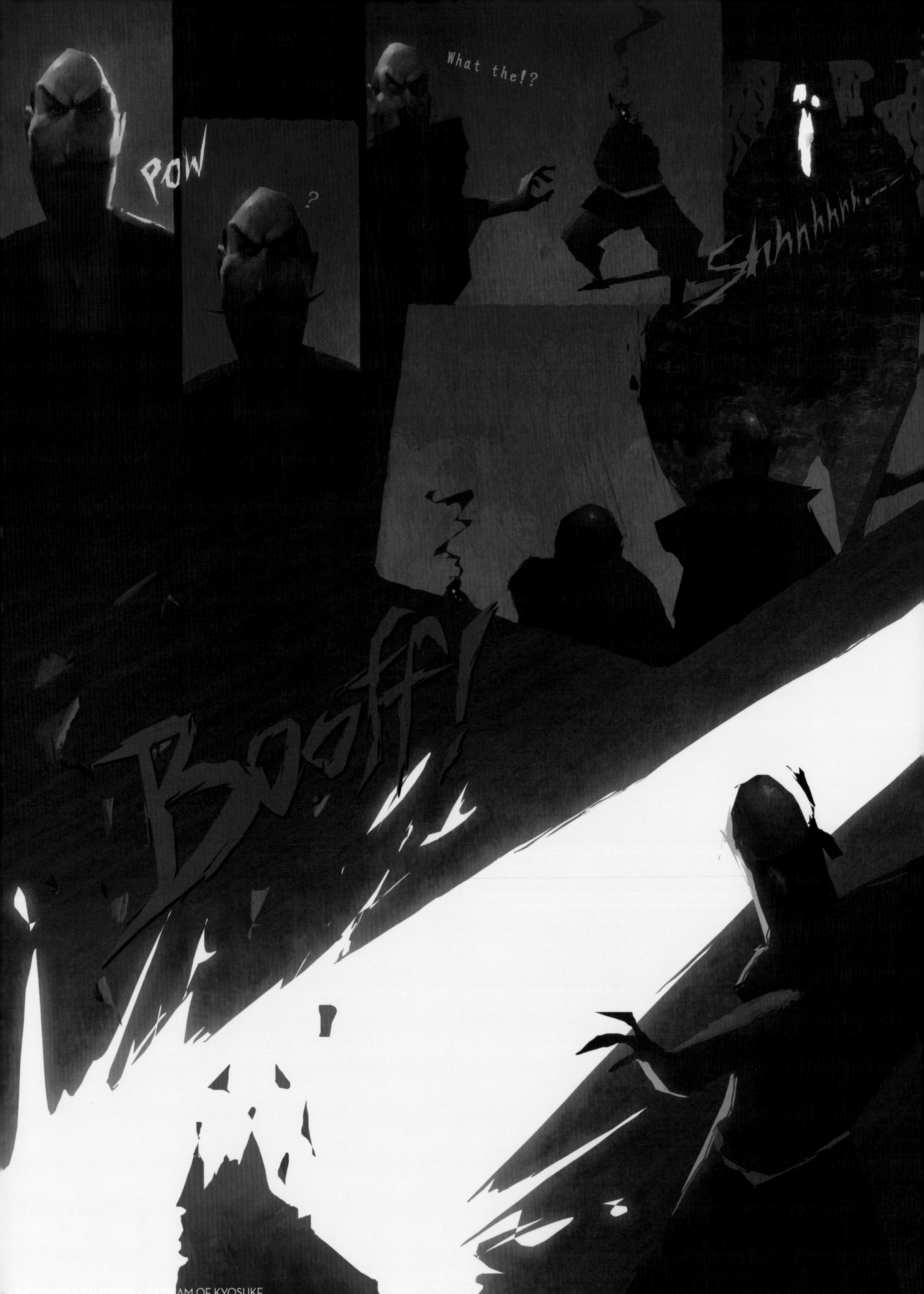
POW
?
What the!?
Shhhhhh...
Booff!

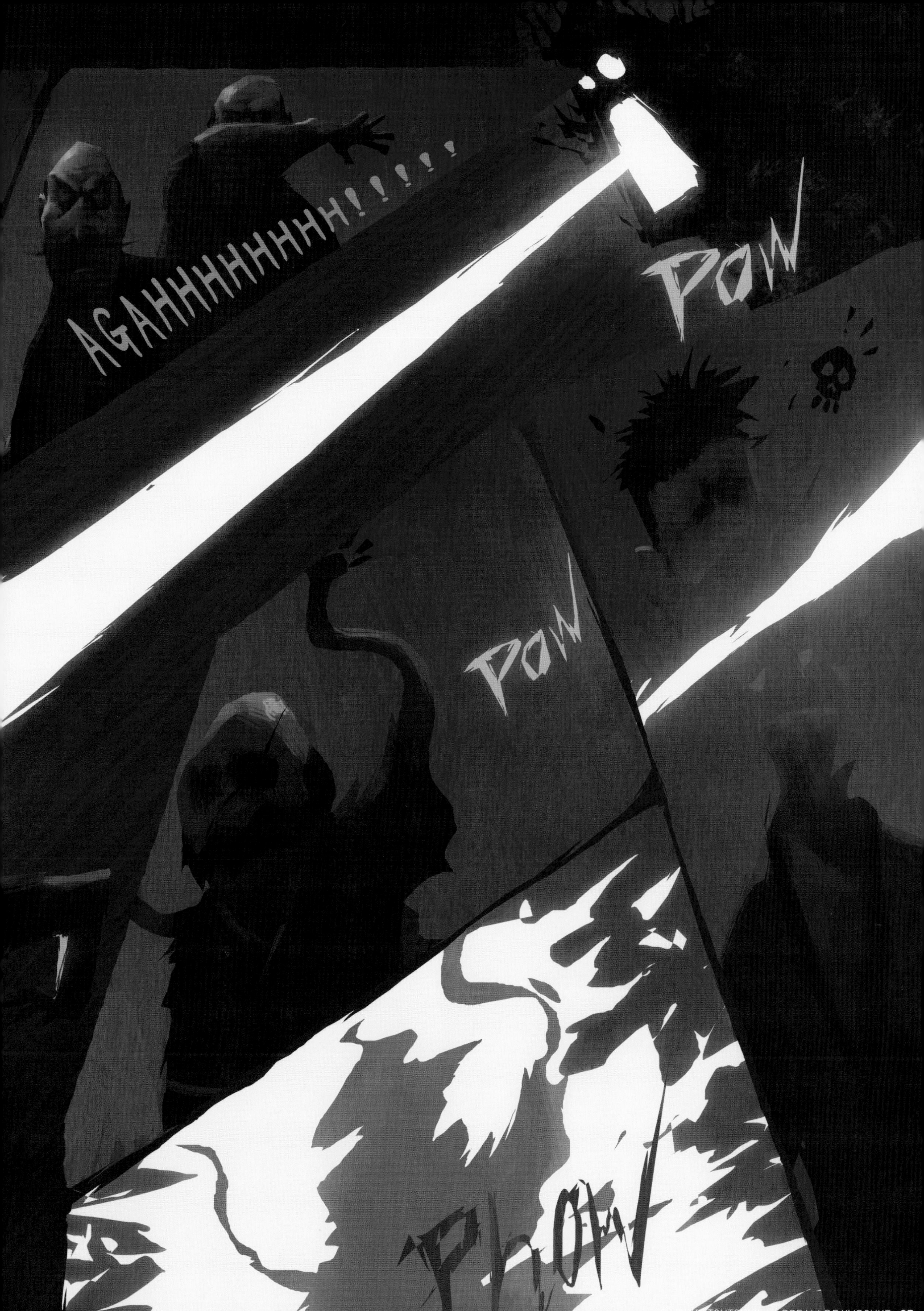
AGAHHHHHHHH!!!!!!
POW
POW
PLOW

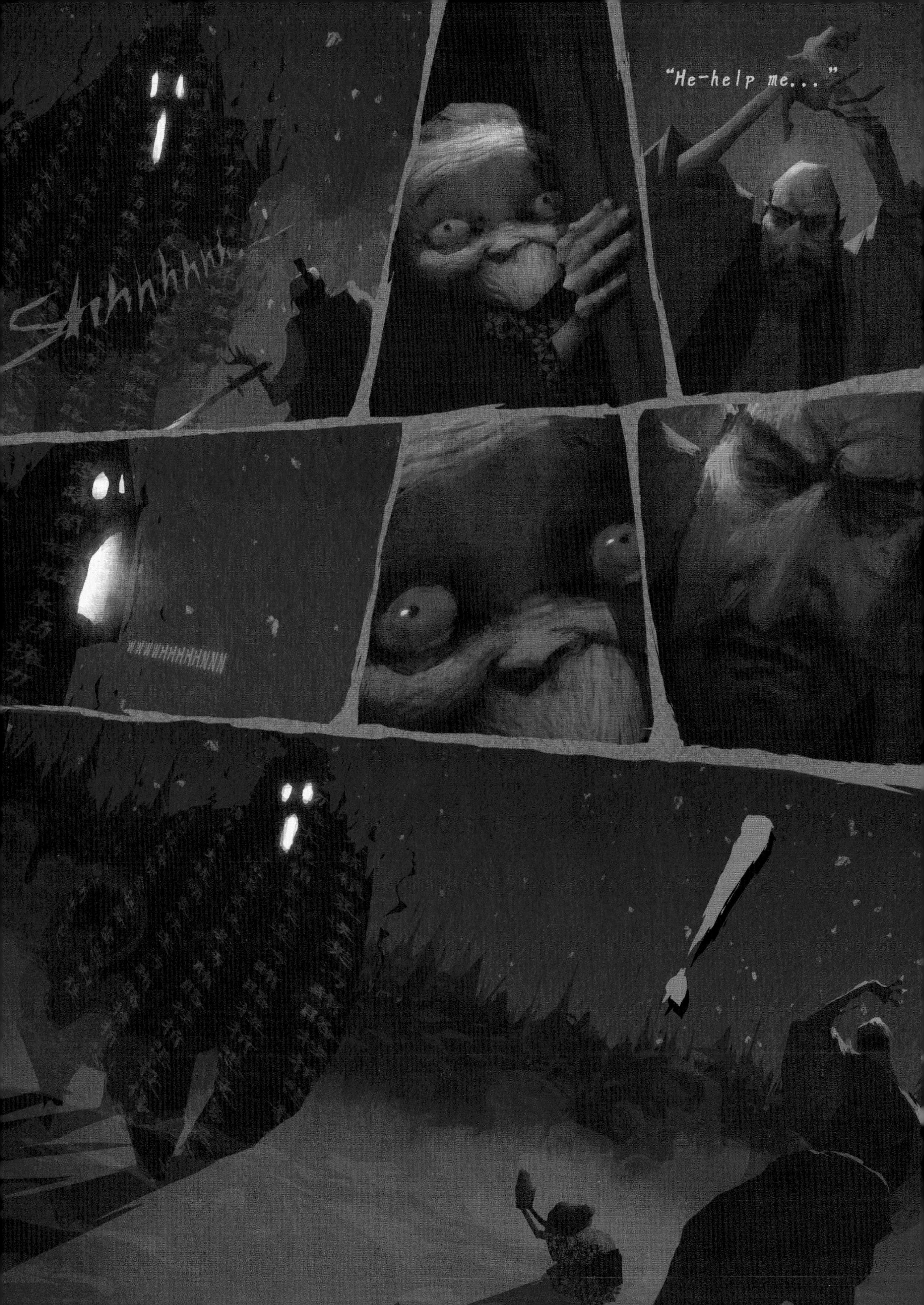
Shhhhhh...
"He-help me..."
WWWHHHHHNN

"P-p-pppleeease, d-ddon't kill...
Ppleease, calm your anger..."

"Granny..."

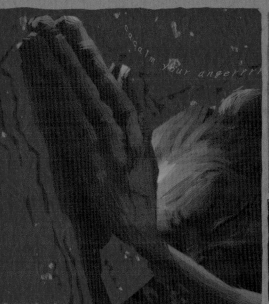

"D,,d.. don't
think
this is

the end,
Kyosuke!"

"Plleeease,
calm your anger down."

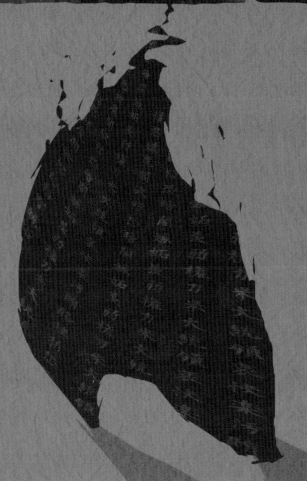

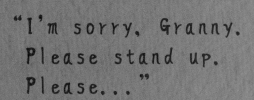

"I'm sorry, Granny.
Please stand up.
Please..."

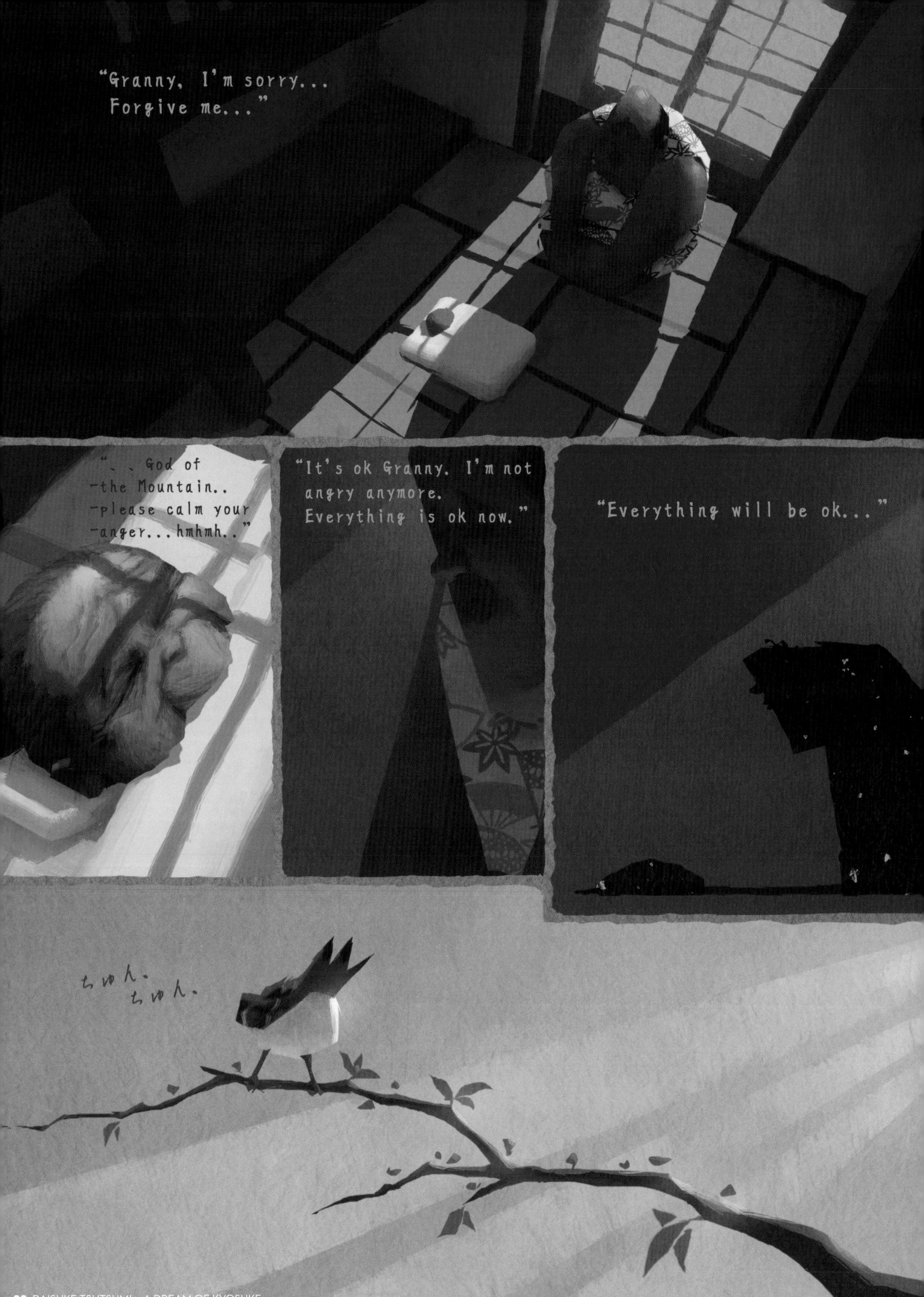
"Granny, I'm sorry...
Forgive me..."
"..God of
-the Mountain..
-please calm your
-anger...hmhmh.."
"It's ok Granny. I'm not
angry anymore.
Everything is ok now."
"Everything will be ok..."
ちゅん。
ちゅん。

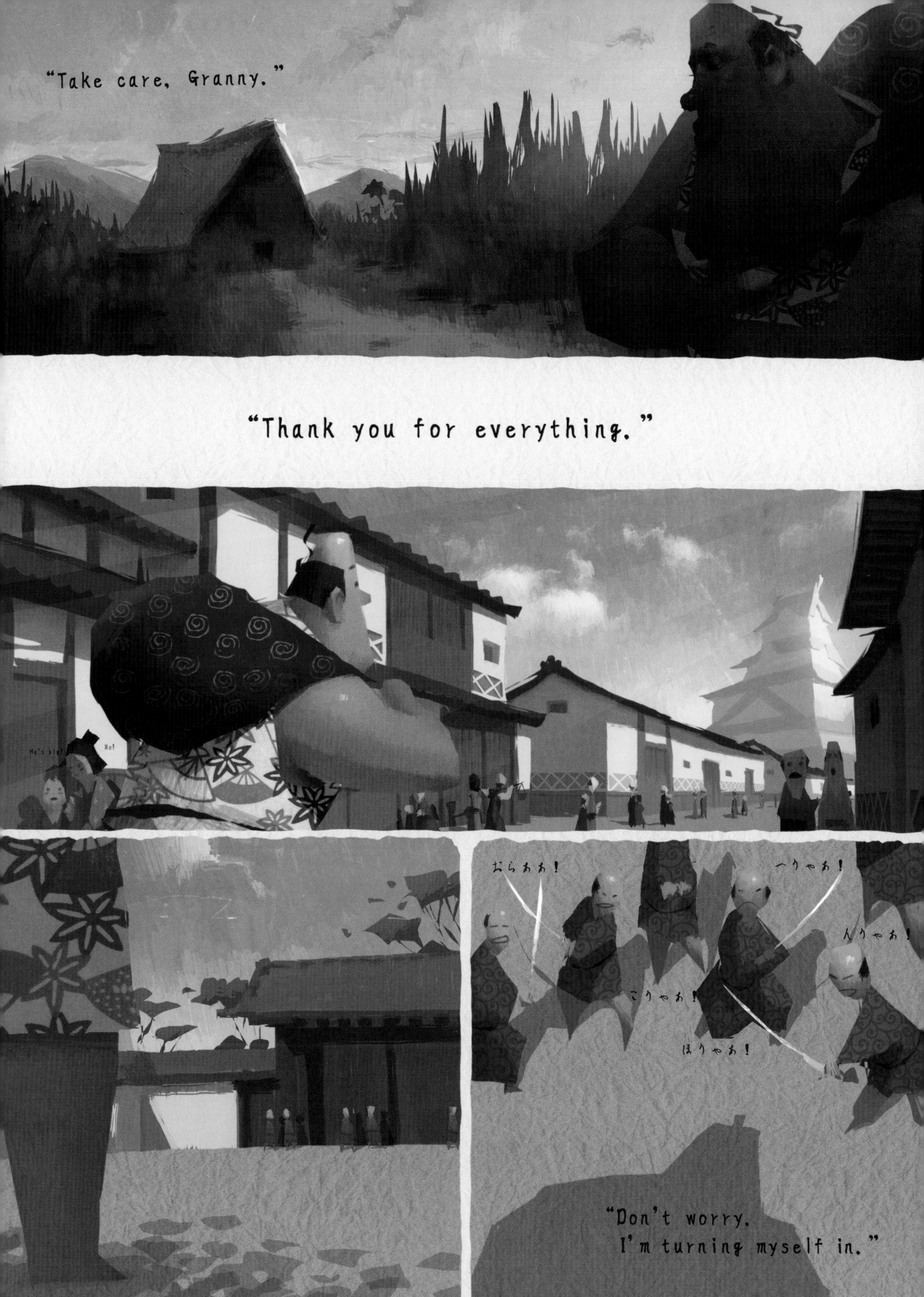
"Take care, Granny."
"Thank you for everything."
He's big!
No!
おらああ！
へりゃあ！
んりゃあ！
こりゃあ！
ほりゃあ！
"Don't worry.
I'm turning myself in."

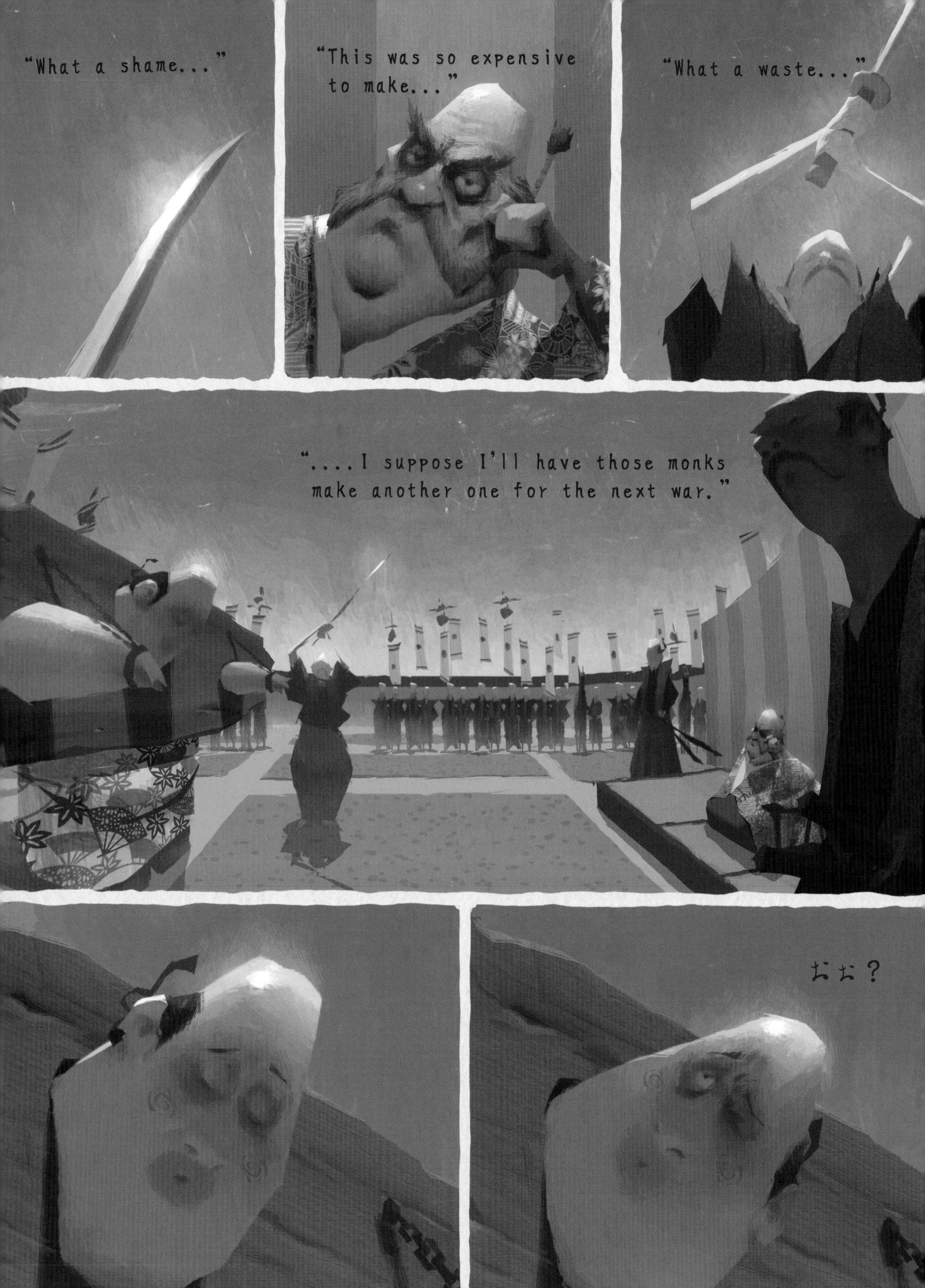
"What a shame..."
"This was so expensive to make..."
"What a waste..."
"....I suppose I'll have those monks make another one for the next war."
おお？

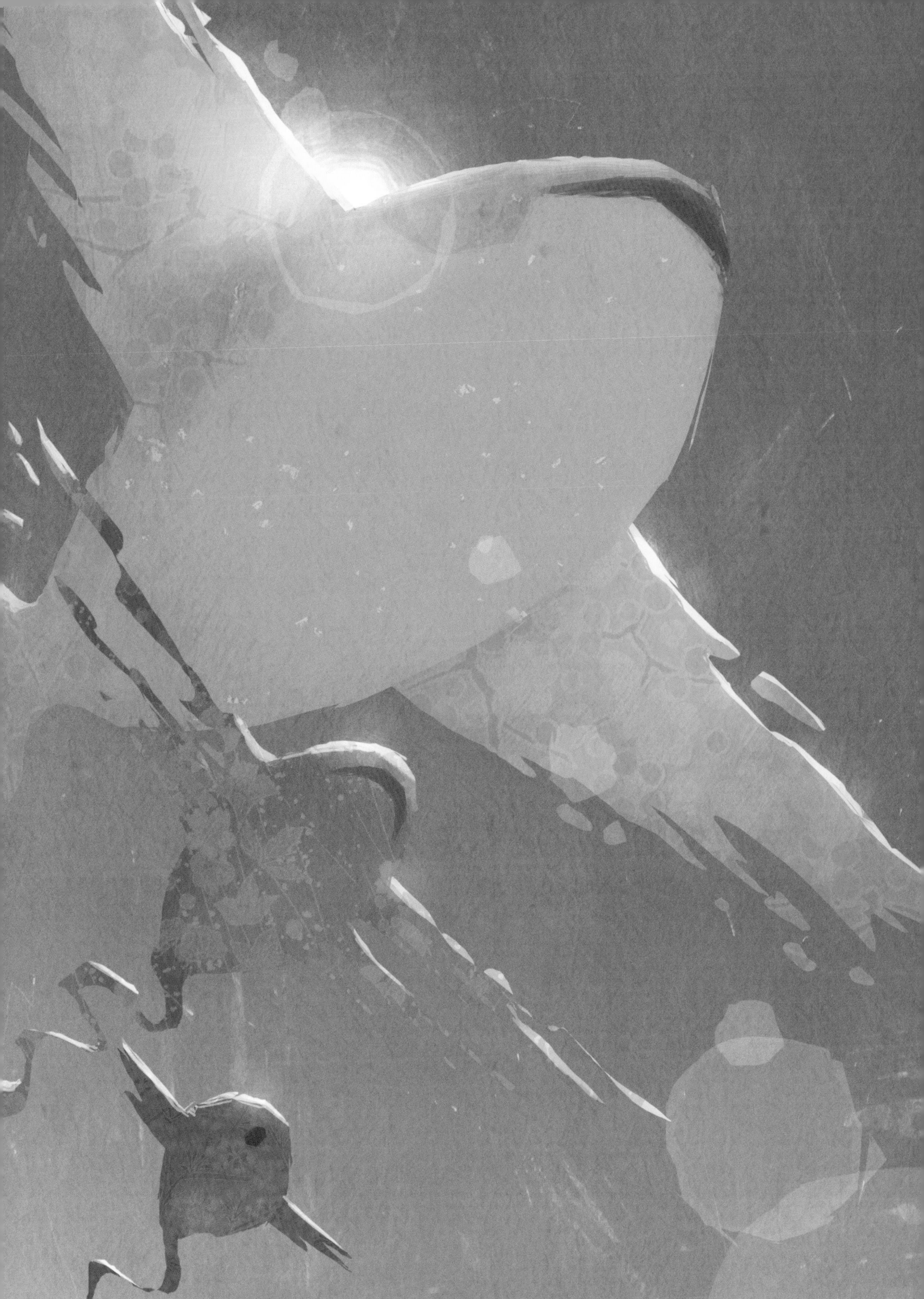

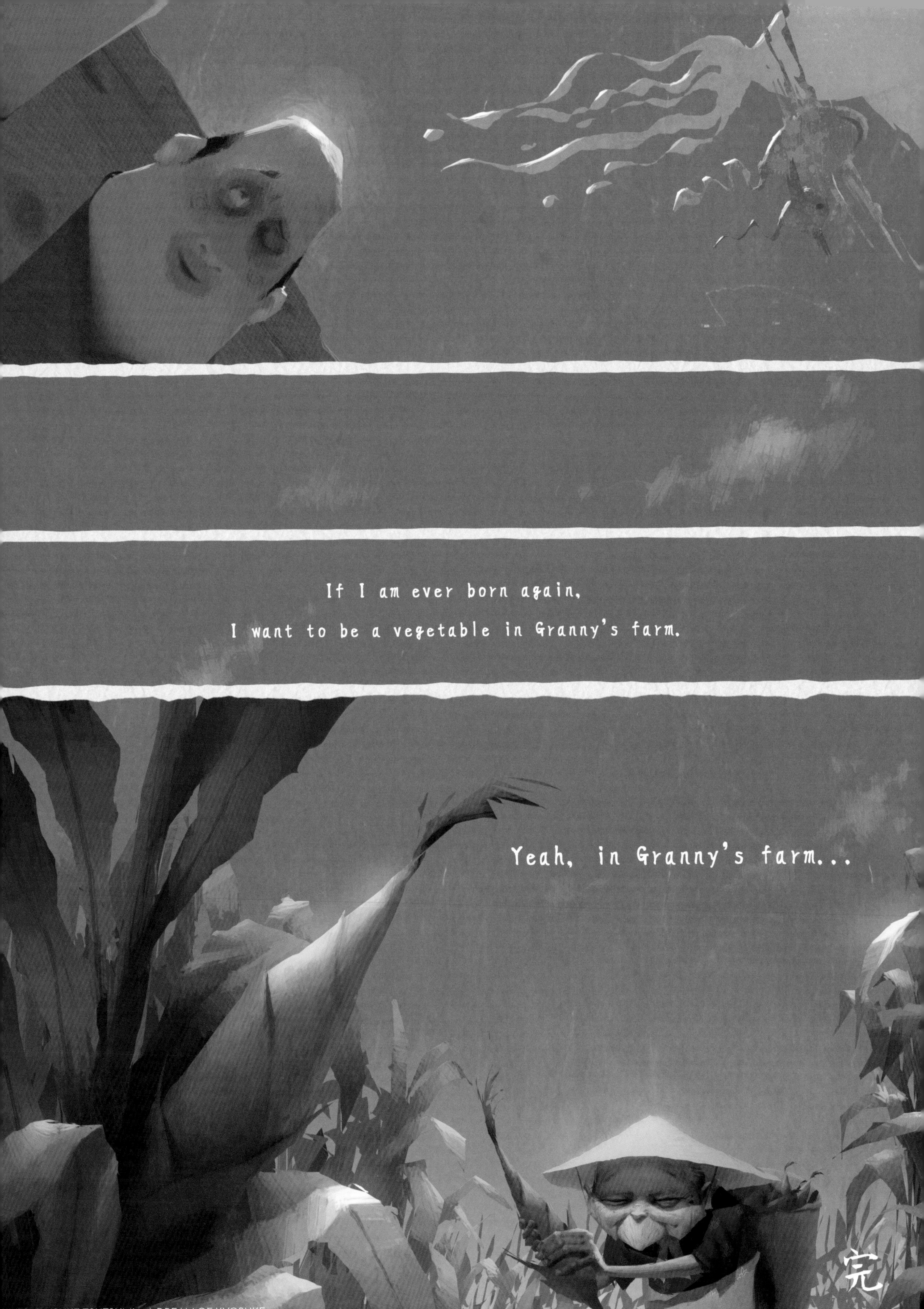
If I am ever born again,
I want to be a vegetable in Granny's farm.
Yeah, in Granny's farm...
完

OUT OF PICTURE

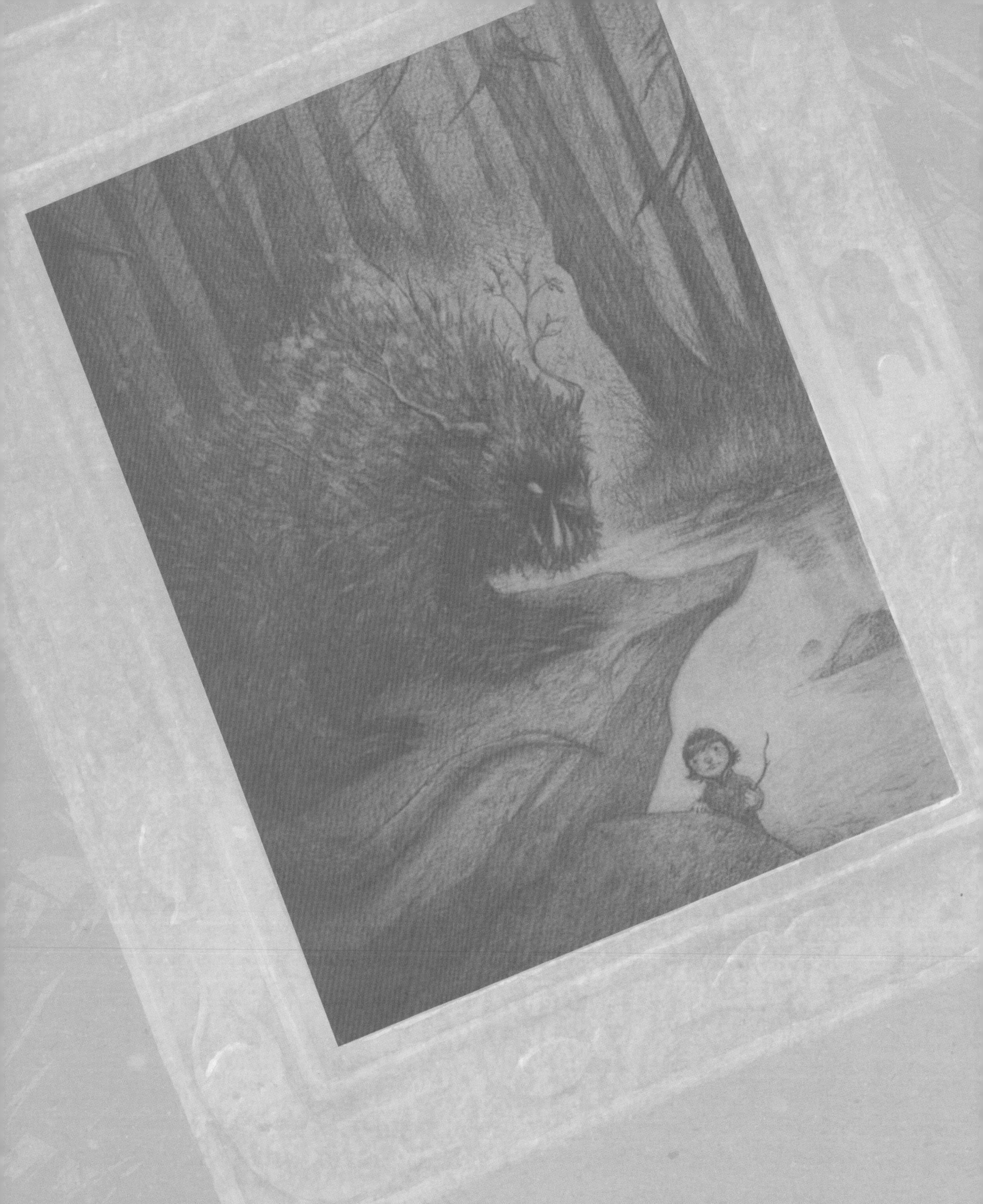

VINCENT NGUYEN

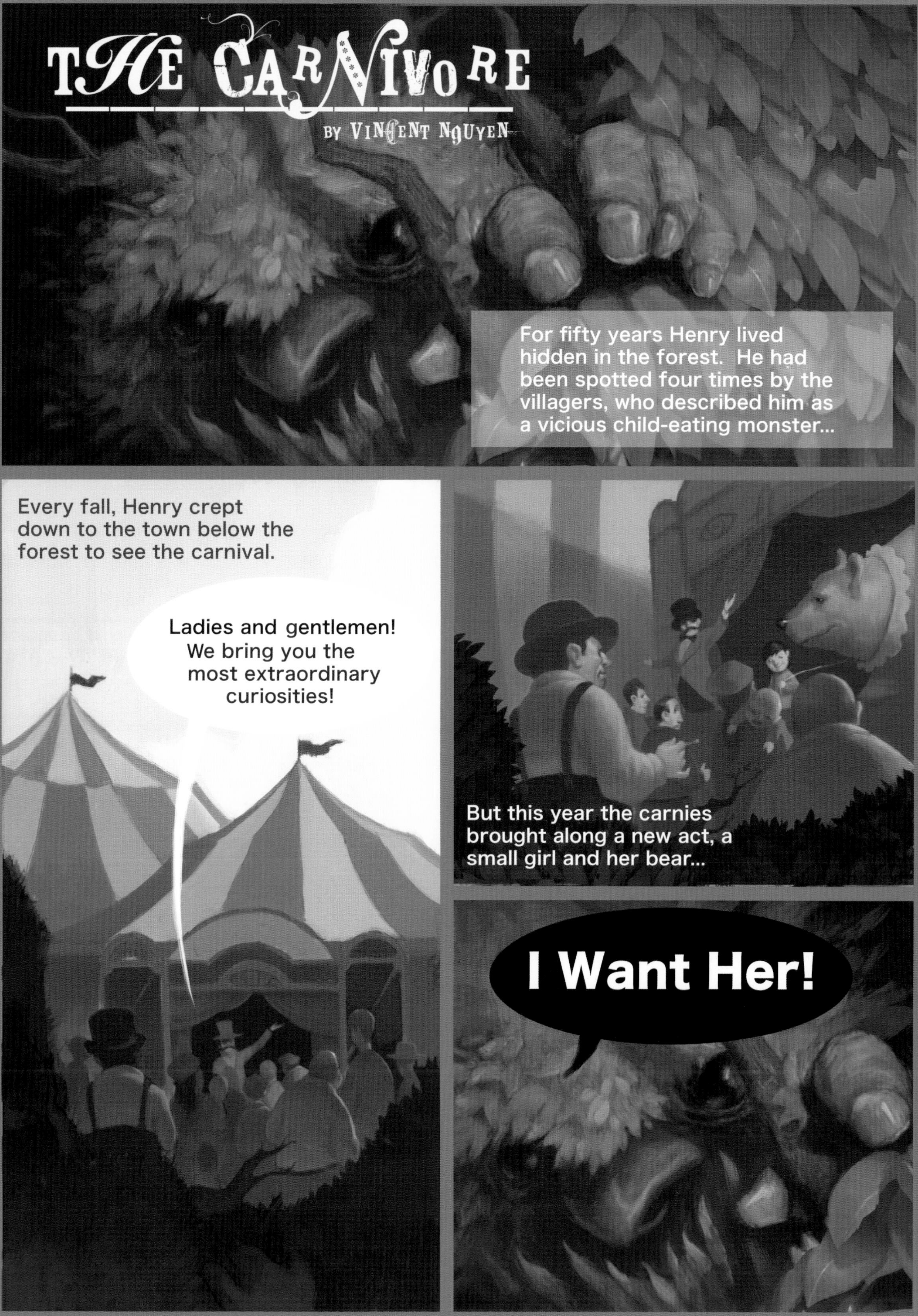
THE CARNIVORE
BY VINCENT NGUYEN
For fifty years Henry lived hidden in the forest. He had been spotted four times by the villagers, who described him as a vicious child-eating monster...
Every fall, Henry crept down to the town below the forest to see the carnival.
Ladies and gentlemen! We bring you the most extraordinary curiosities!
But this year the carnies brought along a new act, a small girl and her bear...
I Want Her!

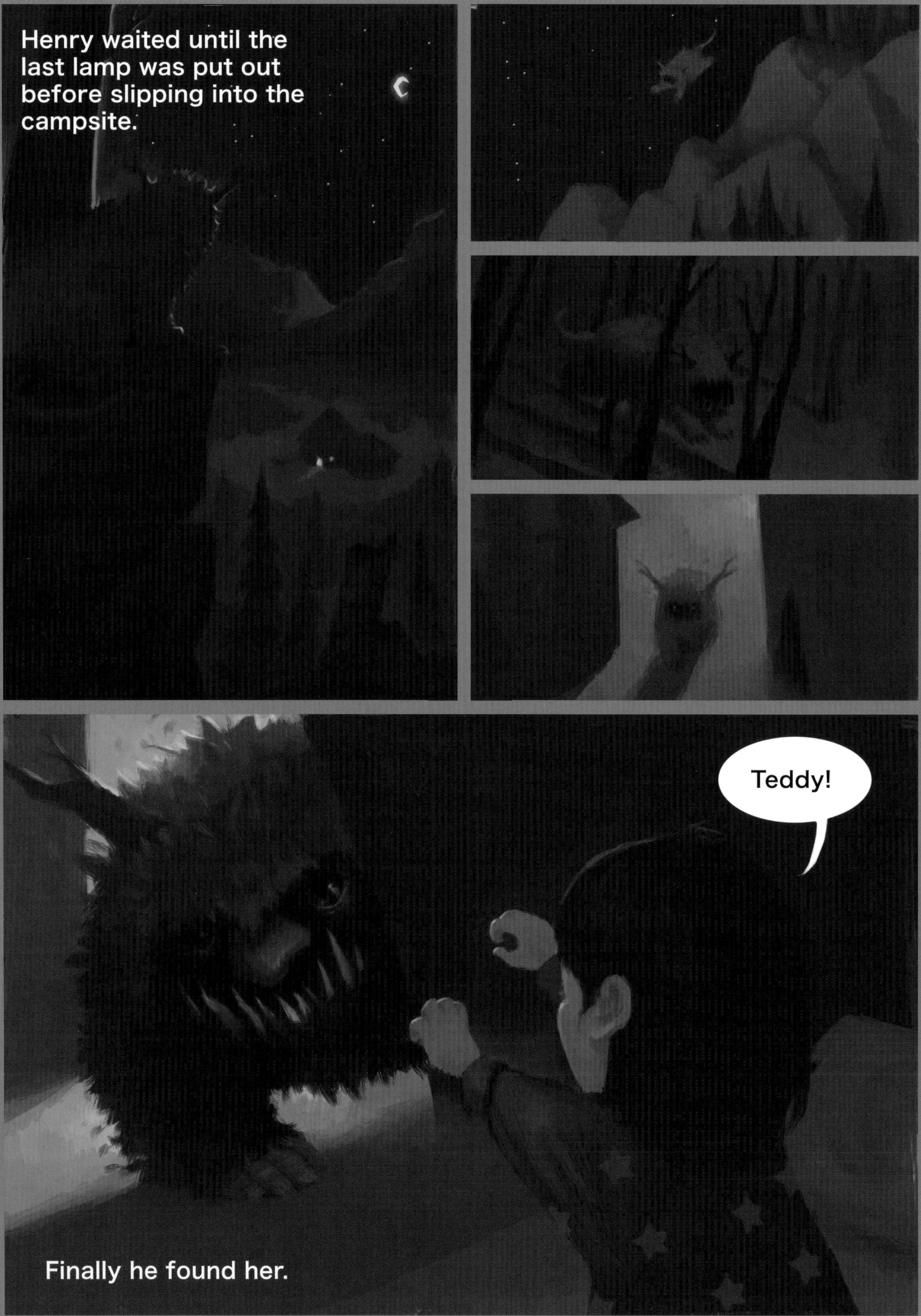
Henry waited until the last lamp was put out before slipping into the campsite.
Teddy!
Finally he found her.

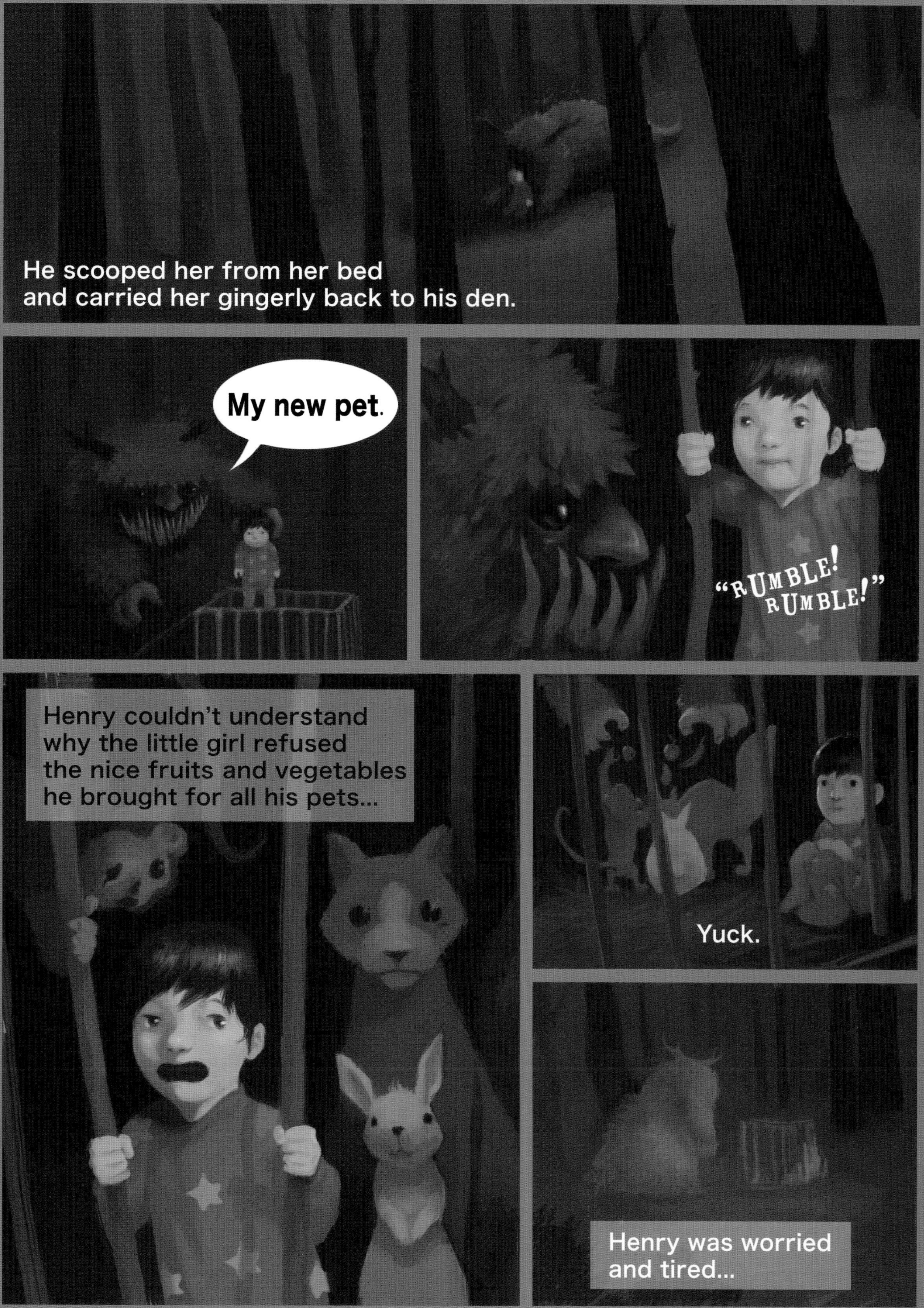
He scooped her from her bed
and carried her gingerly back to his den.
My new pet.
"RUMBLE! RUMBLE!"
Henry couldn't understand why the little girl refused the nice fruits and vegetables he brought for all his pets...
Yuck.
Henry was worried and tired...

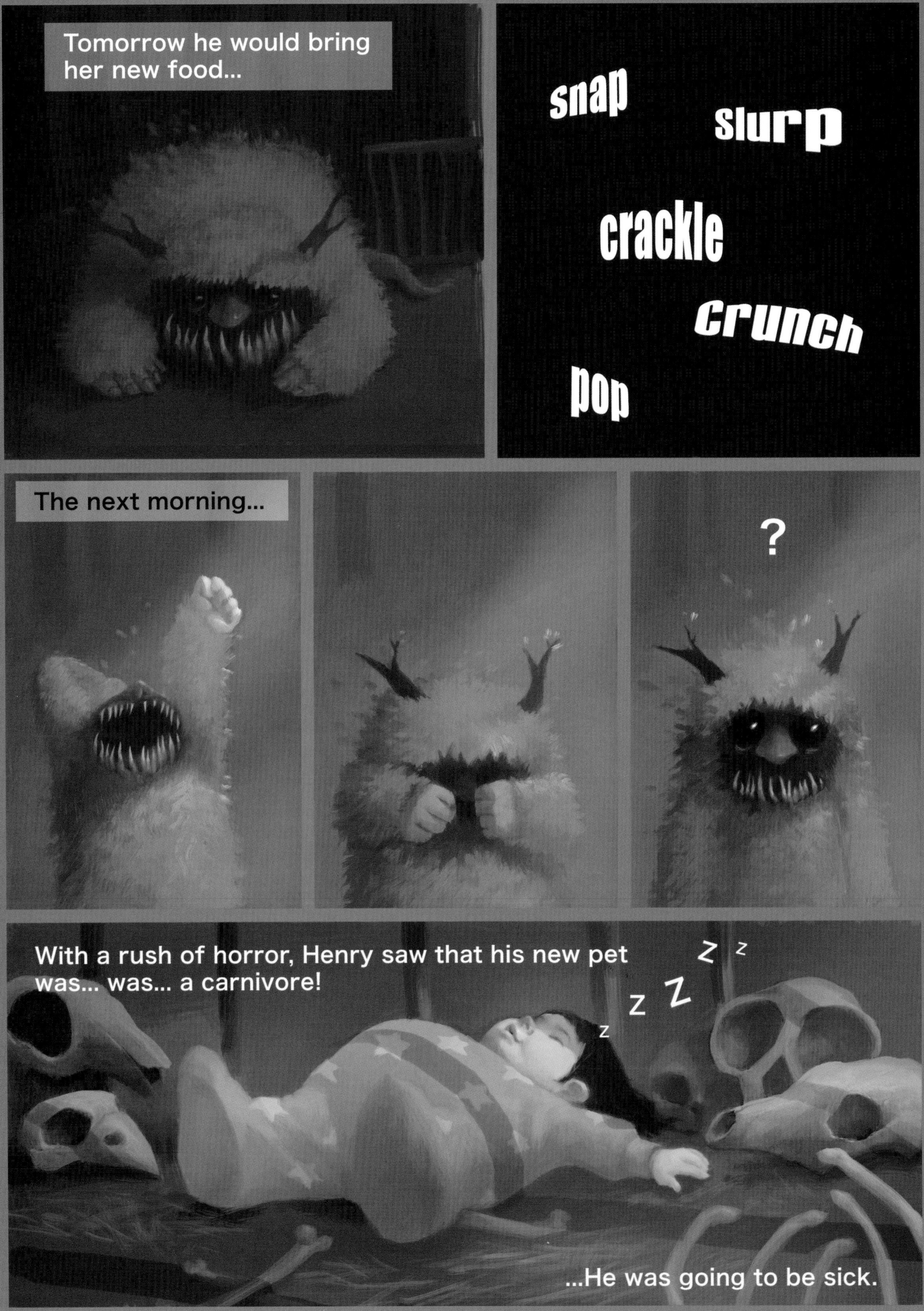

Tomorrow he would bring her new food...
snap
slurp
crackle
crunch
pop
The next morning...
?
With a rush of horror, Henry saw that his new pet was... was... a carnivore!
Z z
Z Z
z
...He was going to be sick.

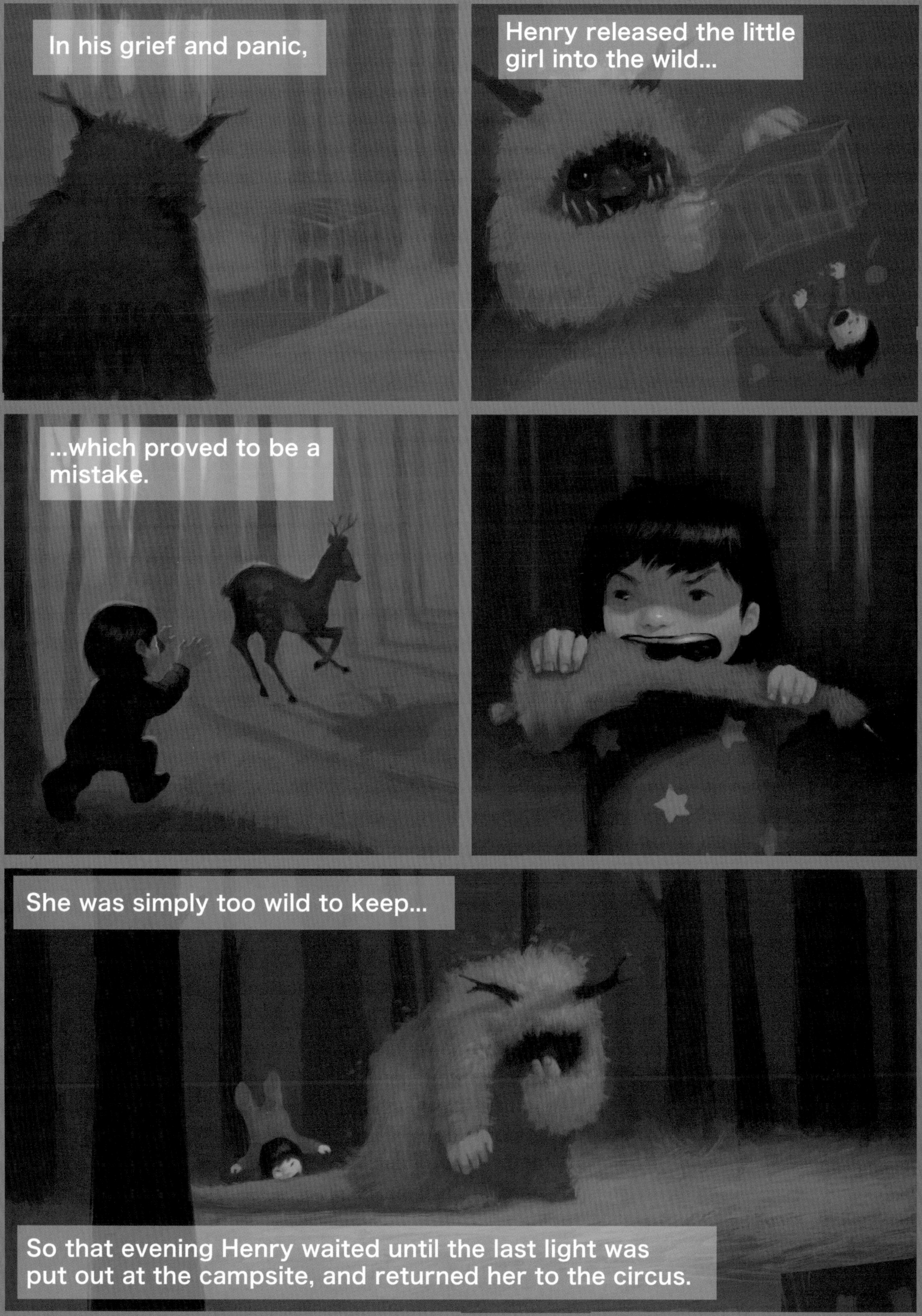
In his grief and panic,
Henry released the little girl into the wild...
...which proved to be a mistake.
She was simply too wild to keep...
So that evening Henry waited until the last light was put out at the campsite, and returned her to the circus.

Ladies and gentlemen! Who among you would dare step in the ring to challenge this big fellow? You, sir?... No?

Perhaps you then, sir?

He still came back to watch her.

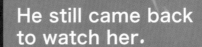

Watch as our little carnivore displays an appetite to rival even that of the mighty bear!

One hundred two and counting!

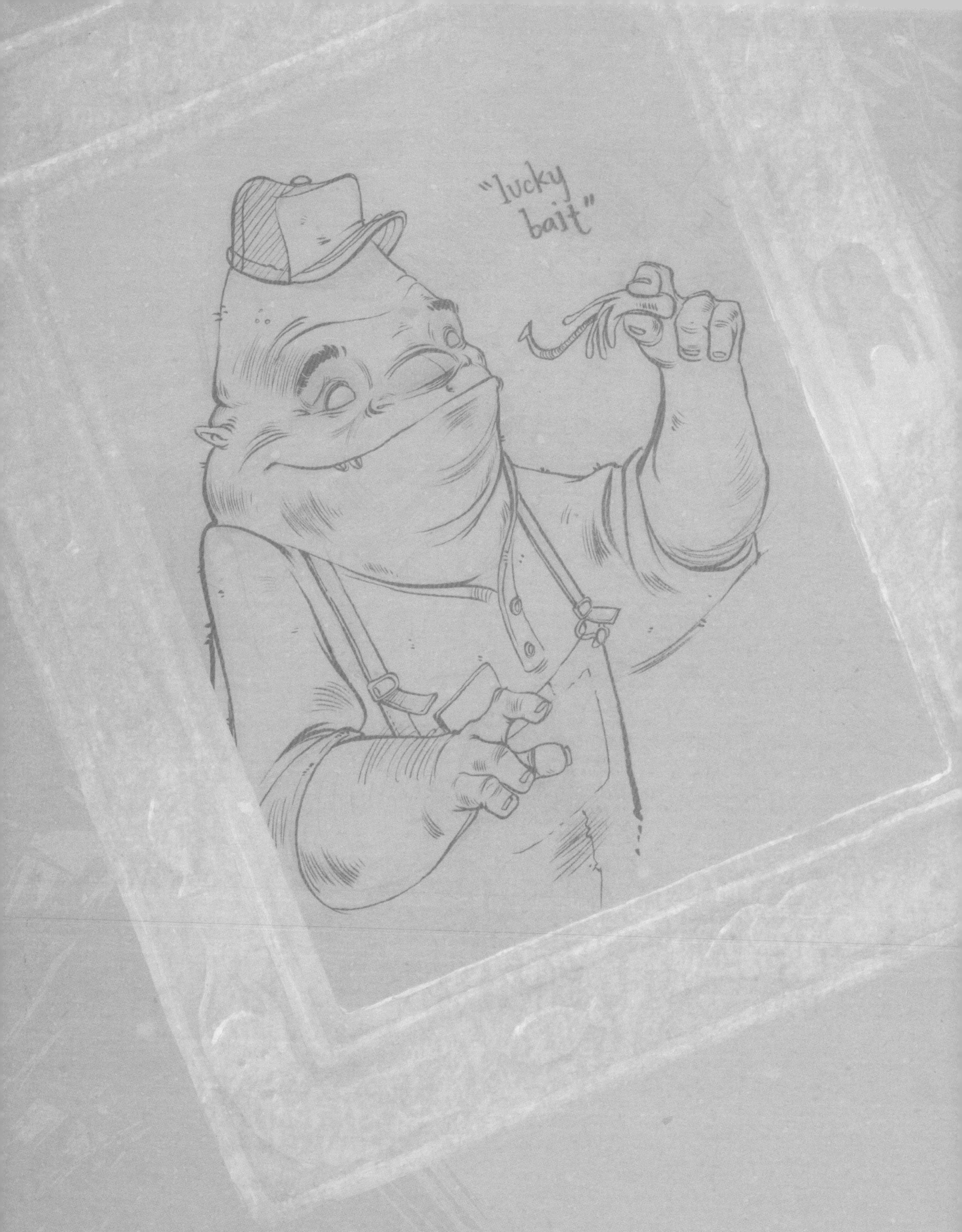
"lucky bait"

WILLIE REAL

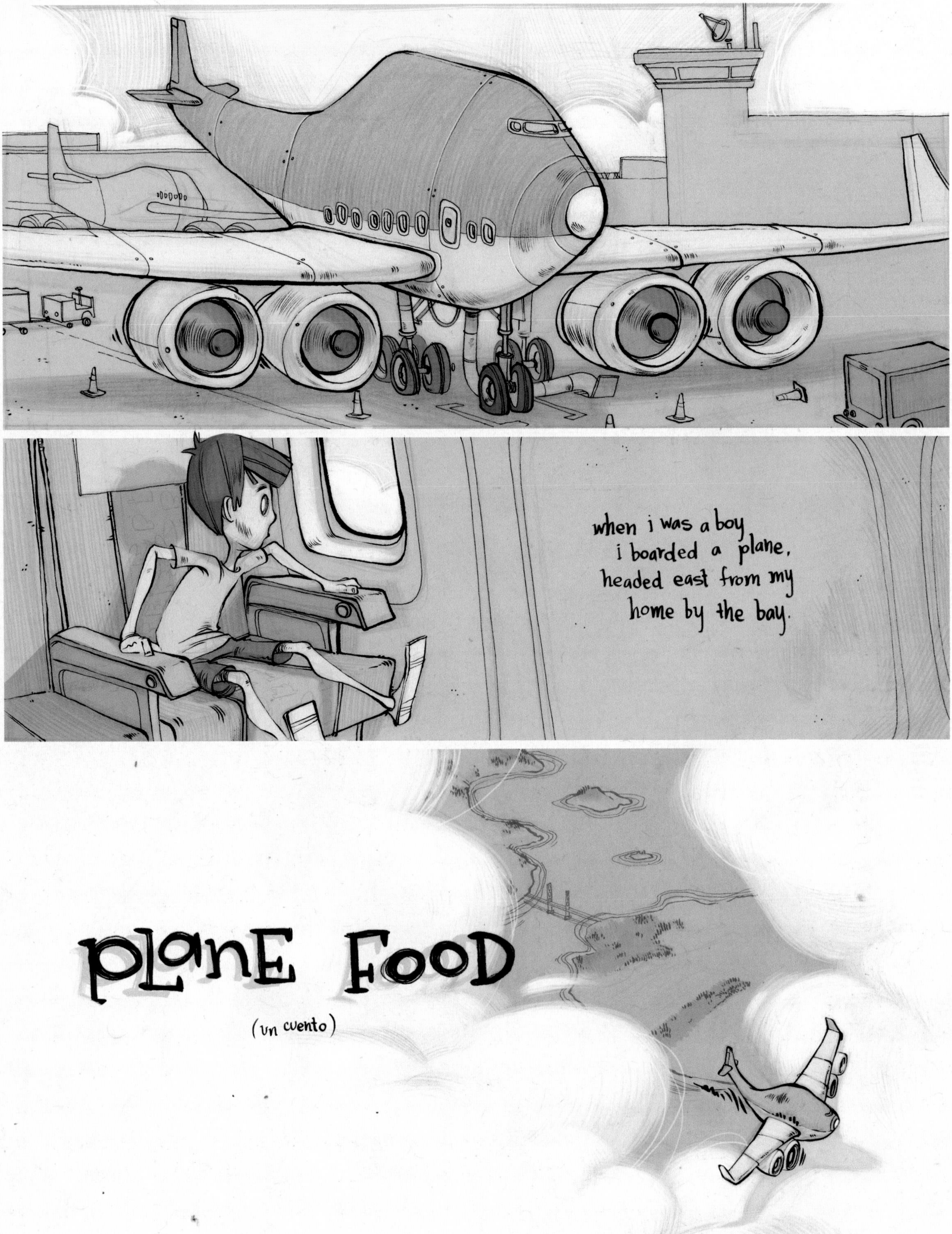
when i was a boy
i boarded a plane,
headed east from my
home by the bay.
PLANE FOOD
(un cuento)

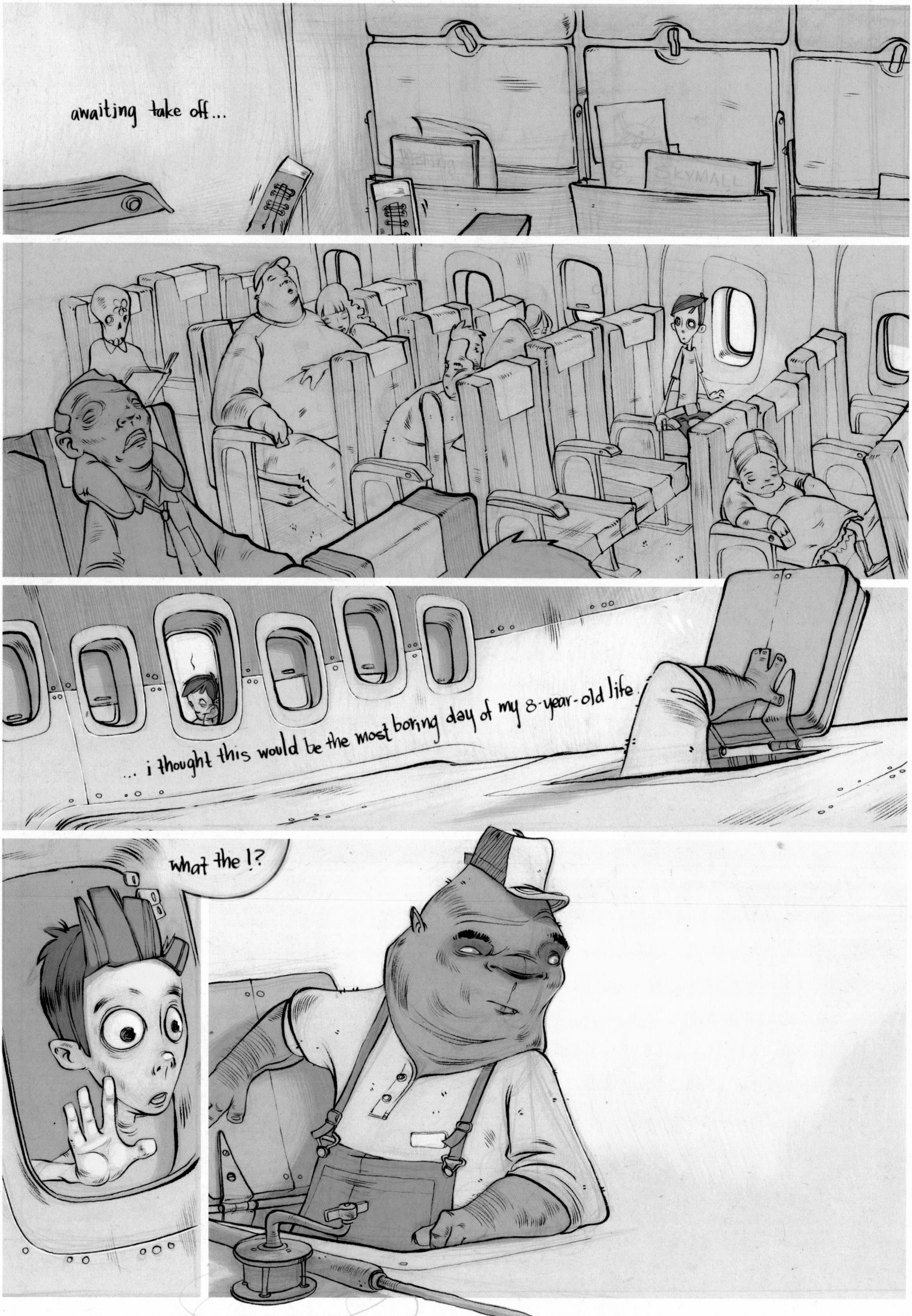
awaiting take off...
... i thought this would be the most boring day of my 8-year-old life
what the !?

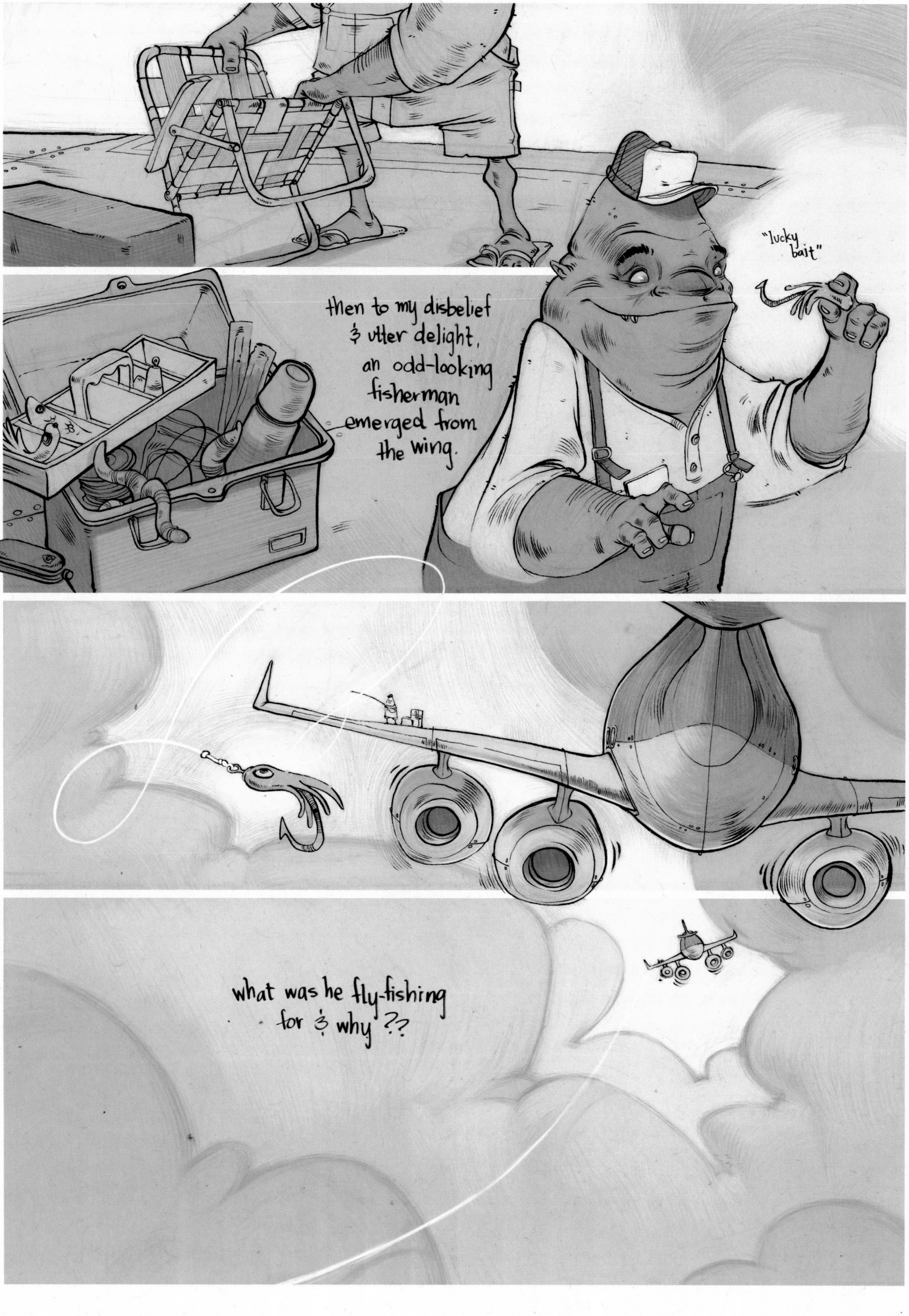
then to my disbelief
& utter delight,
an odd-looking
fisherman
emerged from
the wing.
"lucky bait"
what was he fly-fishing
for & why ??

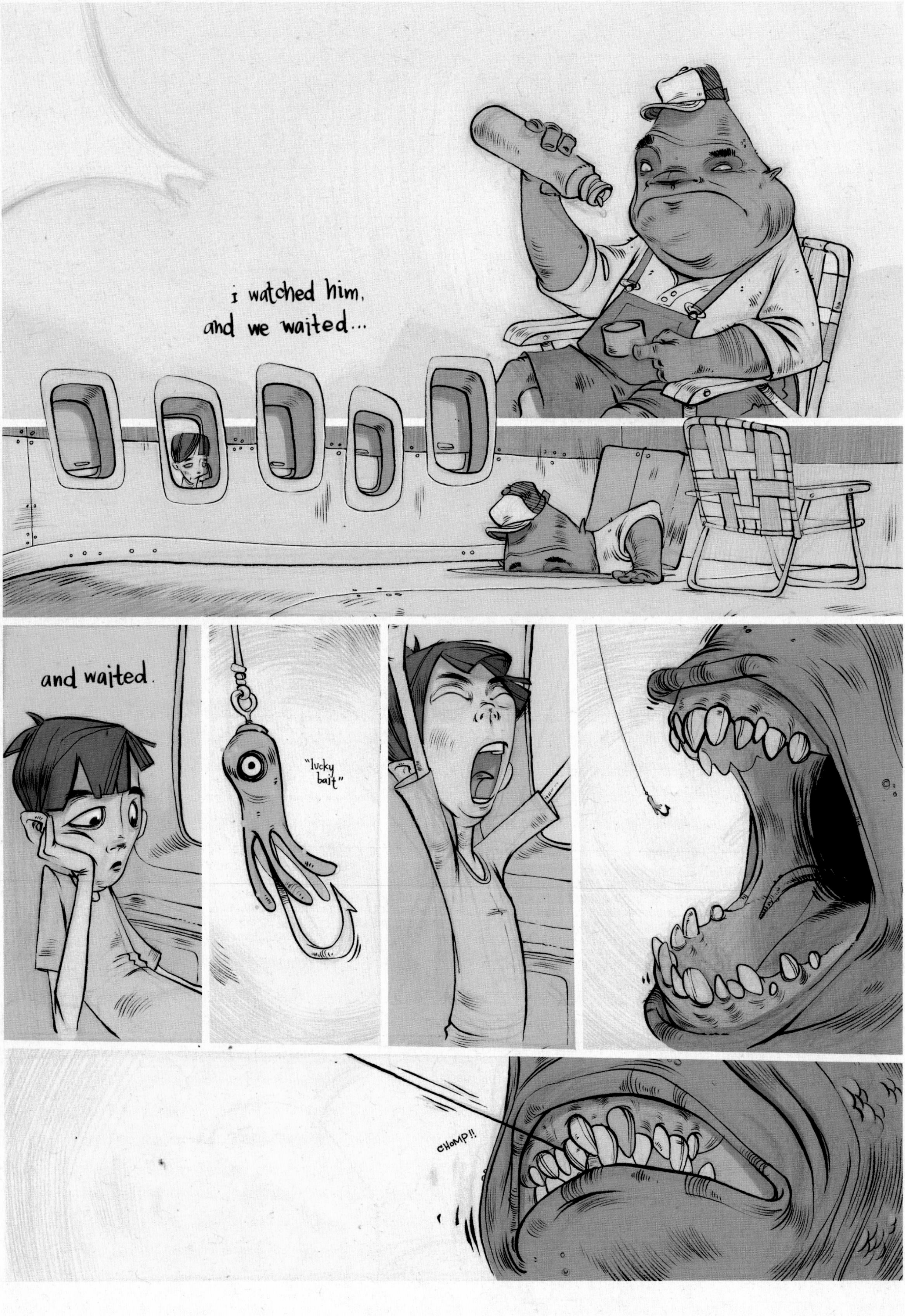
i watched him,
and we waited...
and waited.
"lucky
bait"
CHOMP!!

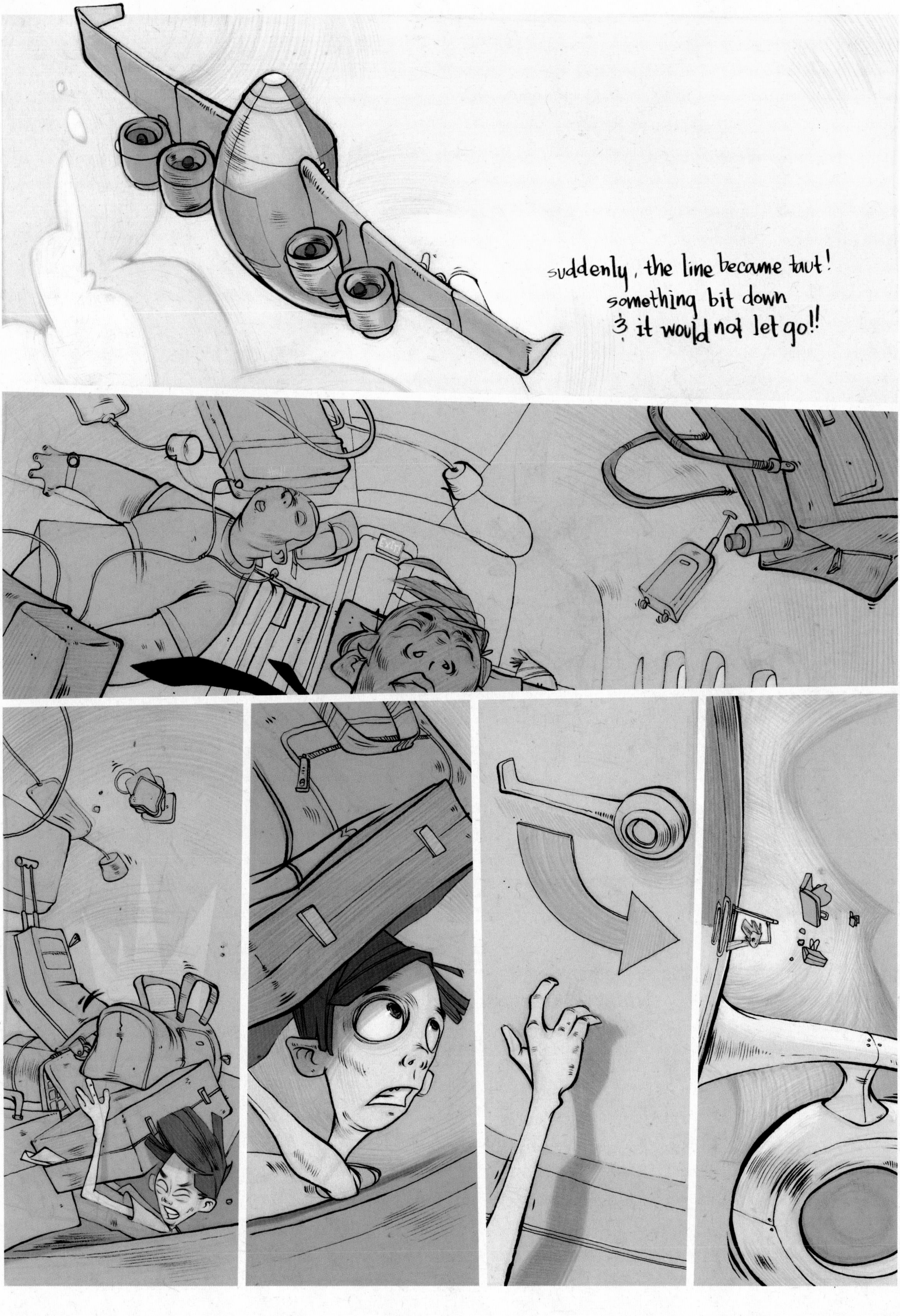
suddenly, the line became taut!
something bit down
& it would not let go!!
EXIT

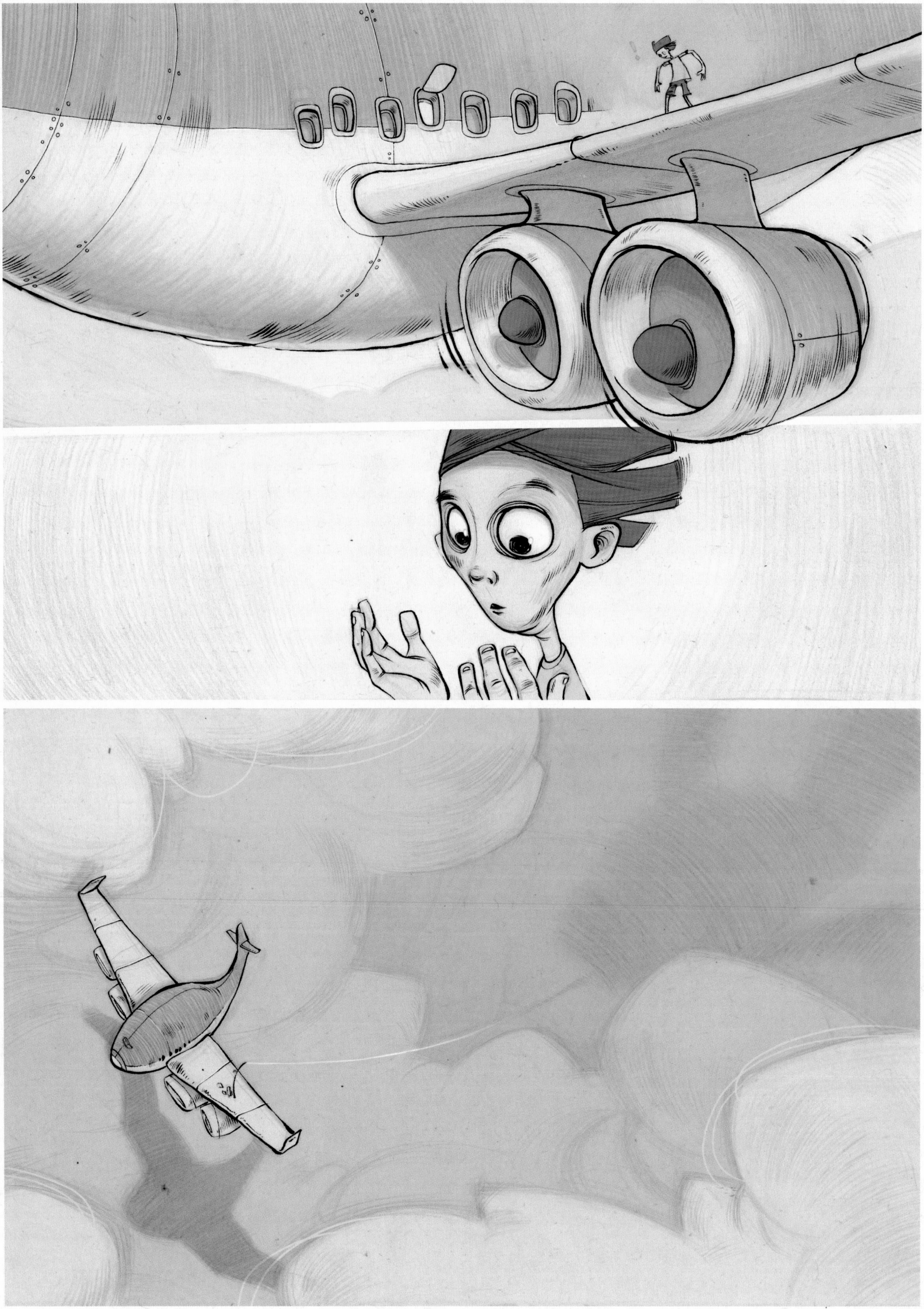

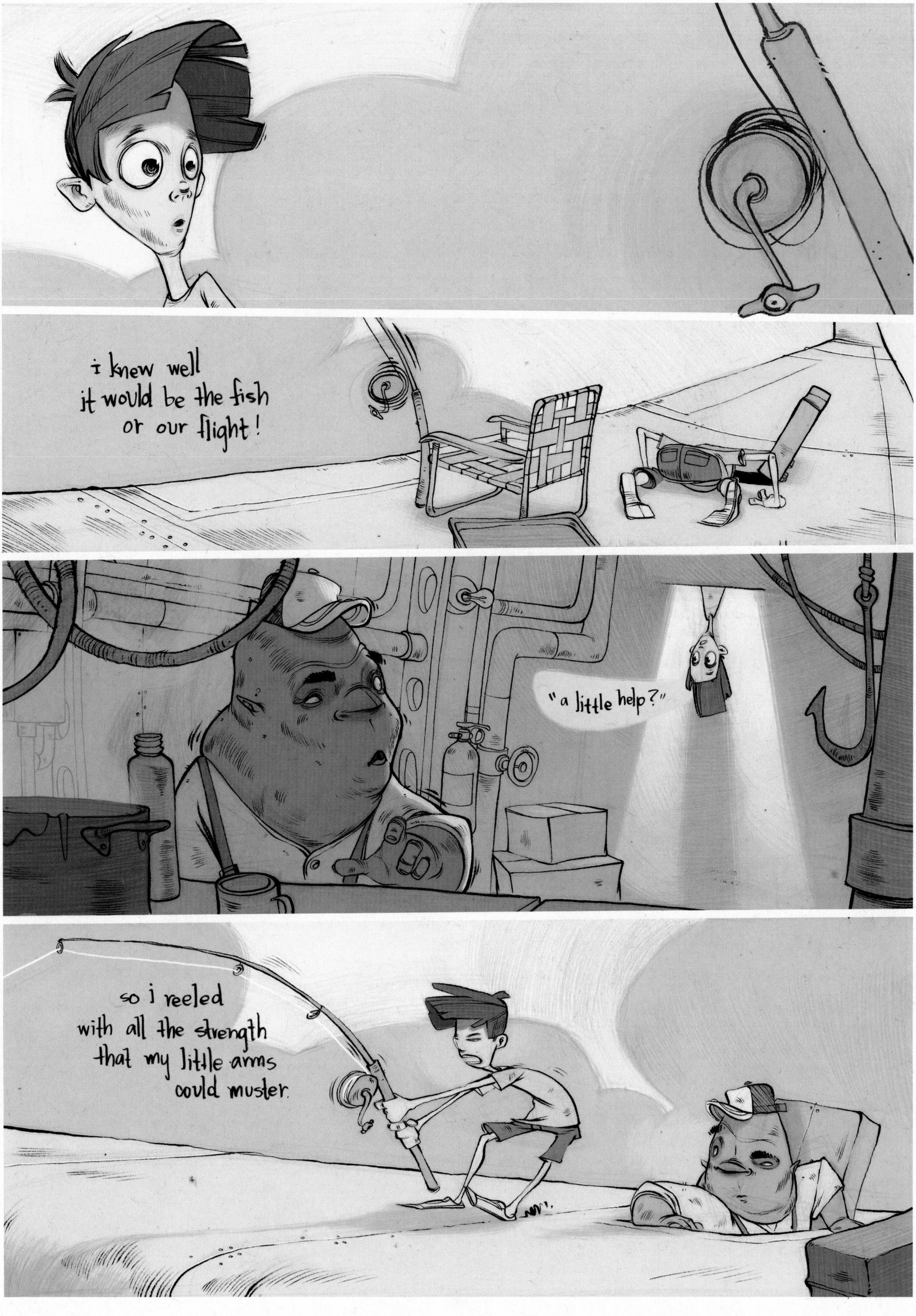
i knew well
it would be the fish
or our flight!
"a little help?"
so i reeled
with all the strength
that my little arms
could muster.

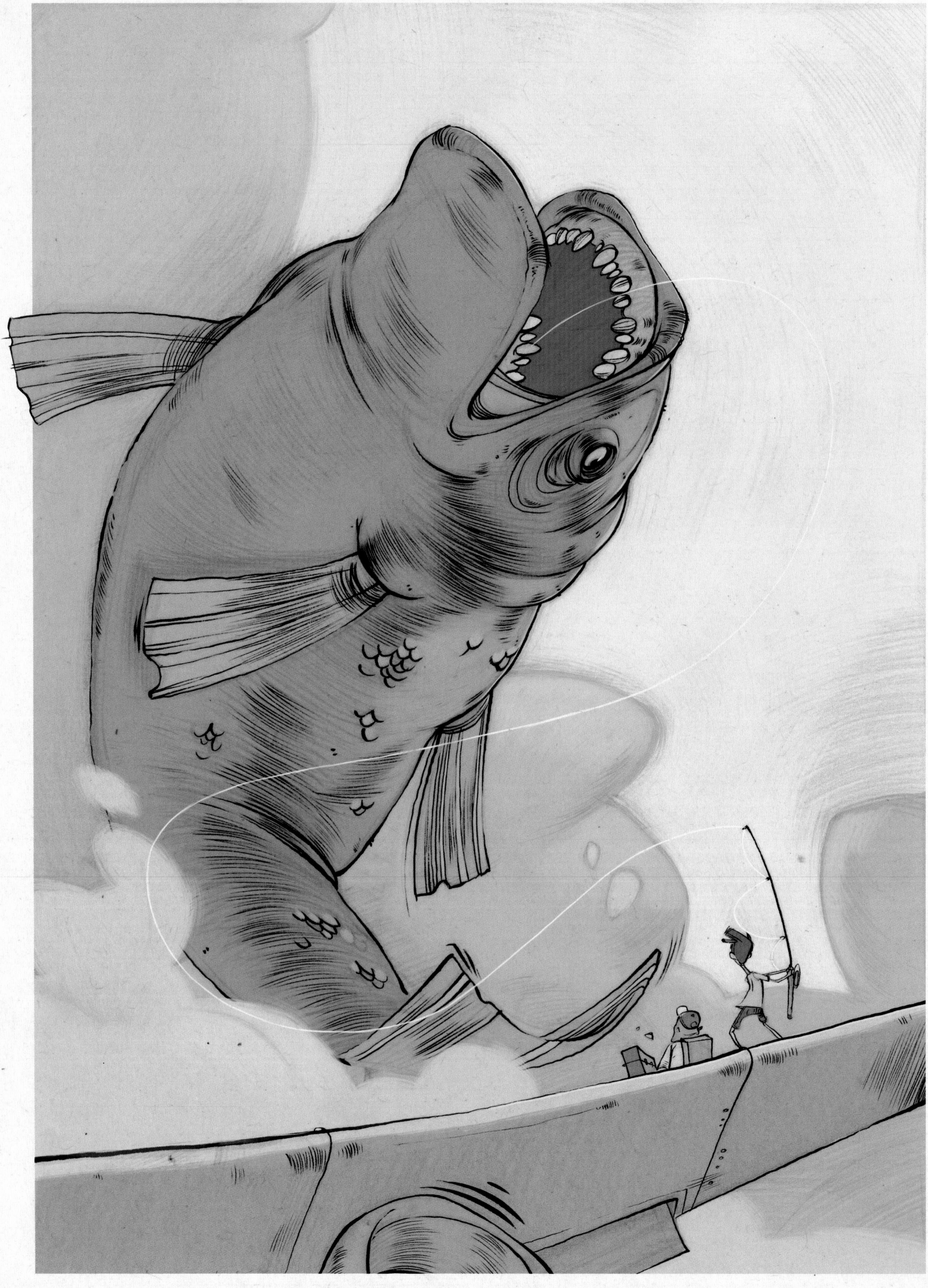

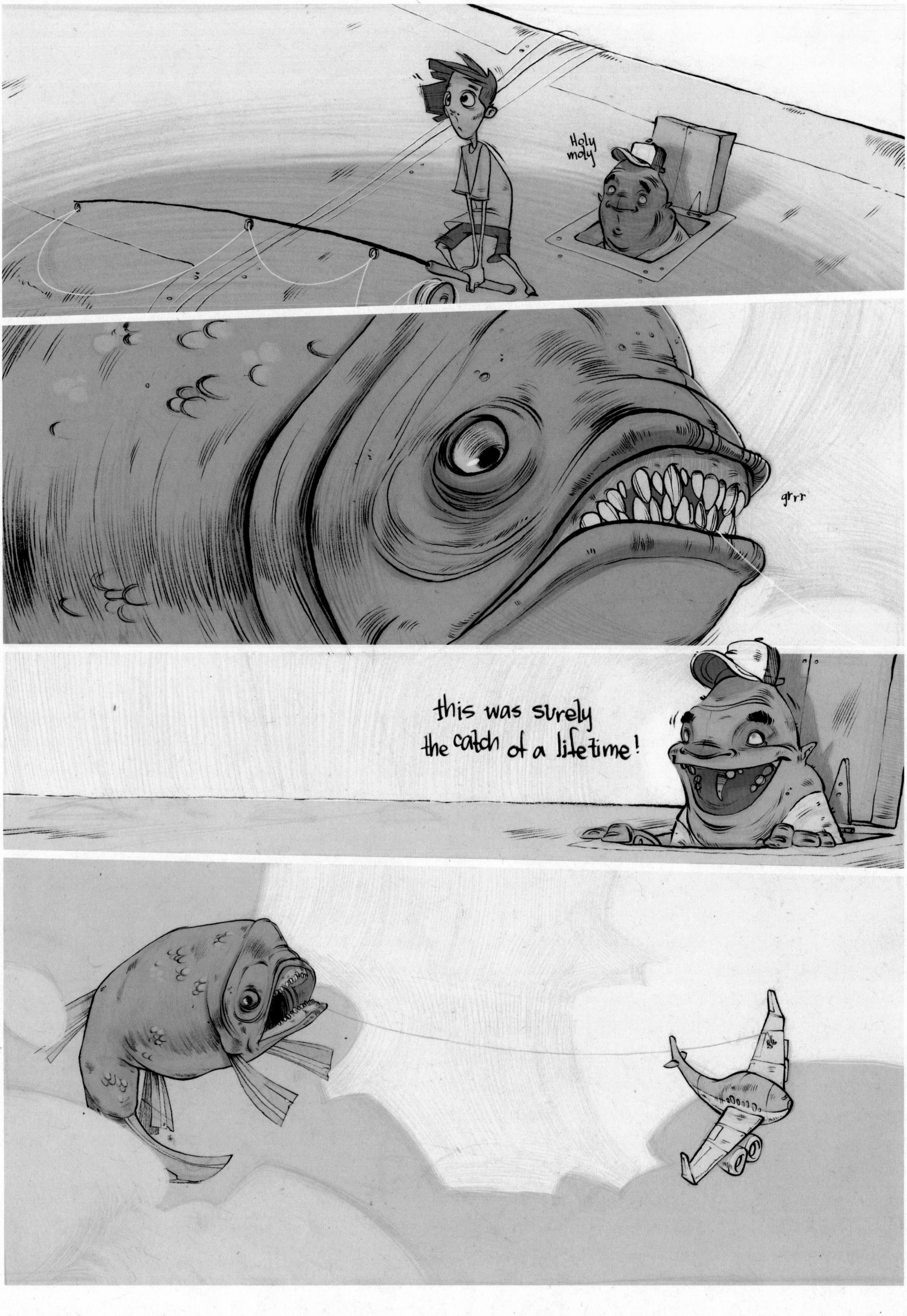
Holy moly
grrr
this was surely the catch of a lifetime!

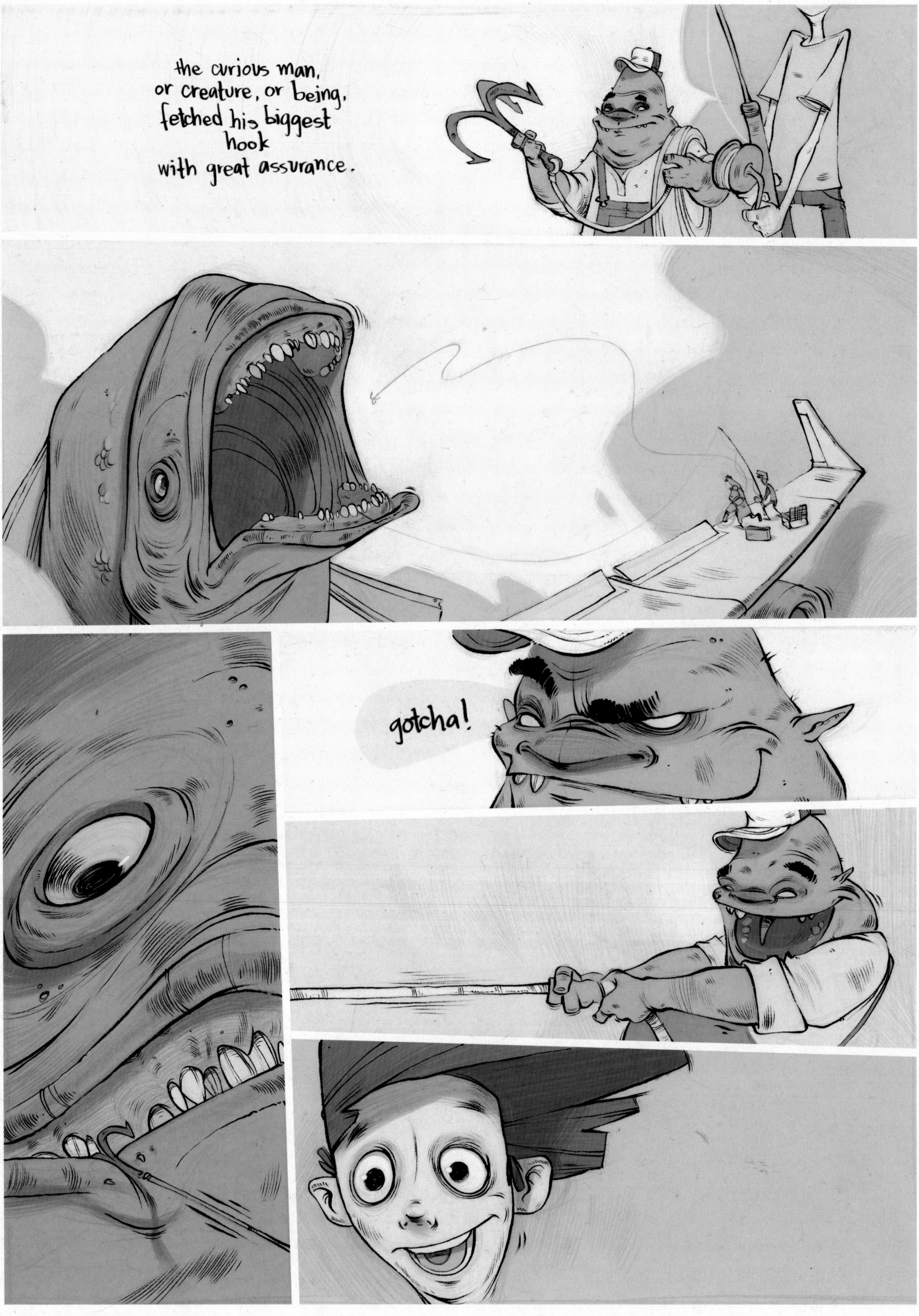
the curious man,
or creature, or being,
fetched his biggest
hook
with great assurance.
gotcha!

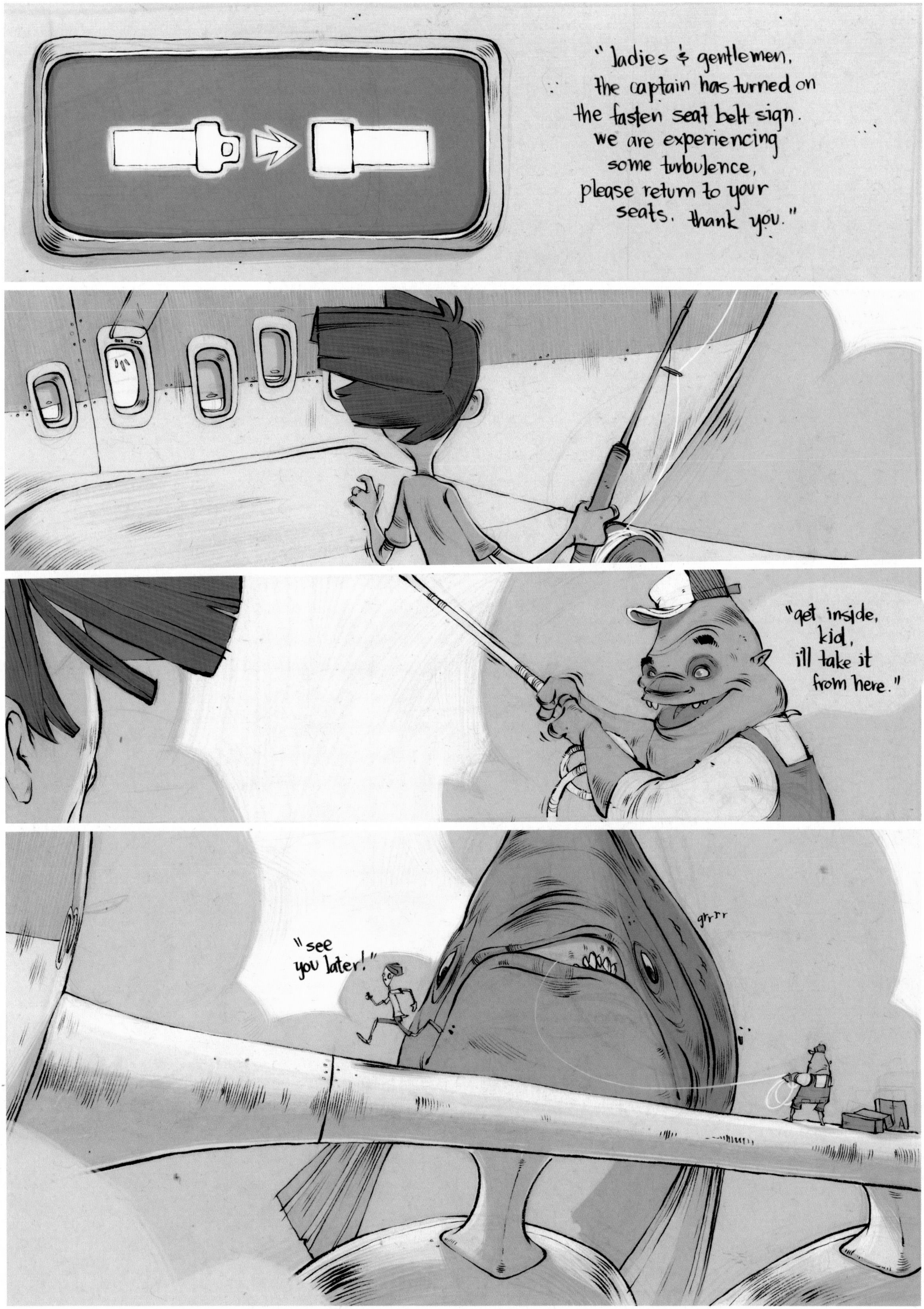
"ladies & gentlemen, the captain has turned on the fasten seat belt sign. we are experiencing some turbulence, please return to your seats. thank you."
"get inside, kid, i'll take it from here."
grrrr
"see you later!"

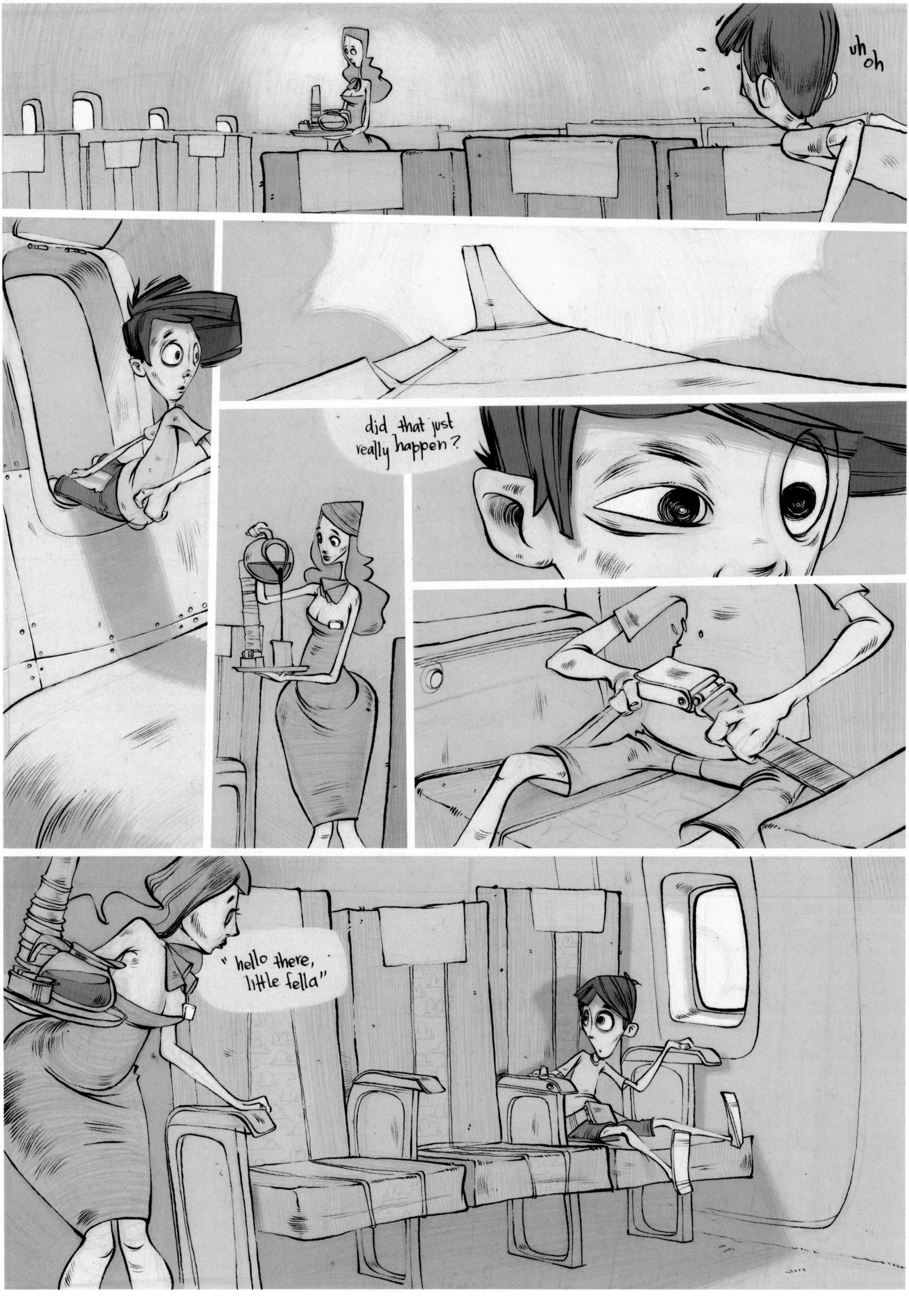
uh oh
did that just really happen?
" hello there, little fella"

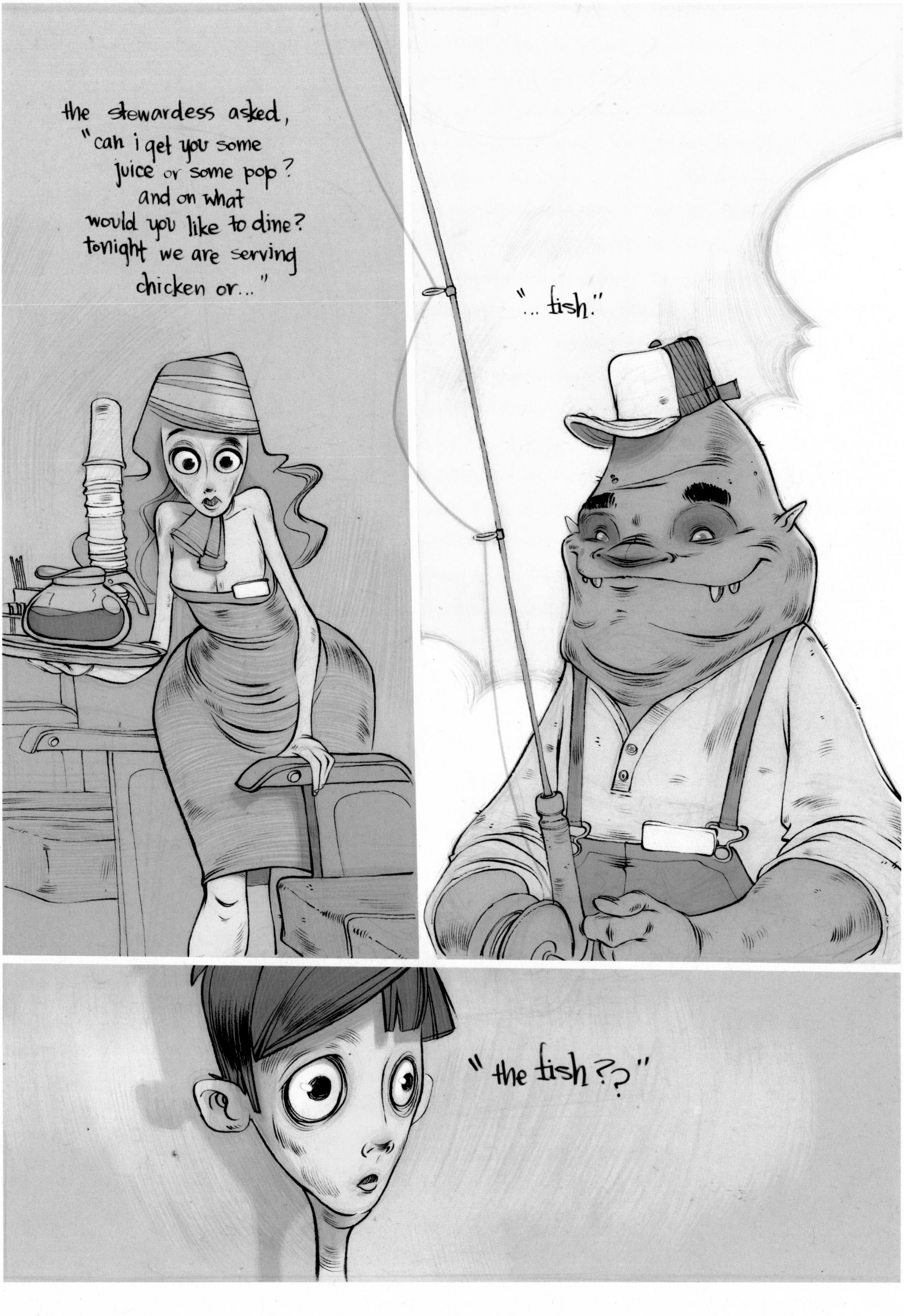
the stewardess asked,
"can i get you some juice or some pop? and on what would you like to dine? tonight we are serving chicken or..."
"... fish."
"the fish??"

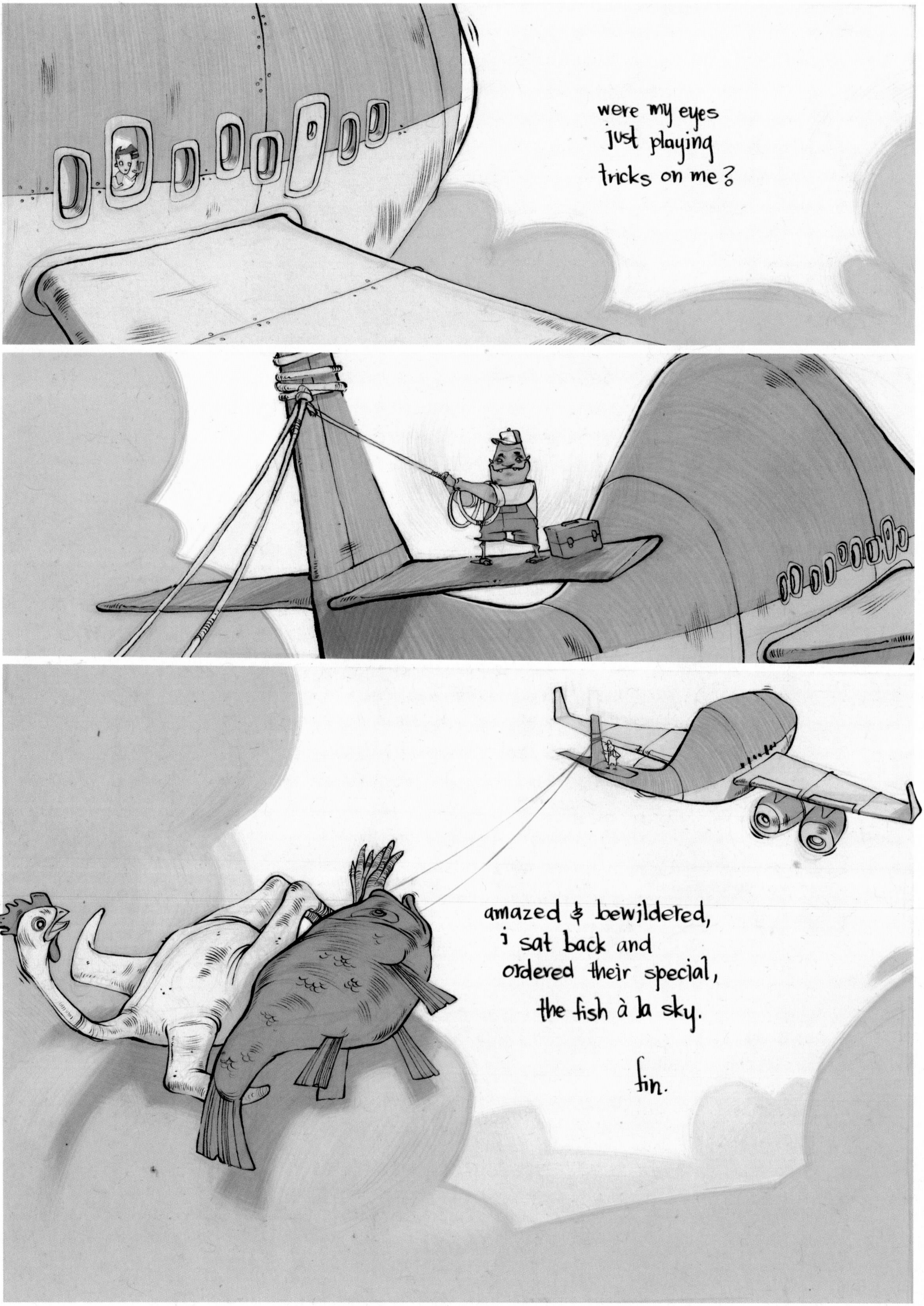
were my eyes just playing tricks on me?
amazed & bewildered, i sat back and ordered their special, the fish à la sky.
fin.

no chickens were harmed in this tale... the fish, on the other hand, wasn't so lucky.

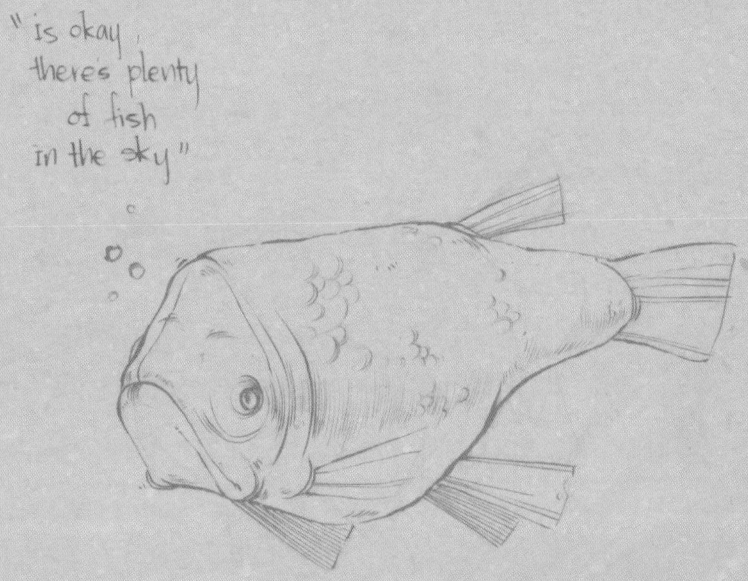
"is okay, there's plenty of fish in the sky"

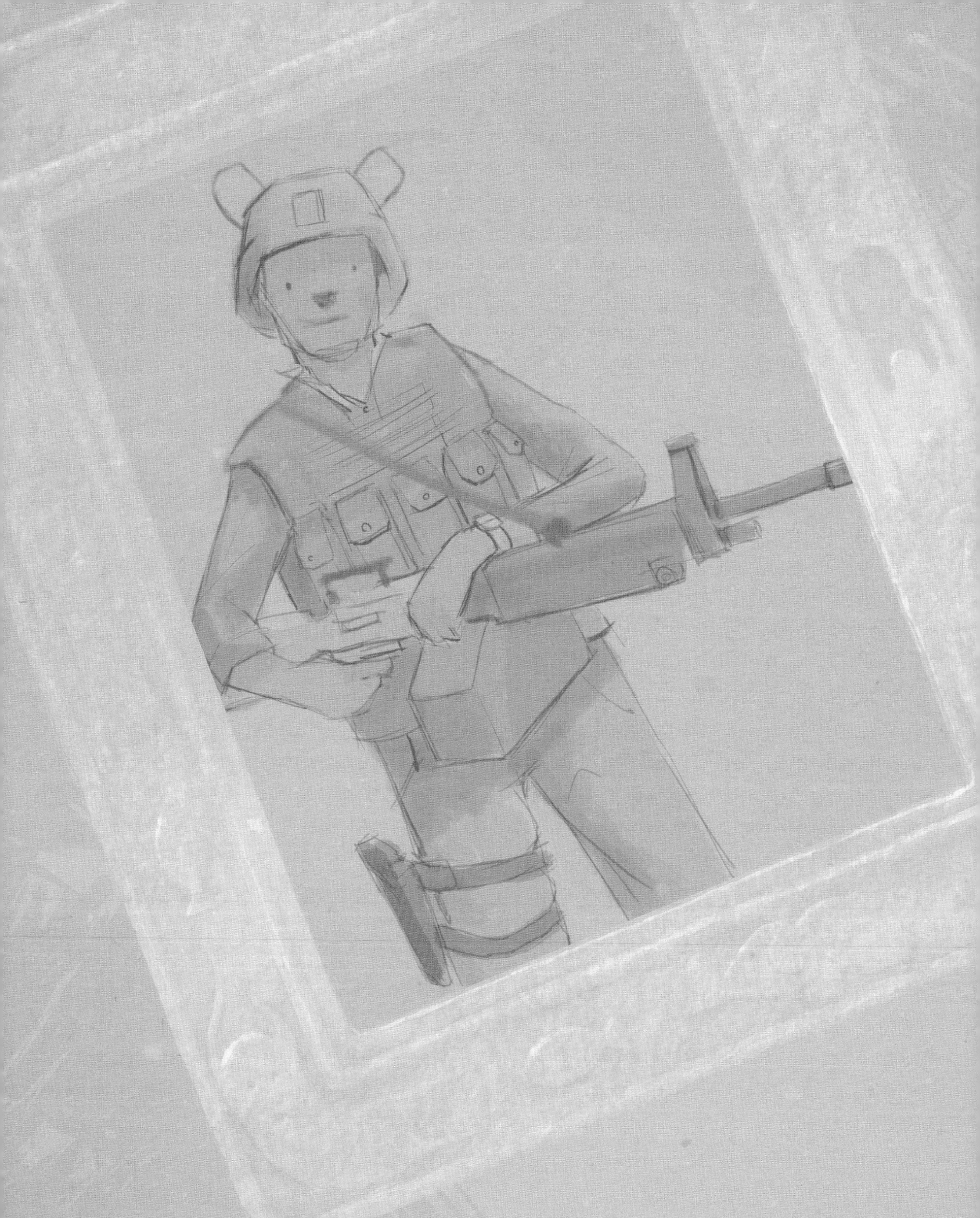

DAVID GORDON

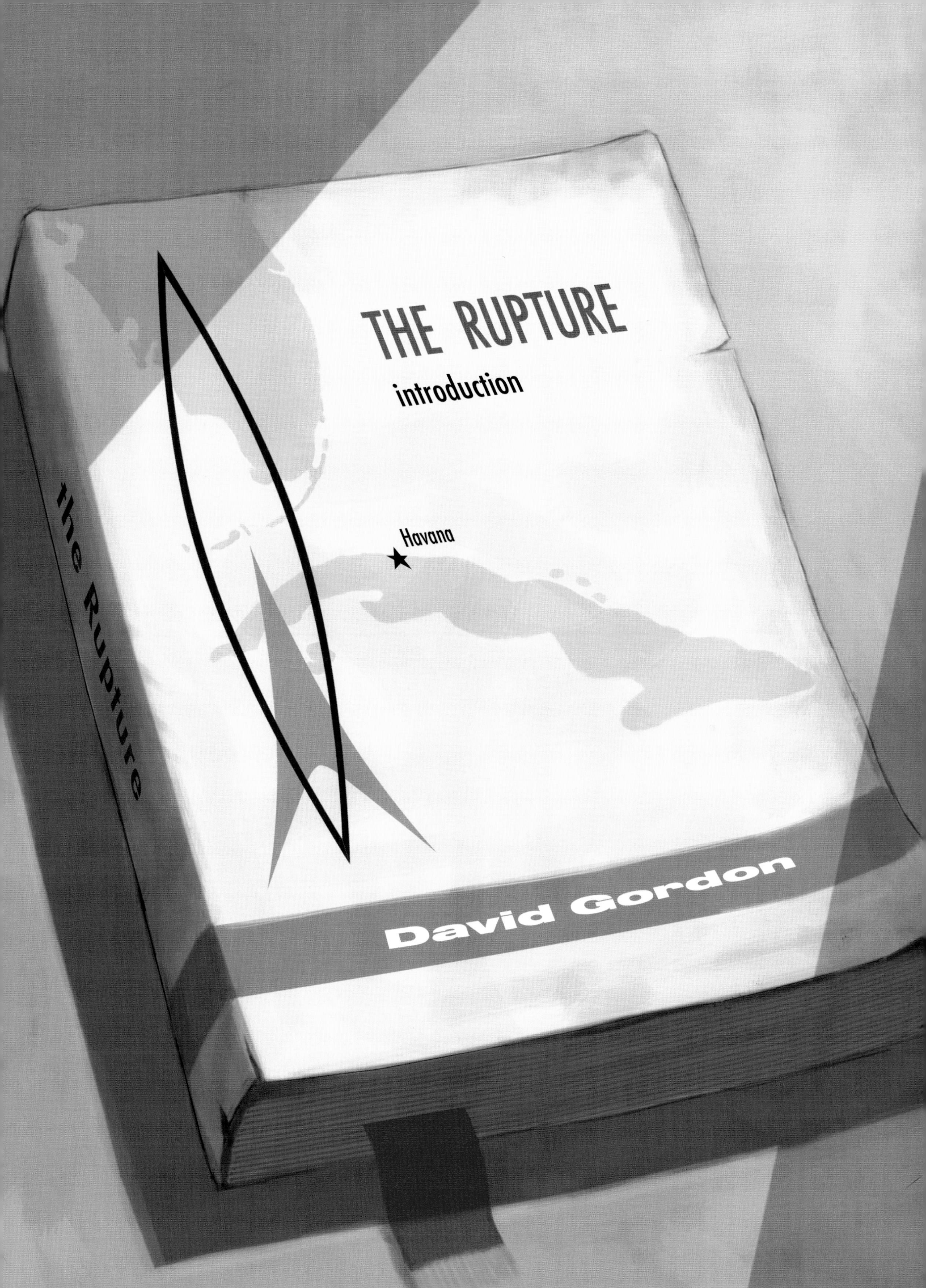
THE RUPTURE
introduction
Havana
the Rupture
David Gordon

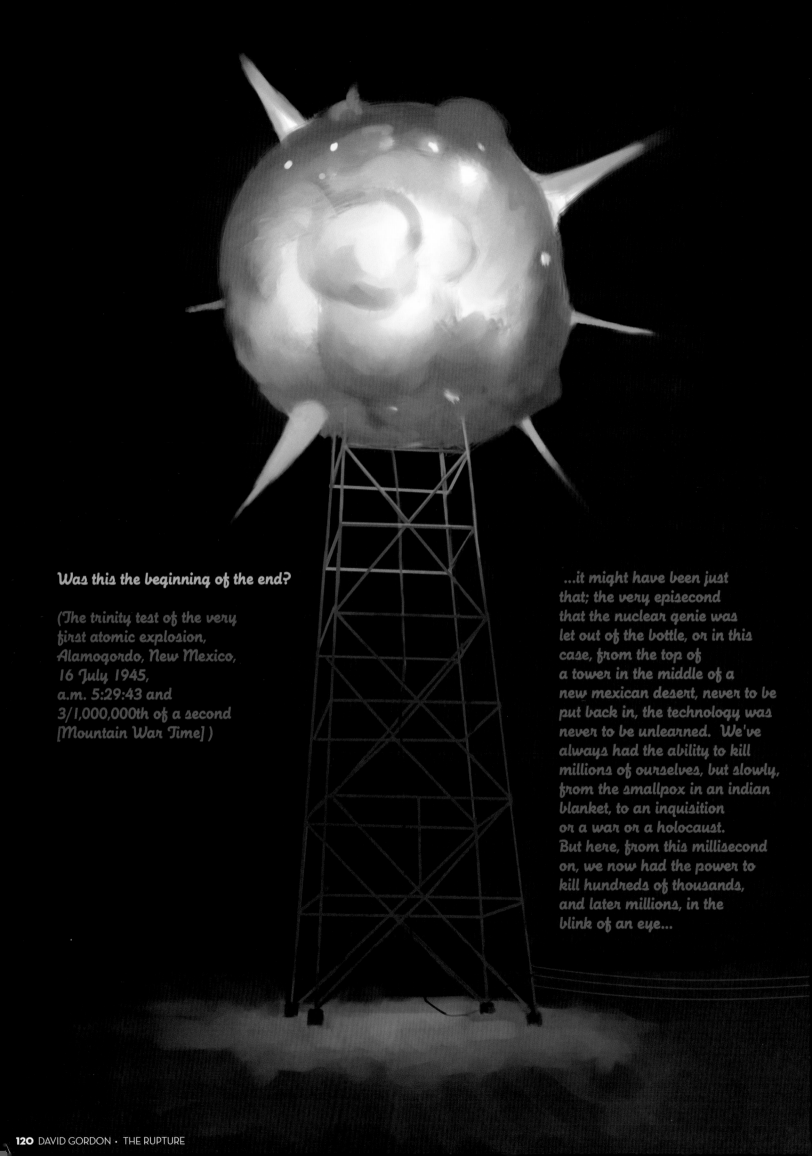

Was this the beginning of the end?

(The trinity test of the very
first atomic explosion,
Alamogordo, New Mexico,
16 July 1945,
a.m. 5:29:43 and
3/1,000,000th of a second
[Mountain War Time])

...it might have been just
that; the very episecond
that the nuclear genie was
let out of the bottle, or in this
case, from the top of
a tower in the middle of a
new mexican desert, never to be
put back in, the technology was
never to be unlearned. We've
always had the ability to kill
millions of ourselves, but slowly,
from the smallpox in an indian
blanket, to an inquisition
or a war or a holocaust.
But here, from this millisecond
on, we now had the power to
kill hundreds of thousands,
and later millions, in the
blink of an eye...

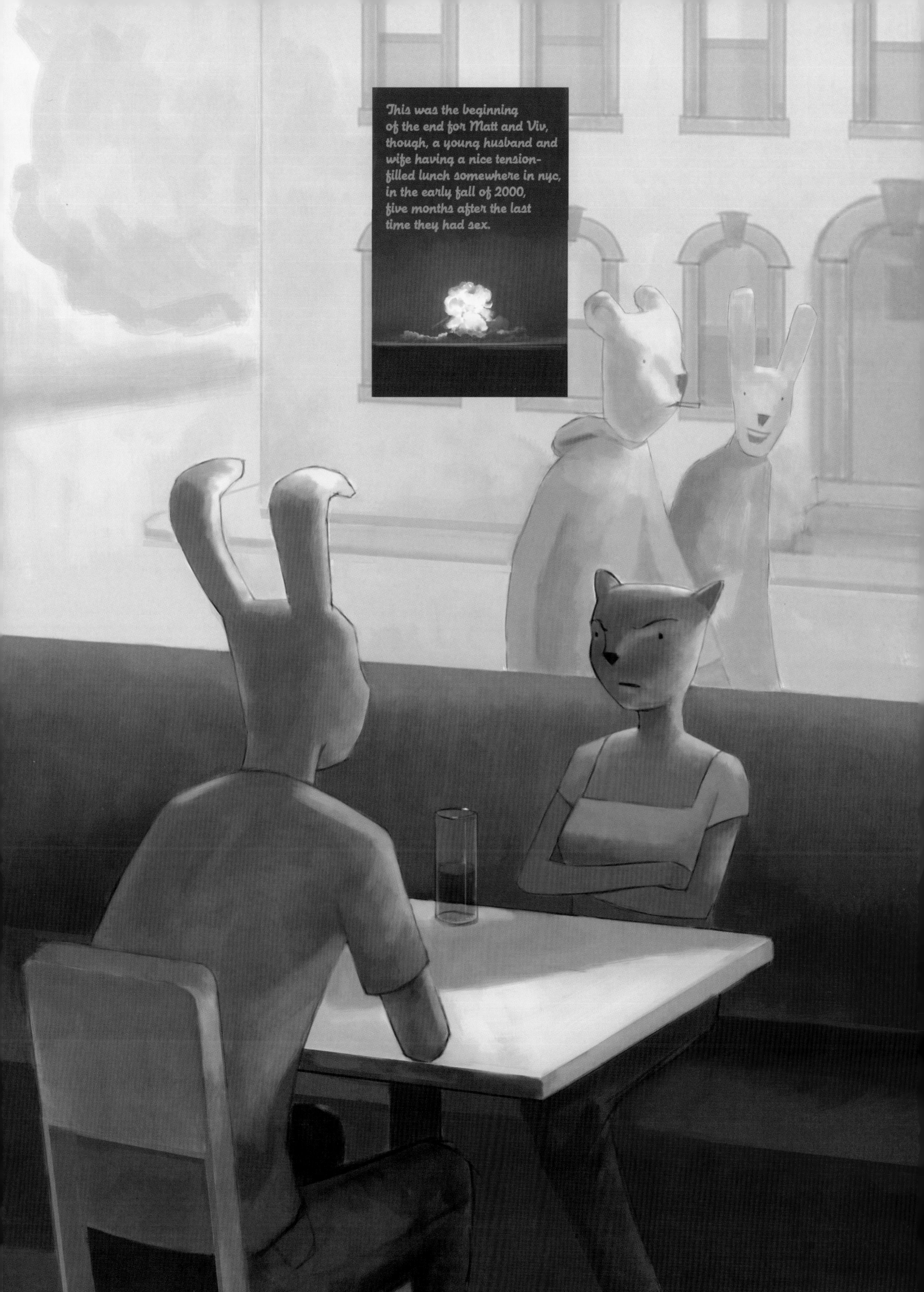
This was the beginning of the end for Matt and Viv, though, a young husband and wife having a nice tension-filled lunch somewhere in nyc, in the early fall of 2000, five months after the last time they had sex.

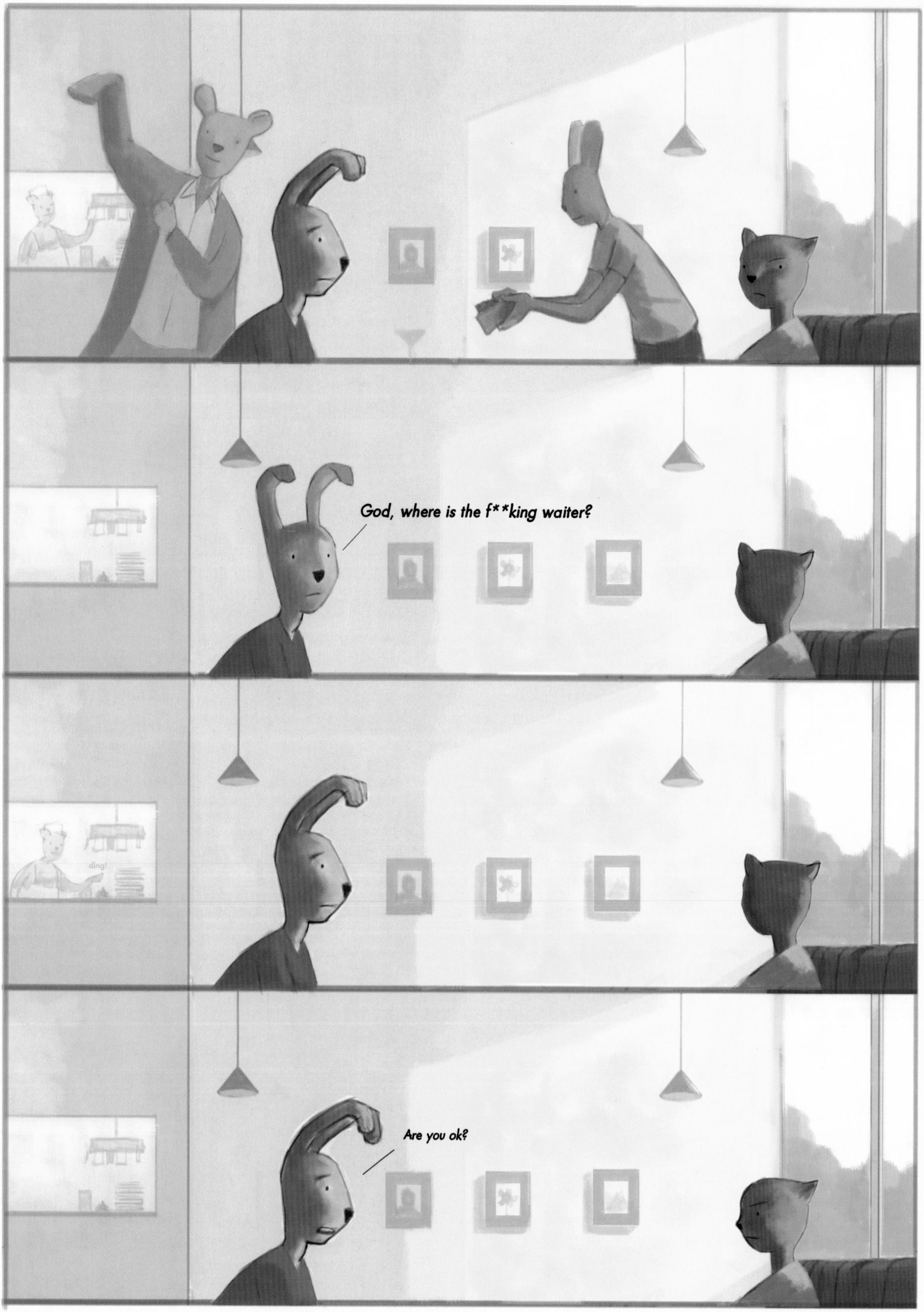
God, where is the f**king waiter?
ding!
Are you ok?

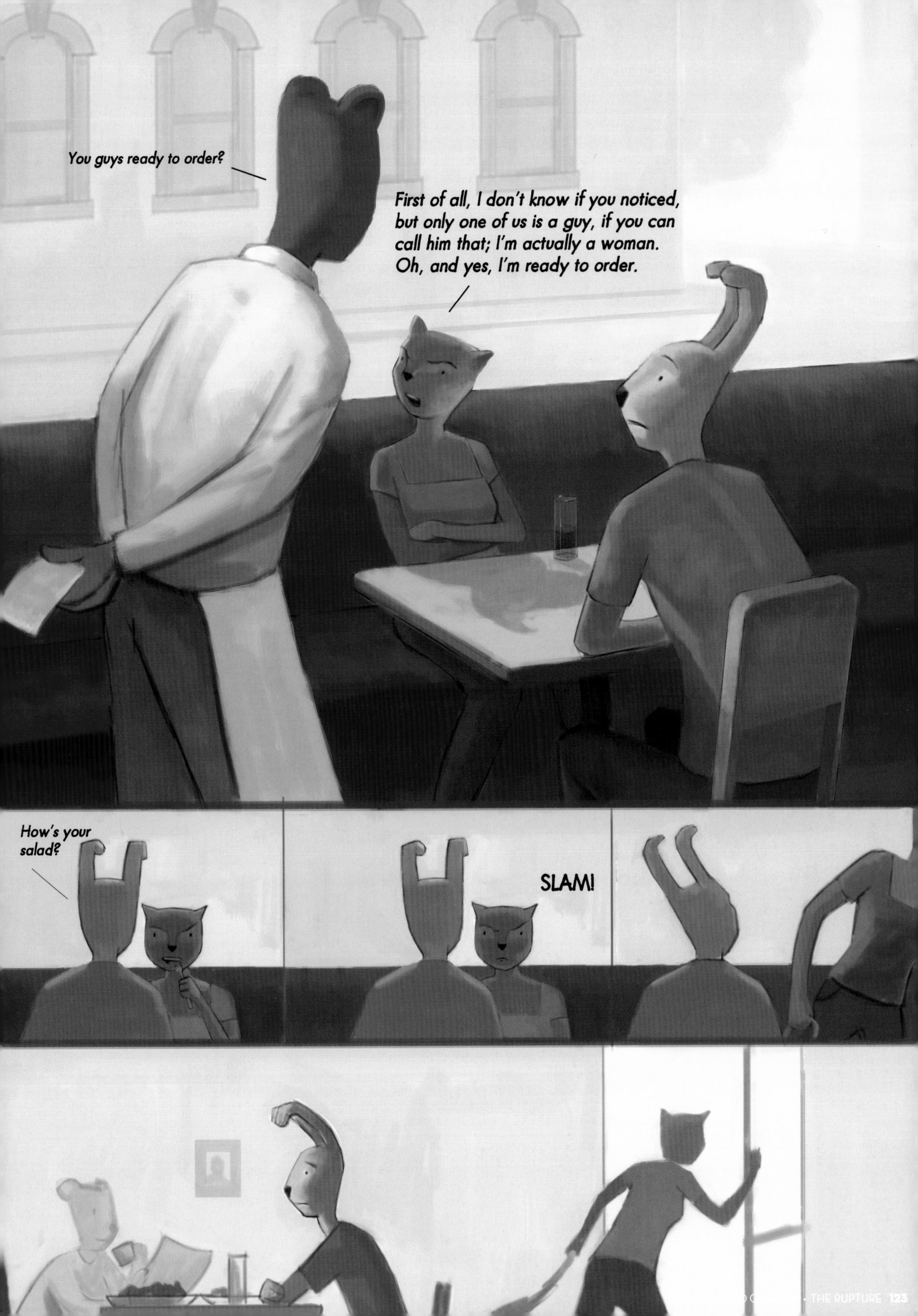

You guys ready to order?
First of all, I don't know if you noticed, but only one of us is a guy, if you can call him that; I'm actually a woman. Oh, and yes, I'm ready to order.
How's your salad?
SLAM!

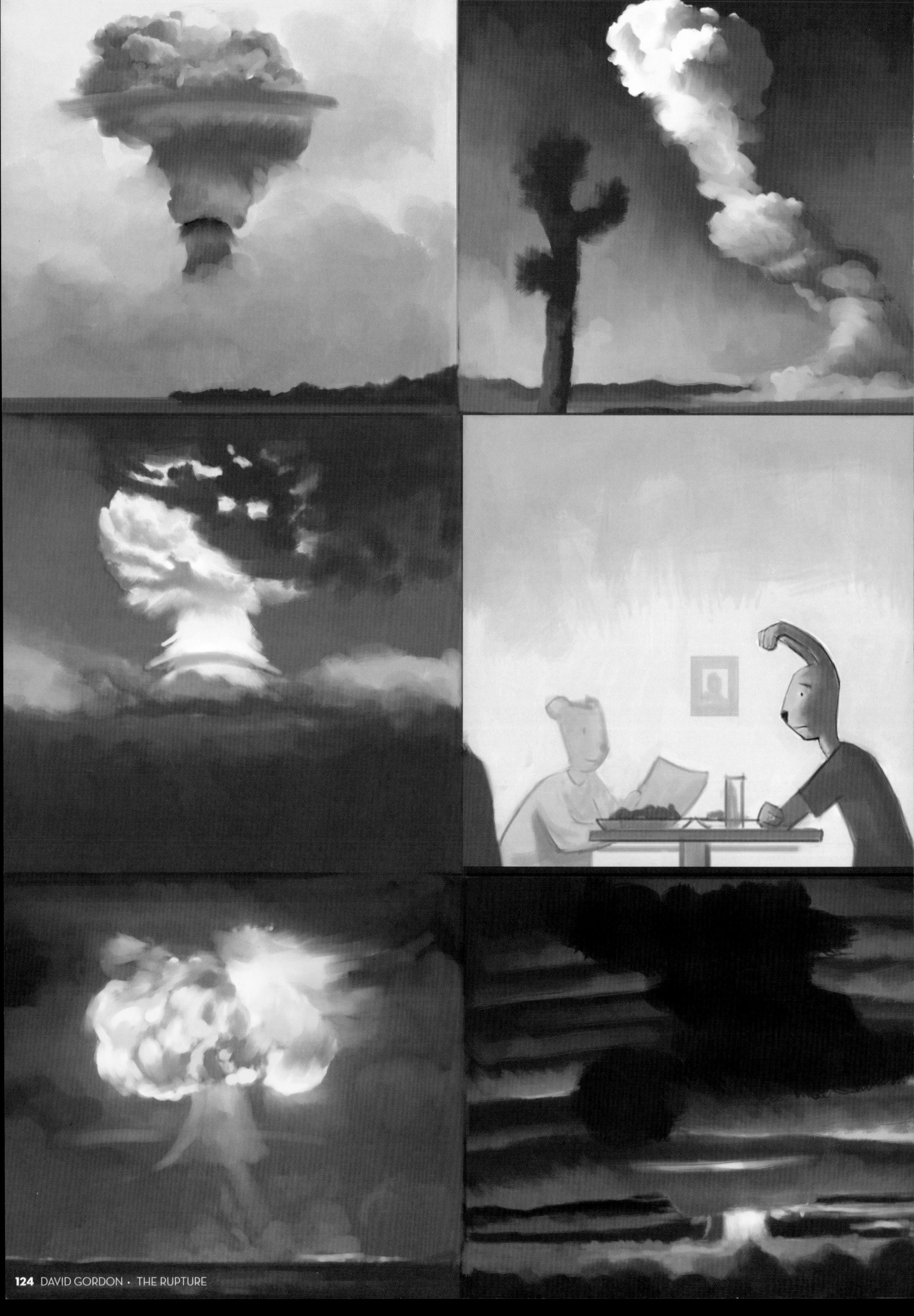

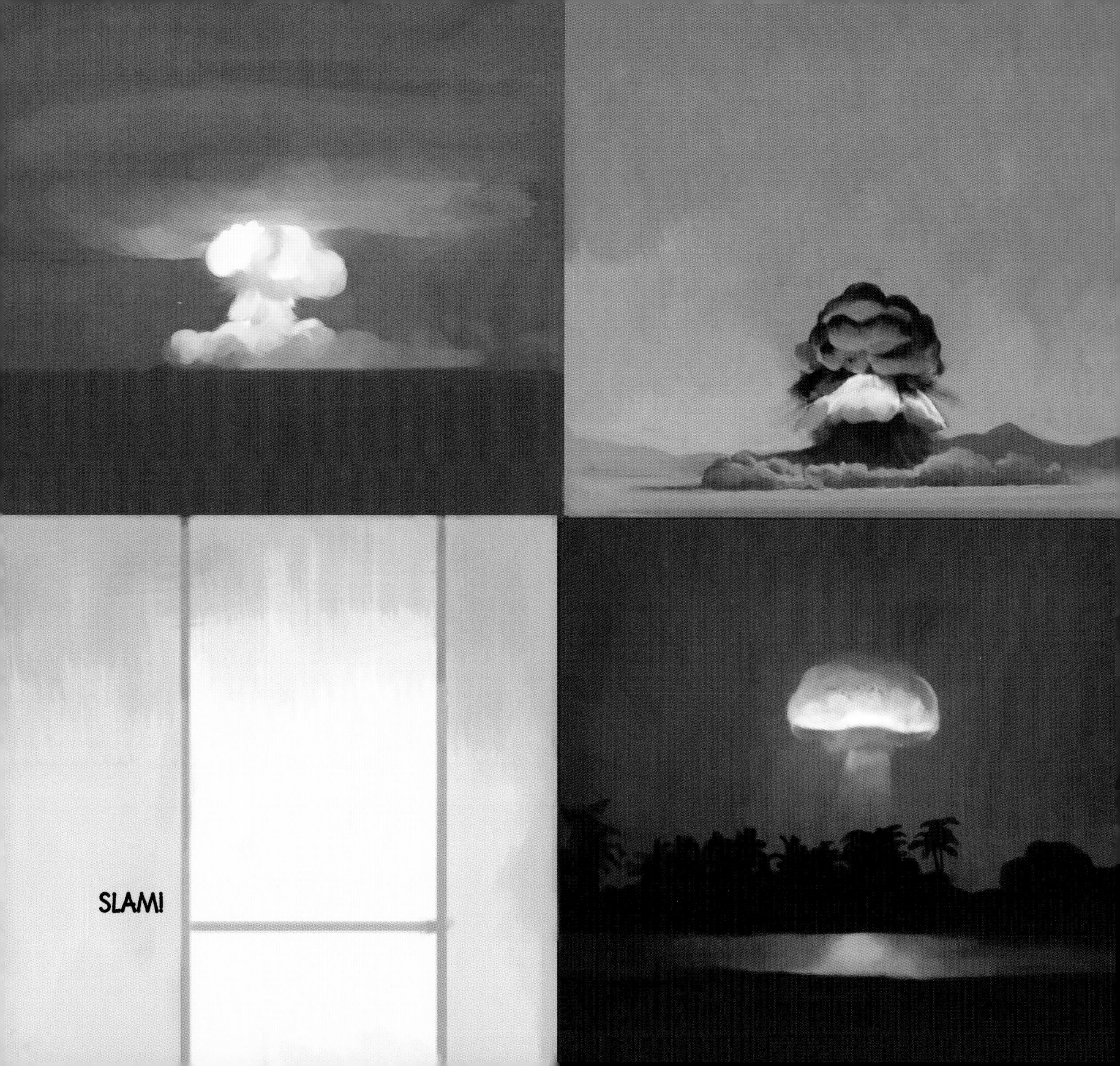
SLAM!

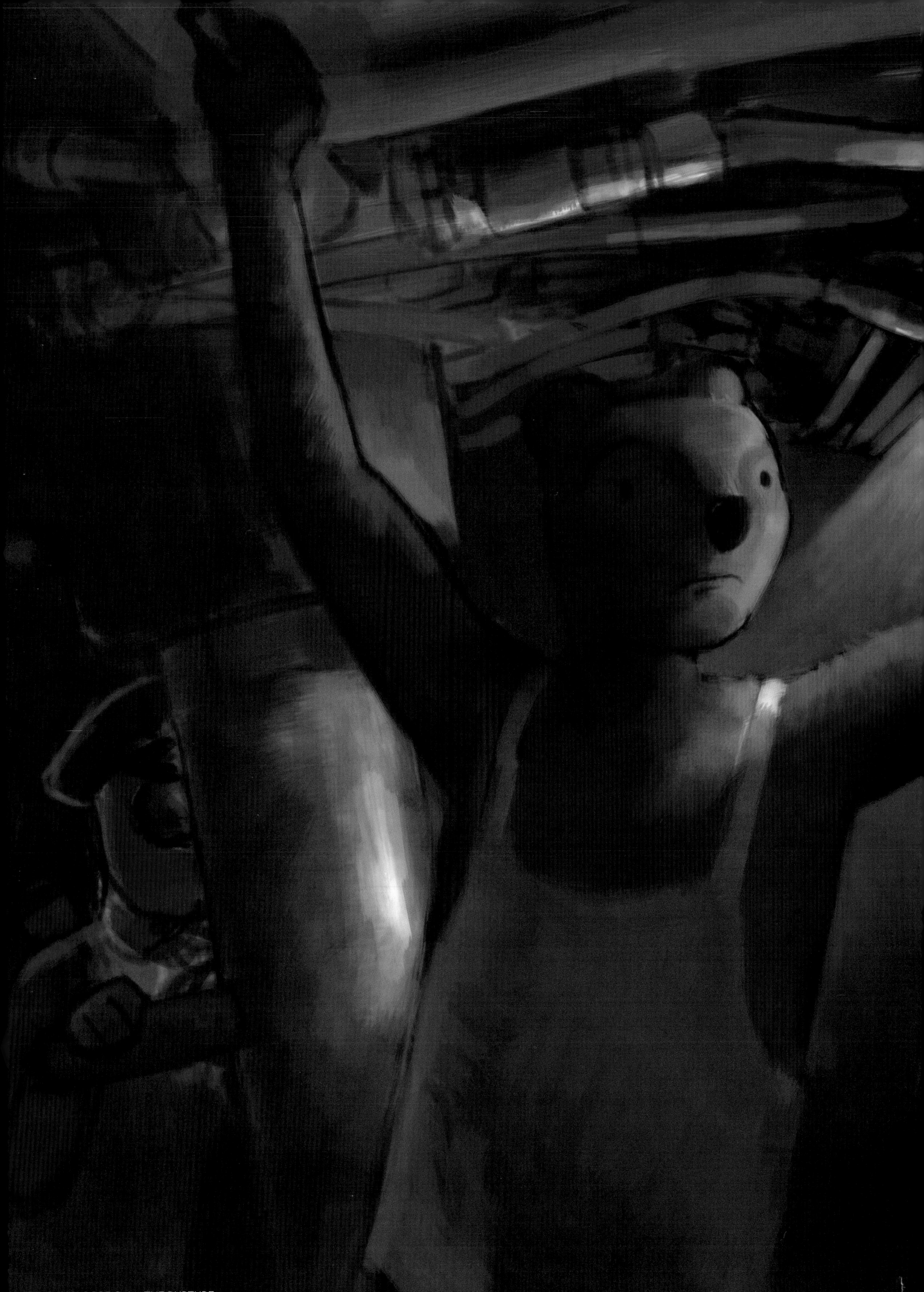

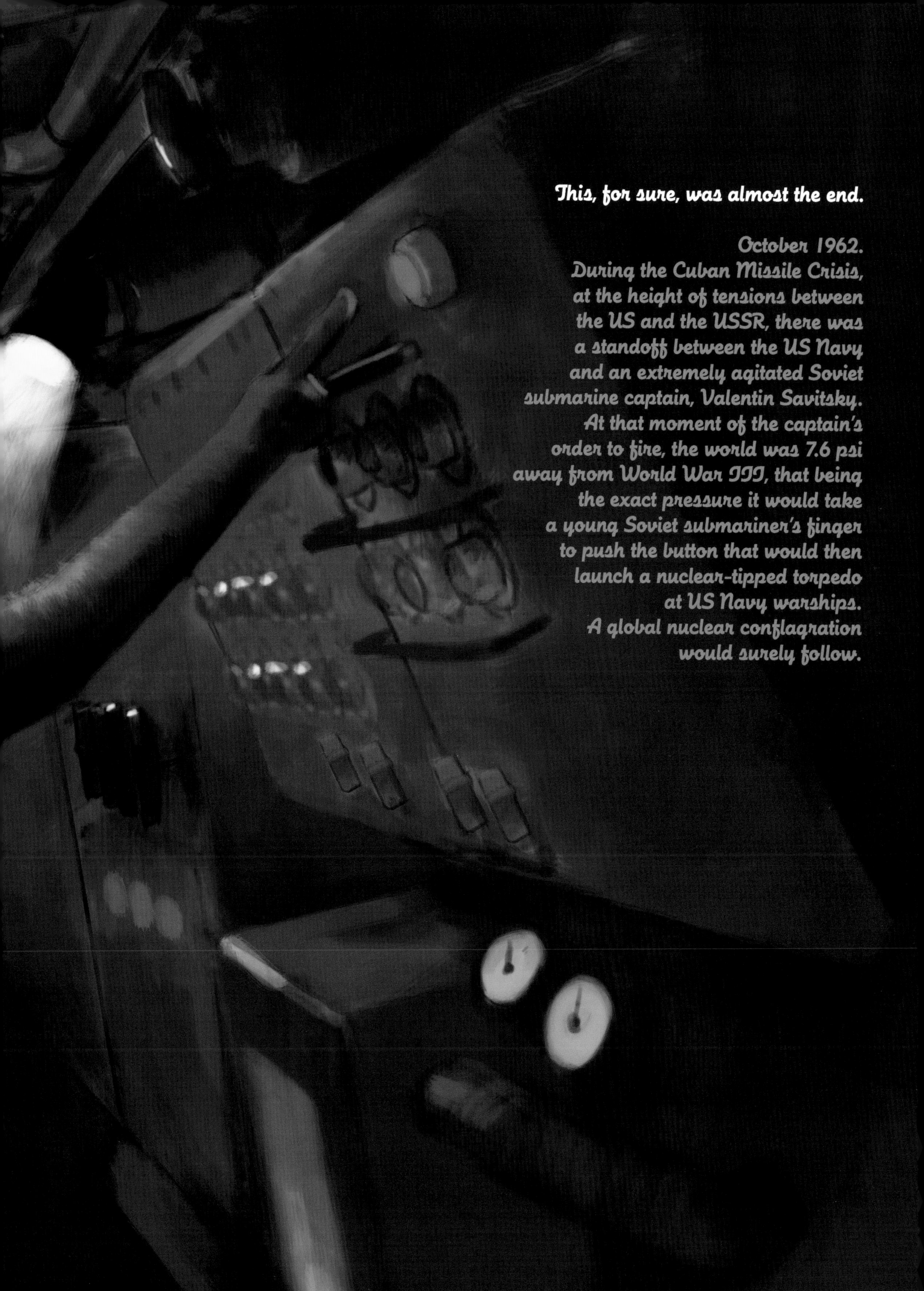

This, for sure, was almost the end.

October 1962.
During the Cuban Missile Crisis, at the height of tensions between the US and the USSR, there was a standoff between the US Navy and an extremely agitated Soviet submarine captain, Valentin Savitsky. At that moment of the captain's order to fire, the world was 7.6 psi away from World War III, that being the exact pressure it would take a young Soviet submariner's finger to push the button that would then launch a nuclear-tipped torpedo at US Navy warships. A global nuclear conflagration would surely follow.

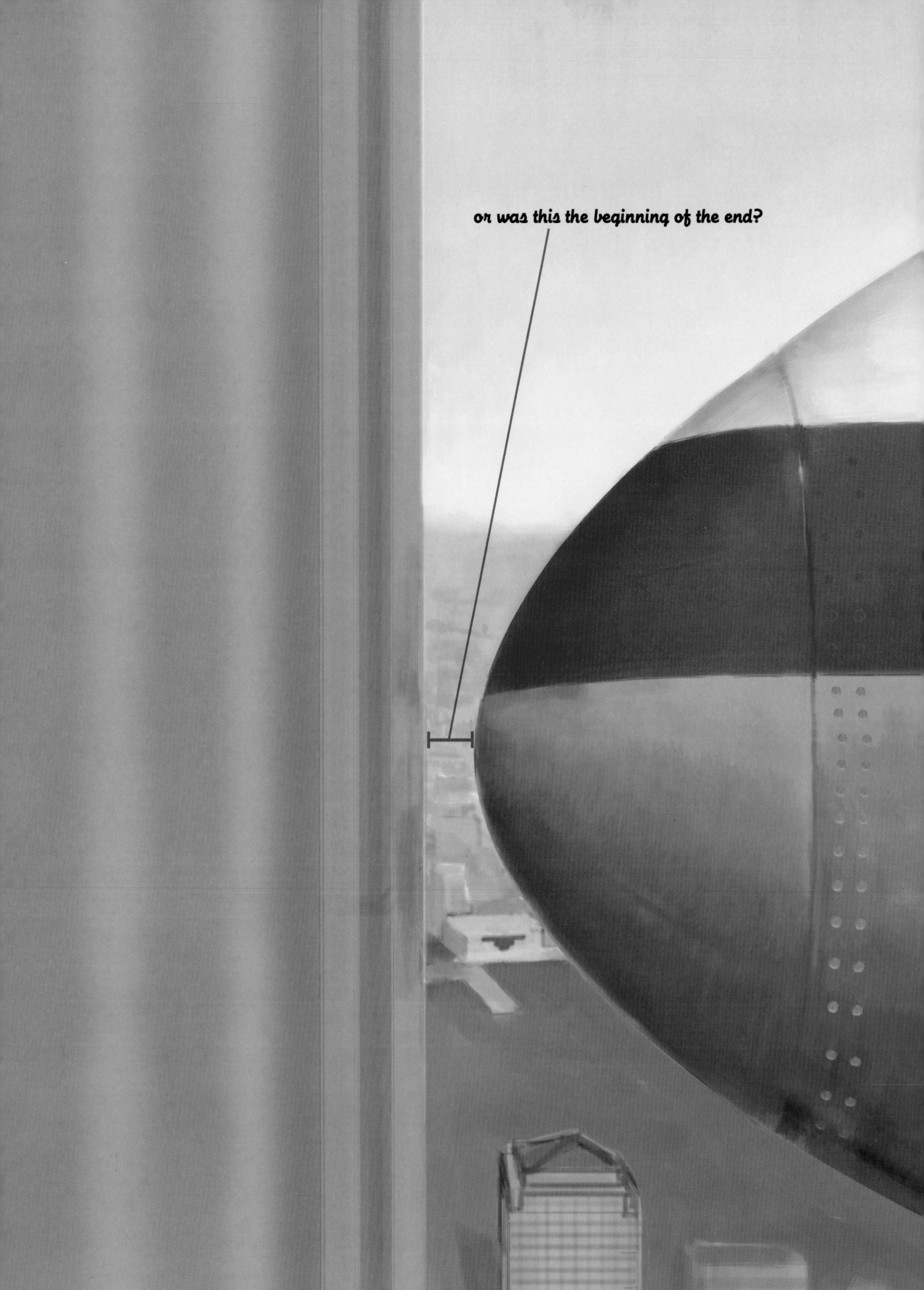
or was this the beginning of the end?

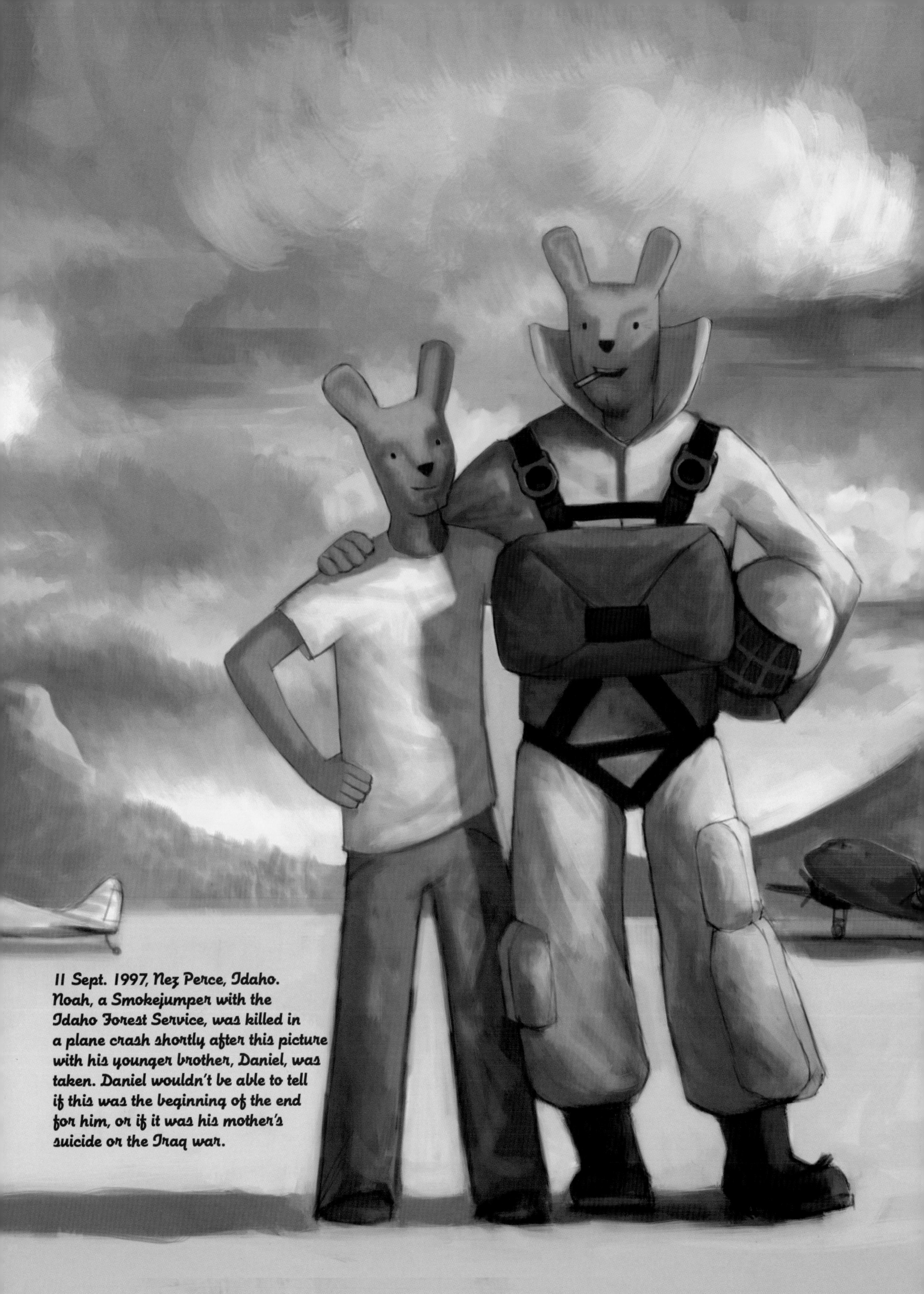

11 Sept. 1997, Nez Perce, Idaho. Noah, a Smokejumper with the Idaho Forest Service, was killed in a plane crash shortly after this picture with his younger brother, Daniel, was taken. Daniel wouldn't be able to tell if this was the beginning of the end for him, or if it was his mother's suicide or the Iraq war.

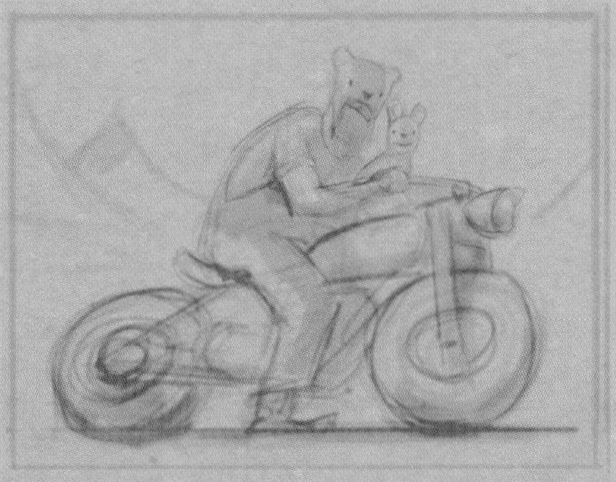

OUT OF PICTURE

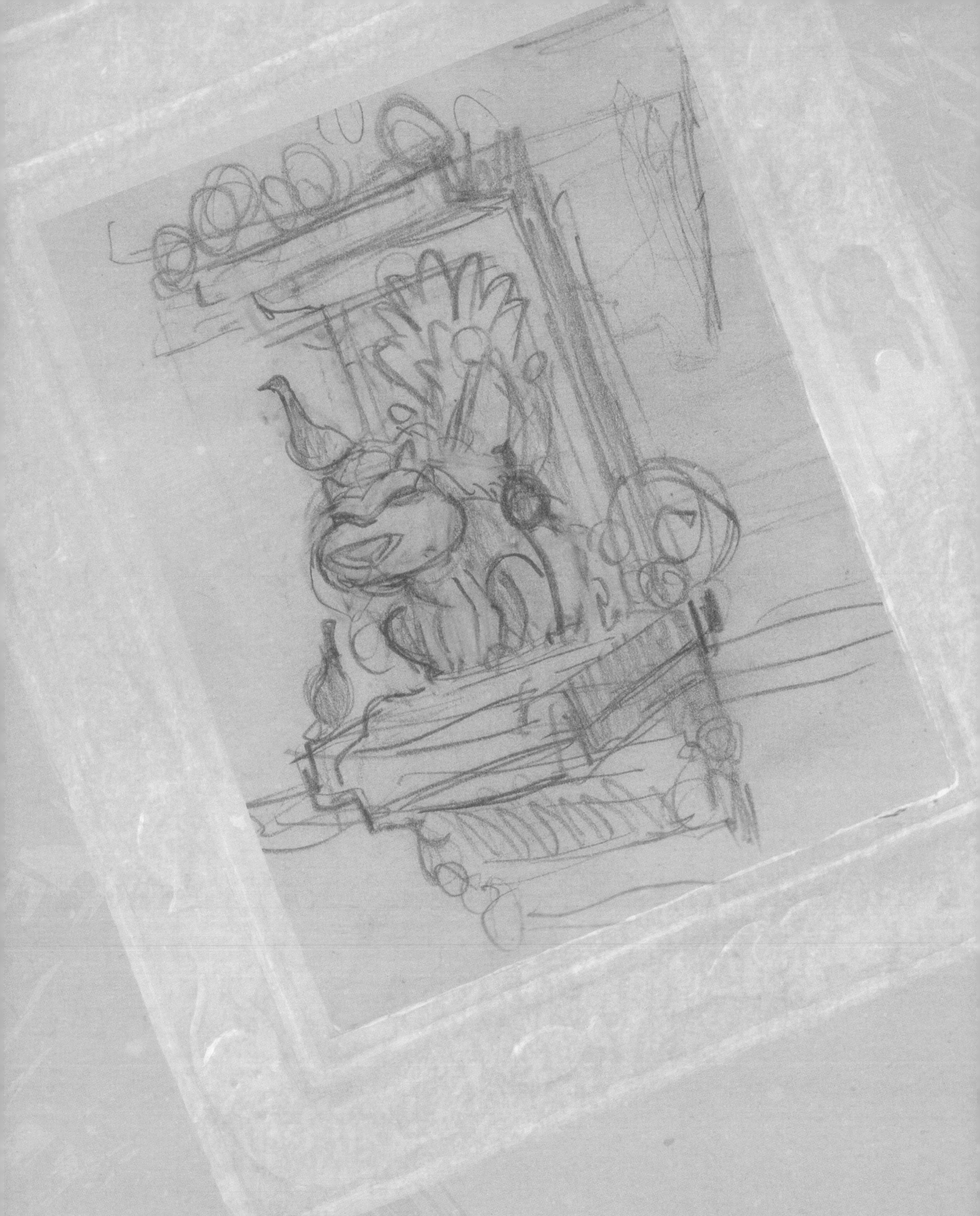

NASH DUNNIGAN

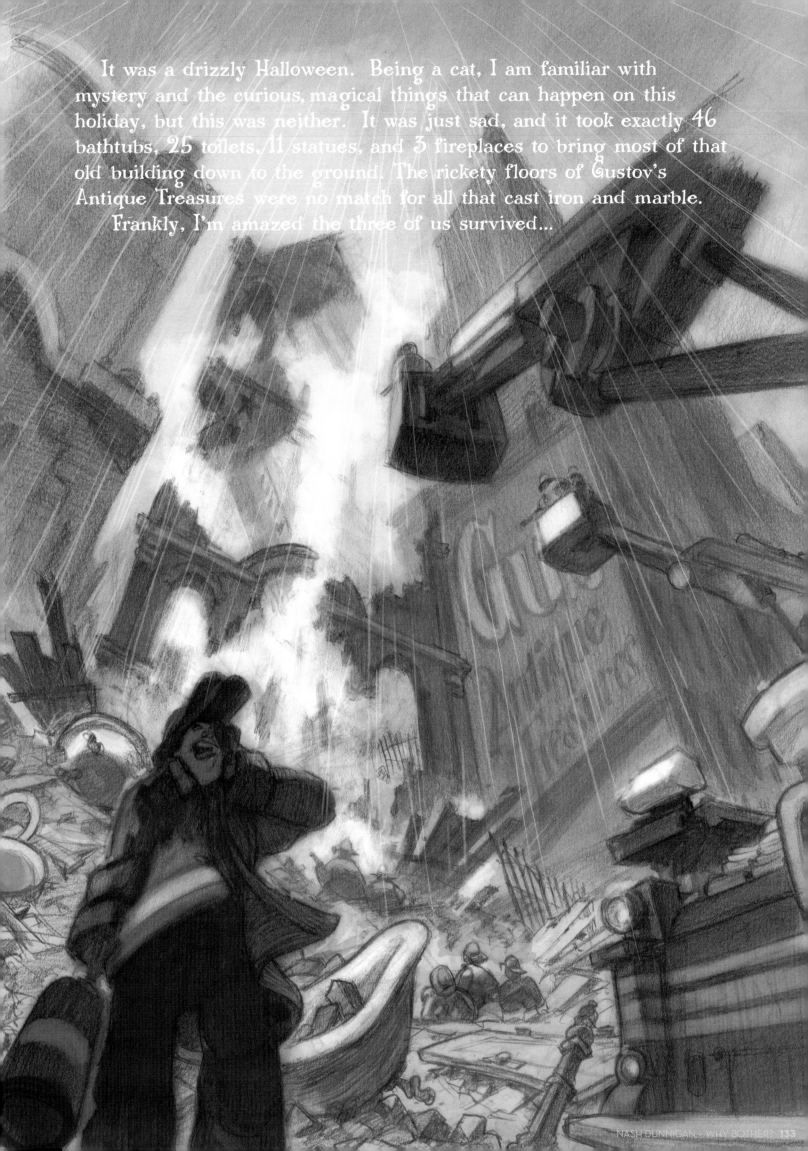

It was a drizzly Halloween. Being a cat, I am familiar with mystery and the curious, magical things that can happen on this holiday, but this was neither. It was just sad, and it took exactly 46 bathtubs, 25 toilets, 11 statues, and 3 fireplaces to bring most of that old building down to the ground. The rickety floors of Gustov's Antique Treasures were no match for all that cast iron and marble.

Frankly, I'm amazed the three of us survived...

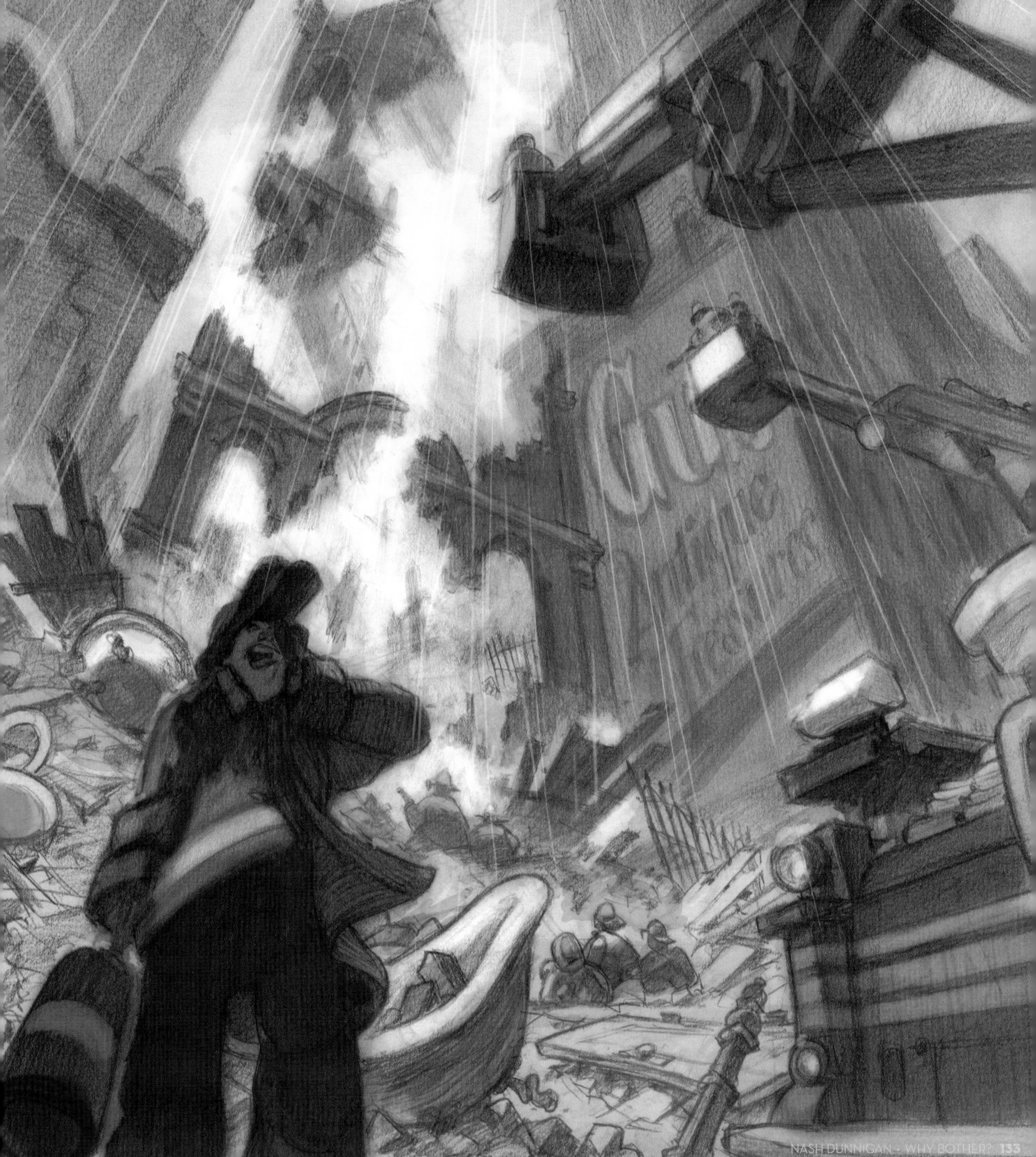

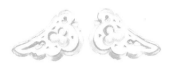

WHY BOTHER?

A Tale of Urban Relocation

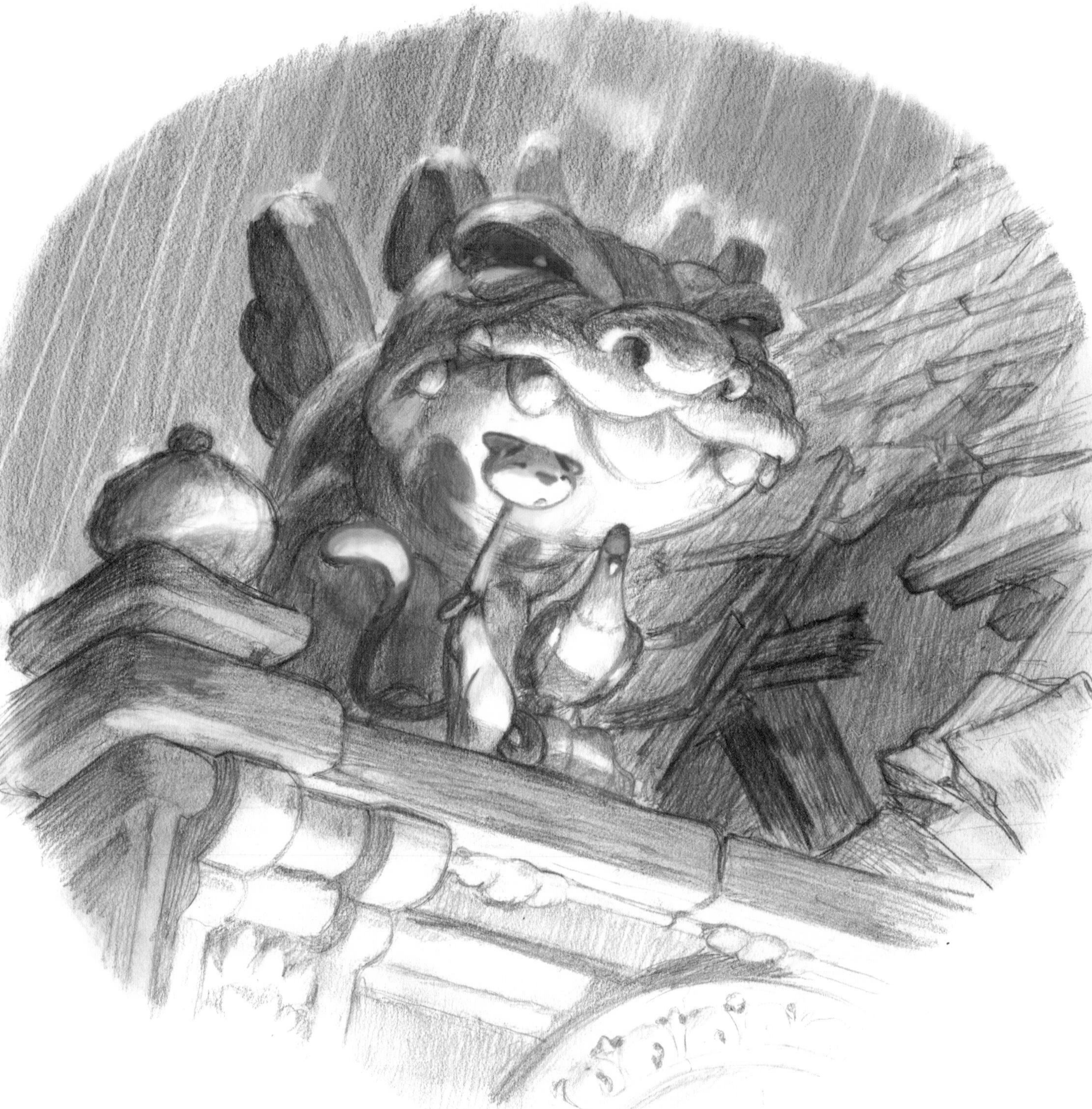

by Nash Dunnigan

I just couldn't believe he was gone. Gus was a saint. He had saved the three of us. Pigeon had blown in from across the Atlantic during a storm with a broken wing. I had sprained my paw from one too many rooftop hops, and Rufus, our resident grouch, was saved from the wrecking ball and brought here to live with us too. We were a family, but in an instant, we found ourselves all alone.

Pigeon, not known for his subtlety or sensitivity, said gruffly, "Look, buddy, we're all sad. Gustov was family and all, but he is gone, and unless we leave tonight, we will come down with this building."

"Have a heart, Pigeon," I said. "Rufus, Halloween is the one night of the year when gargoyles can go wherever they want to. If we don't go tonight, you won't get another chance. Please..."

Rufus just looked down at the street below and said, "Why bother?" Pigeon shook his head and flew off, swallowed up by the mist.

Rufus and I solemnly sat as the rain slowly gave way to the evening fog. It looked as if it was going to be a long Halloween night, and I had all but written off Pigeon, when much to my surprise, the little feathered pessimist came fluttering back to the rooftop. And he was not alone.

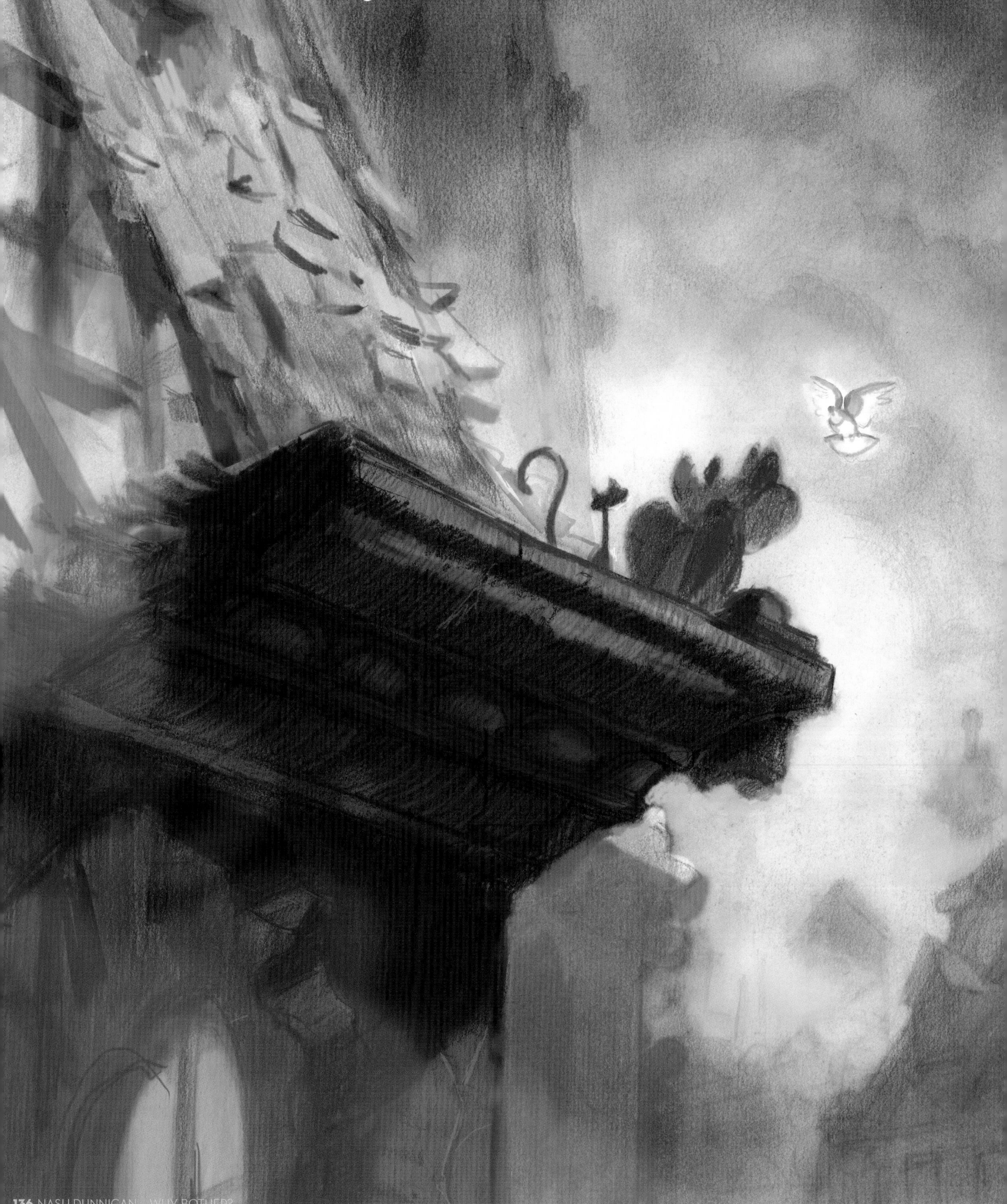

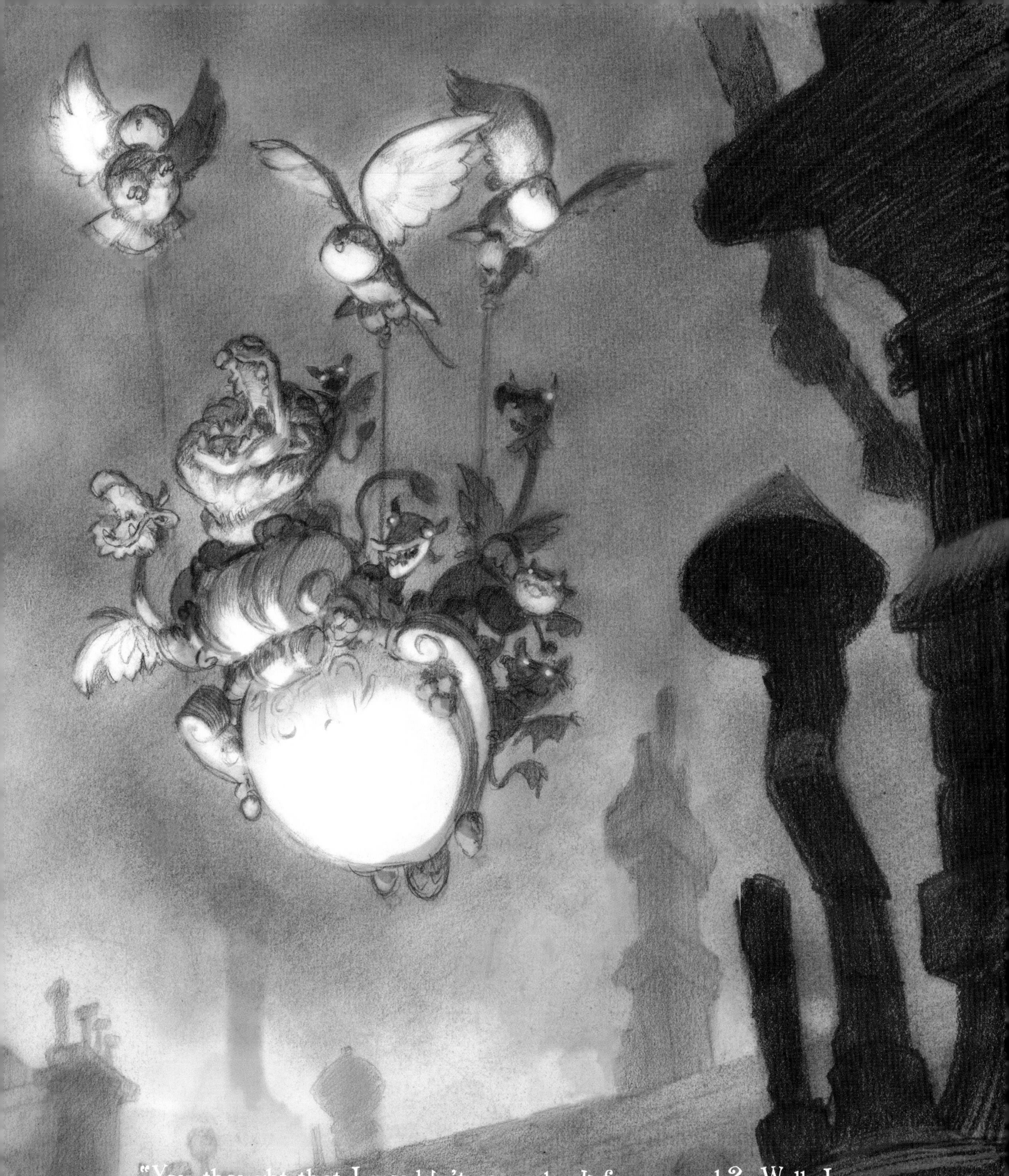

"You thought that I wouldn't come back for you, eh? Well, I wasn't going to let you bring the whole BLOCK down with your sour moods. Besides, it's Halloween, and these guys missed you!" Flying in the crest from the old Midtown Bank and held aloft by the owls of the sewing factory were all of Rufus's old buddies. Even the lions from the library had awakened to help their friends!

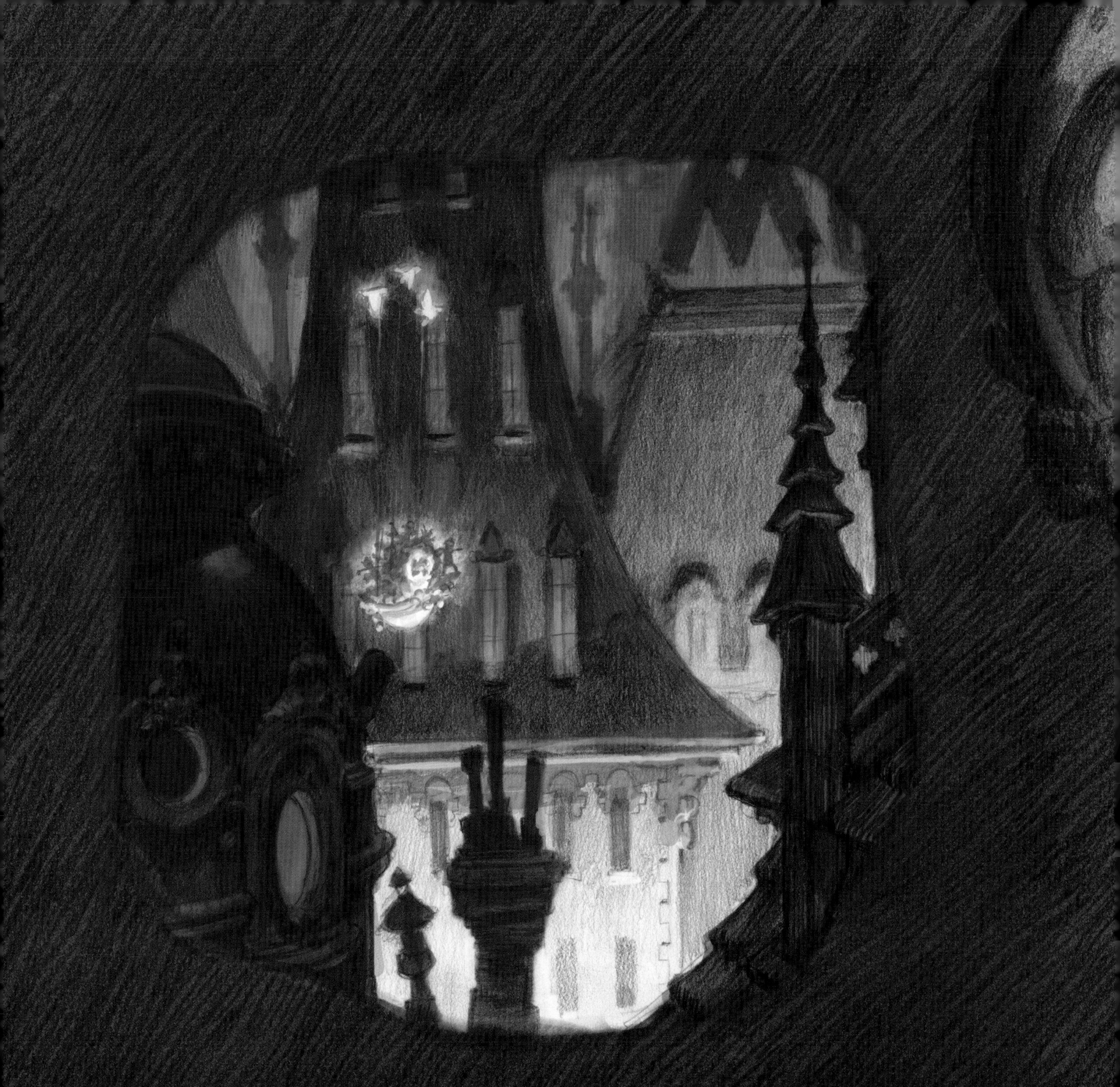

Gargoyles are fond of breaking into song, when they have occasion to get together, and that Halloween was a special night.

"Fate has plucked us from our roosts all right,
even though we are made of stone.
We must awaken and wander this magical night
to find our dear friends a home, a home,
to find our dear friends a home!"

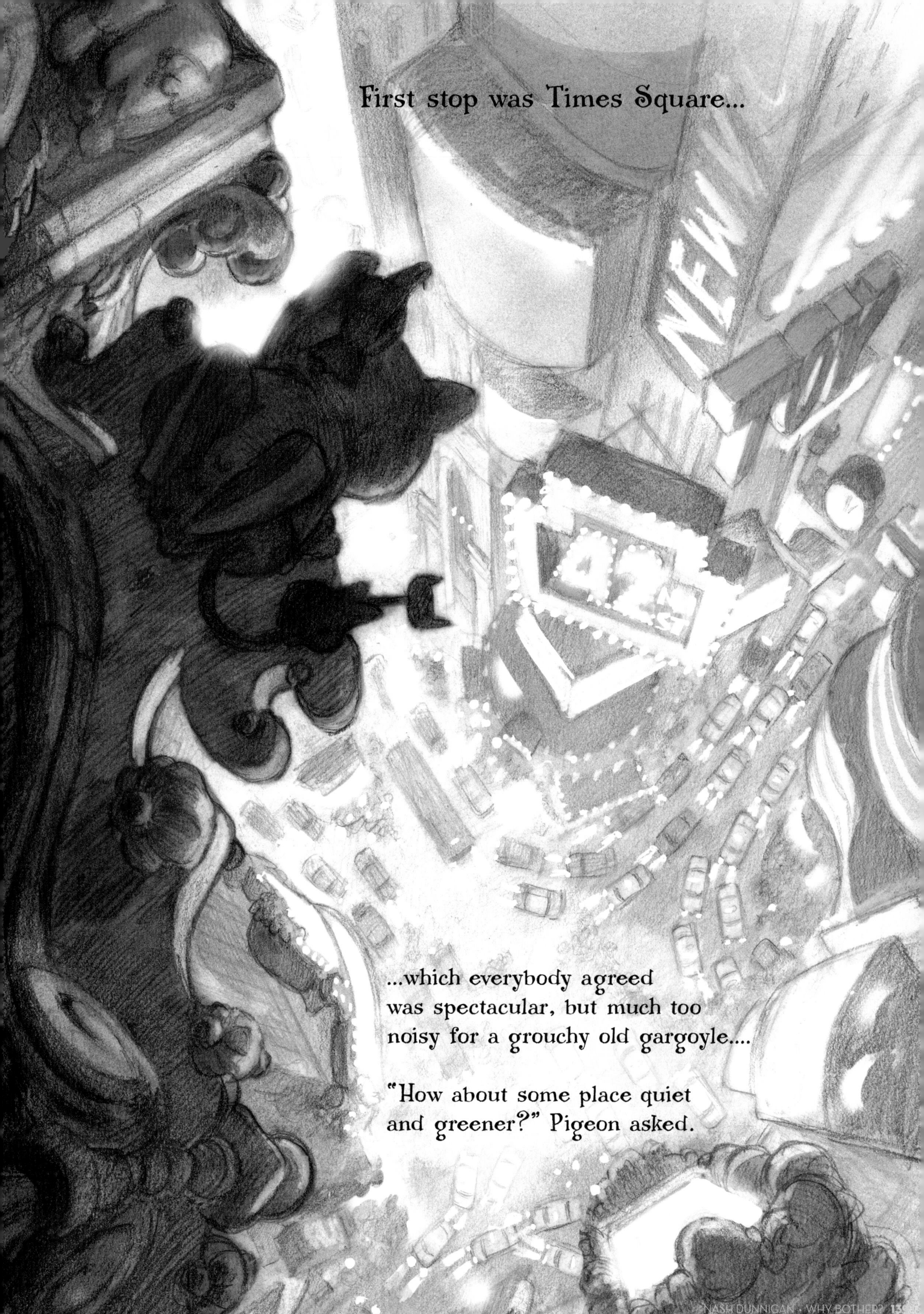
NEW
42

First stop was Times Square...

...which everybody agreed
was spectacular, but much too
noisy for a grouchy old gargoyle....

"How about some place quiet
and greener?" Pigeon asked.

Our next option was the dog run deep in Central Park. I really thought they would have been happier to see him. "I'm not exactly winning best in show over here, or any other beauty contests!" Rufus yelled over the barking of the dogs.

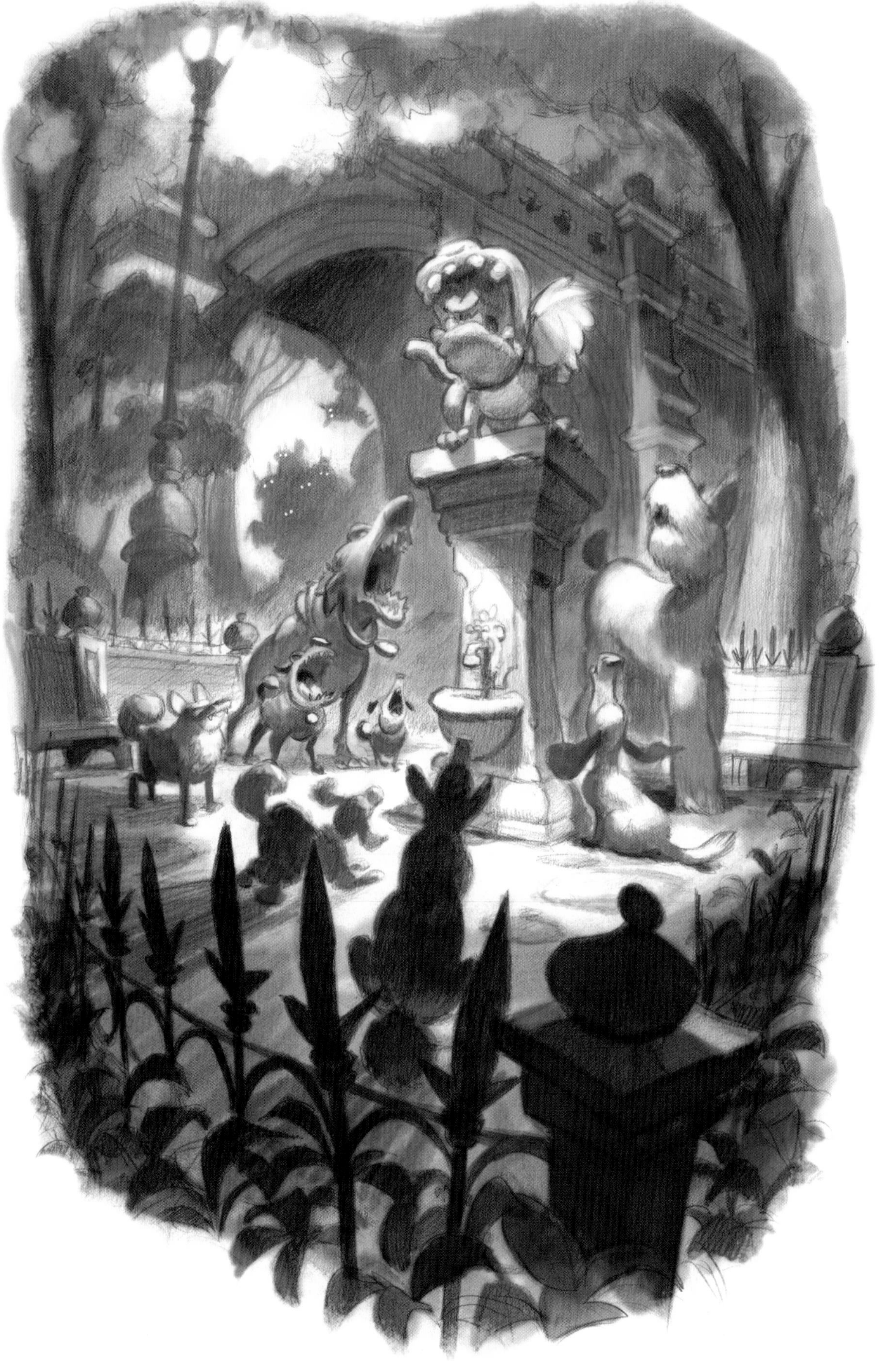

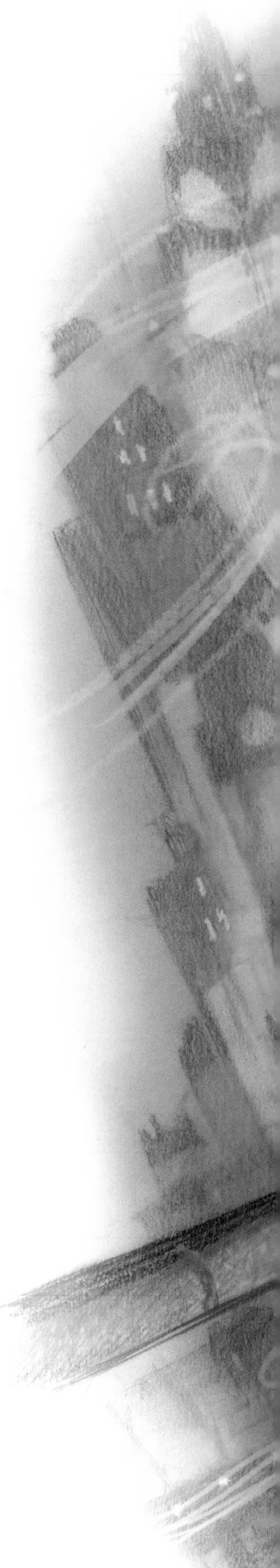

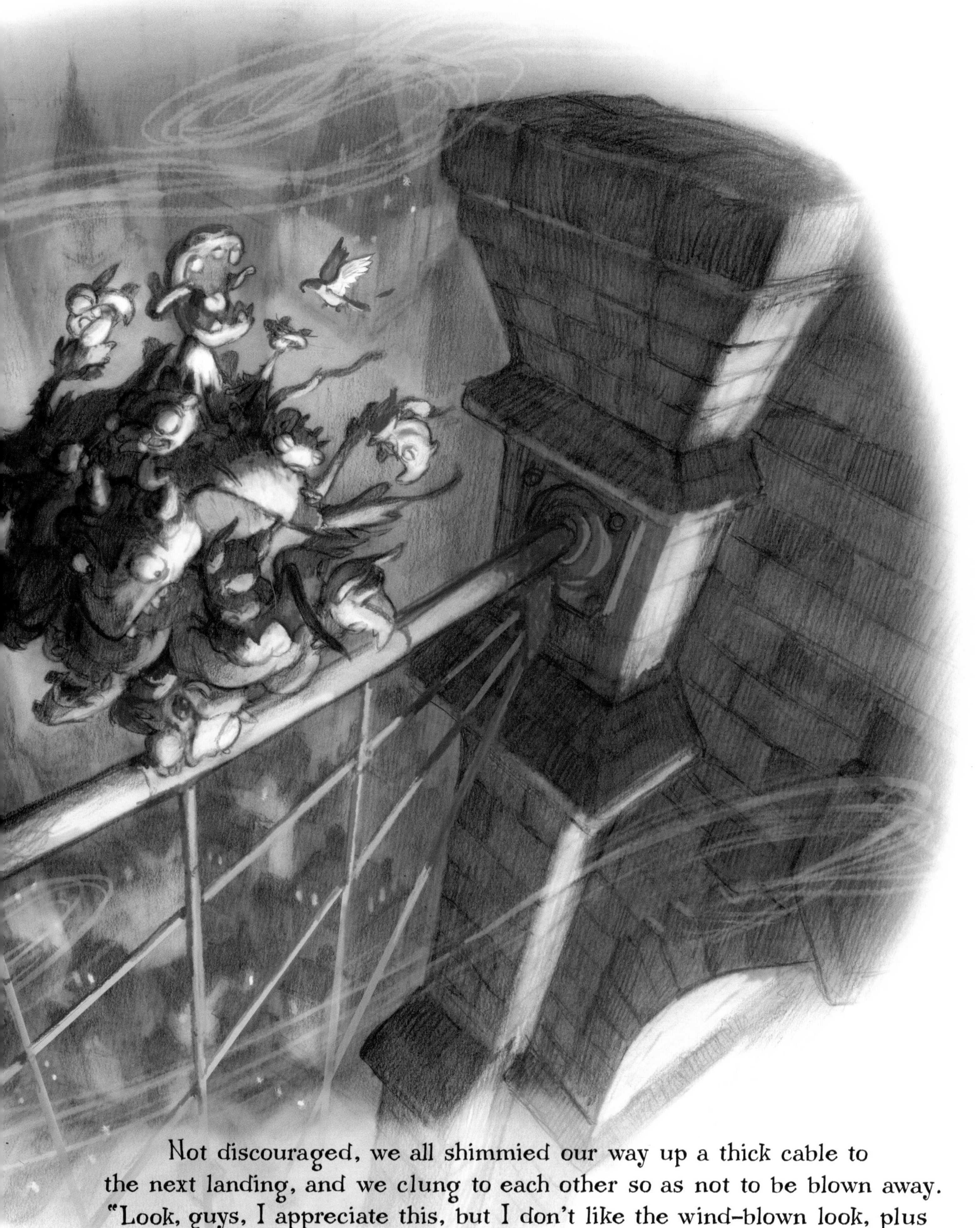

Not discouraged, we all shimmied our way up a thick cable to the next landing, and we clung to each other so as not to be blown away. "Look, guys, I appreciate this, but I don't like the wind-blown look, plus I can't swim!" Rufus screamed. "I'd sink like a rock!"

Well, that was obvious, I thought.

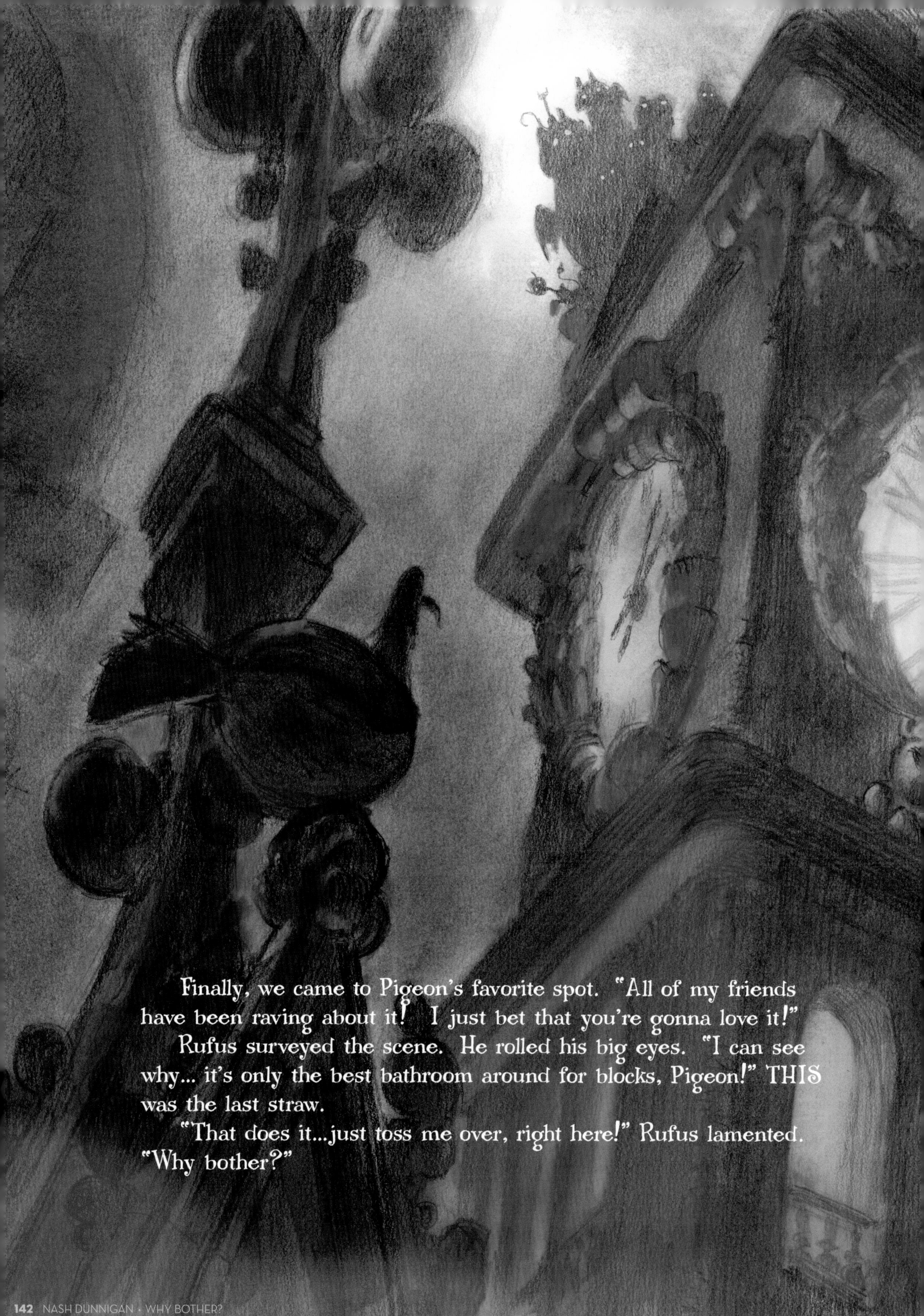

Finally, we came to Pigeon's favorite spot. "All of my friends have been raving about it! I just bet that you're gonna love it!"

Rufus surveyed the scene. He rolled his big eyes. "I can see why... it's only the best bathroom around for blocks, Pigeon!" THIS was the last straw.

"That does it...just toss me over, right here!" Rufus lamented. "Why bother?"

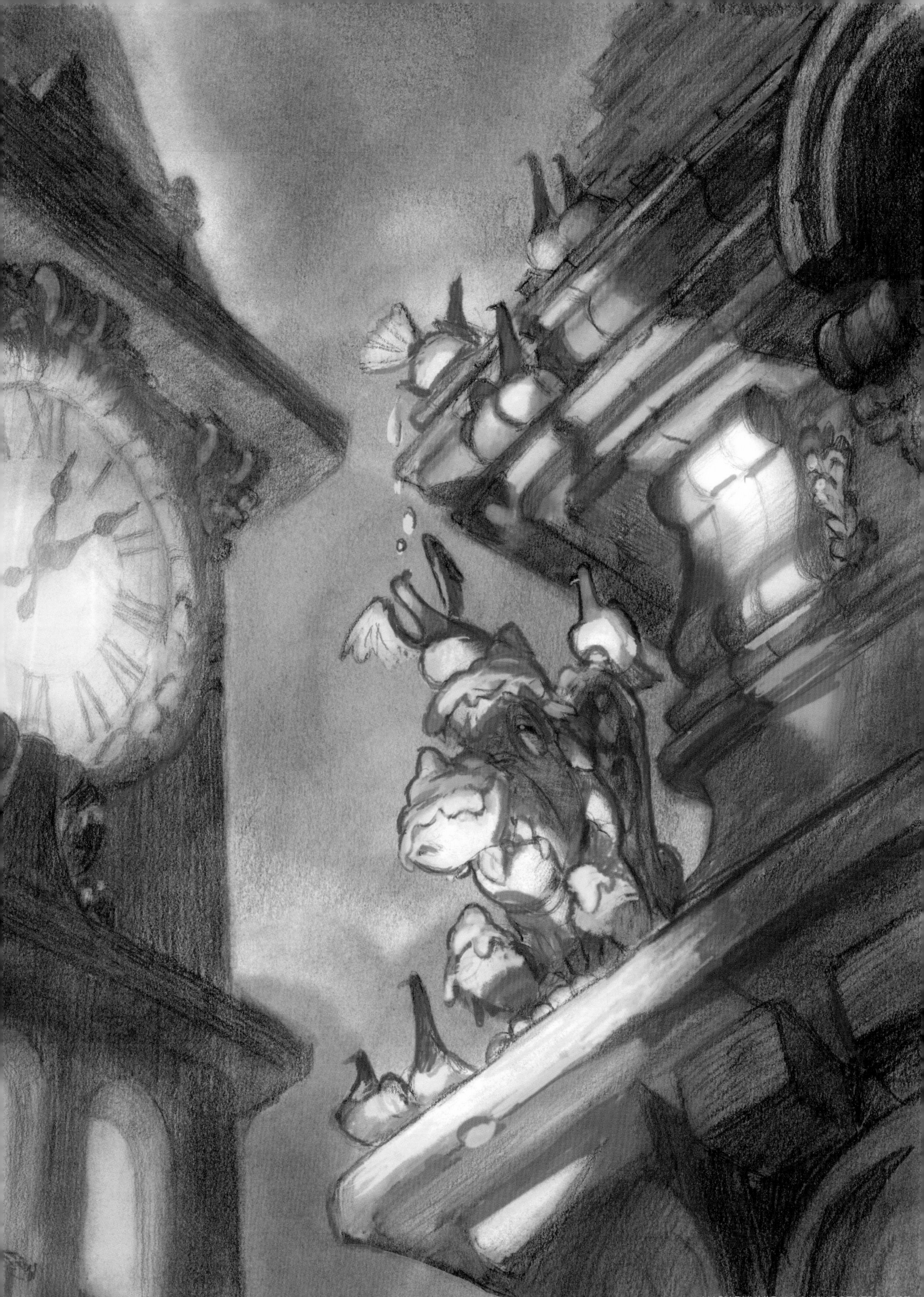

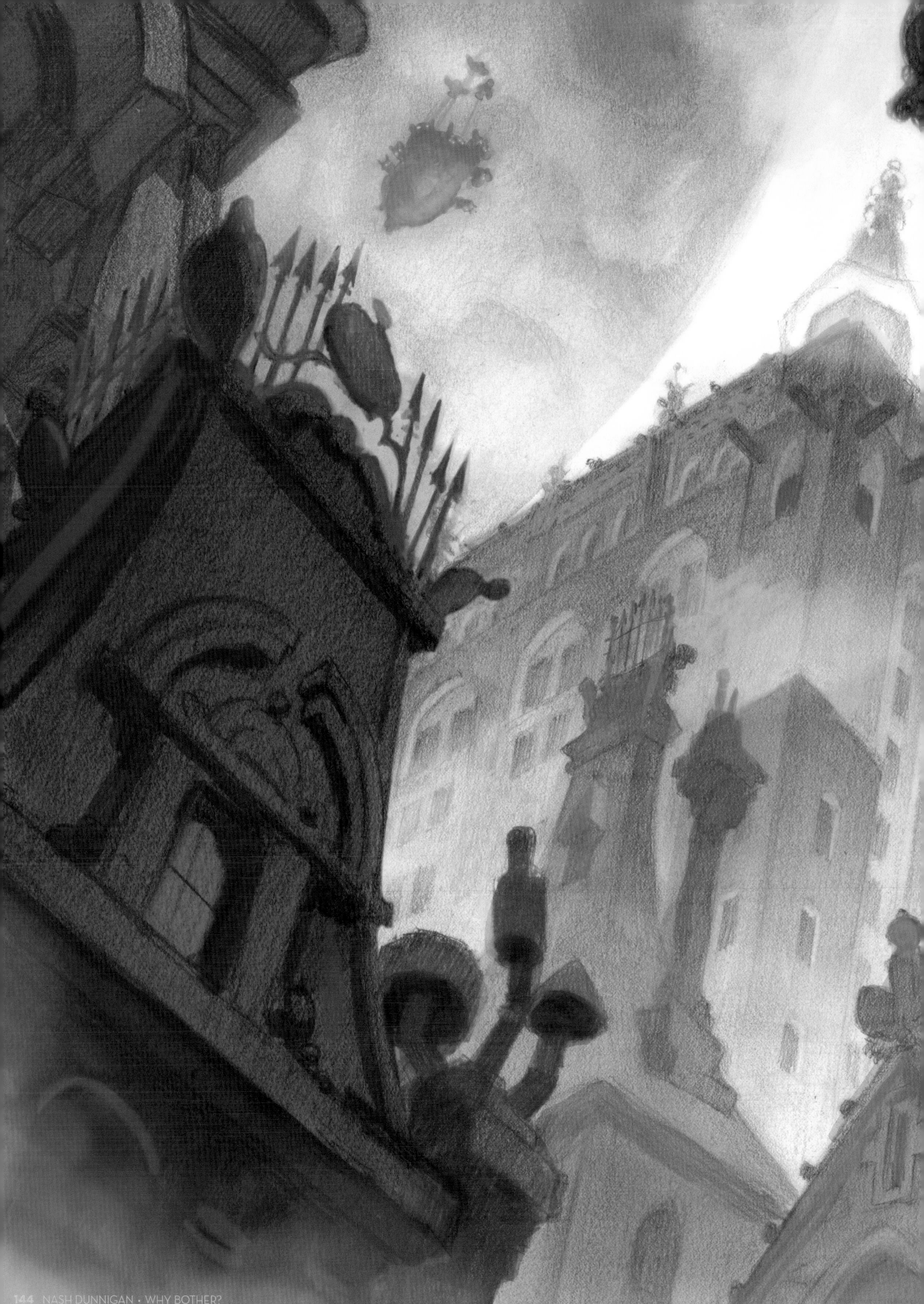

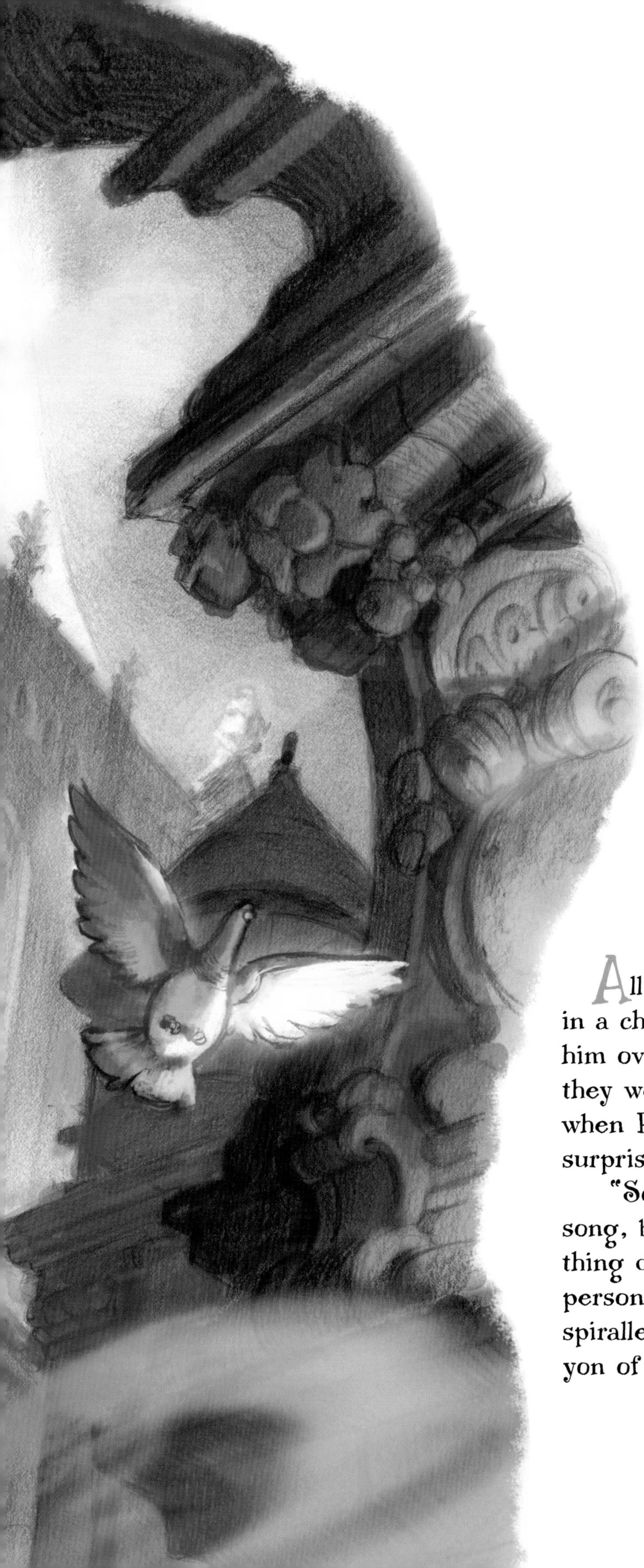

All the gargoyles began to sing in a chorus, "Oh, why bother, just toss him over..." and I really thought that they were getting ready to heave him, when Pigeon saw something quite surprising.

"Sorry to interrupt such a festive song, but I think that there is something down there Rufus should see personally!" And with that, Pigeon spiralled downward through the canyon of skyscrapers as if on a mission.

Somehow, Pigeon found us a home. It was a Halloween
store that stayed open 365 days a year! Rufus planted himself
right above the door that night, and the rest is history. I was adopted
by the owner, a most delightful lady with a most interesting hat.
Even Pigeon got into the act. But confidentially, I think Rufus is the
happiest of us all. He finds no greater delight than scaring the
daylights out of everyone who walks through those doors...

The End

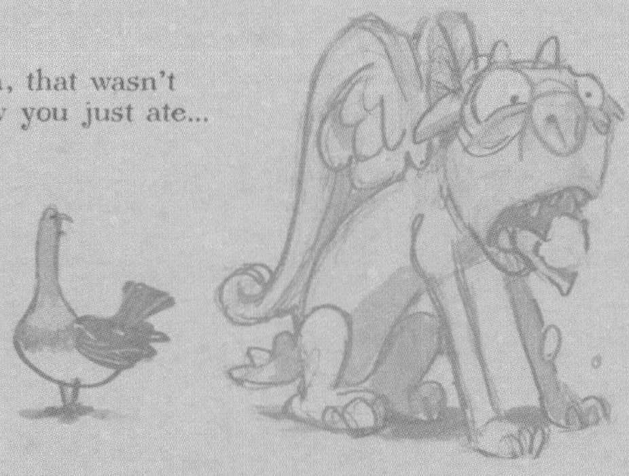
Um, that wasn't
snow you just ate...

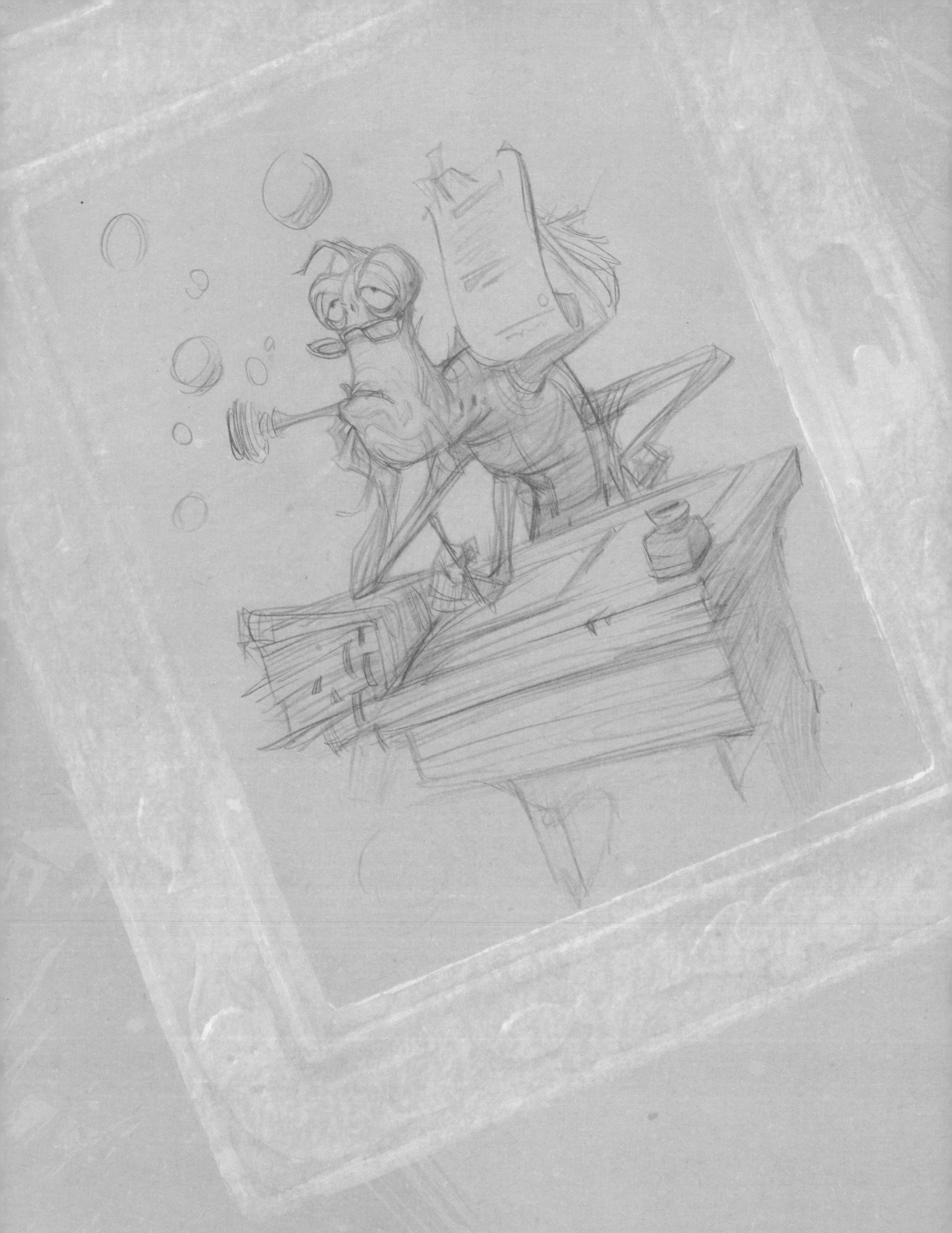

SANG JUN LEE

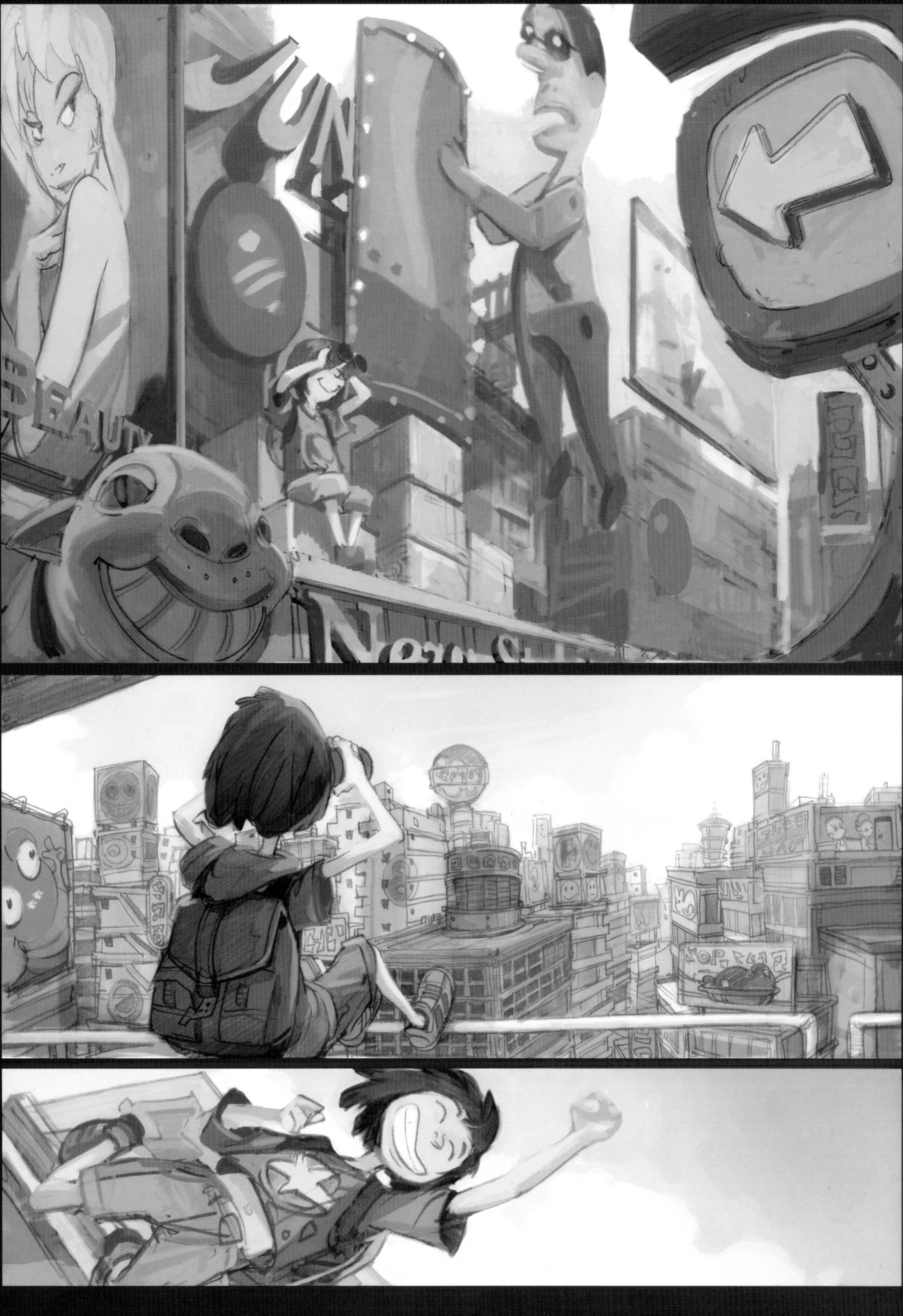
BEAUTY

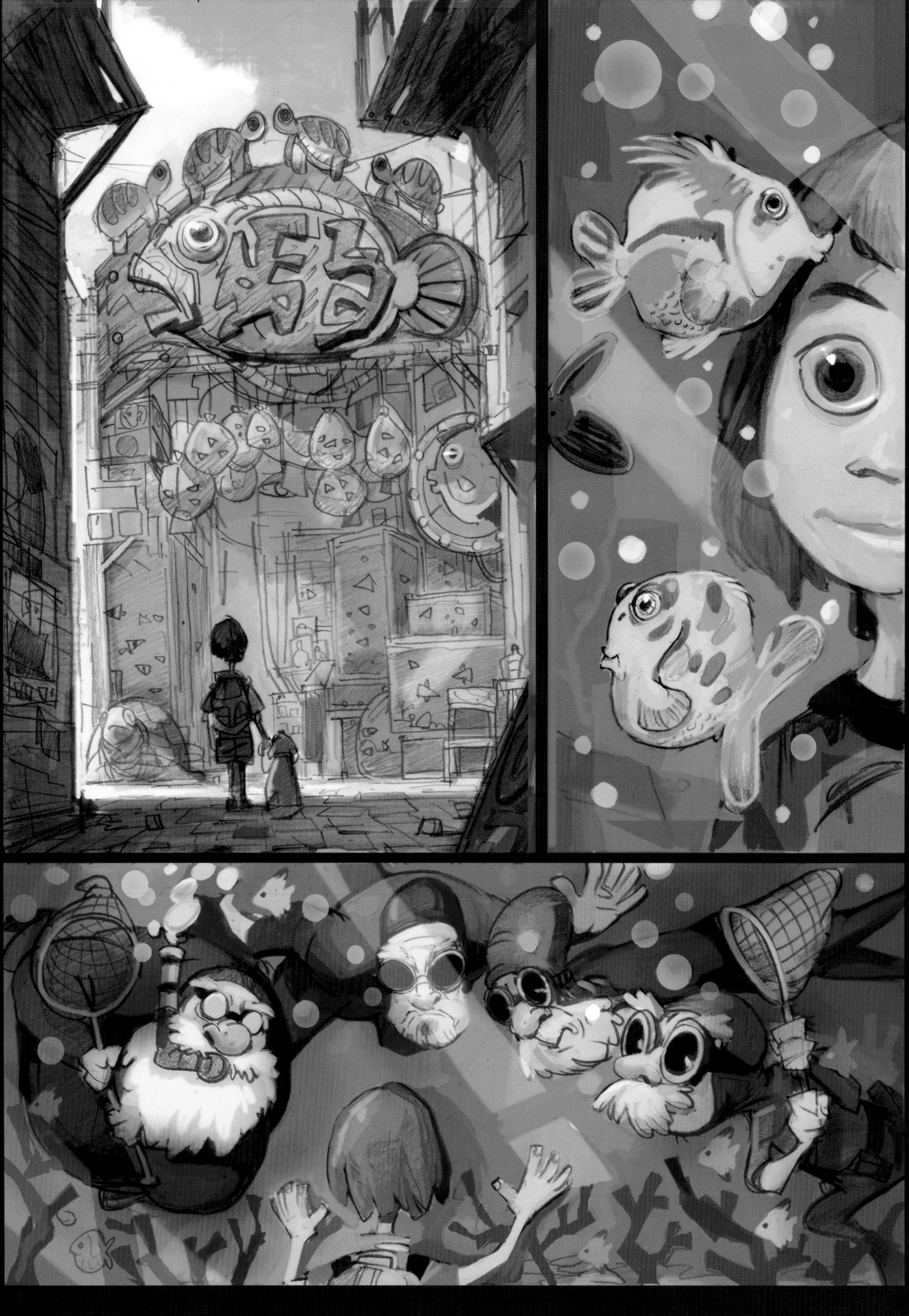

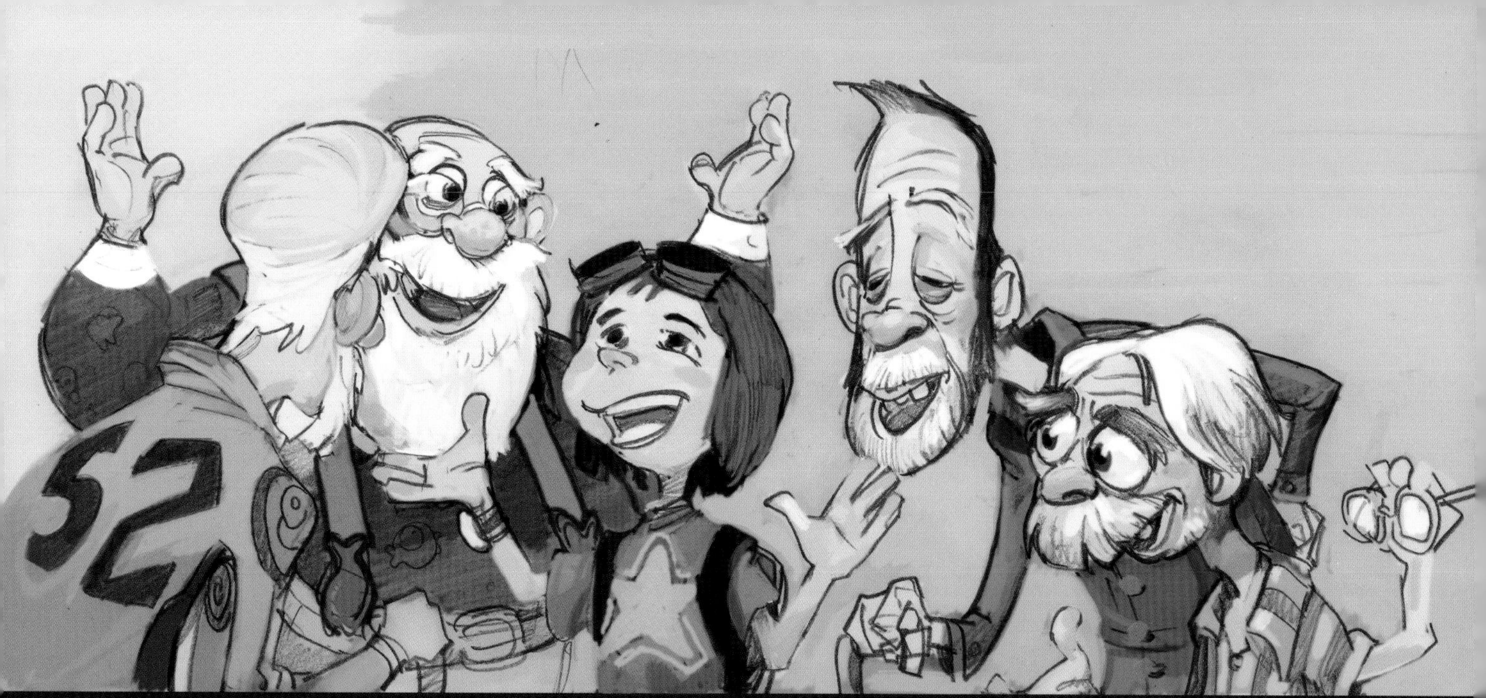
52

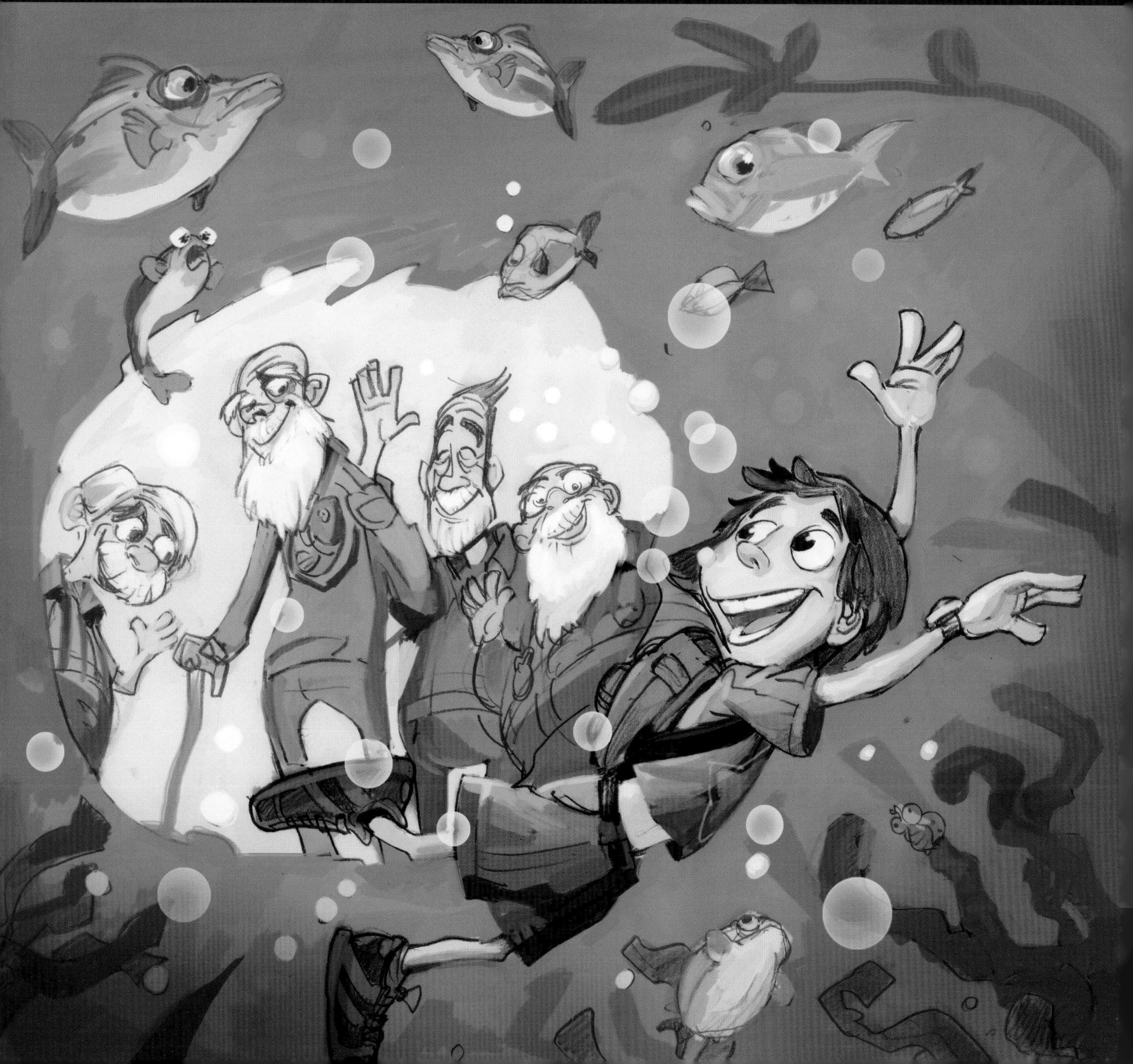

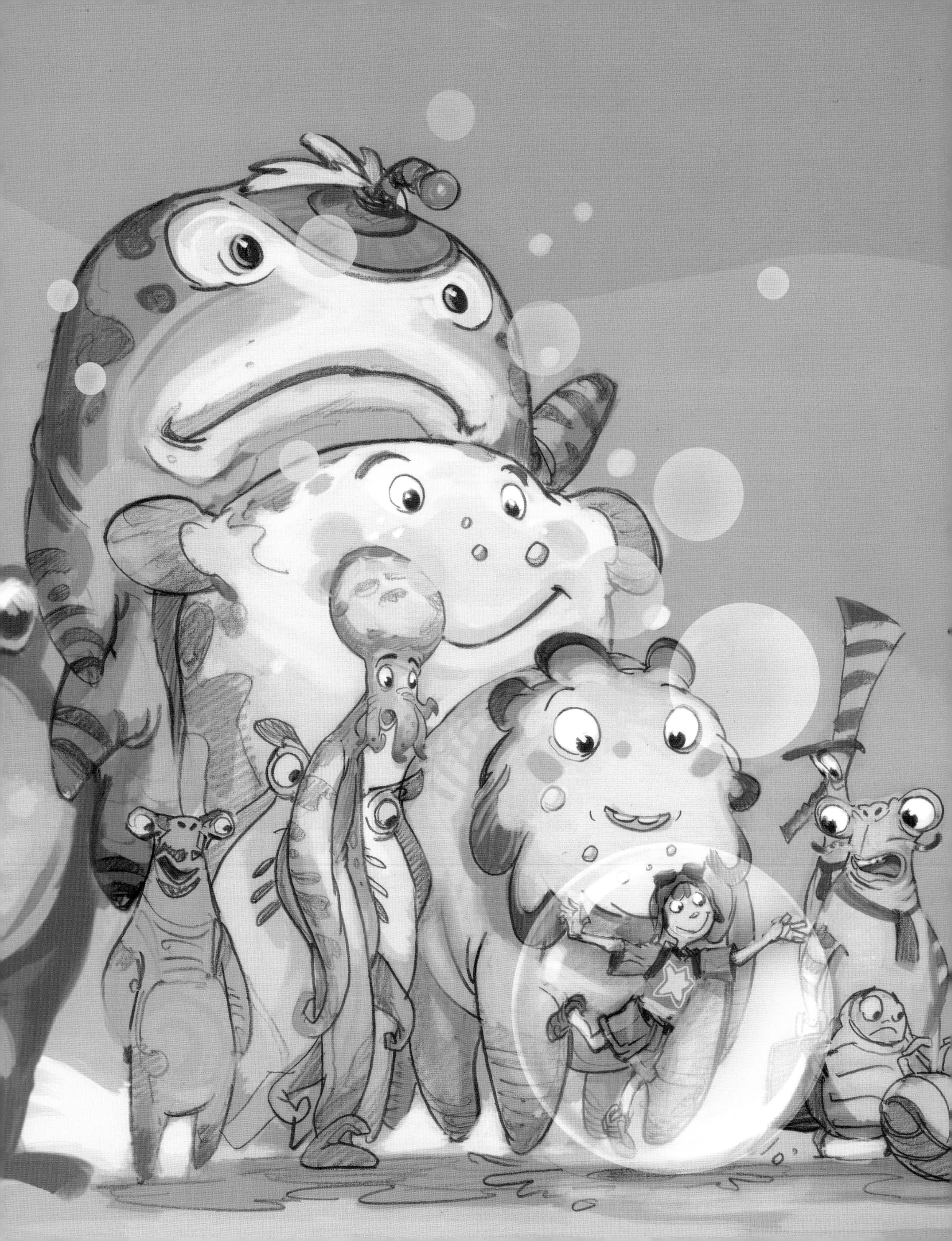

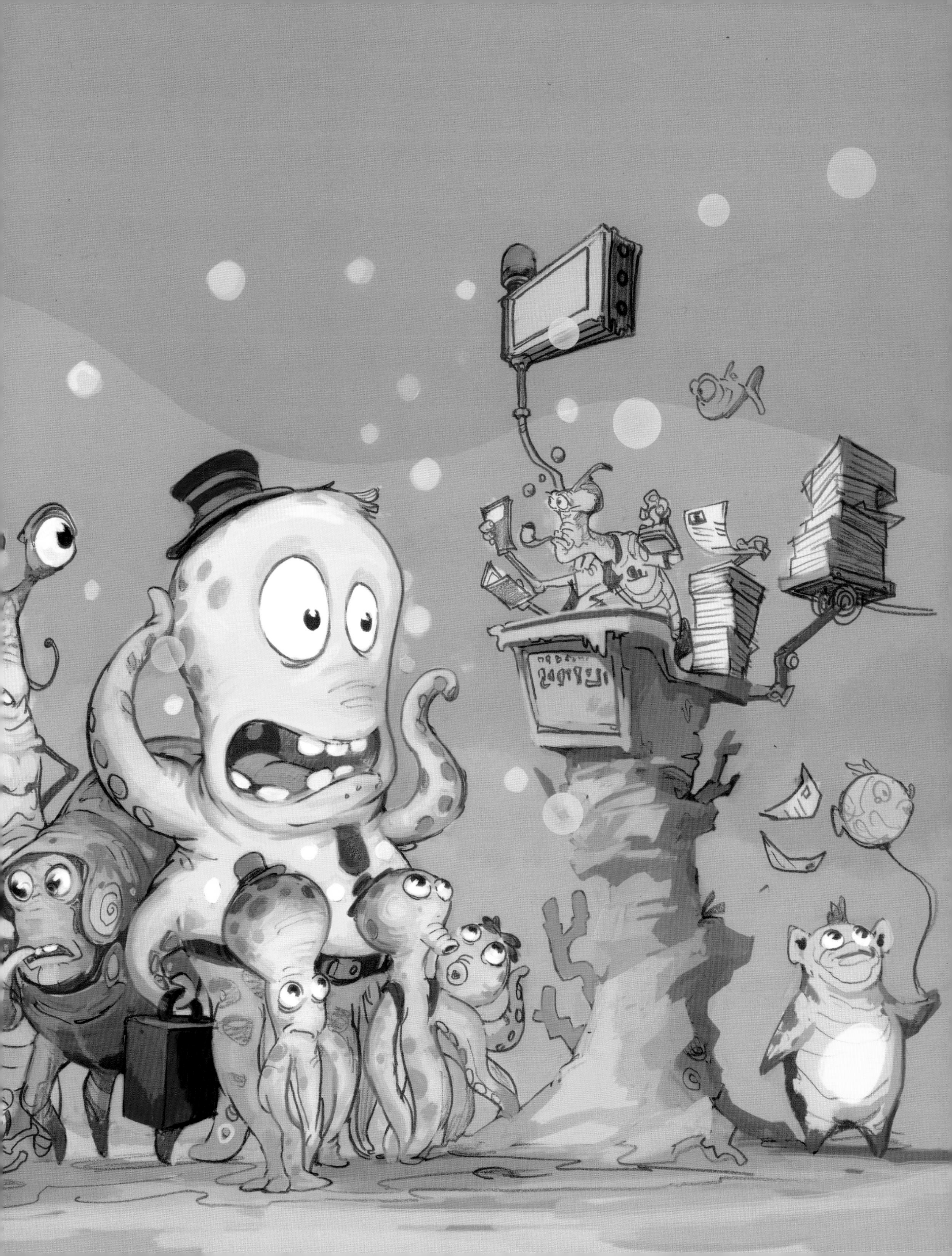

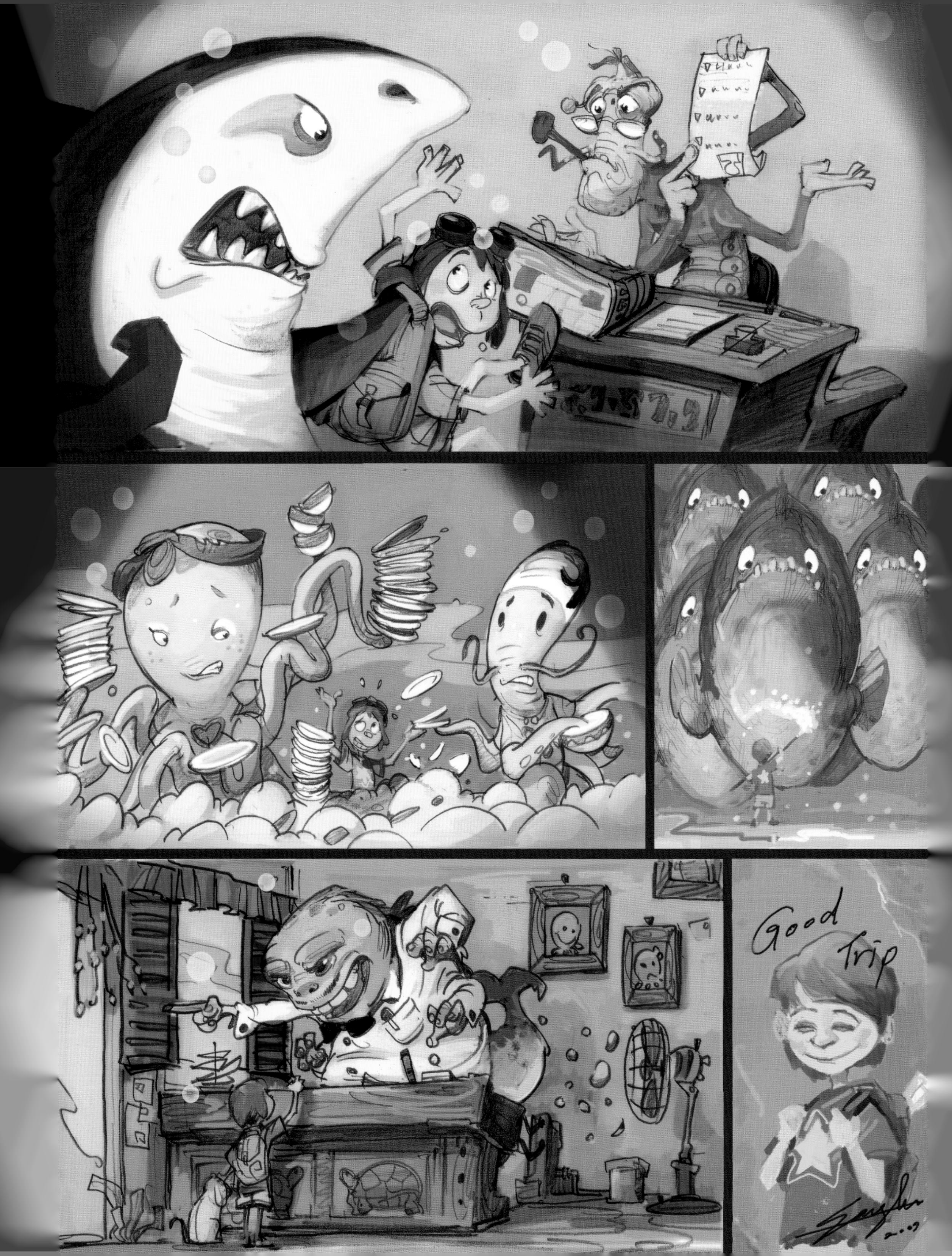
Good
Trip

MICHAEL KNAPP

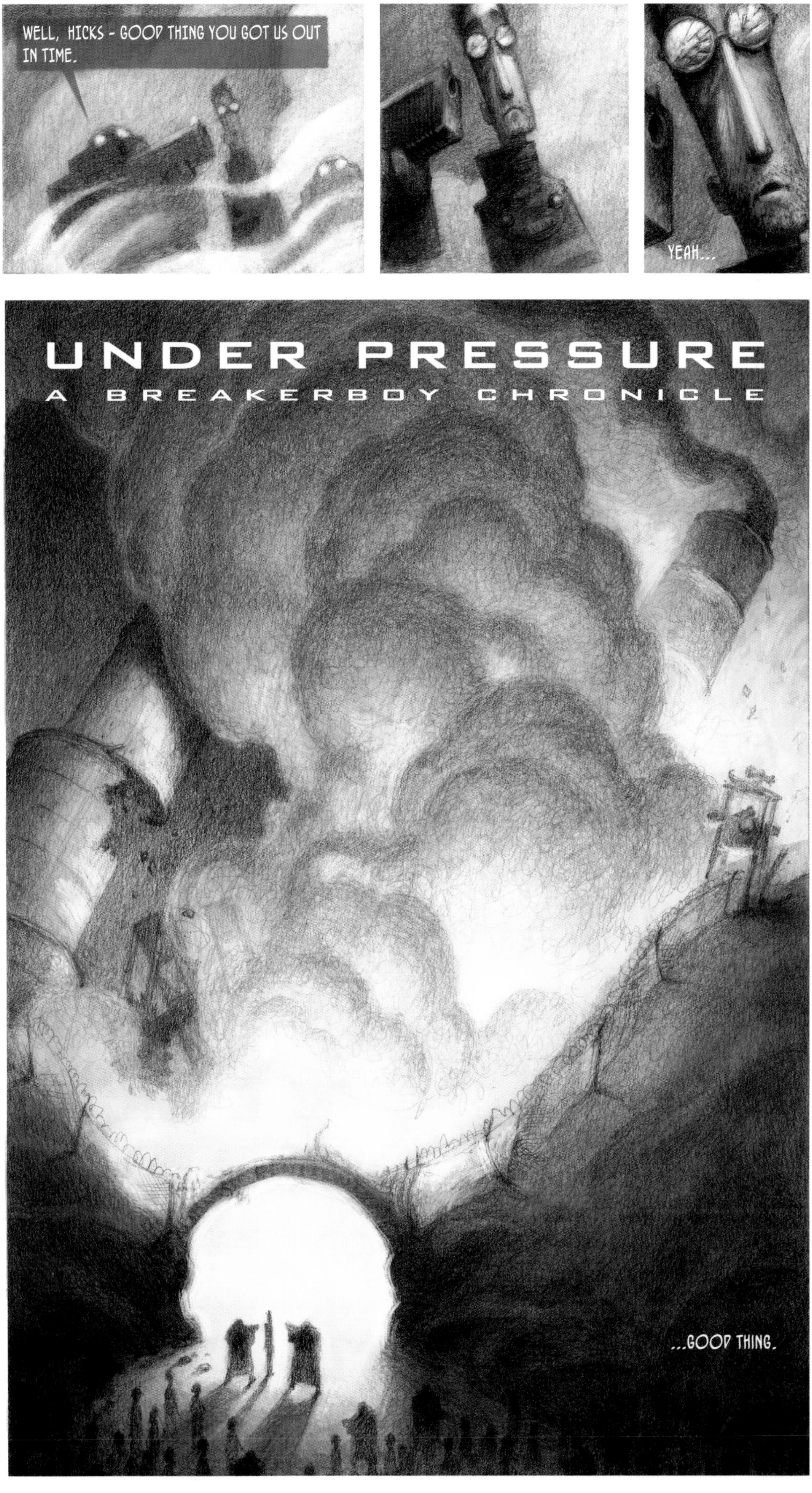
WELL, HICKS - GOOD THING YOU GOT US OUT IN TIME.
YEAH...
UNDER PRESSURE
A BREAKERBOY CHRONICLE
...GOOD THING.

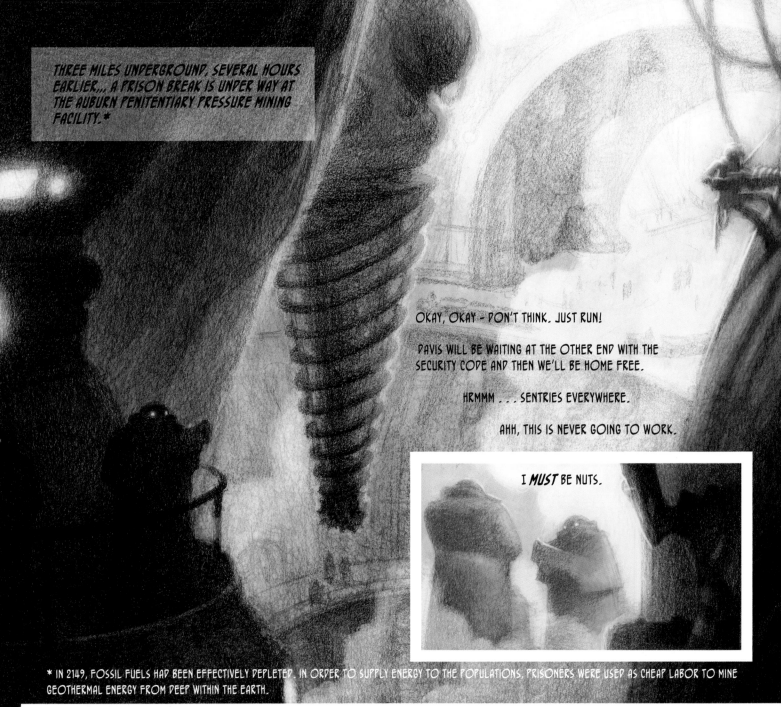

THREE MILES UNDERGROUND, SEVERAL HOURS EARLIER... A PRISON BREAK IS UNDER WAY AT THE AUBURN PENITENTIARY PRESSURE MINING FACILITY. *

OKAY, OKAY - DON'T THINK. JUST RUN!

DAVIS WILL BE WAITING AT THE OTHER END WITH THE SECURITY CODE AND THEN WE'LL BE HOME FREE.

HRMMM . . . . SENTRIES EVERYWHERE.

AHH, THIS IS NEVER GOING TO WORK.

I *MUST* BE NUTS.

* IN 2149, FOSSIL FUELS HAD BEEN EFFECTIVELY DEPLETED. IN ORDER TO SUPPLY ENERGY TO THE POPULATIONS, PRISONERS WERE USED AS CHEAP LABOR TO MINE GEOTHERMAL ENERGY FROM DEEP WITHIN THE EARTH.

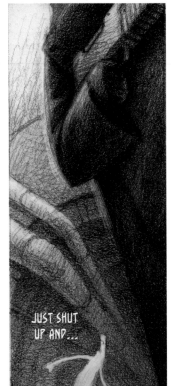

JUST SHUT UP AND...

GO!!!

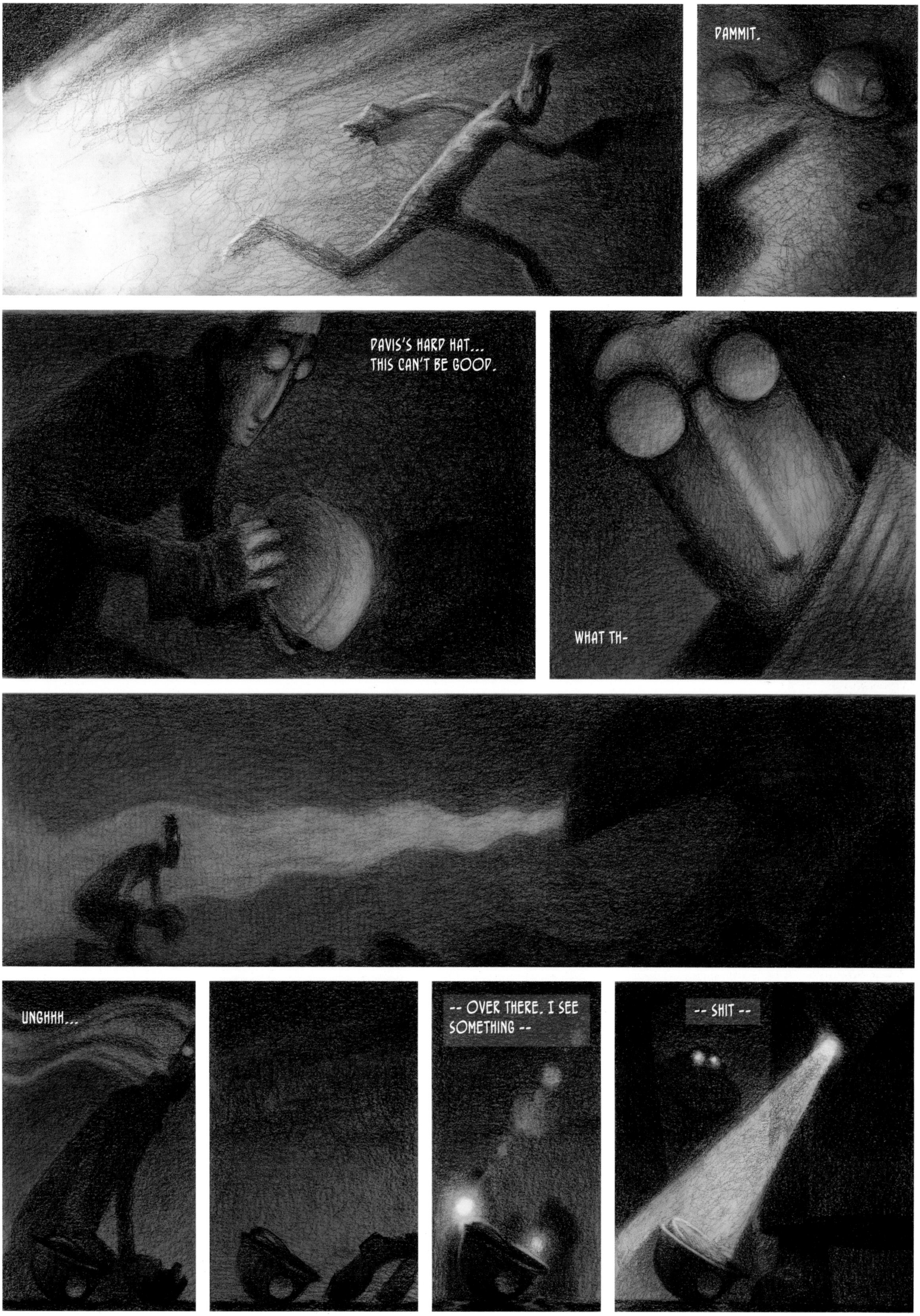
DAMMIT.
DAVIS'S HARD HAT... THIS CAN'T BE GOOD.
WHAT TH-
UNGHHH...
-- OVER THERE. I SEE SOMETHING --
-- SHIT --

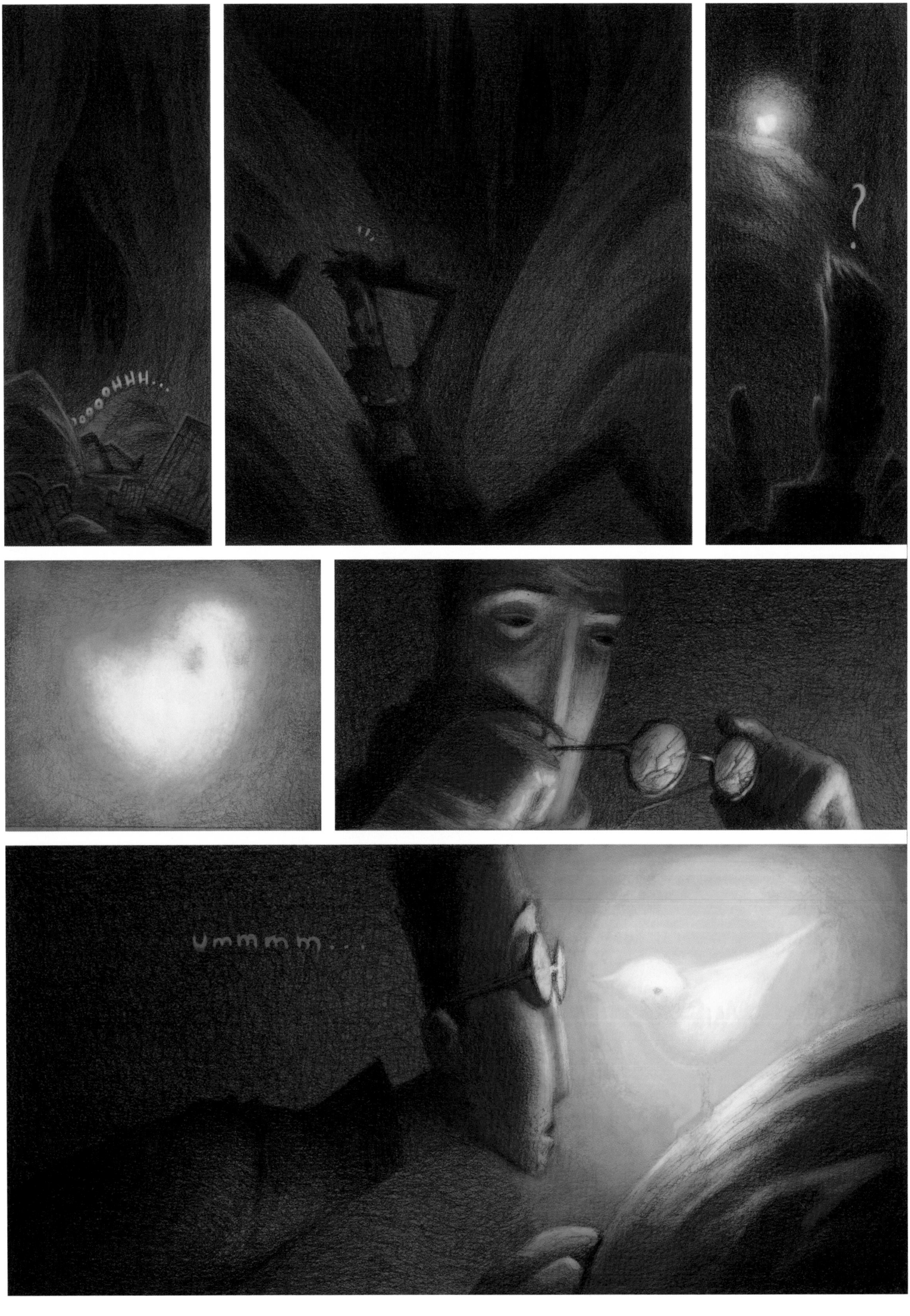
ooooOOHHH...
?
Ummmm...

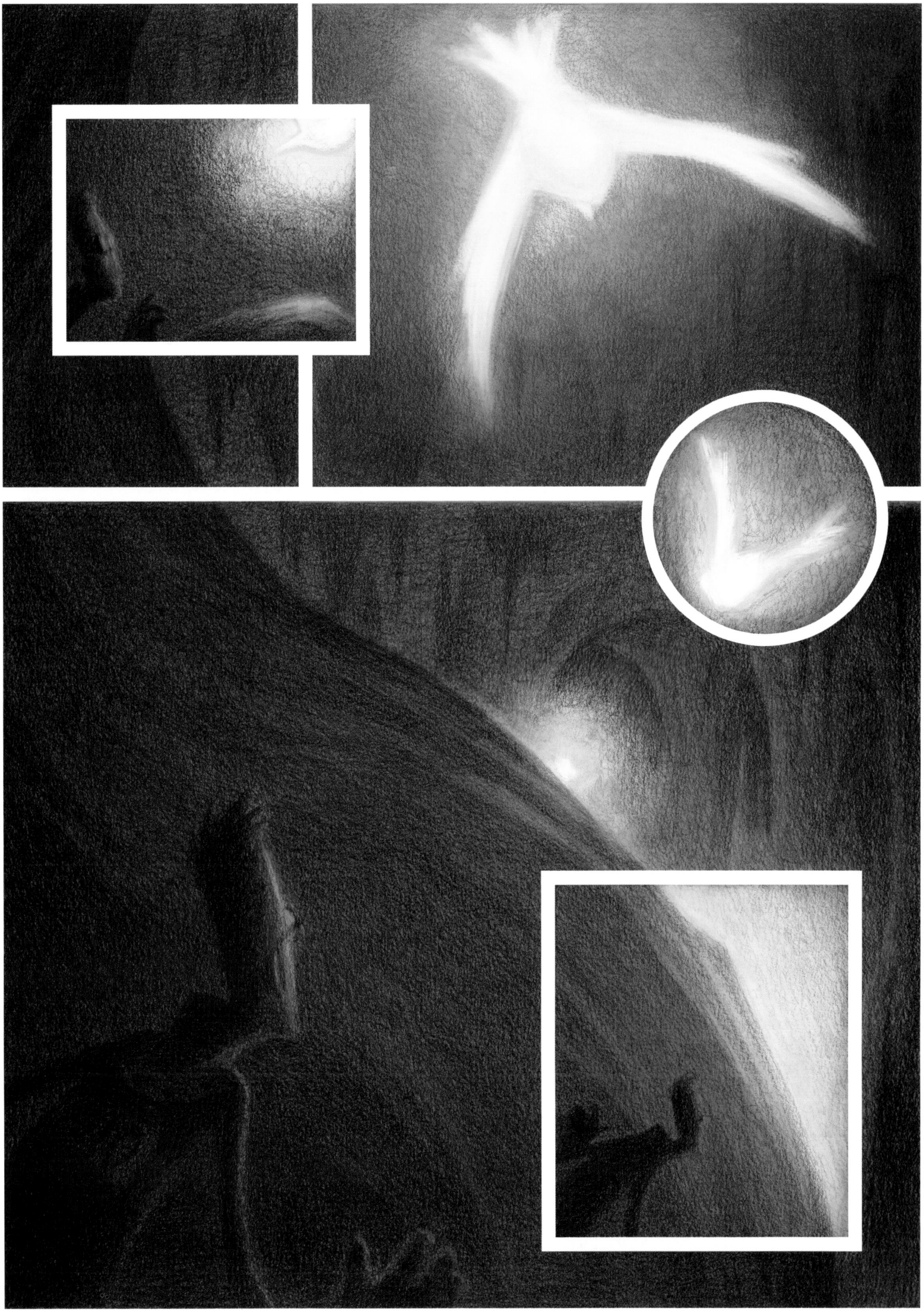

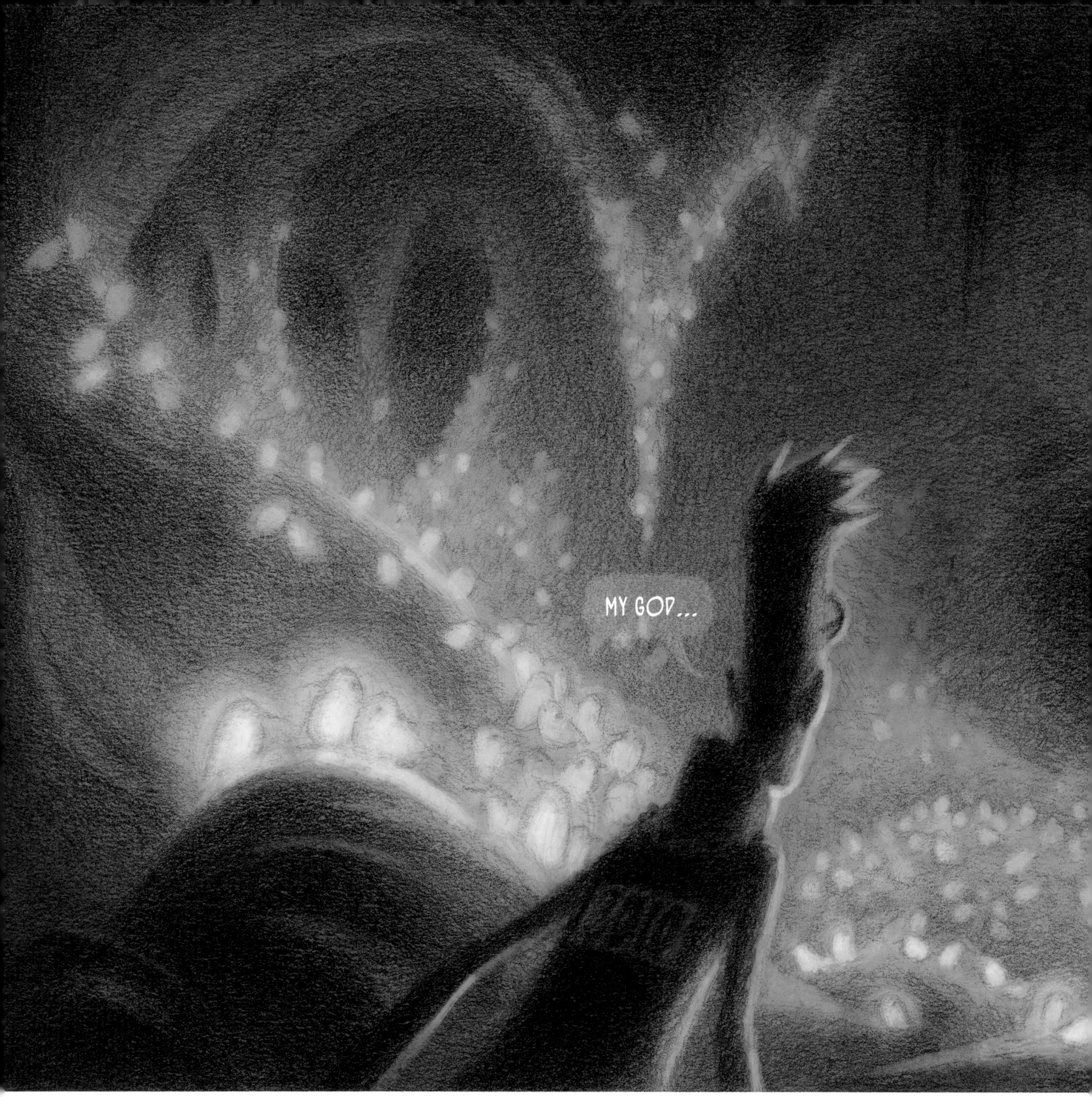
MY GOD...

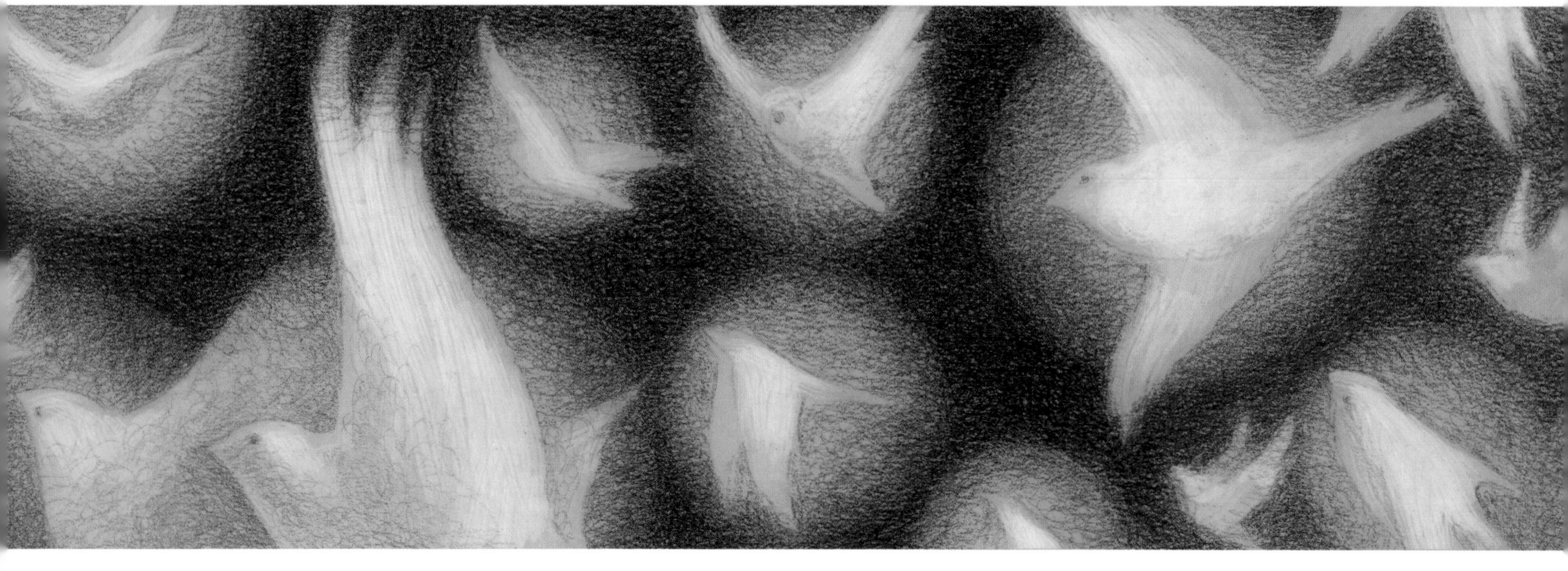

DAVIS?

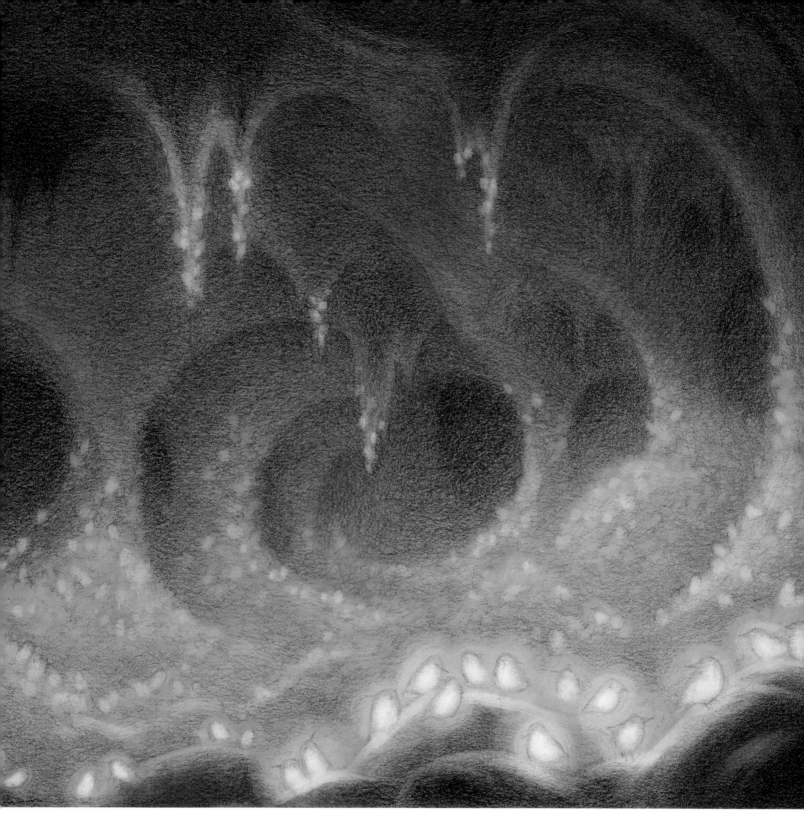

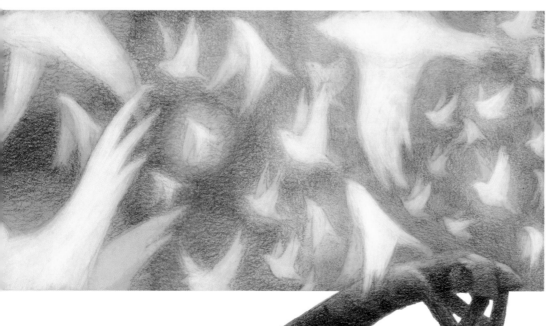

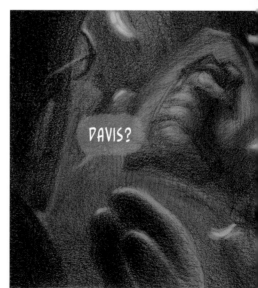

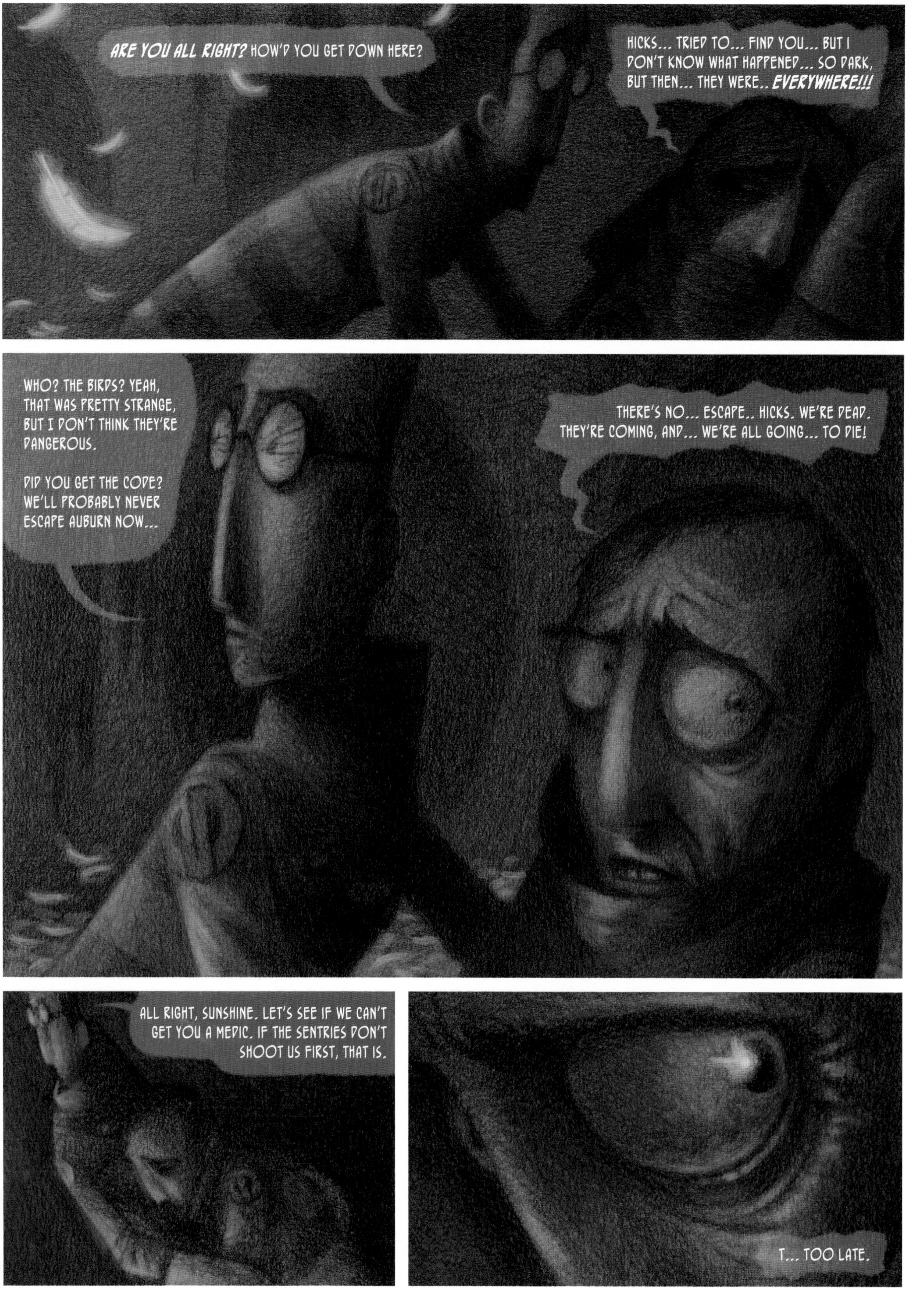

ARE YOU ALL RIGHT? HOW'D YOU GET DOWN HERE?
HICKS... TRIED TO... FIND YOU... BUT I DON'T KNOW WHAT HAPPENED... SO DARK, BUT THEN... THEY WERE.. EVERYWHERE!!!
WHO? THE BIRDS? YEAH, THAT WAS PRETTY STRANGE, BUT I DON'T THINK THEY'RE DANGEROUS.
DID YOU GET THE CODE? WE'LL PROBABLY NEVER ESCAPE AUBURN NOW...
THERE'S NO... ESCAPE.. HICKS. WE'RE DEAD. THEY'RE COMING, AND... WE'RE ALL GOING... TO DIE!
ALL RIGHT, SUNSHINE. LET'S SEE IF WE CAN'T GET YOU A MEDIC. IF THE SENTRIES DON'T SHOOT US FIRST, THAT IS.
T... TOO LATE.

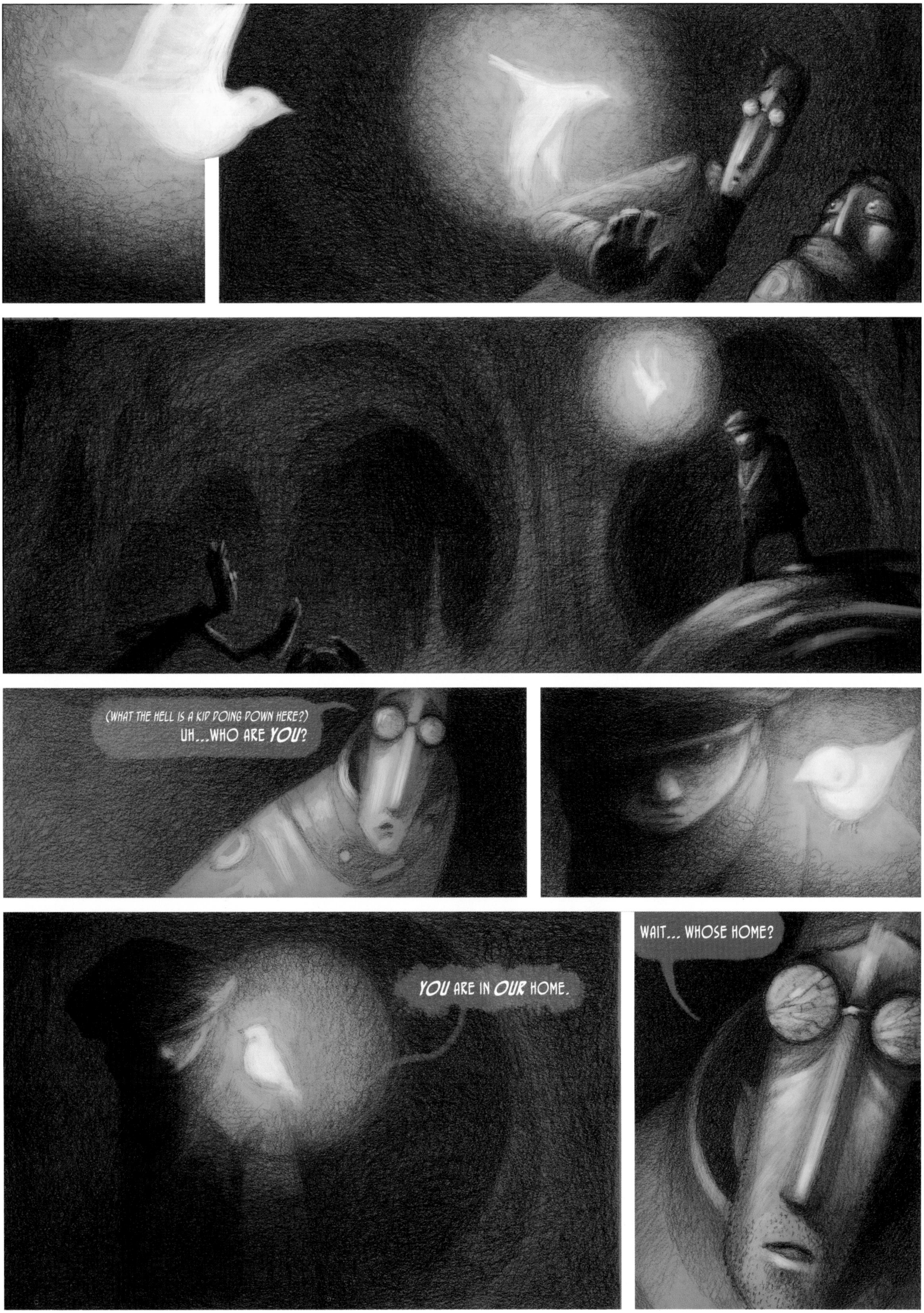
(WHAT THE HELL IS A KID DOING DOWN HERE?)
UH...WHO ARE YOU?
YOU ARE IN OUR HOME.
WAIT... WHOSE HOME?

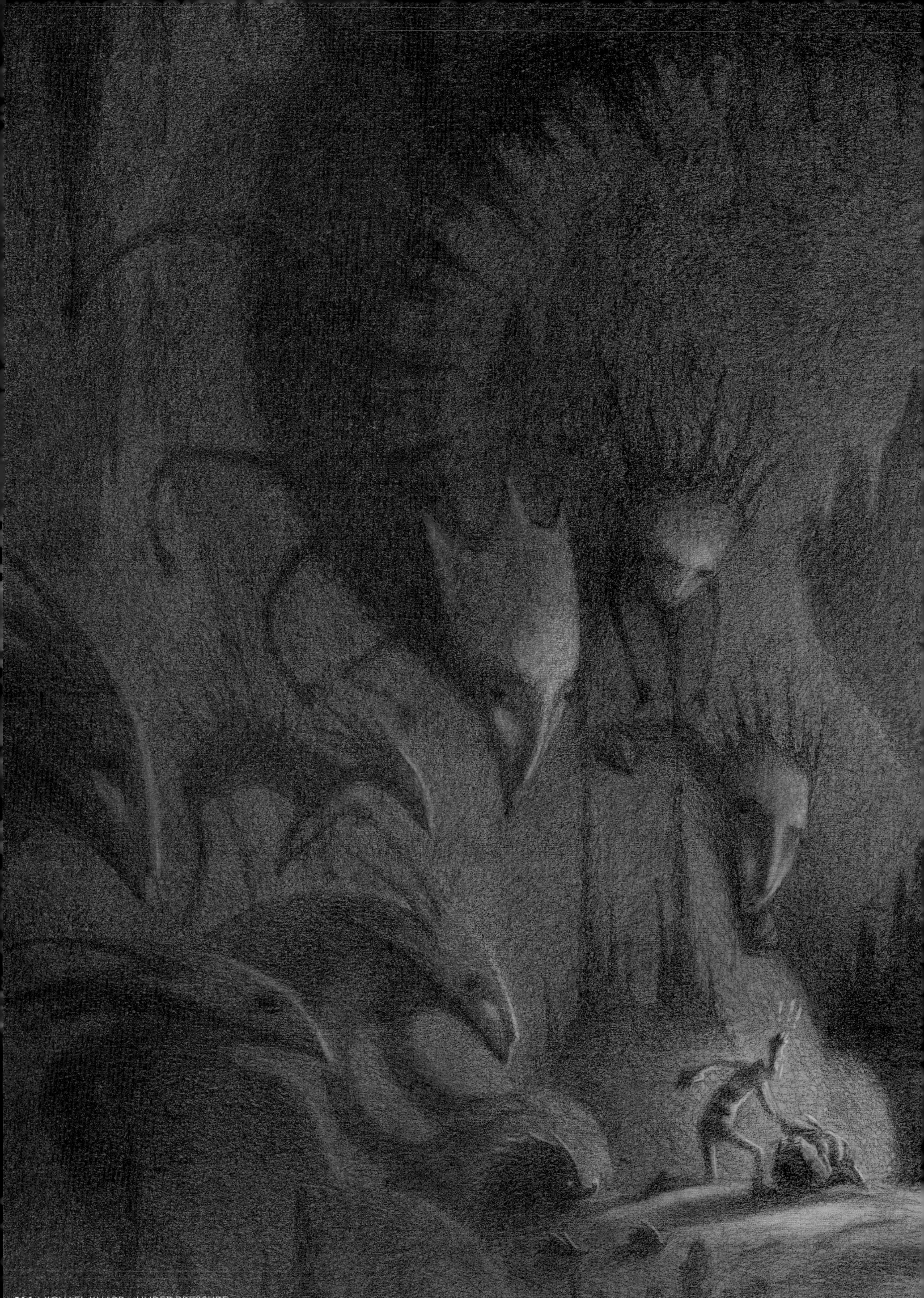

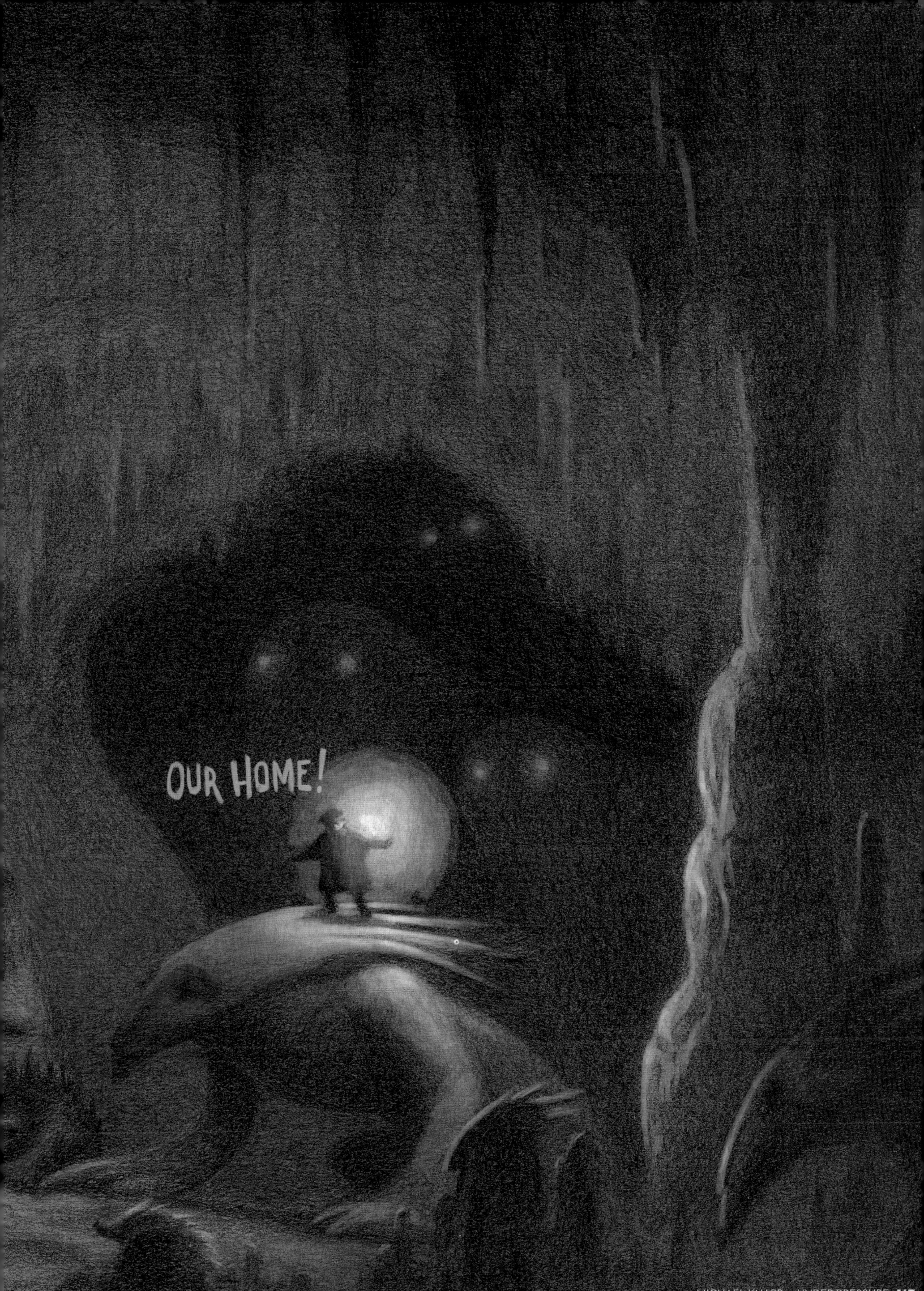
OUR HOME!

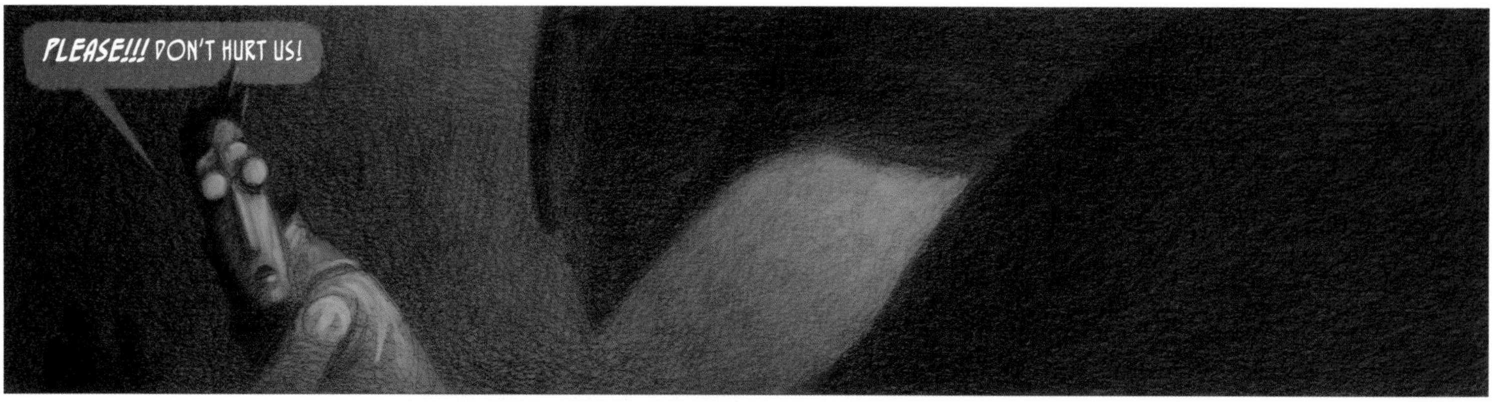
PLEASE!!! DON'T HURT US!

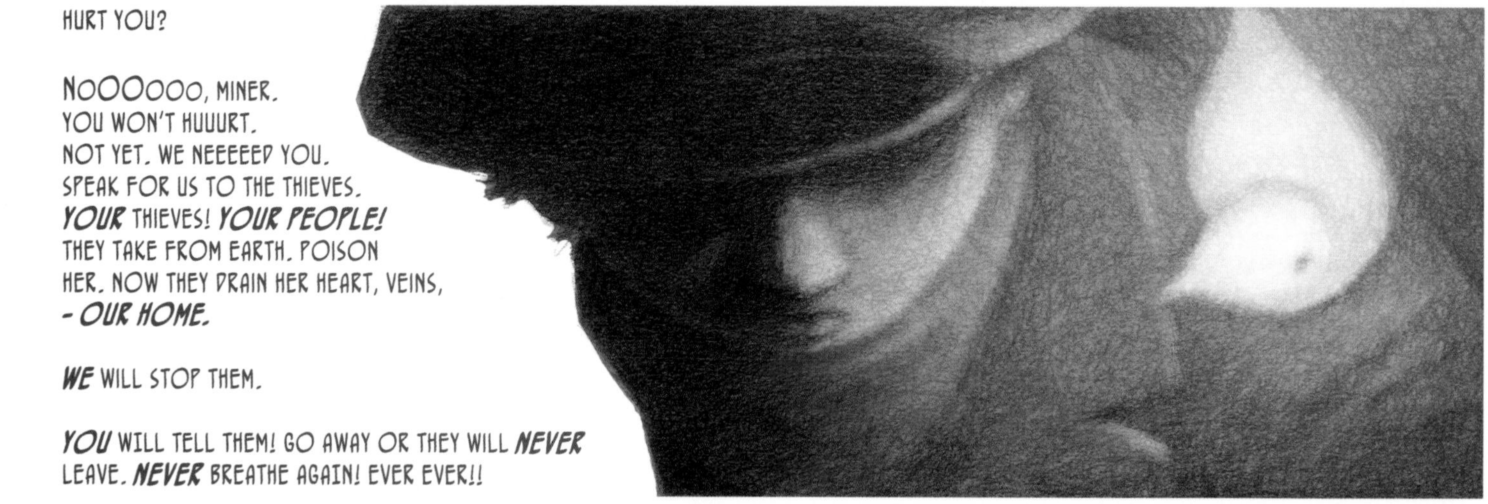
HURT YOU?
NOOOooo, MINER.
YOU WON'T HUUURT.
NOT YET. WE NEEEEED YOU.
SPEAK FOR US TO THE THIEVES.
YOUR THIEVES! YOUR PEOPLE!
THEY TAKE FROM EARTH. POISON
HER. NOW THEY DRAIN HER HEART, VEINS,
- OUR HOME.
WE WILL STOP THEM.
YOU WILL TELL THEM! GO AWAY OR THEY WILL NEVER
LEAVE. NEVER BREATHE AGAIN! EVER EVER!!

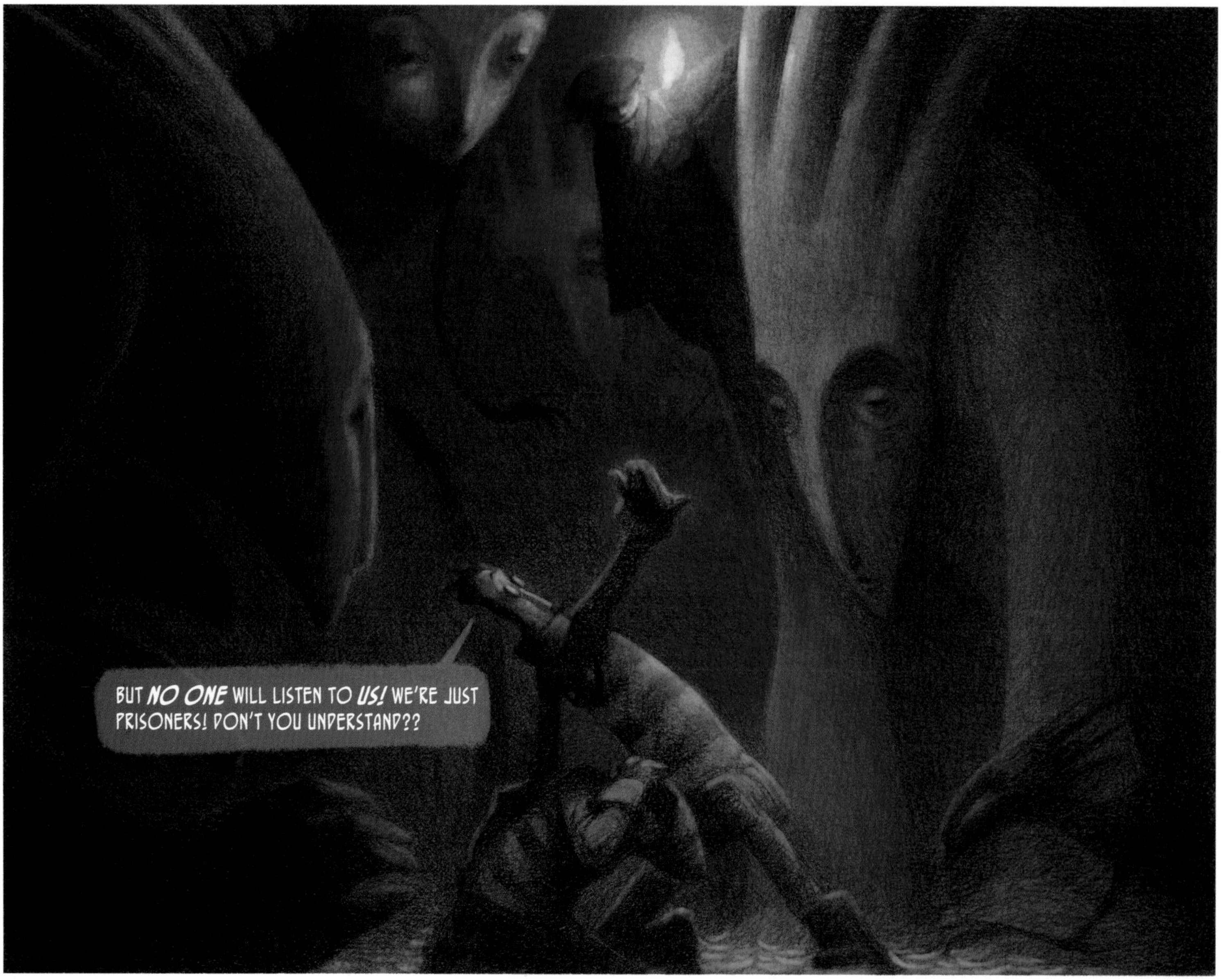
BUT NO ONE WILL LISTEN TO US! WE'RE JUST
PRISONERS! DON'T YOU UNDERSTAND??

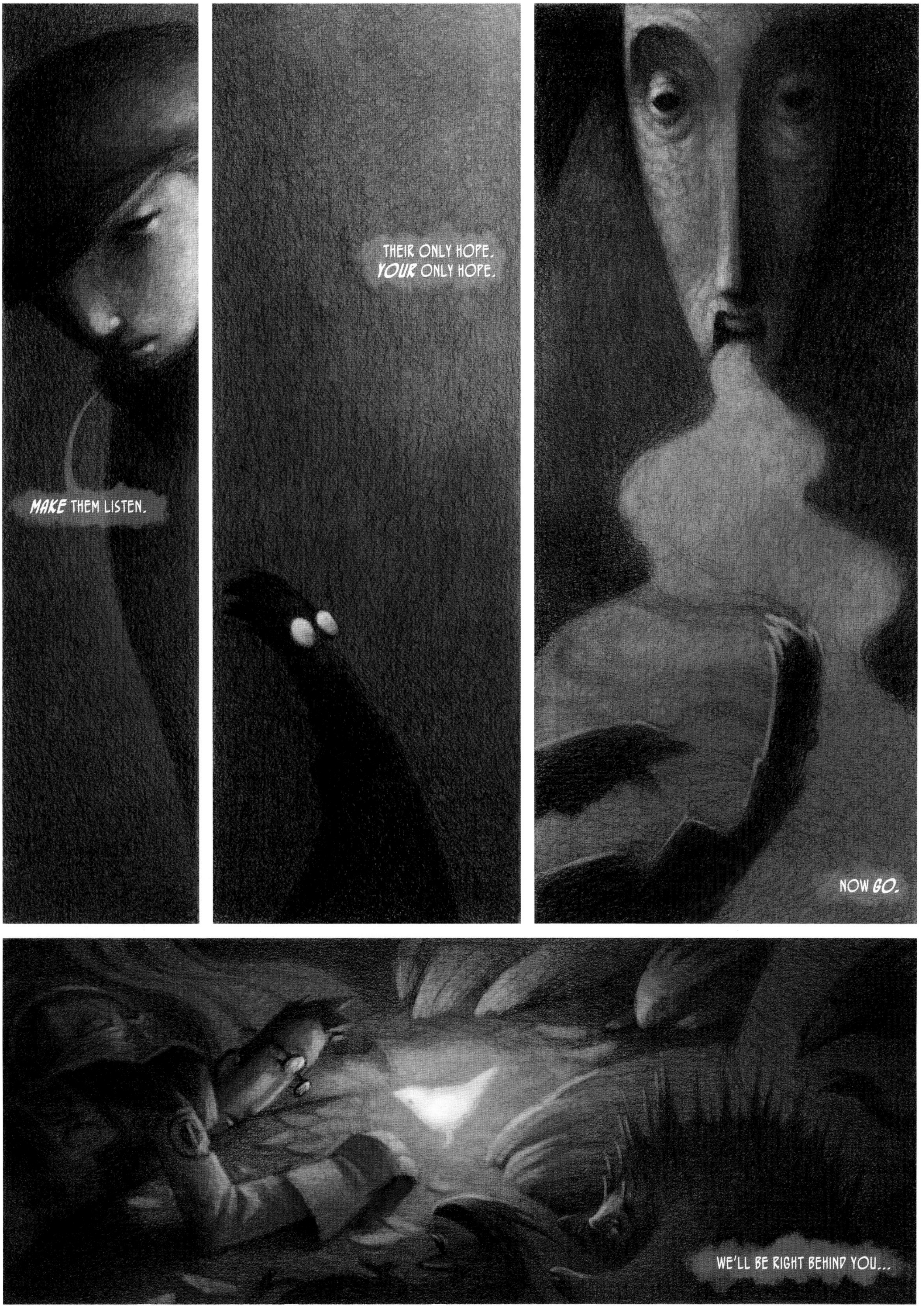
MAKE THEM LISTEN.
THEIR ONLY HOPE.
YOUR ONLY HOPE.
NOW GO.
WE'LL BE RIGHT BEHIND YOU...

GASP!

OH, GREAT. WE'RE BACK.

WELL, DAVIS WON'T BE RUNNING ANYMORE. CRAZY BASTARD - I *TOLD* HIM TO CALM THE HELL DOWN.

WHAT WAS ALL THAT TALK ABOUT MONSTERS?

GOOD MORNING, HICKS! FEEL LIKE RUNNING, TOO?

DIDN'T GET TOO FAR, *DID YOU?* WELL, GO AHEAD, *RUN!* SEE IF YOU CAN GET FARTHER THAN YOUR PAL HERE.

DAVIS?!?

IDIOTS!!! HE WAS RIGHT! WE HAVE TO GET OUT *NOW!*

THEY'RE COMING!!!

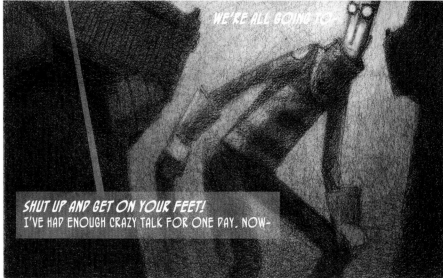

WE'RE ALL GOING TO—

SHUT UP AND GET ON YOUR FEET! I'VE HAD ENOUGH CRAZY TALK FOR ONE DAY. NOW—

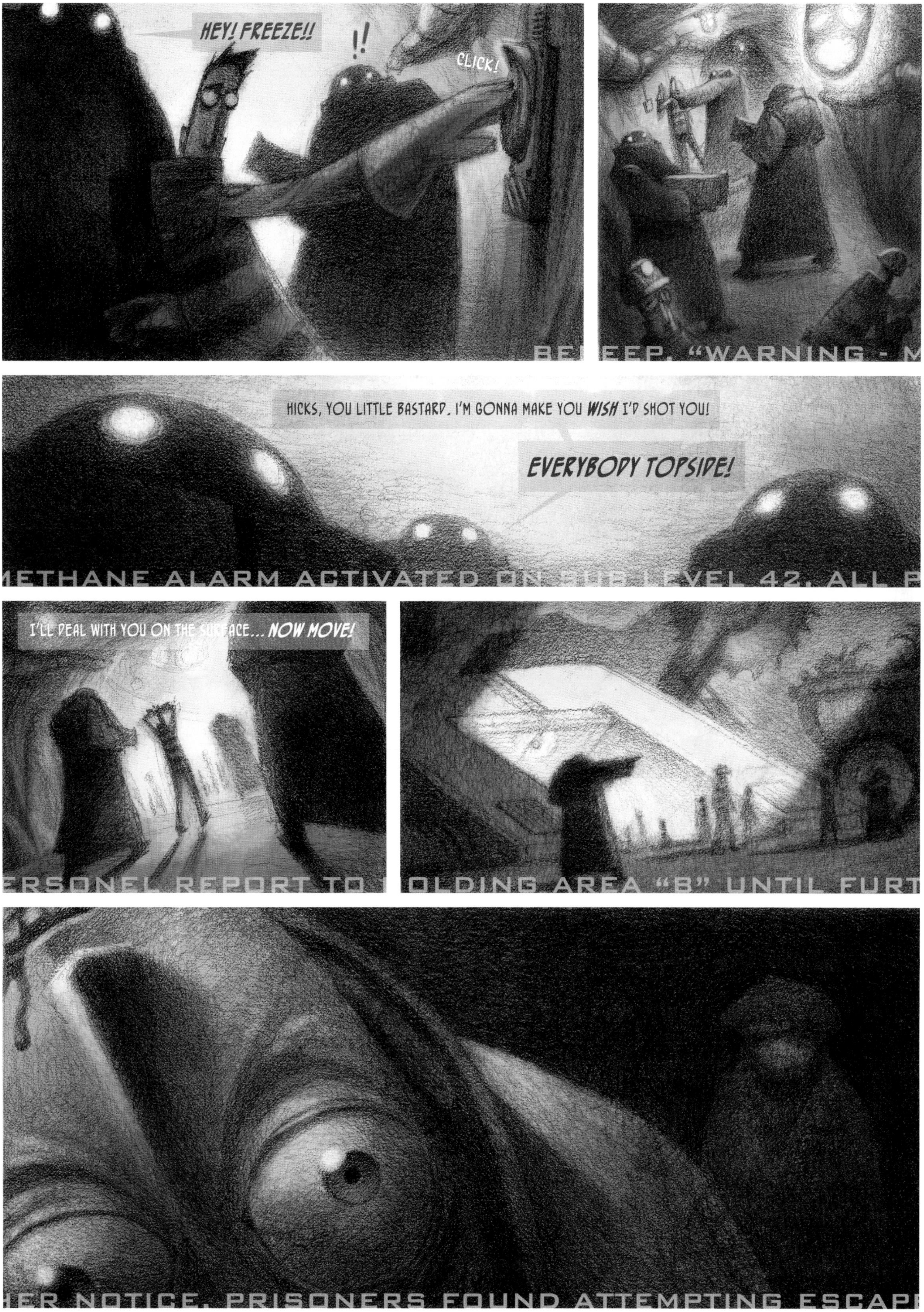
HEY! FREEZE!!
!!
CLICK!
BEEEEP. "WARNING - M
HICKS, YOU LITTLE BASTARD. I'M GONNA MAKE YOU WISH I'D SHOT YOU!
EVERYBODY TOPSIDE!
METHANE ALARM ACTIVATED ON SUB LEVEL 42. ALL P
I'LL DEAL WITH YOU ON THE SURFACE... NOW MOVE!
ERSONEL REPORT TO HOLDING AREA "B" UNTIL FURT
HER NOTICE. PRISONERS FOUND ATTEMPTING ESCAP

WILL BE SHOT ON SIGHT. THIS IS NOT A DRILL - BEE

EEEEP - WARNING, METHANE ALARM ACTIVATED ON SI

WHAT'S THAT SOUND?

LEVEL 42. ALL PERSONEL REPORT TO HOLDING ARE

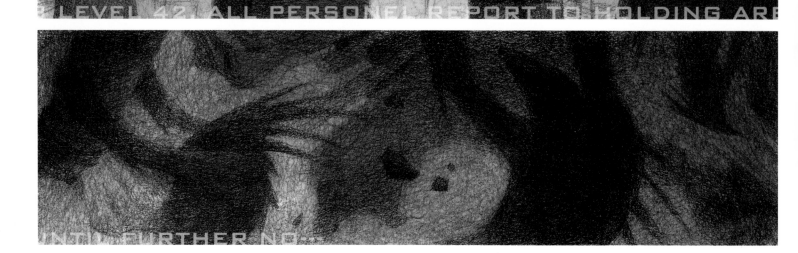

NTIL FURTHER NO--

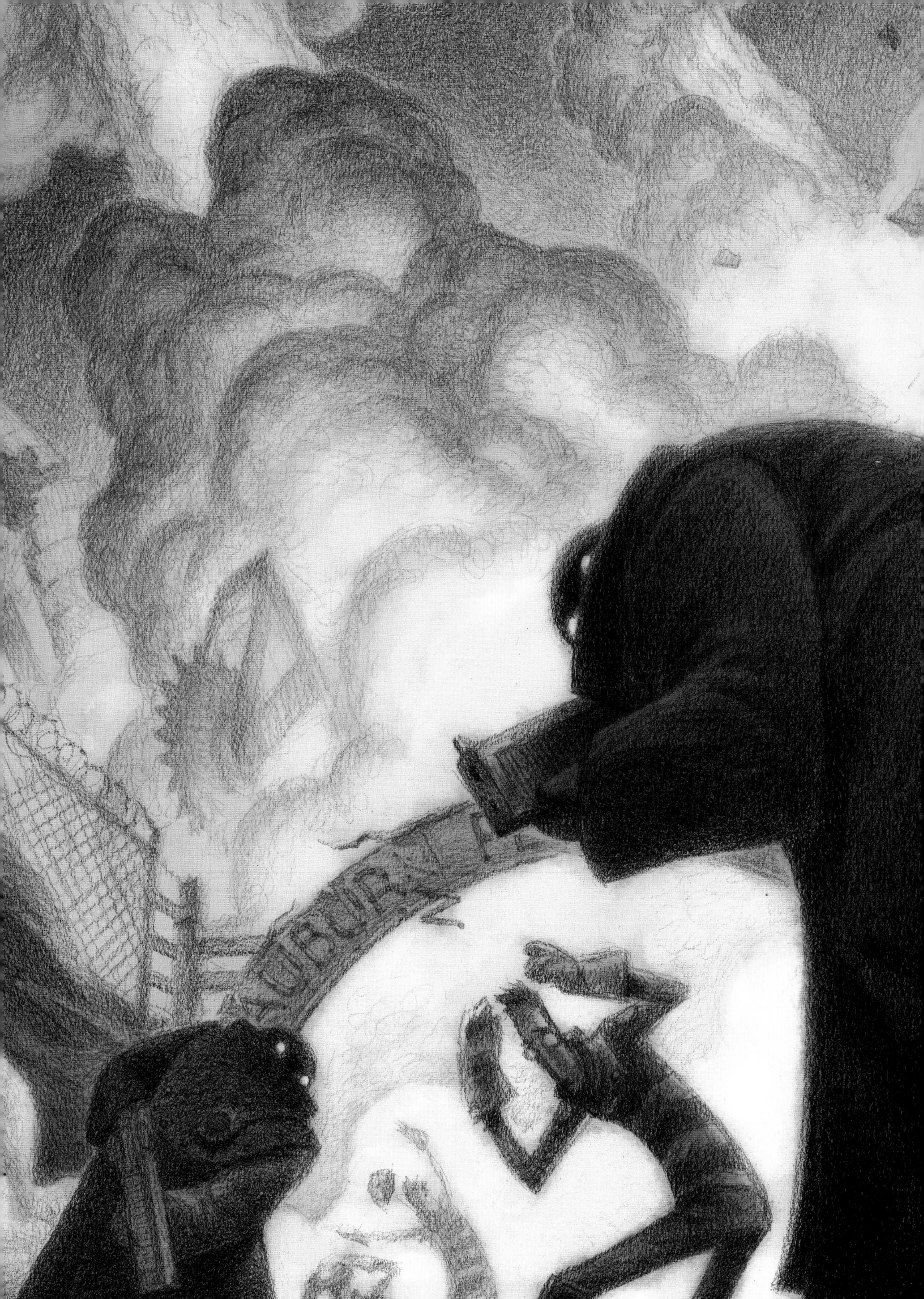

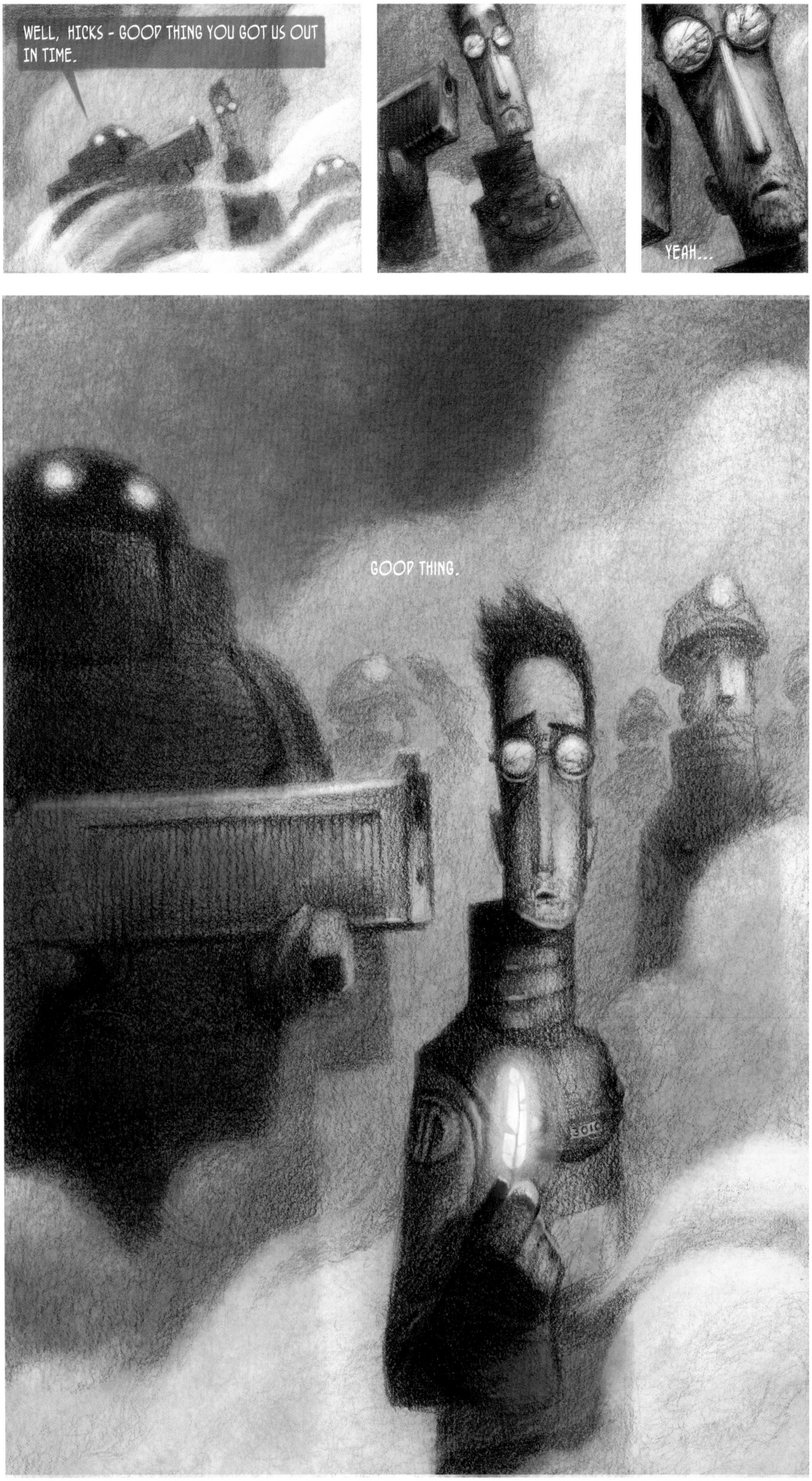
WELL, HICKS - GOOD THING YOU GOT US OUT IN TIME.
YEAH...
GOOD THING.

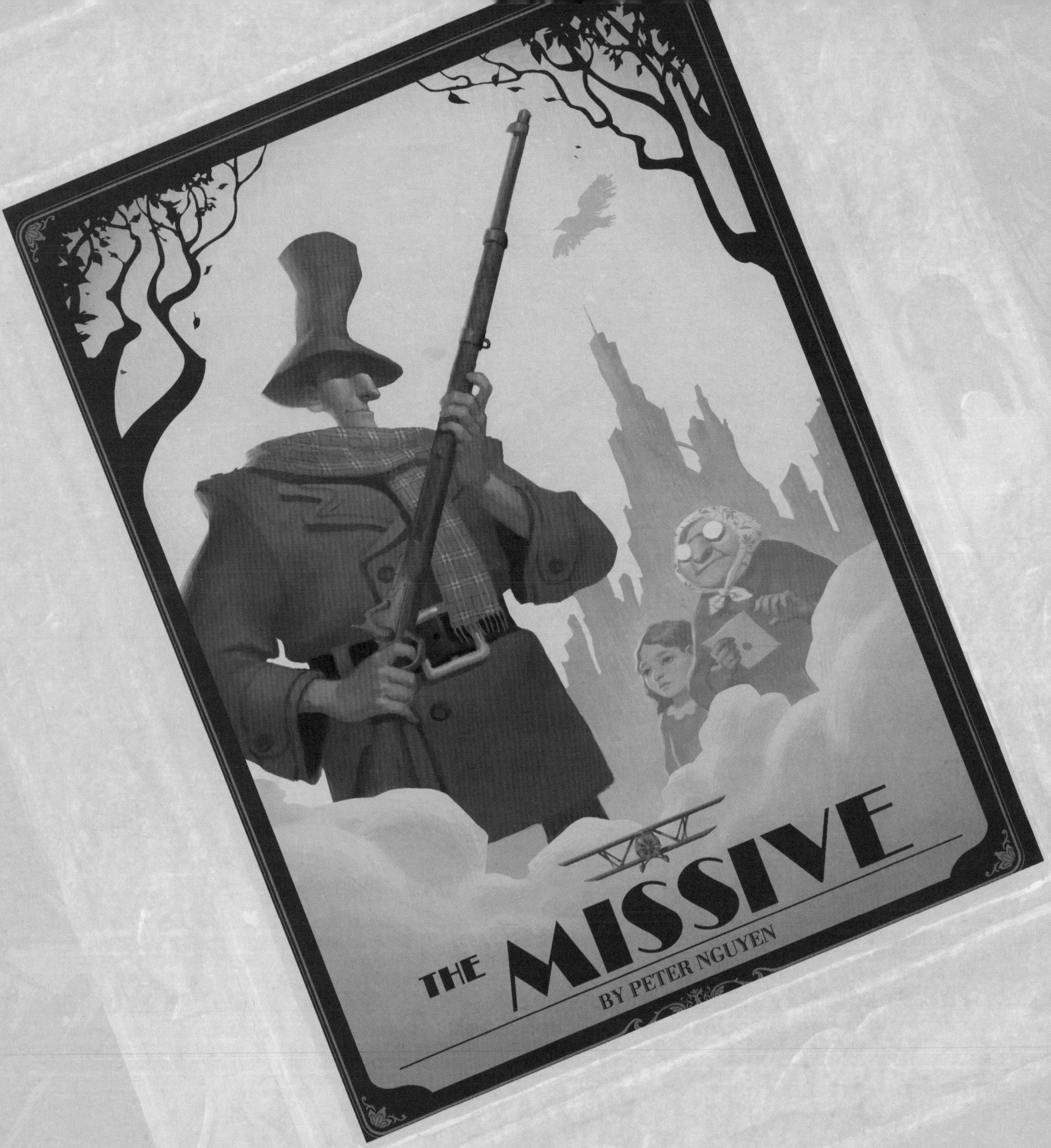
THE MISSIVE
BY PETER NGUYEN

PETER NGUYEN

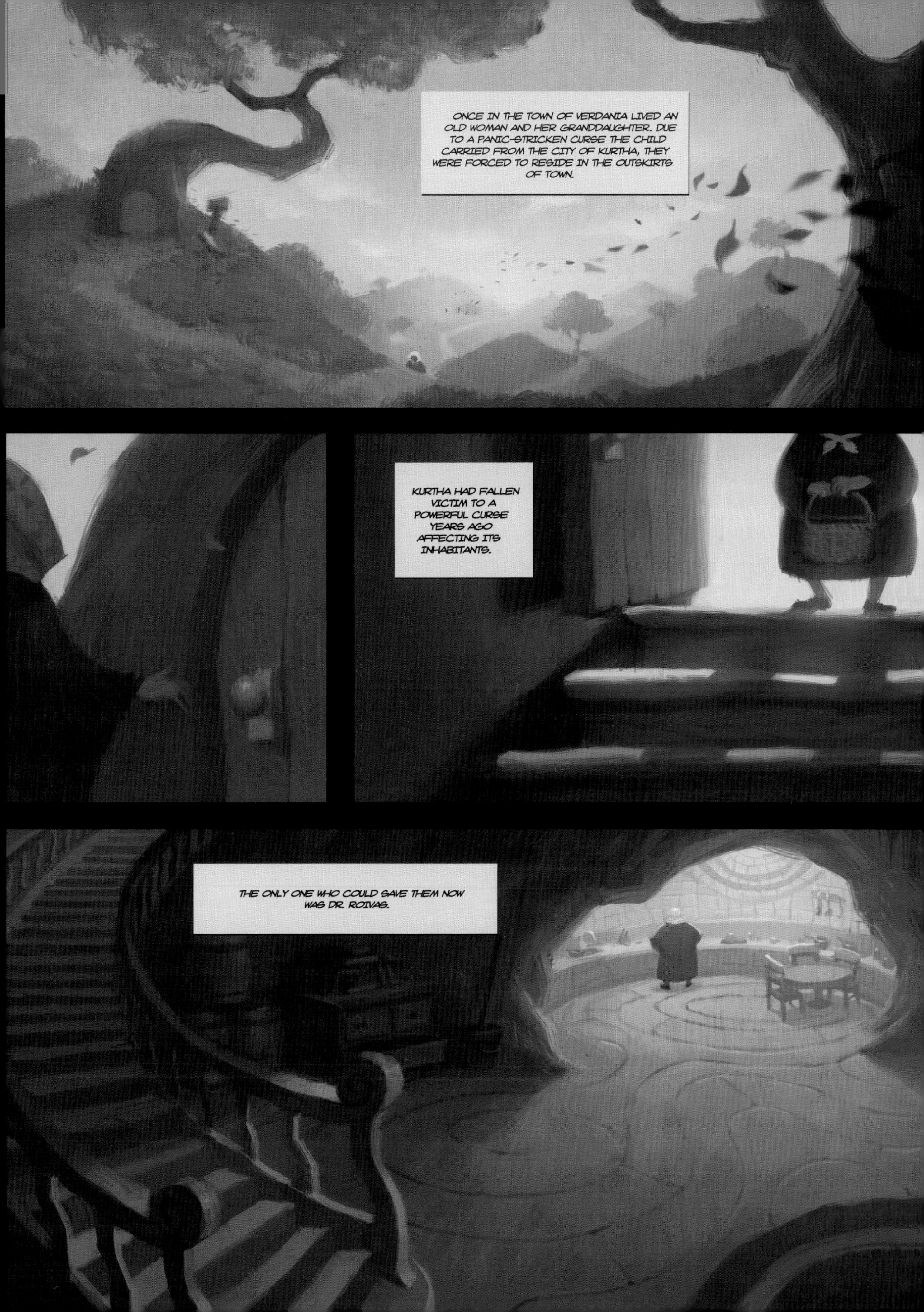
ONCE IN THE TOWN OF VERDANIA LIVED AN OLD WOMAN AND HER GRANDDAUGHTER. DUE TO A PANIC-STRICKEN CURSE THE CHILD CARRIED FROM THE CITY OF KURTHA, THEY WERE FORCED TO RESIDE IN THE OUTSKIRTS OF TOWN.
KURTHA HAD FALLEN VICTIM TO A POWERFUL CURSE YEARS AGO AFFECTING ITS INHABITANTS.
THE ONLY ONE WHO COULD SAVE THEM NOW WAS DR. ROIVAS.

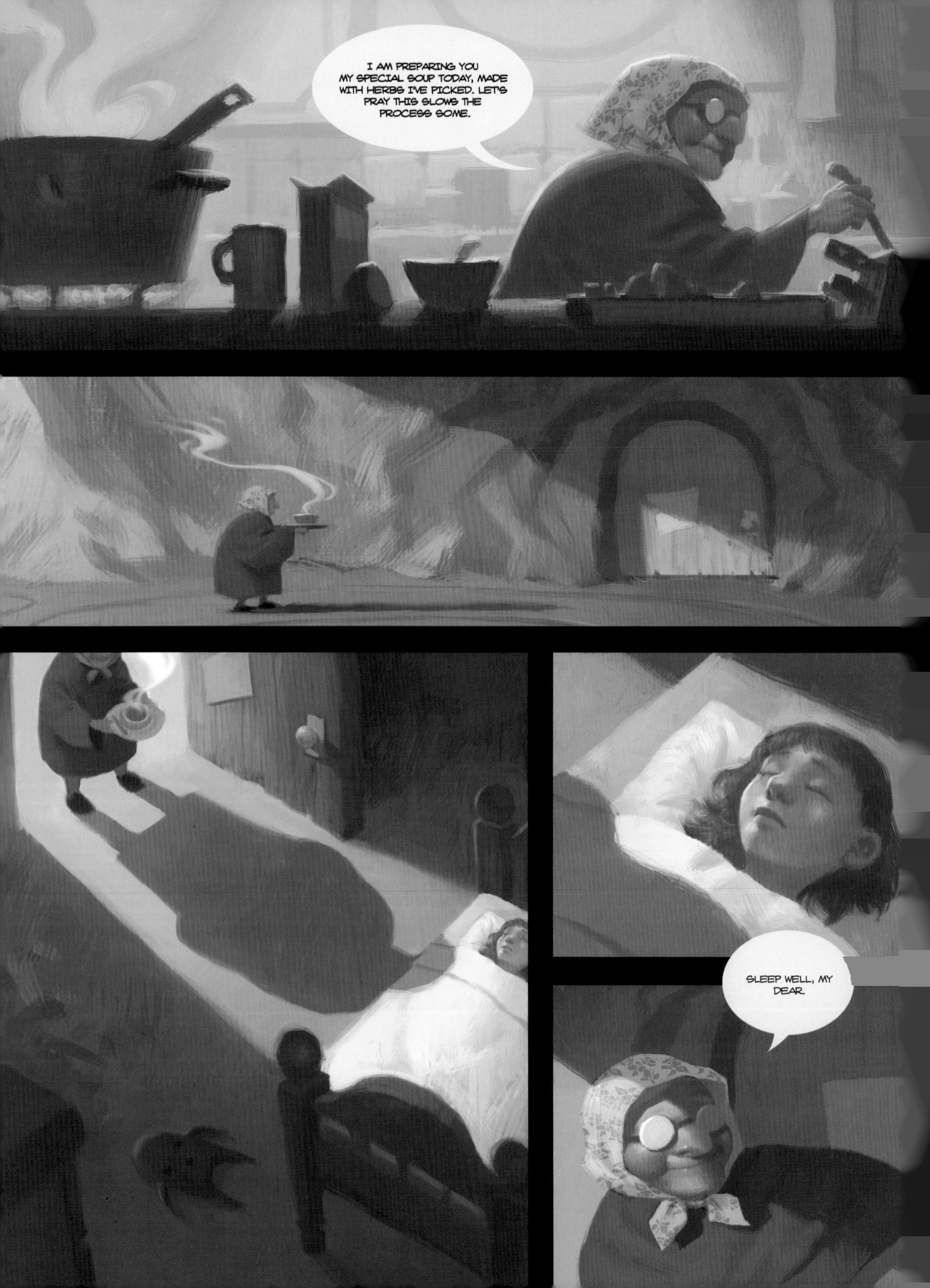
I AM PREPARING YOU MY SPECIAL SOUP TODAY, MADE WITH HERBS I'VE PICKED. LET'S PRAY THIS SLOWS THE PROCESS SOME.
SLEEP WELL, MY DEAR.

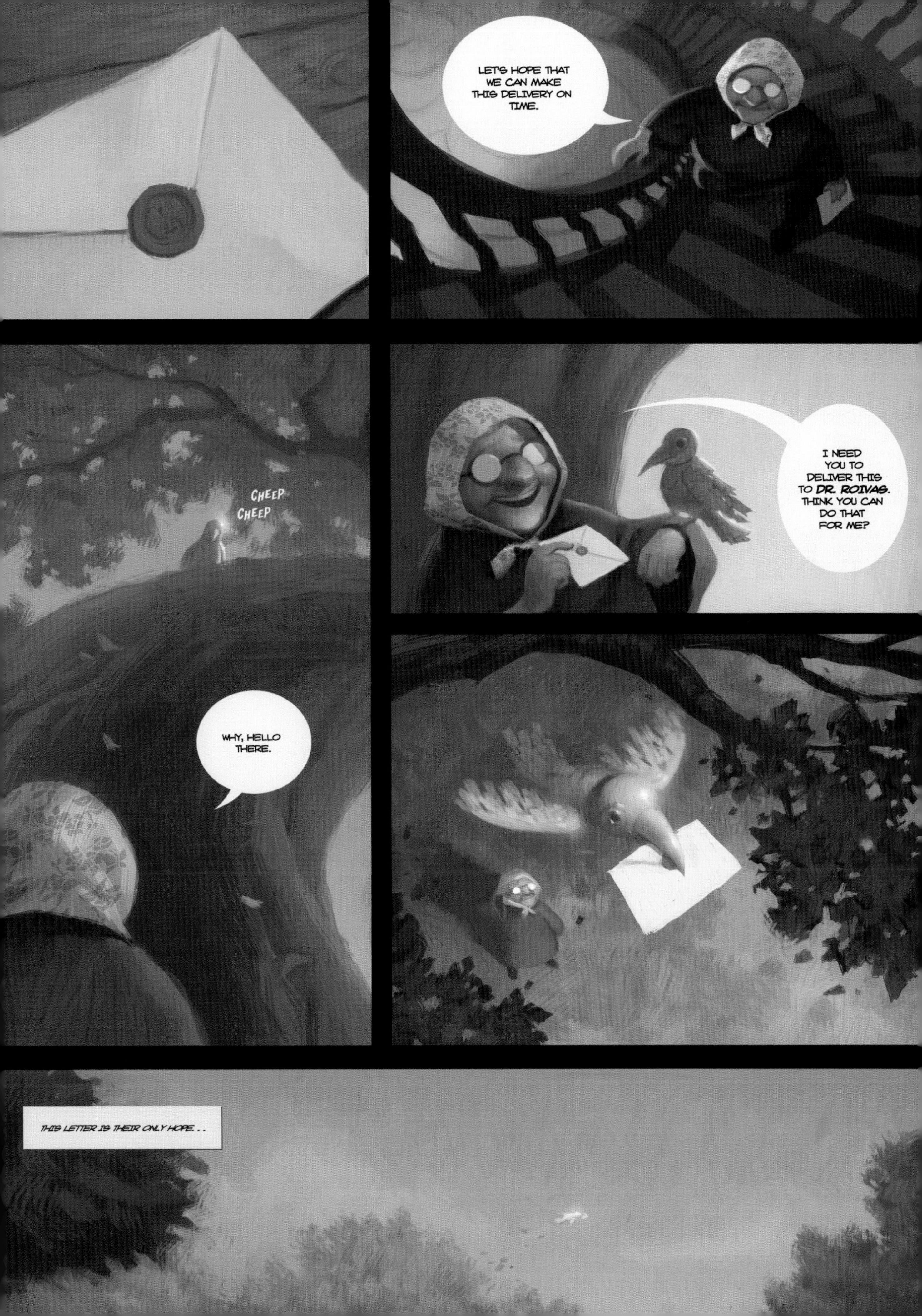
LET'S HOPE THAT WE CAN MAKE THIS DELIVERY ON TIME.
CHEEP CHEEP
WHY, HELLO THERE.
I NEED YOU TO DELIVER THIS TO DR. ROIVAS. THINK YOU CAN DO THAT FOR ME?
THIS LETTER IS THEIR ONLY HOPE. . .

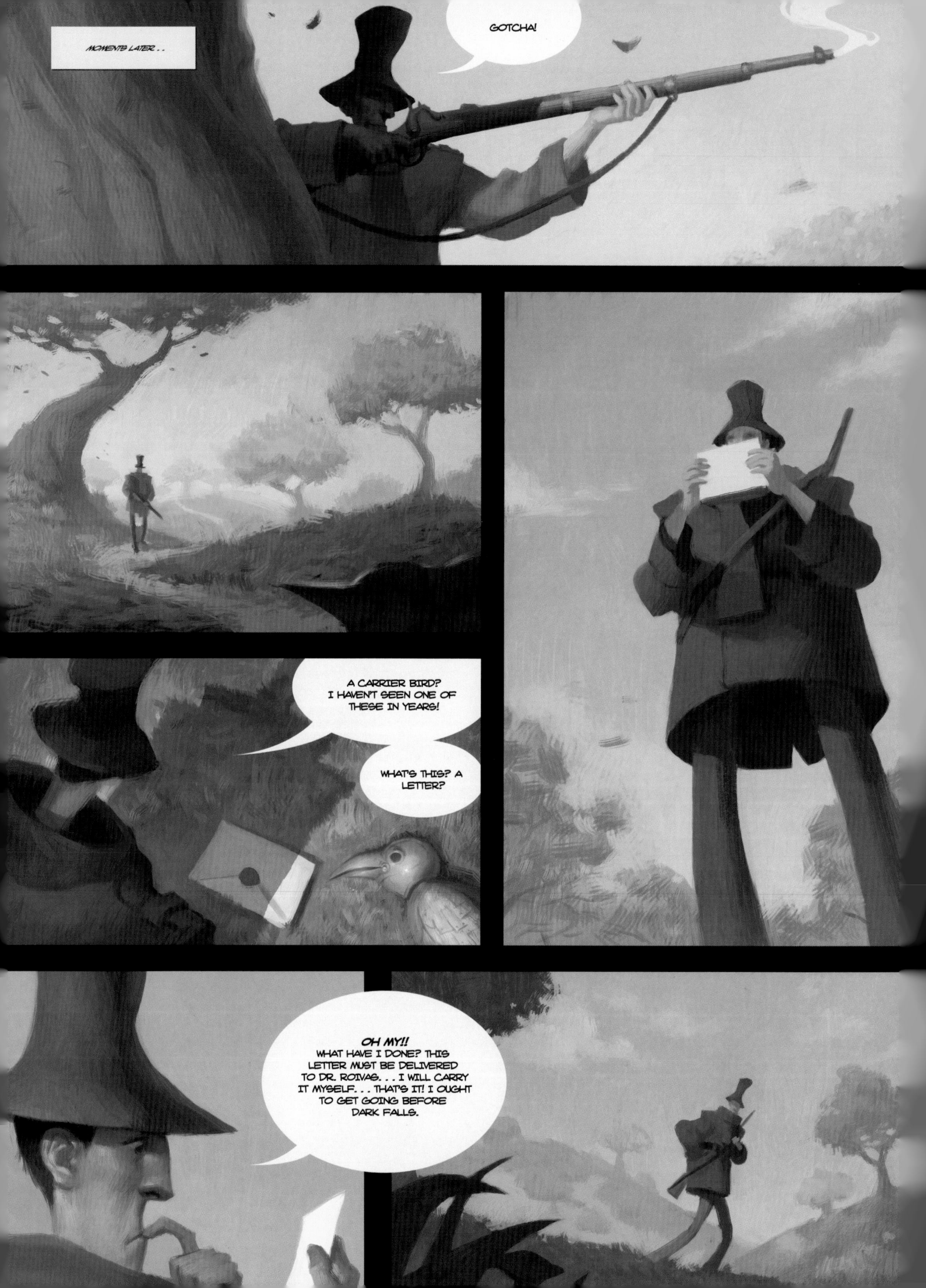
MOMENTS LATER . .
GOTCHA!
A CARRIER BIRD? I HAVEN'T SEEN ONE OF THESE IN YEARS!
WHAT'S THIS? A LETTER?
OH MY!! WHAT HAVE I DONE? THIS LETTER MUST BE DELIVERED TO DR. ROIVAS. . . I WILL CARRY IT MYSELF. . . THAT'S IT! I OUGHT TO GET GOING BEFORE DARK FALLS.

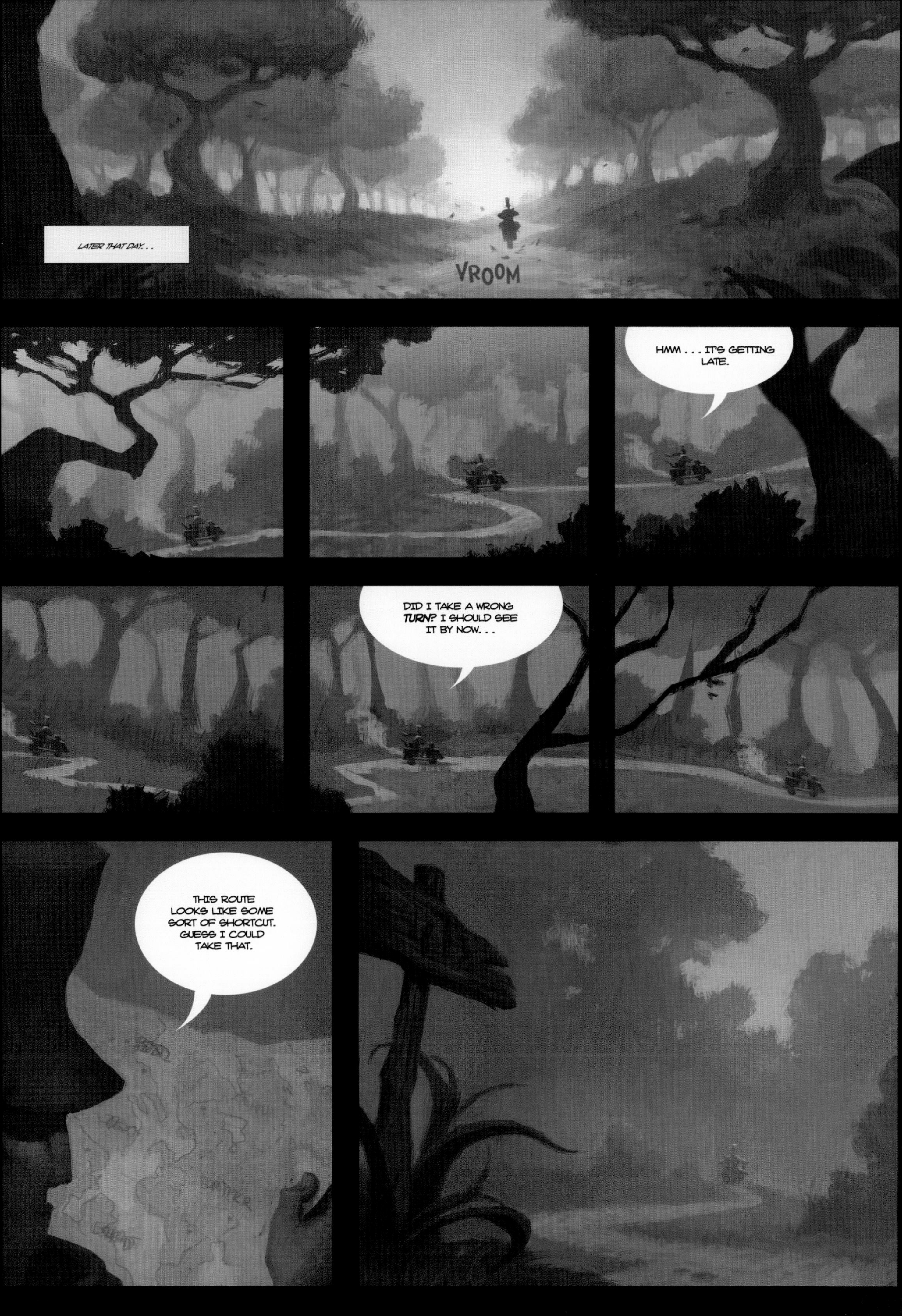
LATER THAT DAY. . .
VROOM
HMM . . . IT'S GETTING LATE.
DID I TAKE A WRONG TURN? I SHOULD SEE IT BY NOW. . .
THIS ROUTE LOOKS LIKE SOME SORT OF SHORTCUT. GUESS I COULD TAKE THAT.

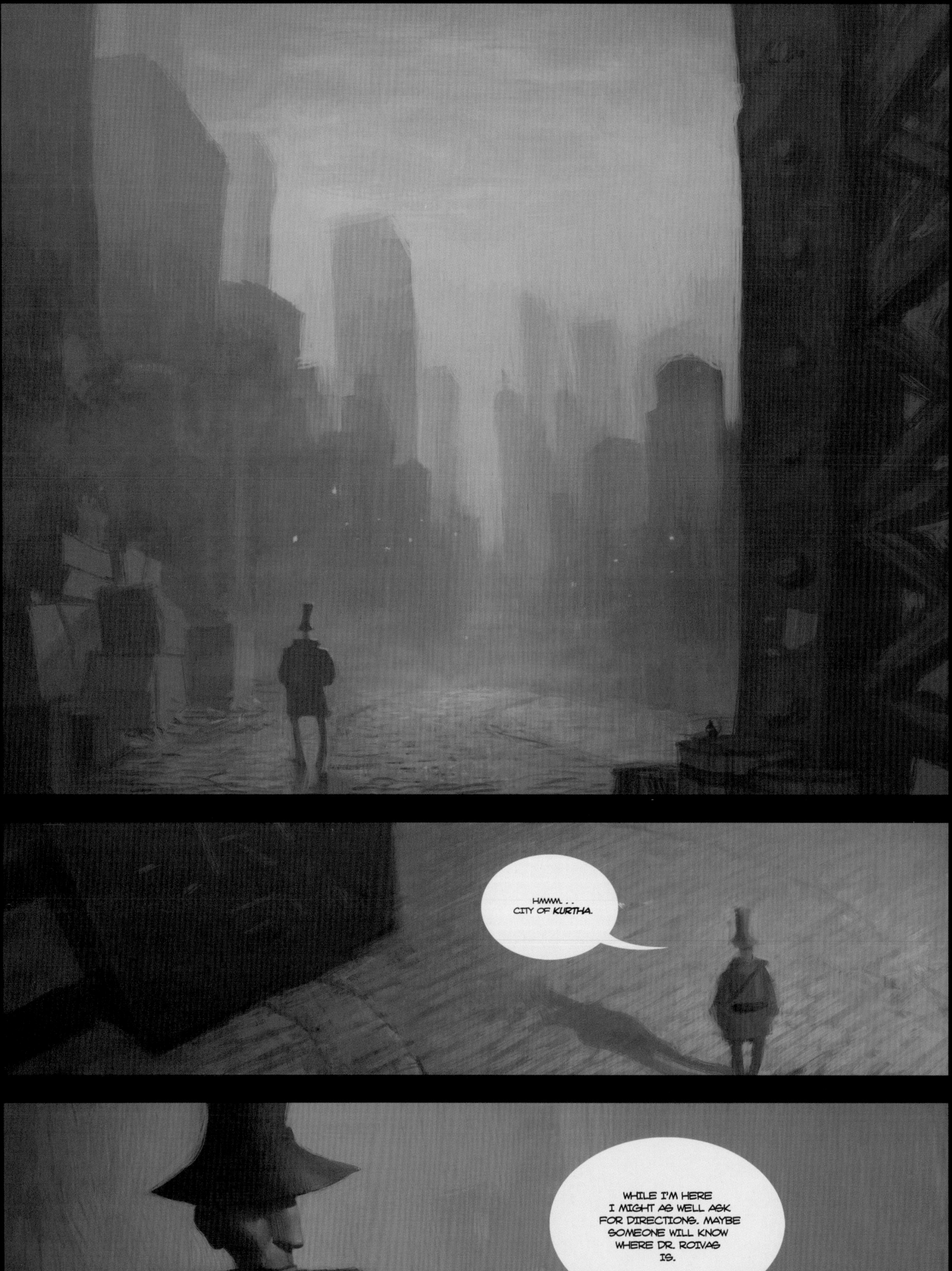
HMMM. . . CITY OF KURTHA.
WHILE I'M HERE I MIGHT AS WELL ASK FOR DIRECTIONS. MAYBE SOMEONE WILL KNOW WHERE DR. ROIVAS IS.

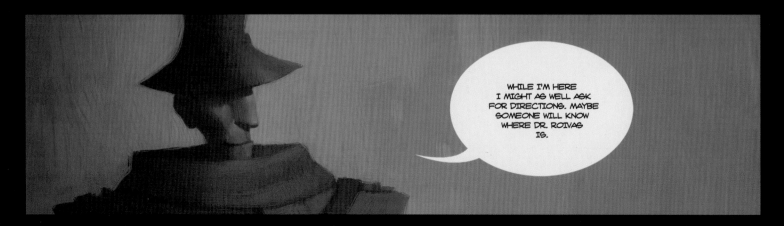

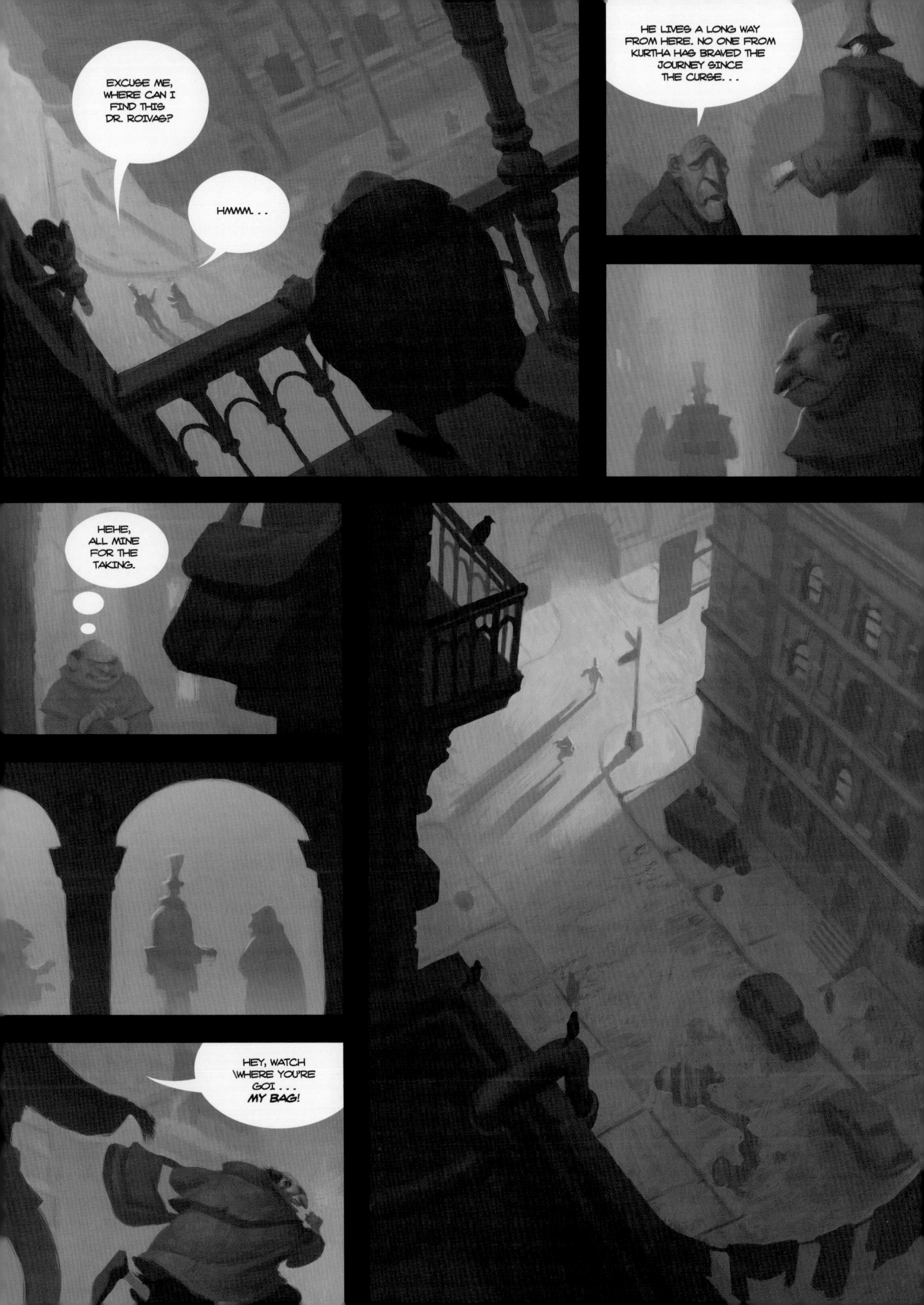
EXCUSE ME, WHERE CAN I FIND THIS DR. ROIVAS?
HMMM. . .
HE LIVES A LONG WAY FROM HERE. NO ONE FROM KURTHA HAS BRAVED THE JOURNEY SINCE THE CURSE. . .
HEHE, ALL MINE FOR THE TAKING.
HEY, WATCH WHERE YOU'RE GOI . . . MY BAG!

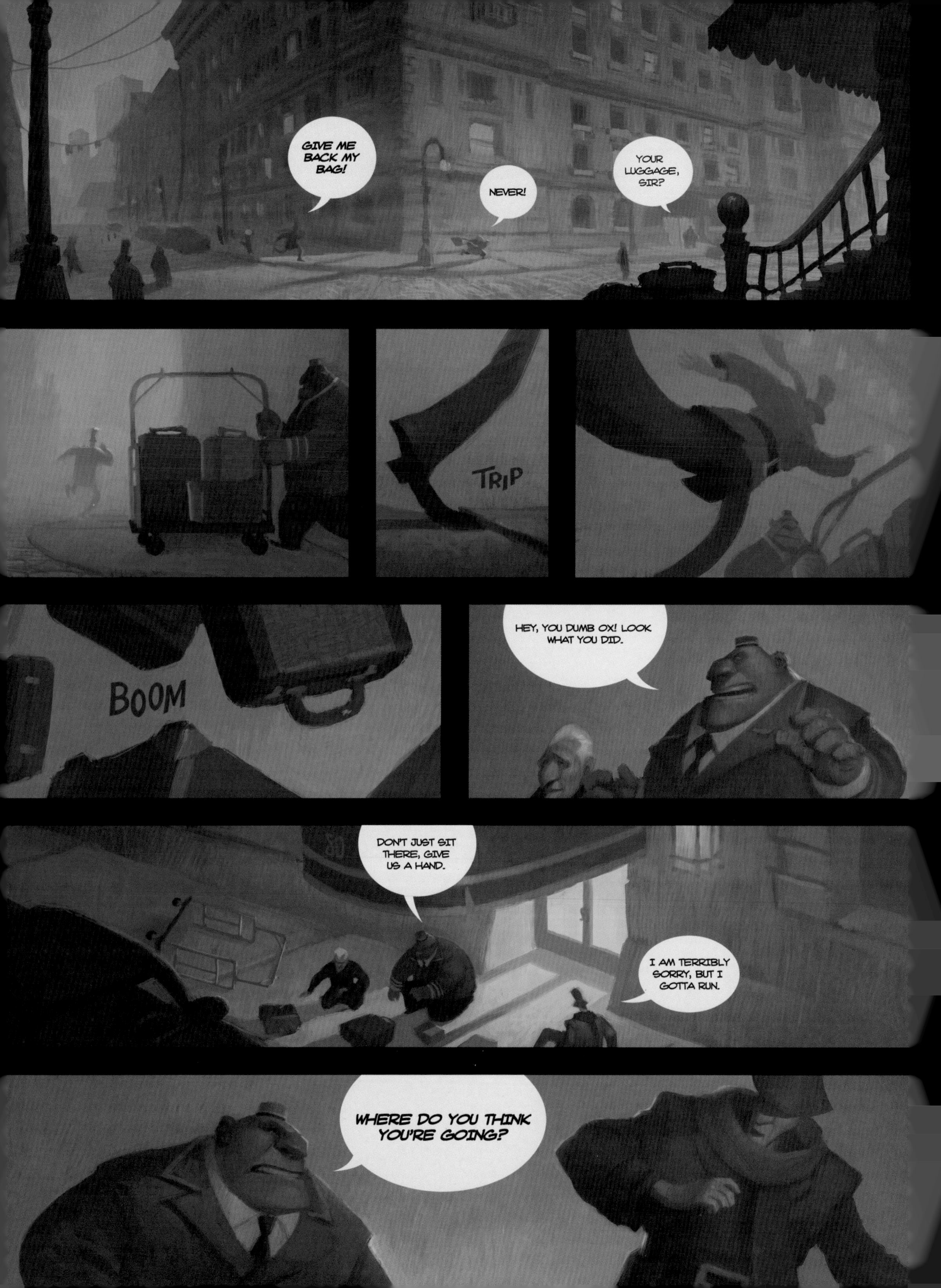
GIVE ME BACK MY BAG!
NEVER!
YOUR LUGGAGE, SIR?
TRIP
BOOM
HEY, YOU DUMB OX! LOOK WHAT YOU DID.
DON'T JUST SIT THERE, GIVE US A HAND.
I AM TERRIBLY SORRY, BUT I GOTTA RUN.
WHERE DO YOU THINK YOU'RE GOING?

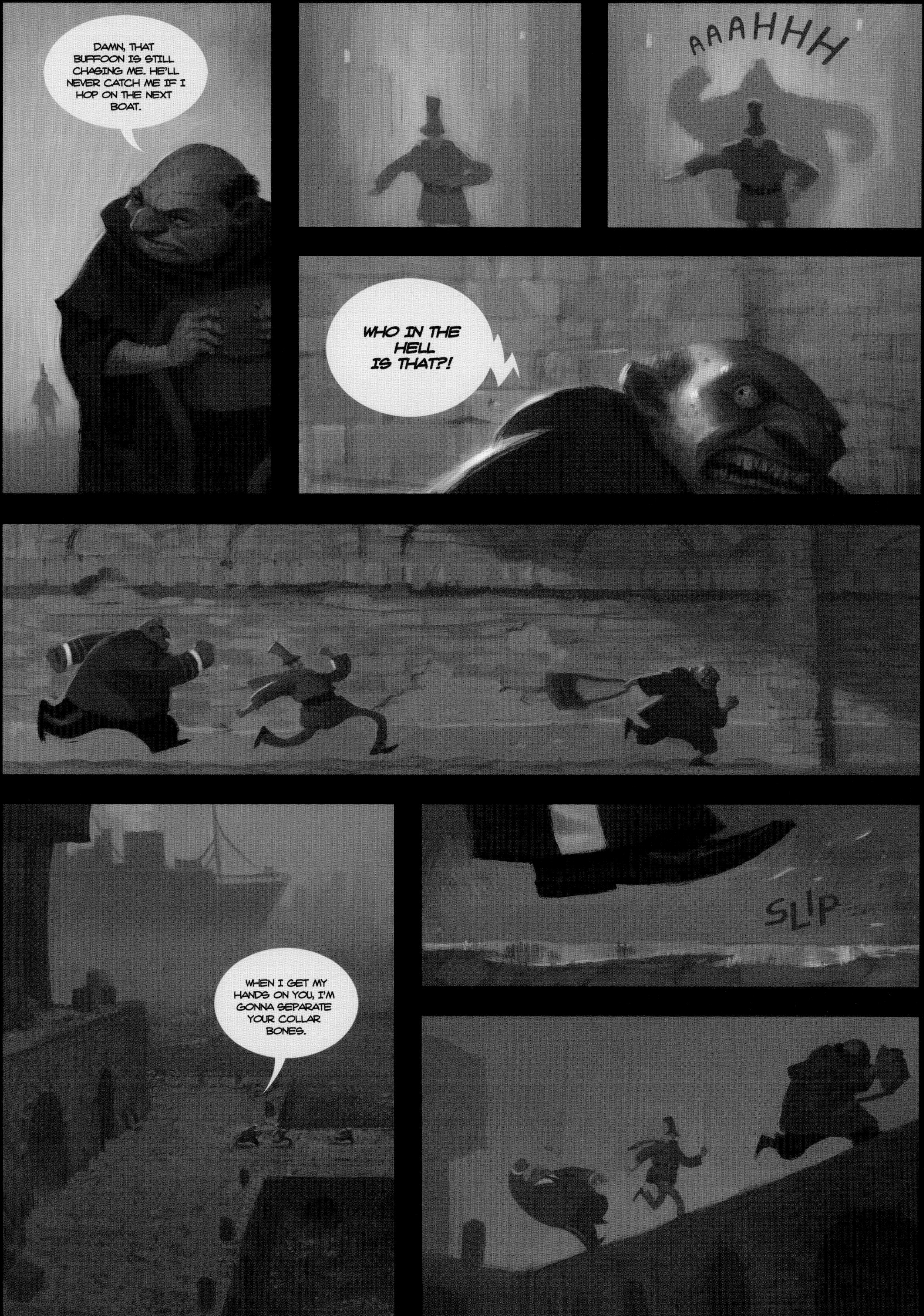
DAMN, THAT BUFFOON IS STILL CHASING ME. HE'LL NEVER CATCH ME IF I HOP ON THE NEXT BOAT.
AAAHHH
WHO IN THE HELL IS THAT?!
WHEN I GET MY HANDS ON YOU, I'M GONNA SEPARATE YOUR COLLAR BONES.
SLIP

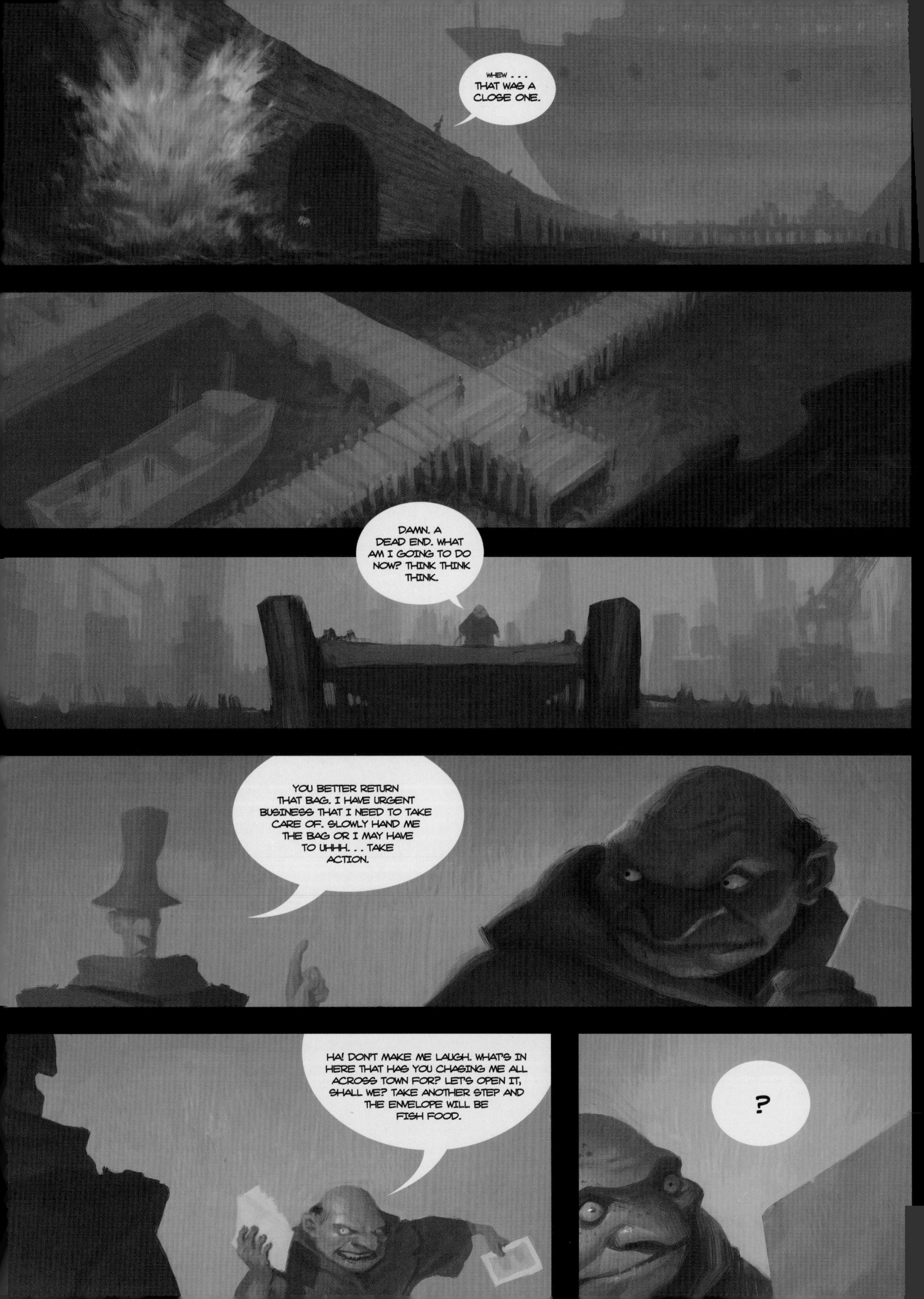
WHEW . . . THAT WAS A CLOSE ONE.
DAMN. A DEAD END. WHAT AM I GOING TO DO NOW? THINK THINK THINK.
YOU BETTER RETURN THAT BAG. I HAVE URGENT BUSINESS THAT I NEED TO TAKE CARE OF. SLOWLY HAND ME THE BAG OR I MAY HAVE TO UHHH. . . TAKE ACTION.
HA! DON'T MAKE ME LAUGH. WHAT'S IN HERE THAT HAS YOU CHASING ME ALL ACROSS TOWN FOR? LET'S OPEN IT, SHALL WE? TAKE ANOTHER STEP AND THE ENVELOPE WILL BE FISH FOOD.
?

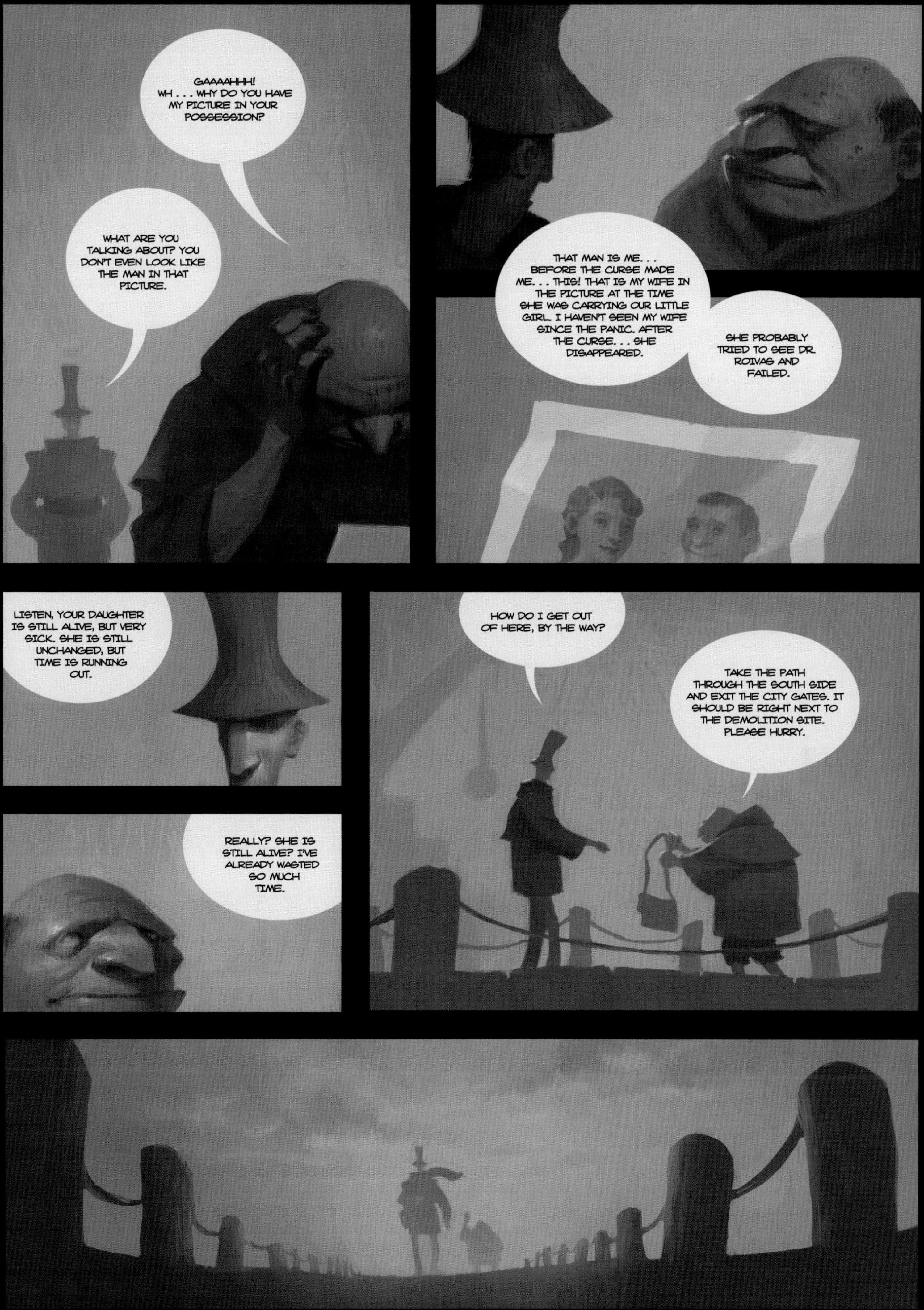
GAAAAHHH! WH . . . WHY DO YOU HAVE MY PICTURE IN YOUR POSSESSION?
WHAT ARE YOU TALKING ABOUT? YOU DON'T EVEN LOOK LIKE THE MAN IN THAT PICTURE.
THAT MAN IS ME. . . BEFORE THE CURSE MADE ME. . . THIS! THAT IS MY WIFE IN THE PICTURE AT THE TIME SHE WAS CARRYING OUR LITTLE GIRL. I HAVEN'T SEEN MY WIFE SINCE THE PANIC. AFTER THE CURSE. . . SHE DISAPPEARED.
SHE PROBABLY TRIED TO SEE DR. ROIVAS AND FAILED.
LISTEN, YOUR DAUGHTER IS STILL ALIVE, BUT VERY SICK. SHE IS STILL UNCHANGED, BUT TIME IS RUNNING OUT.
REALLY? SHE IS STILL ALIVE? I'VE ALREADY WASTED SO MUCH TIME.
HOW DO I GET OUT OF HERE, BY THE WAY?
TAKE THE PATH THROUGH THE SOUTH SIDE AND EXIT THE CITY GATES. IT SHOULD BE RIGHT NEXT TO THE DEMOLITION SITE. PLEASE HURRY.

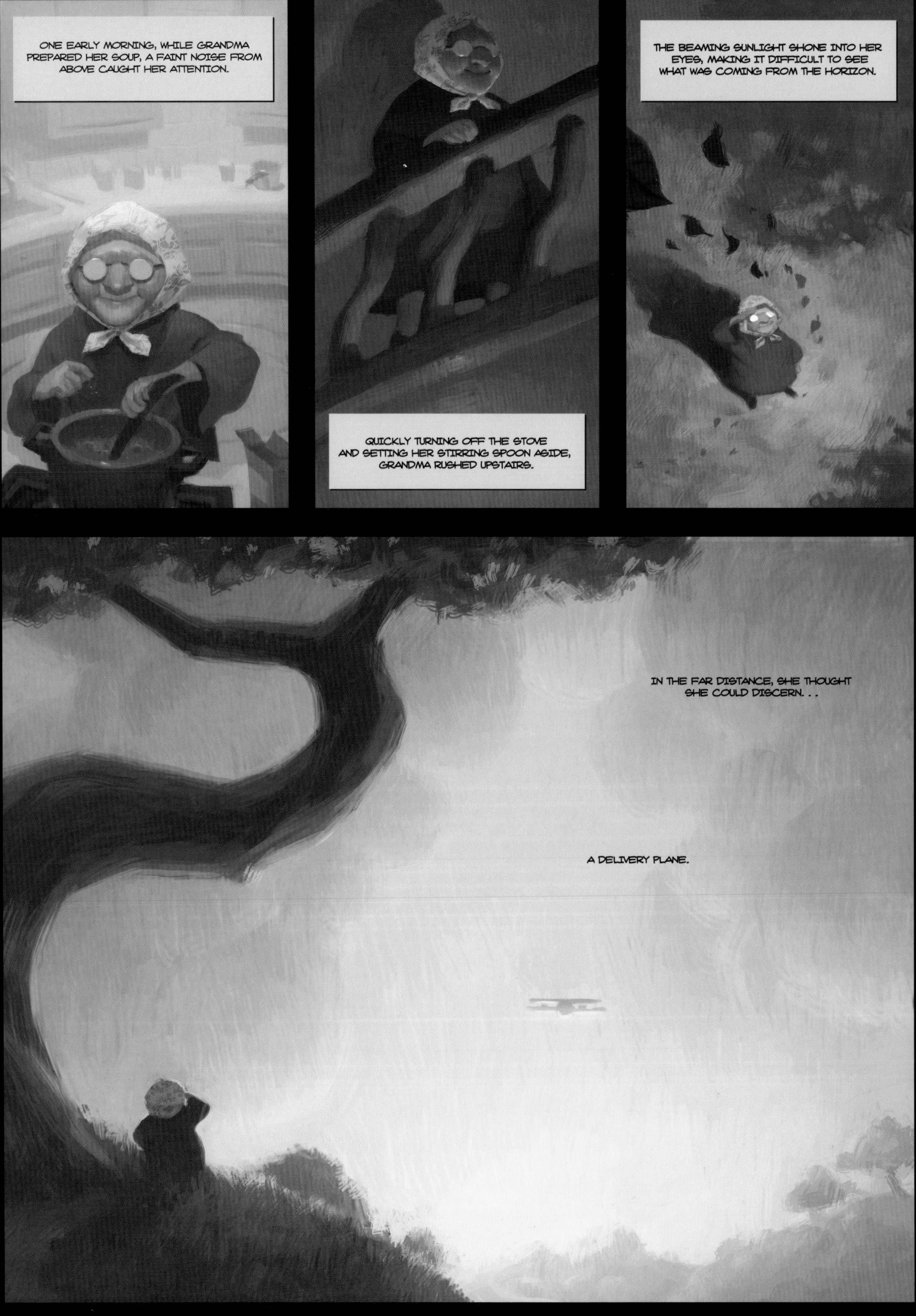
ONE EARLY MORNING, WHILE GRANDMA PREPARED HER SOUP, A FAINT NOISE FROM ABOVE CAUGHT HER ATTENTION.
QUICKLY TURNING OFF THE STOVE AND SETTING HER STIRRING SPOON ASIDE, GRANDMA RUSHED UPSTAIRS.
THE BEAMING SUNLIGHT SHONE INTO HER EYES, MAKING IT DIFFICULT TO SEE WHAT WAS COMING FROM THE HORIZON.
IN THE FAR DISTANCE, SHE THOUGHT SHE COULD DISCERN. . .
A DELIVERY PLANE.

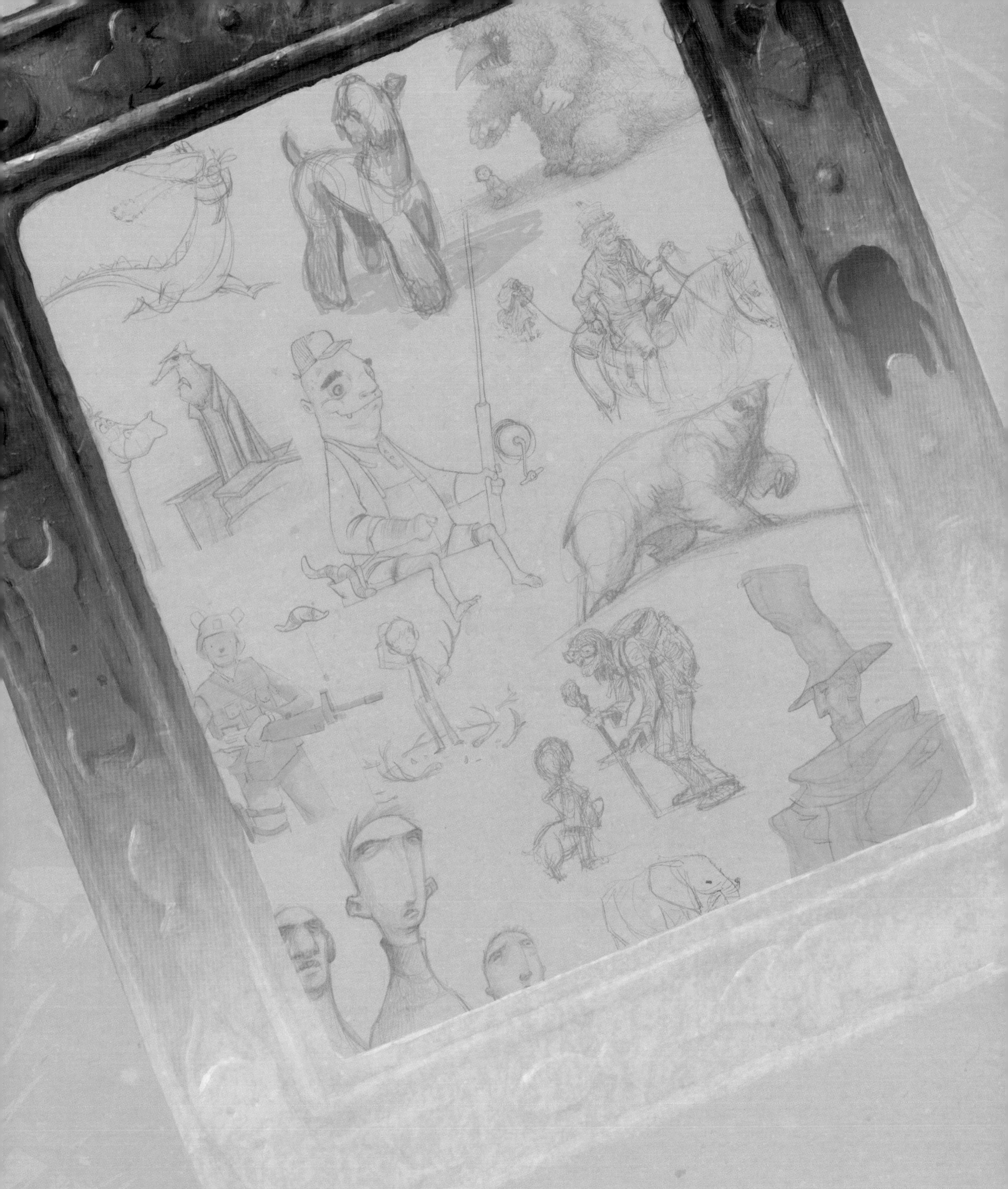

DEVELOPMENT GALLERY

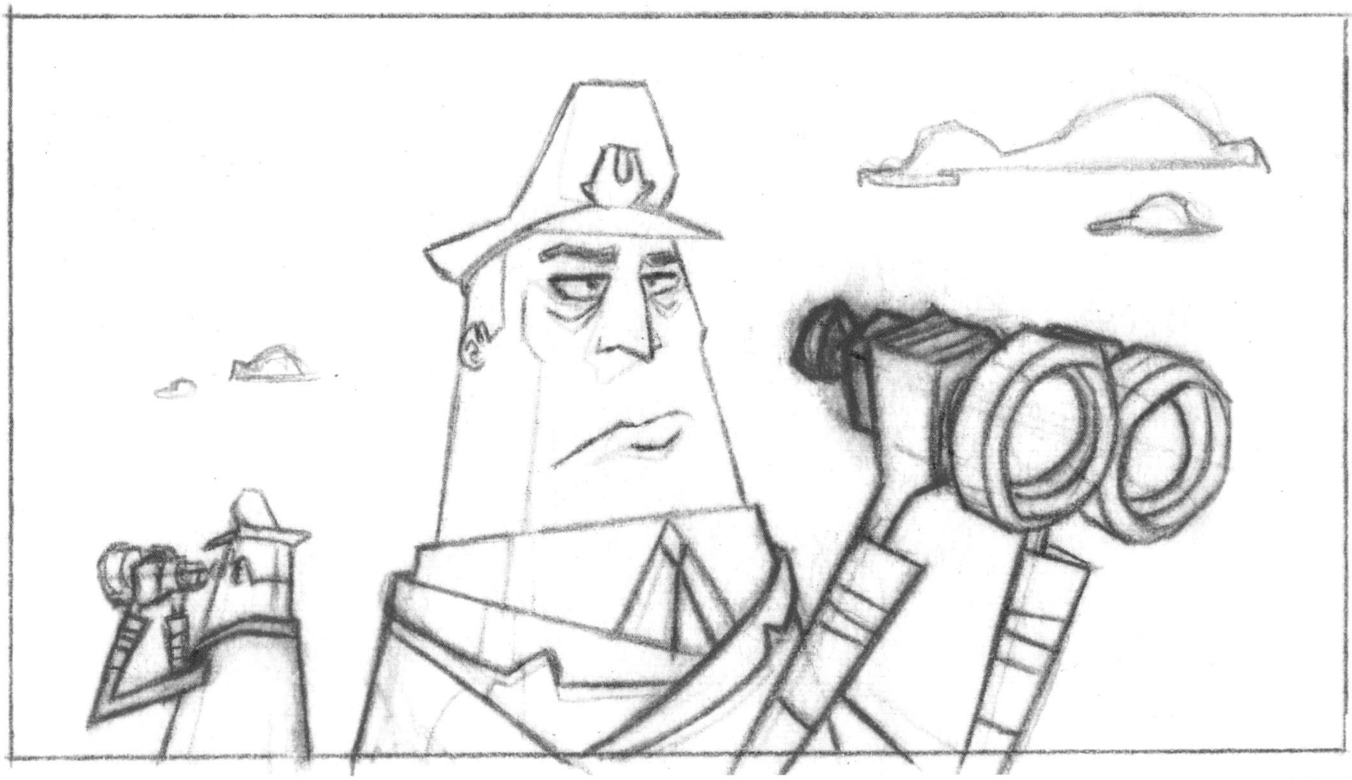

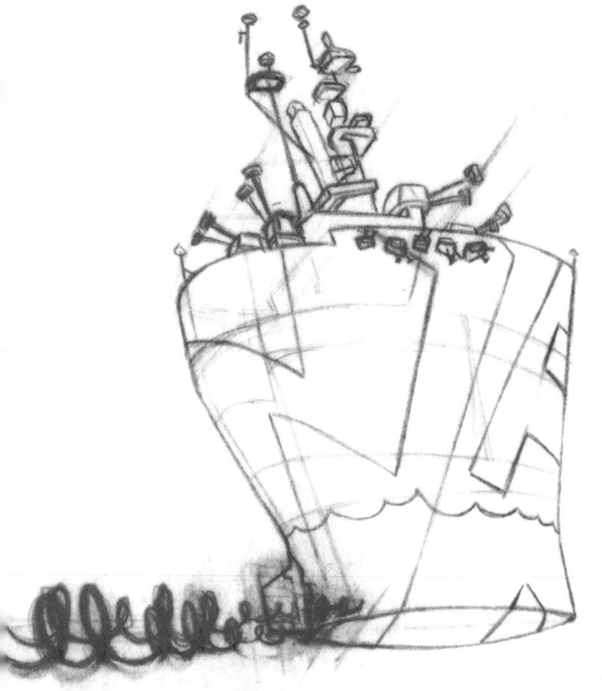

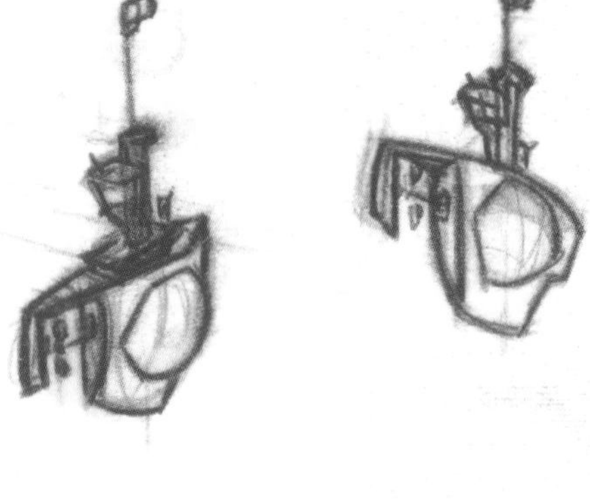

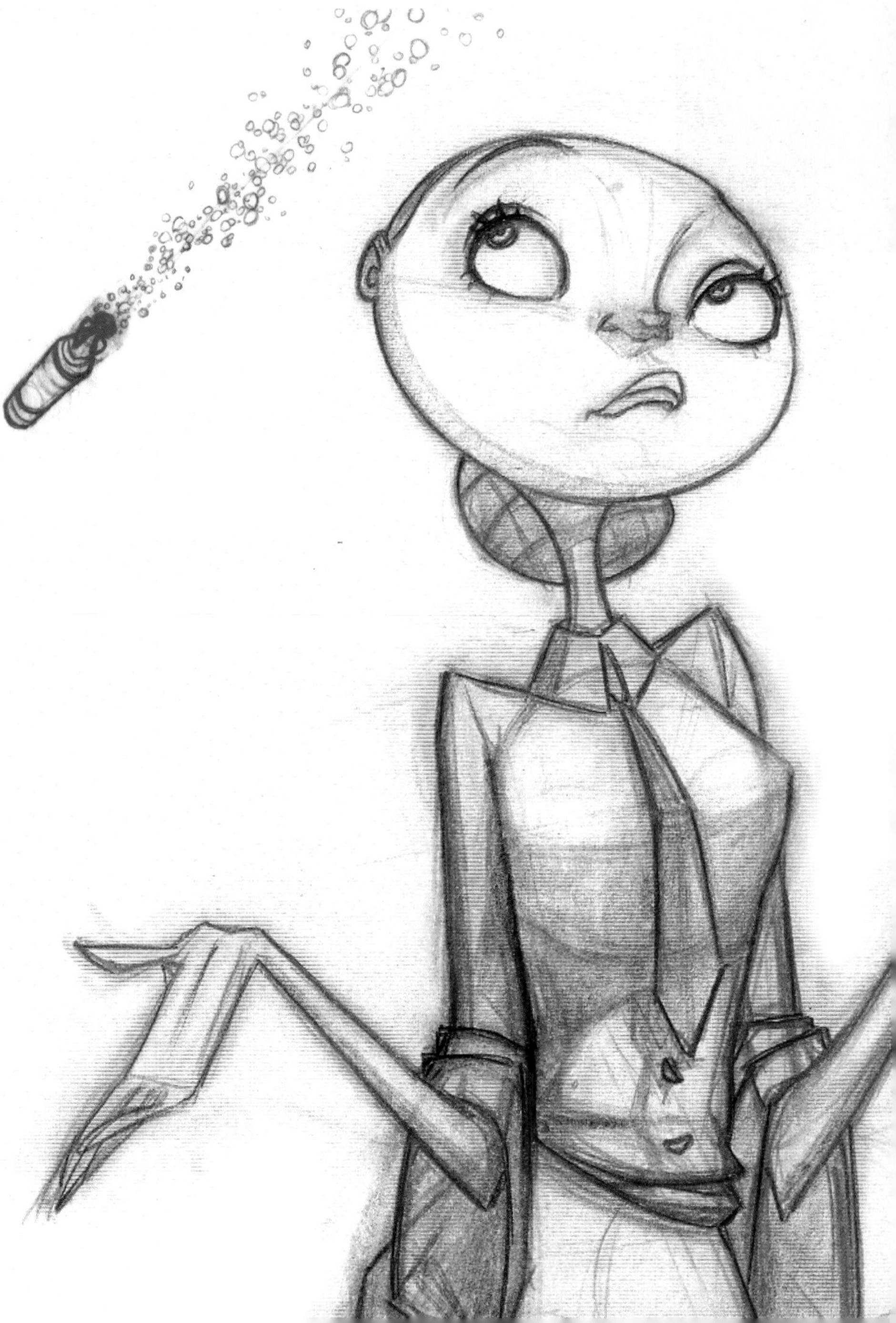

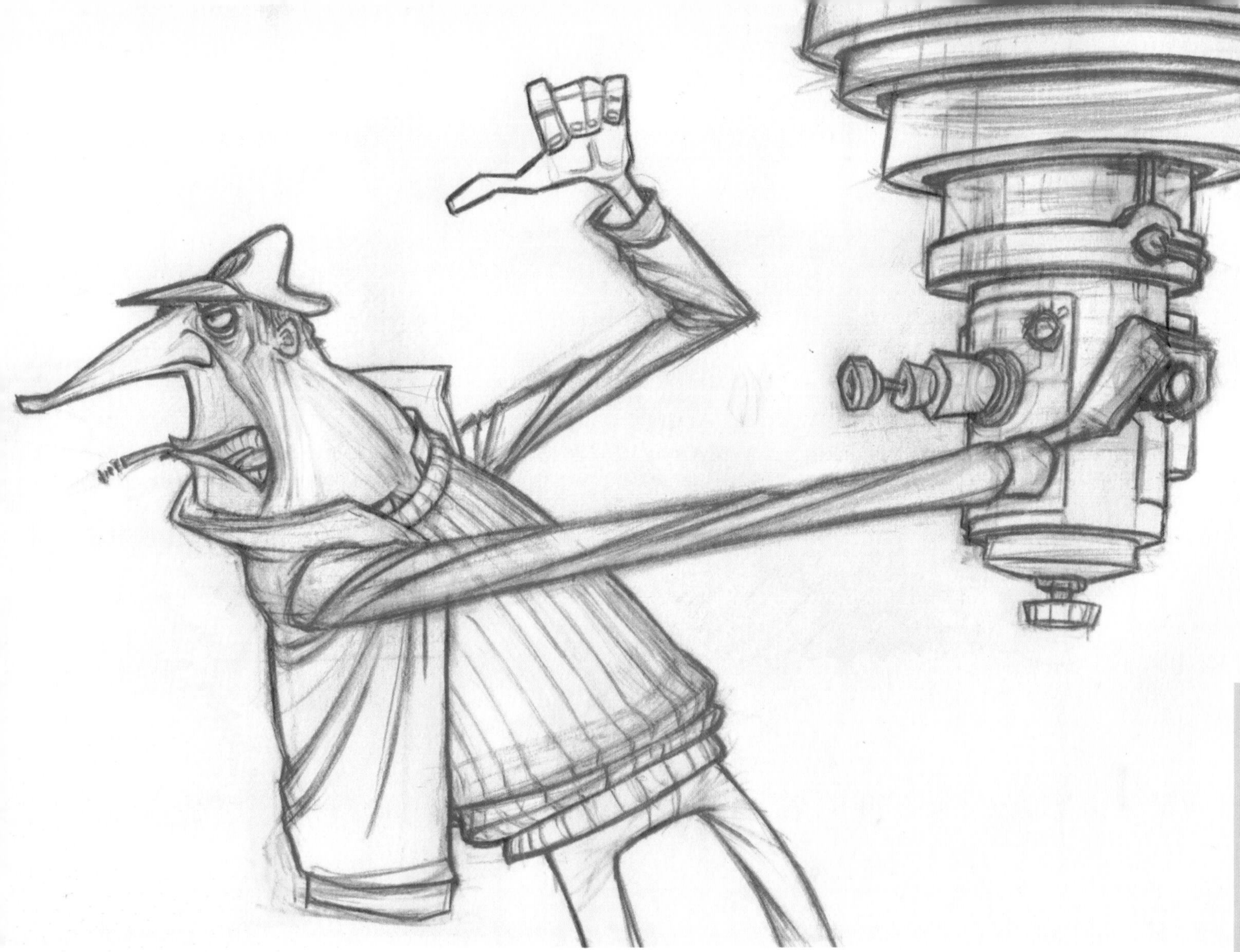

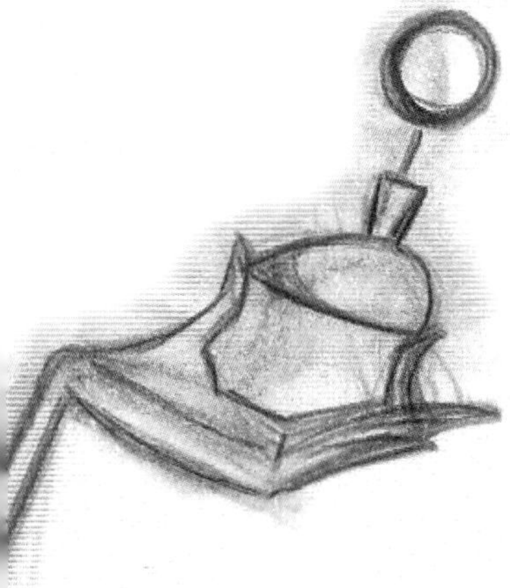

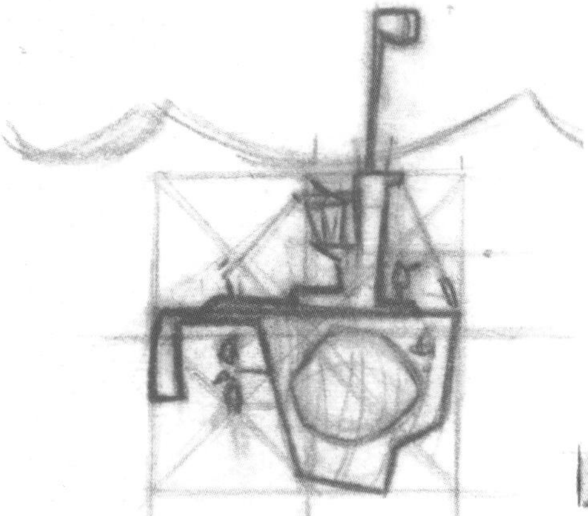

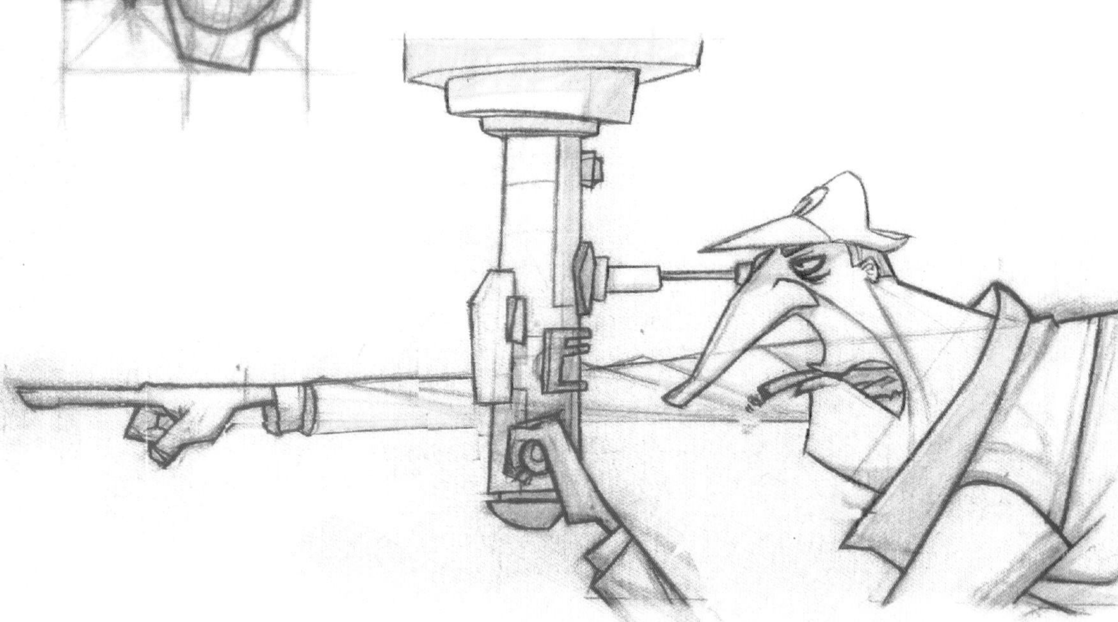

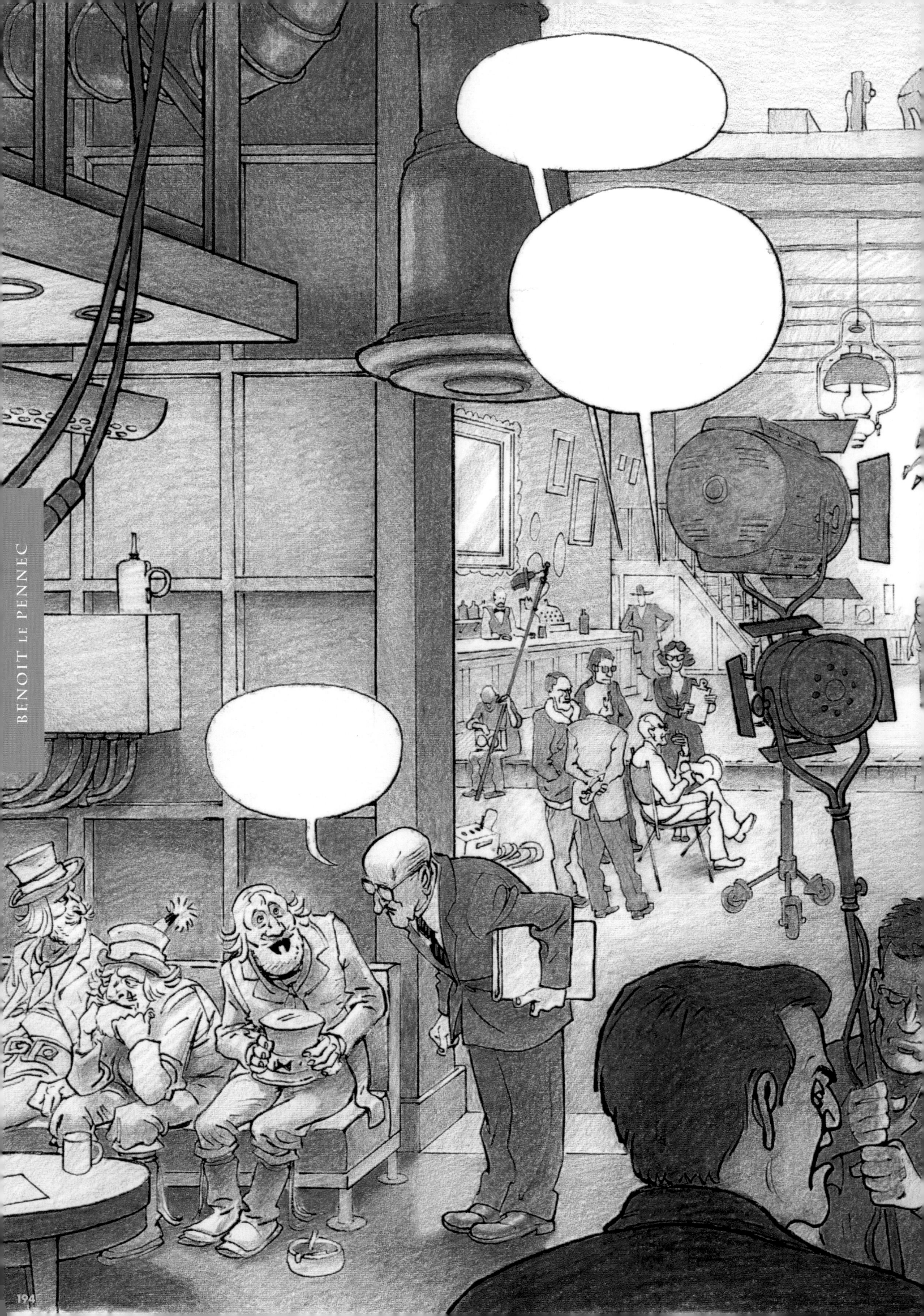

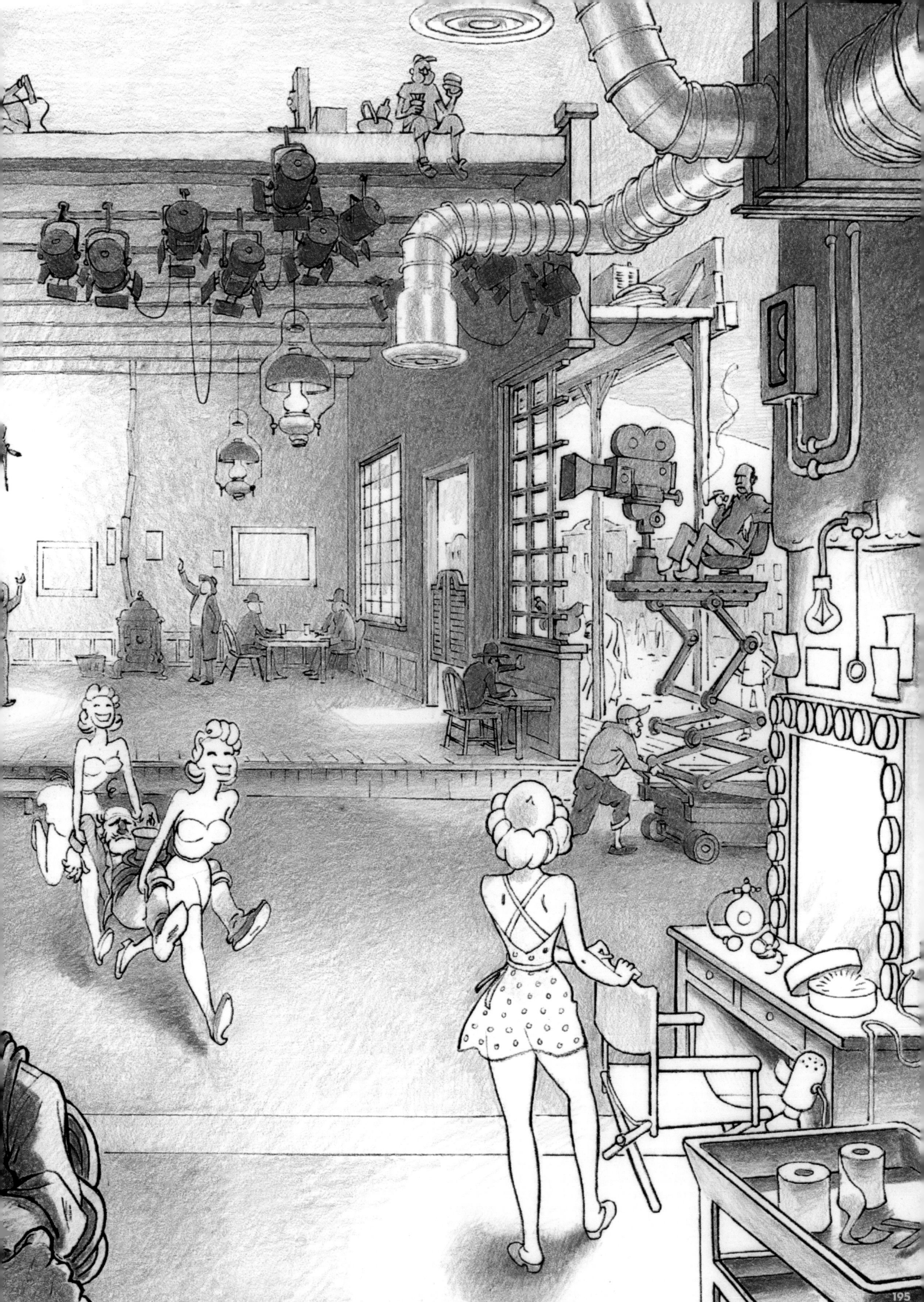

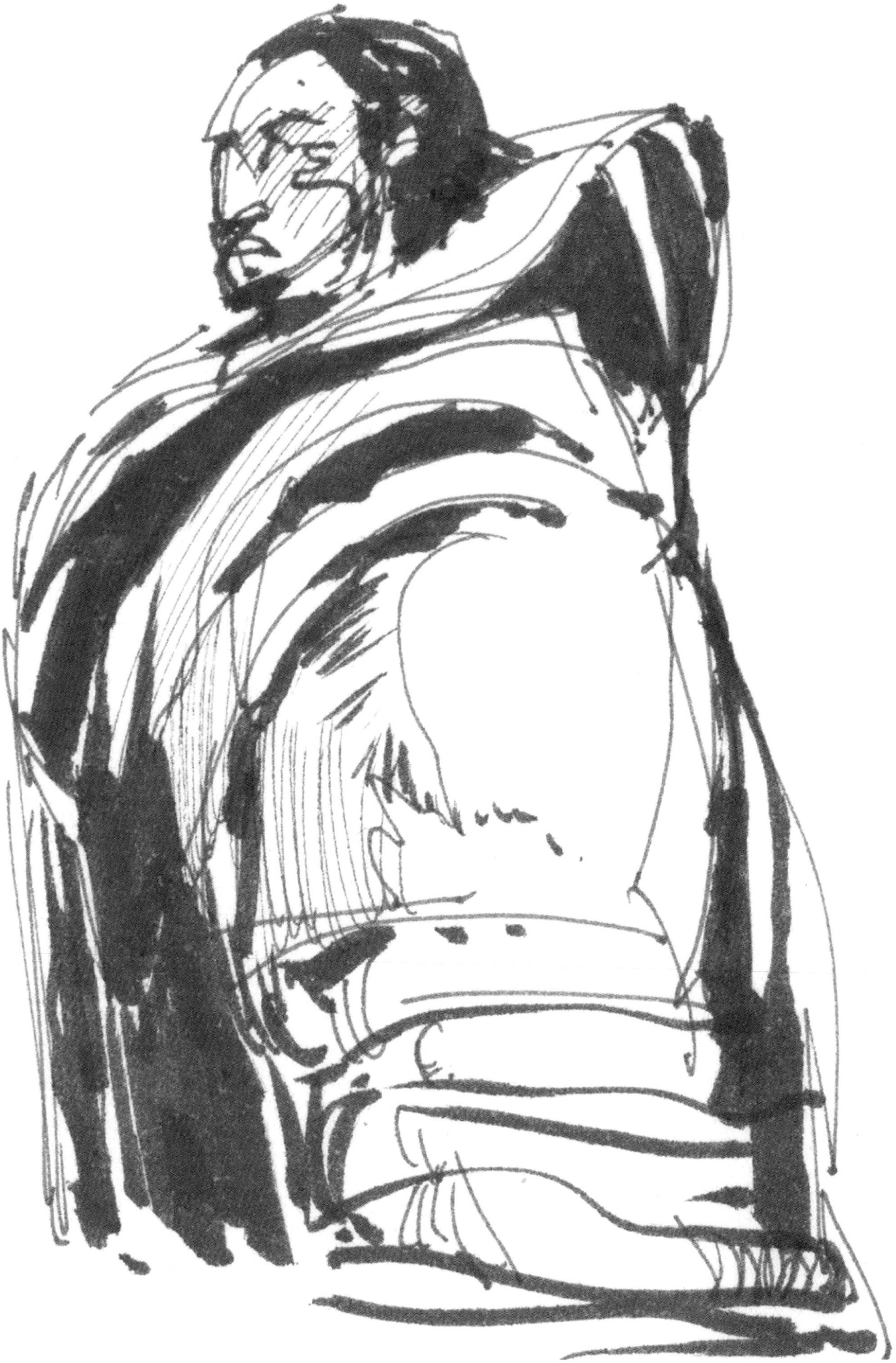

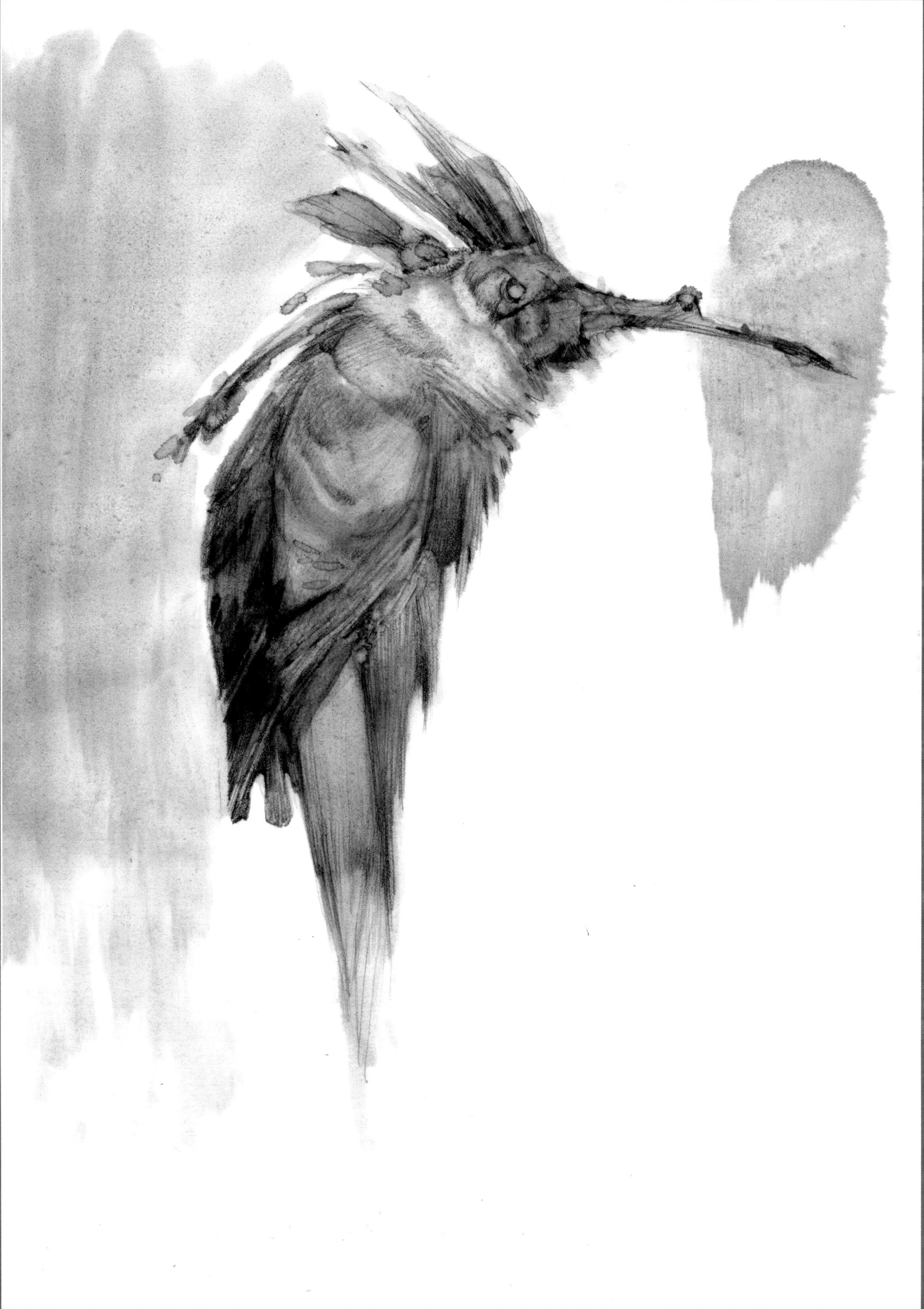

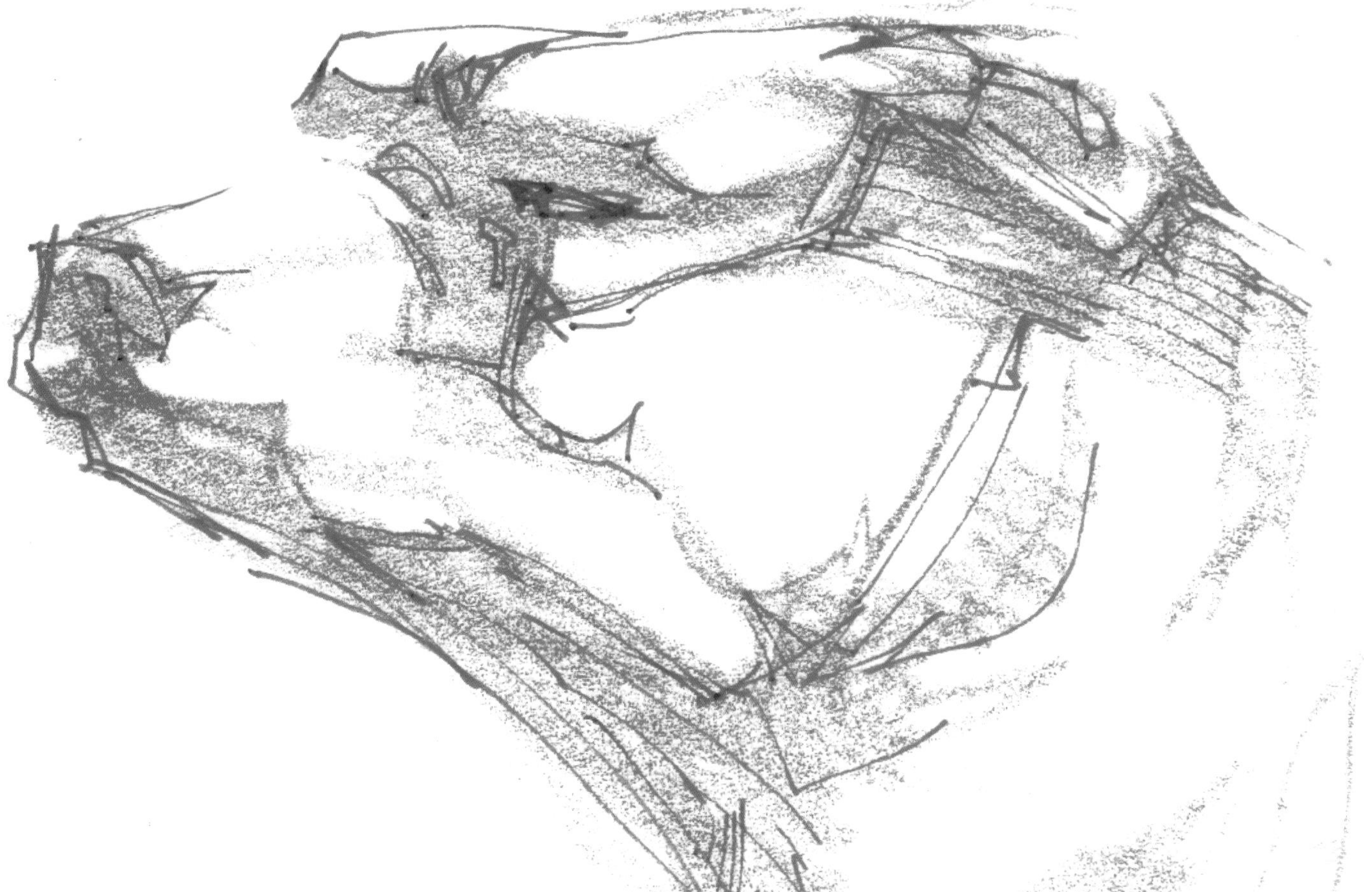

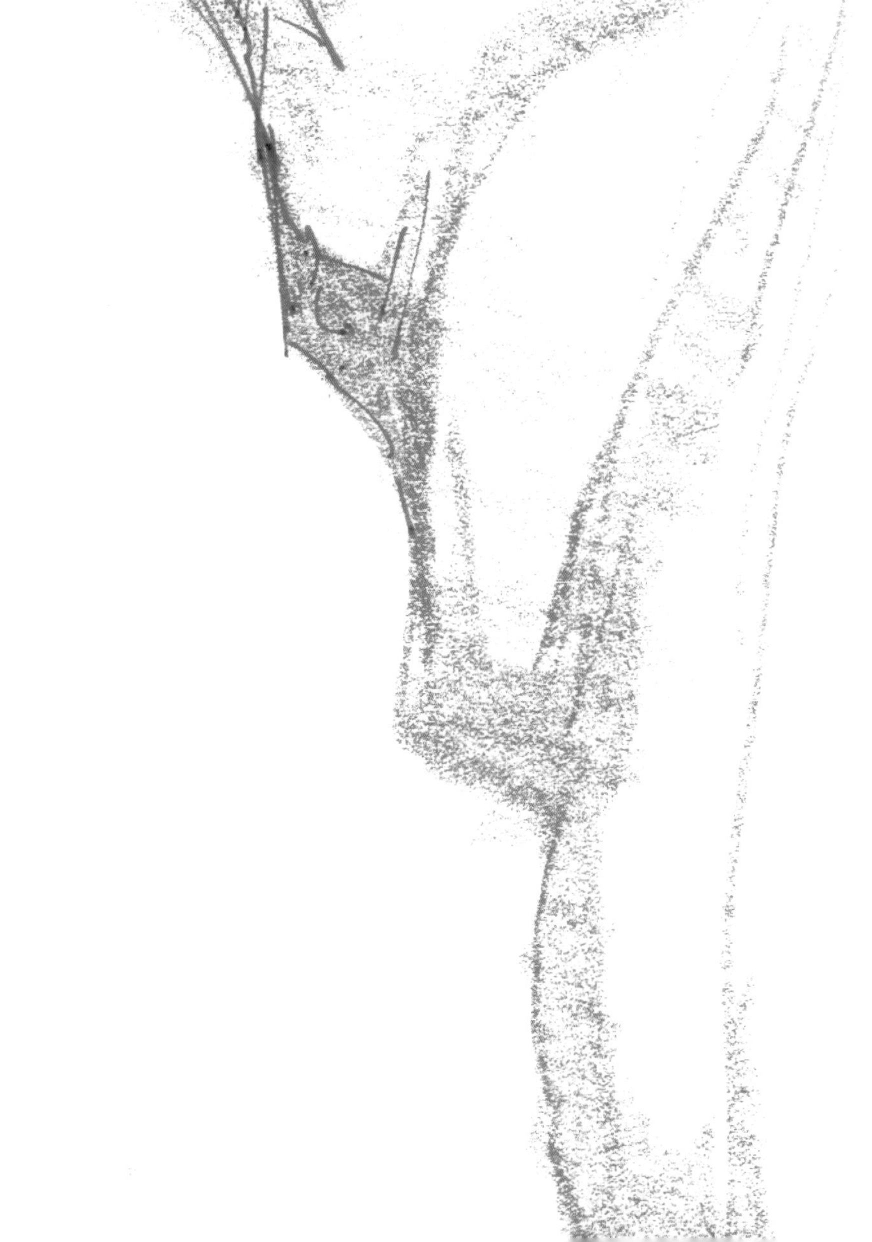

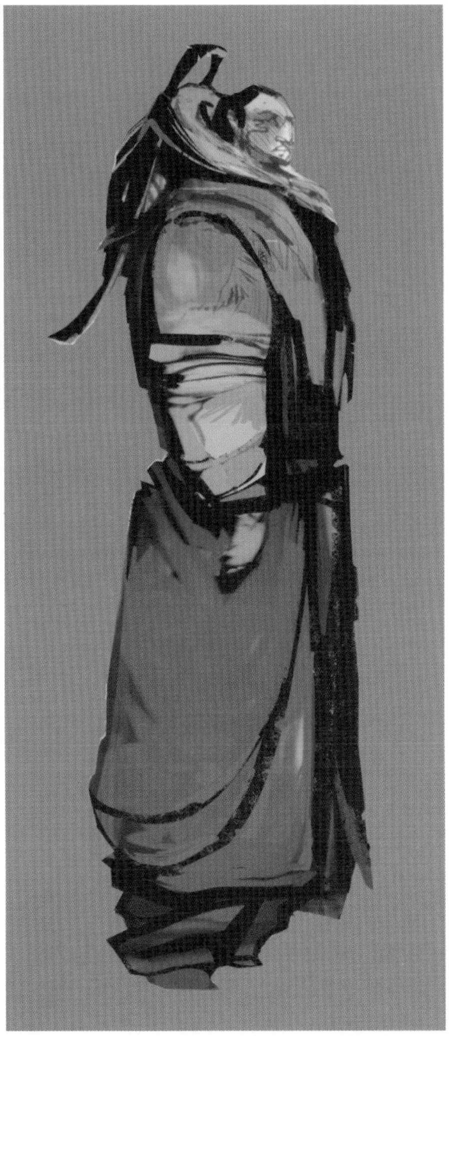

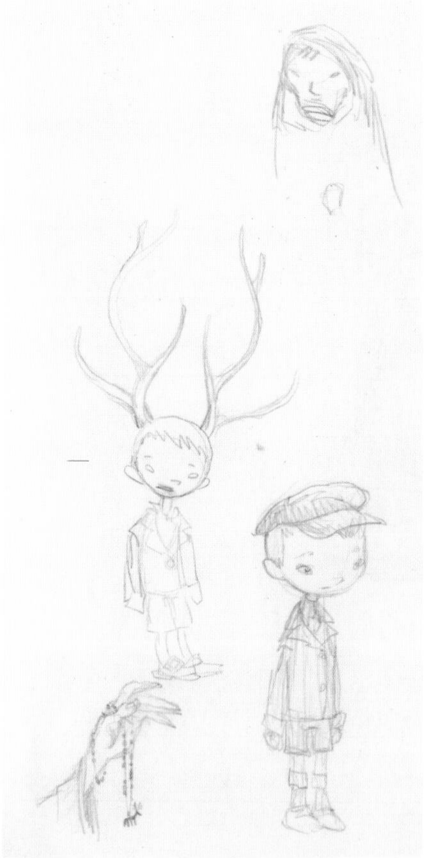

JAKE PARKER

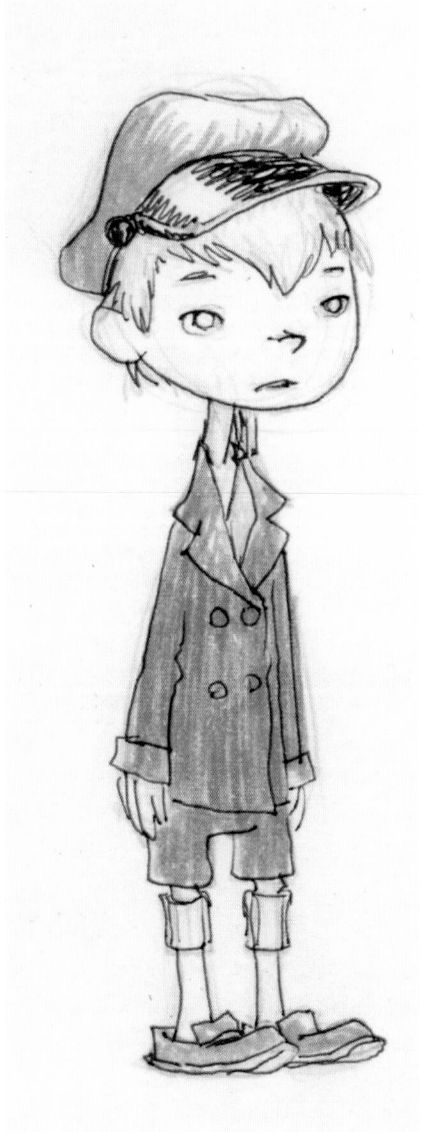

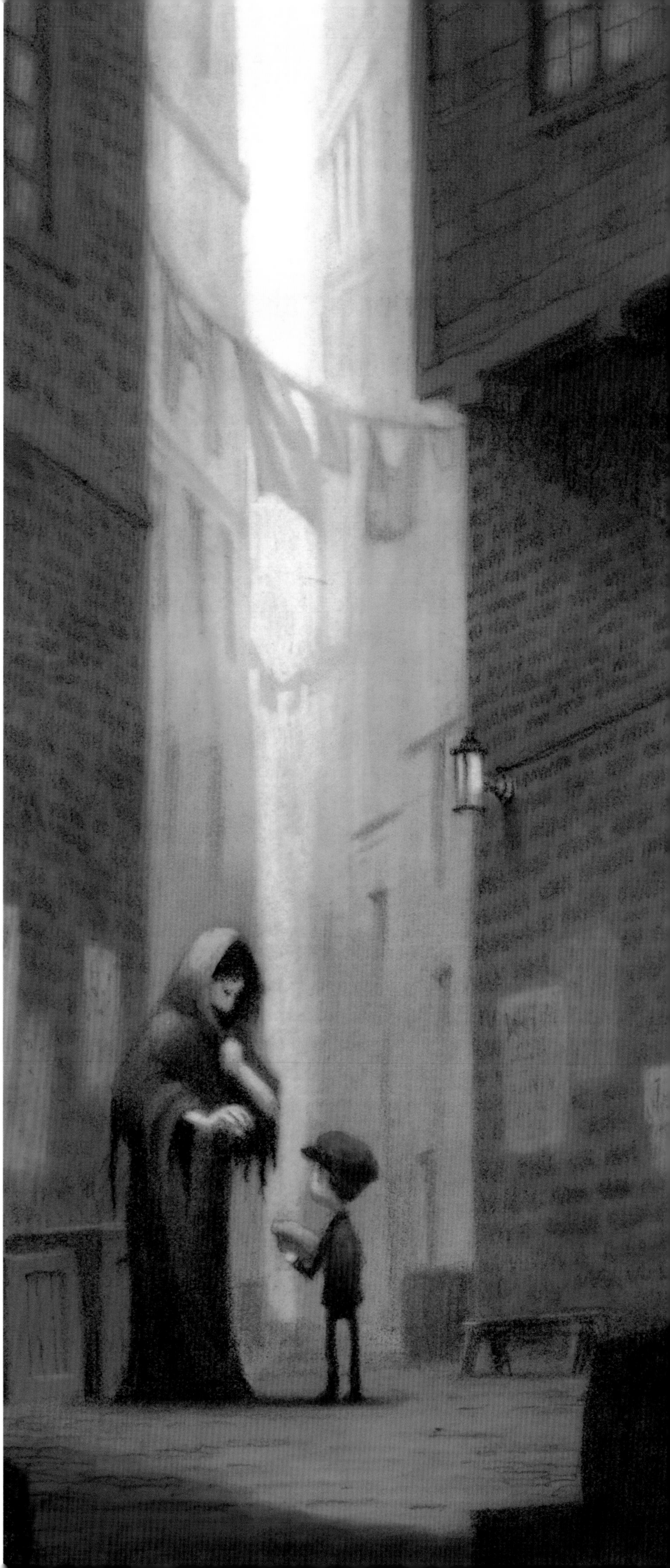

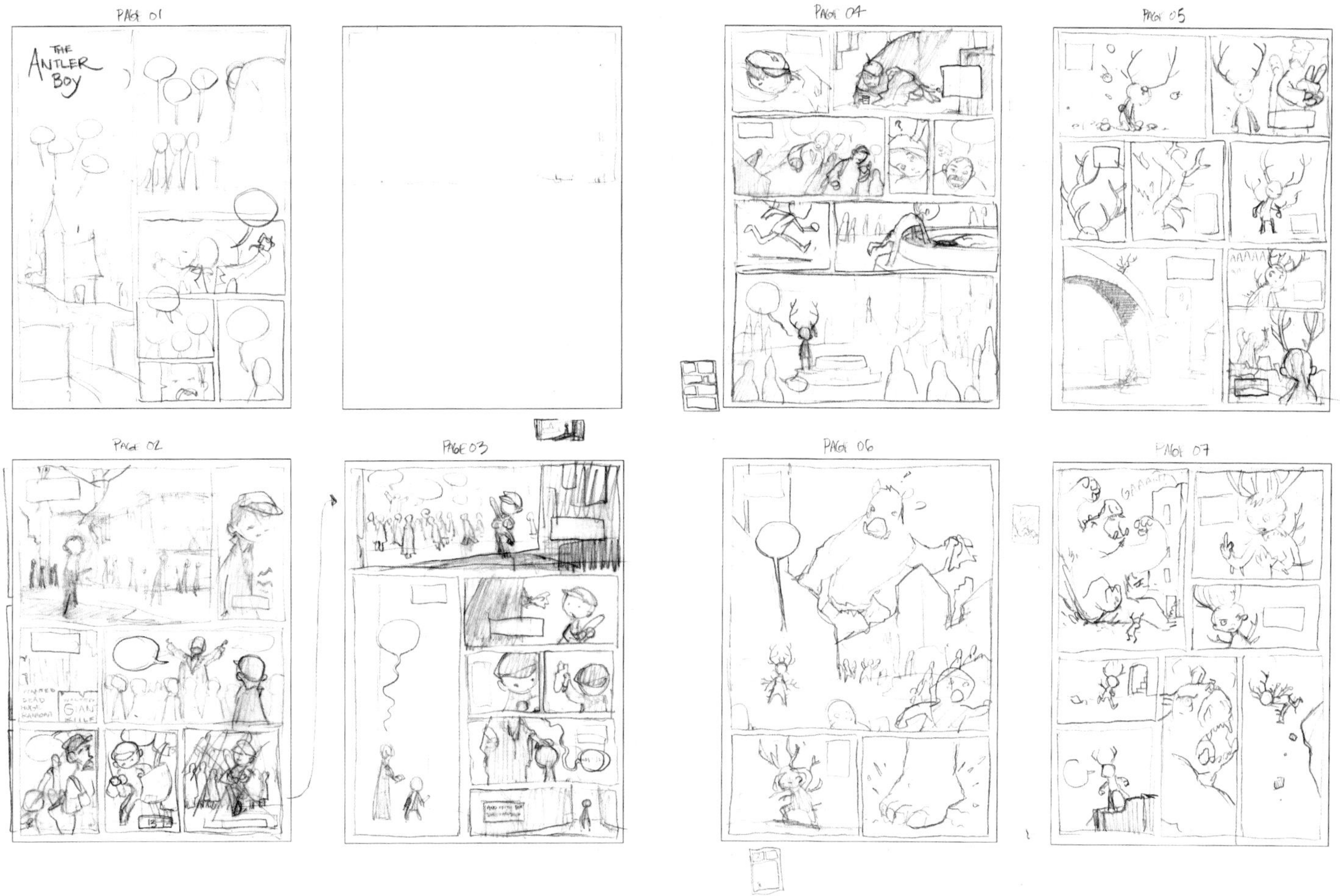
PAGE 01
THE ANTLER BOY
PAGE 04
PAGE 05
PAGE 02
PAGE 03
PAGE 06
PAGE 07

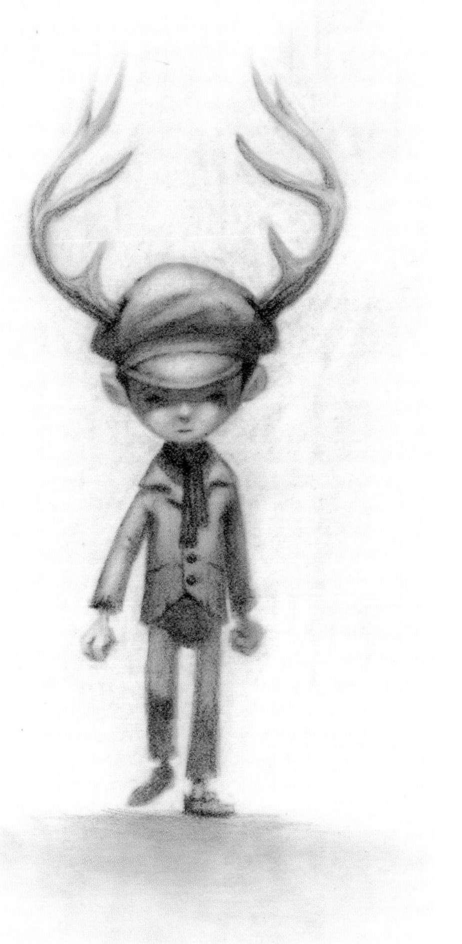

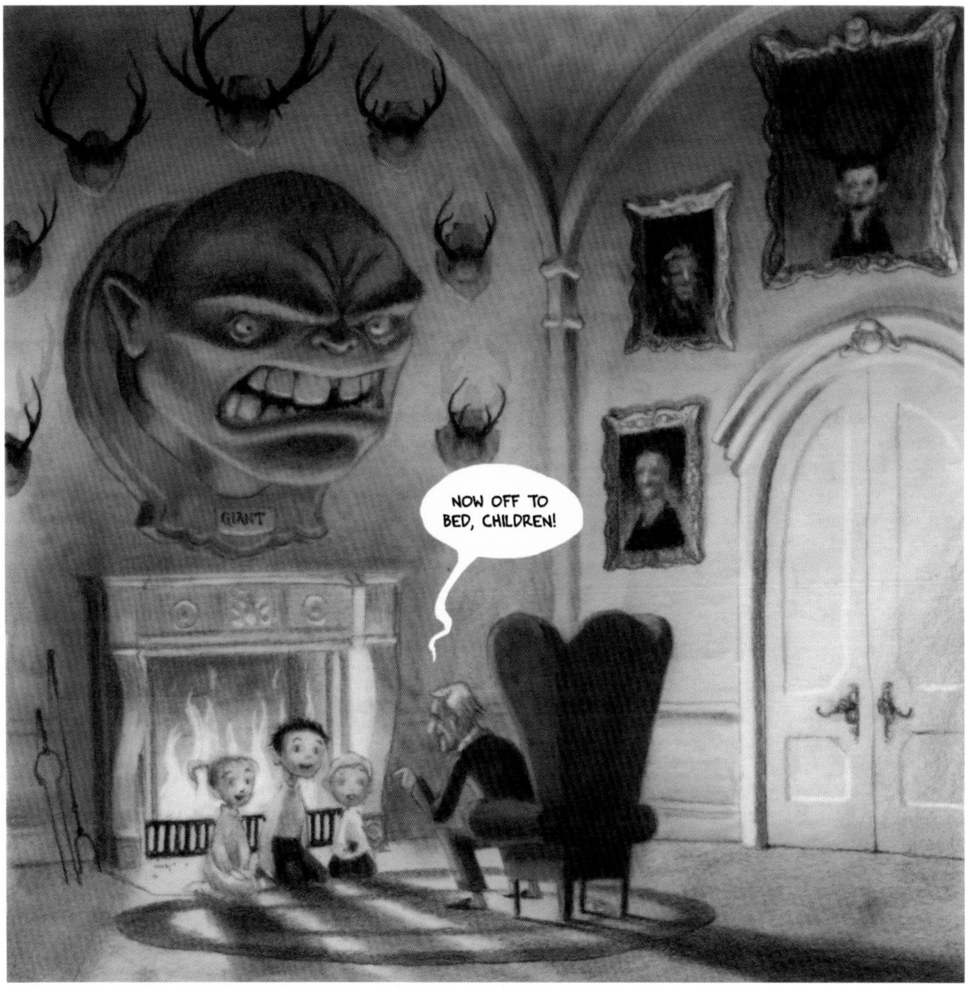
GIANT
NOW OFF TO BED, CHILDREN!

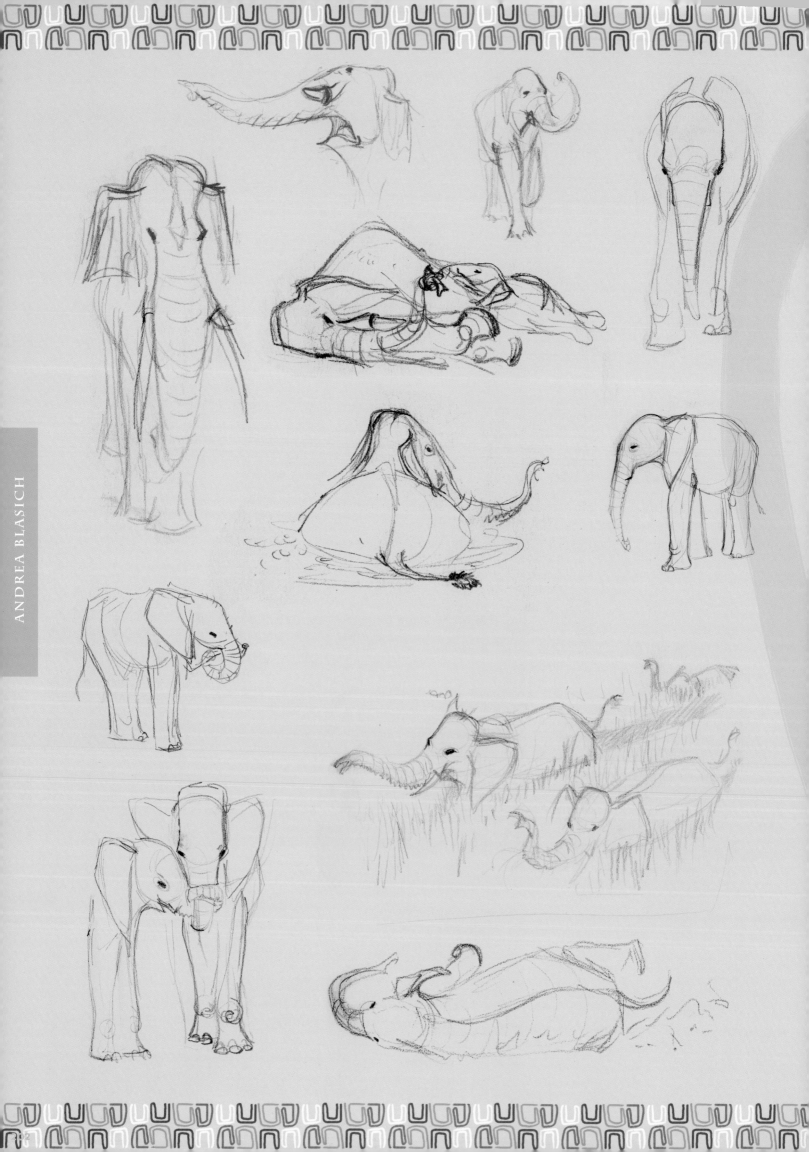

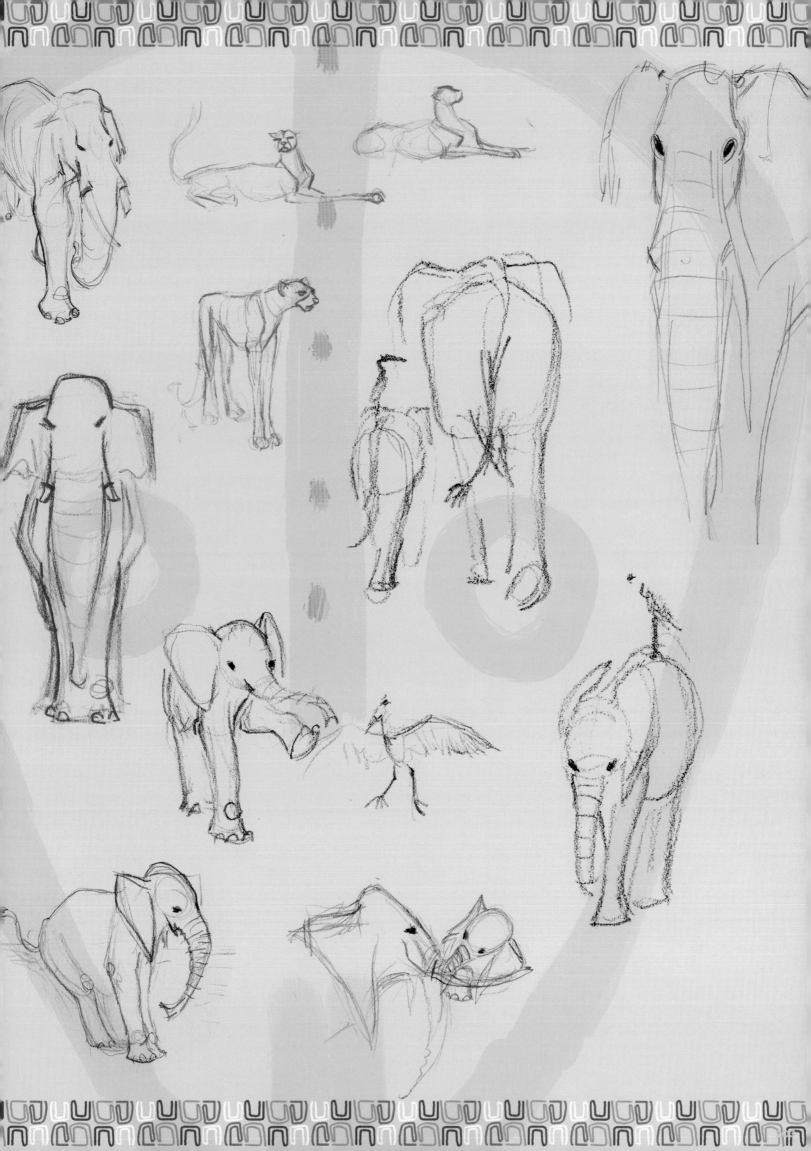

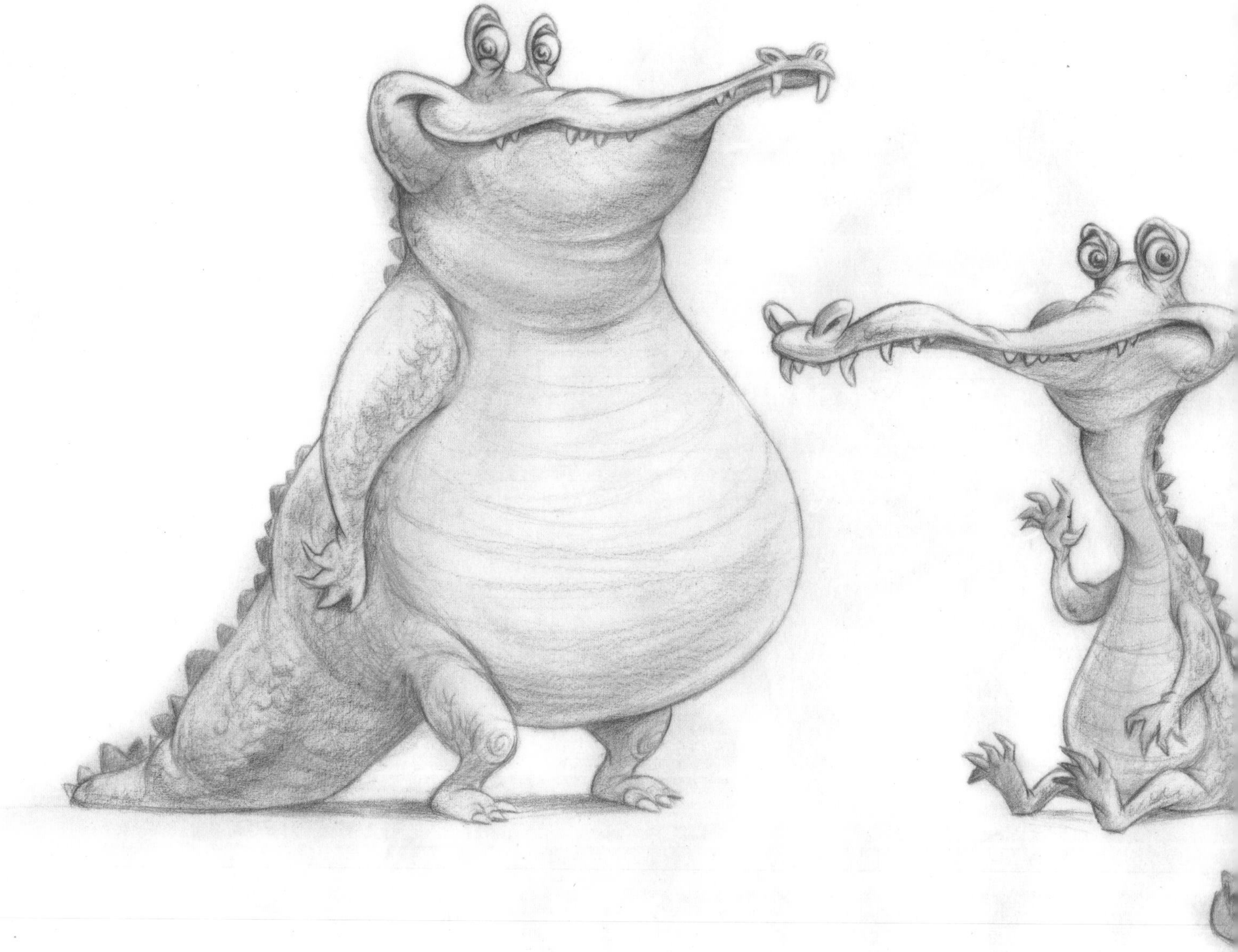

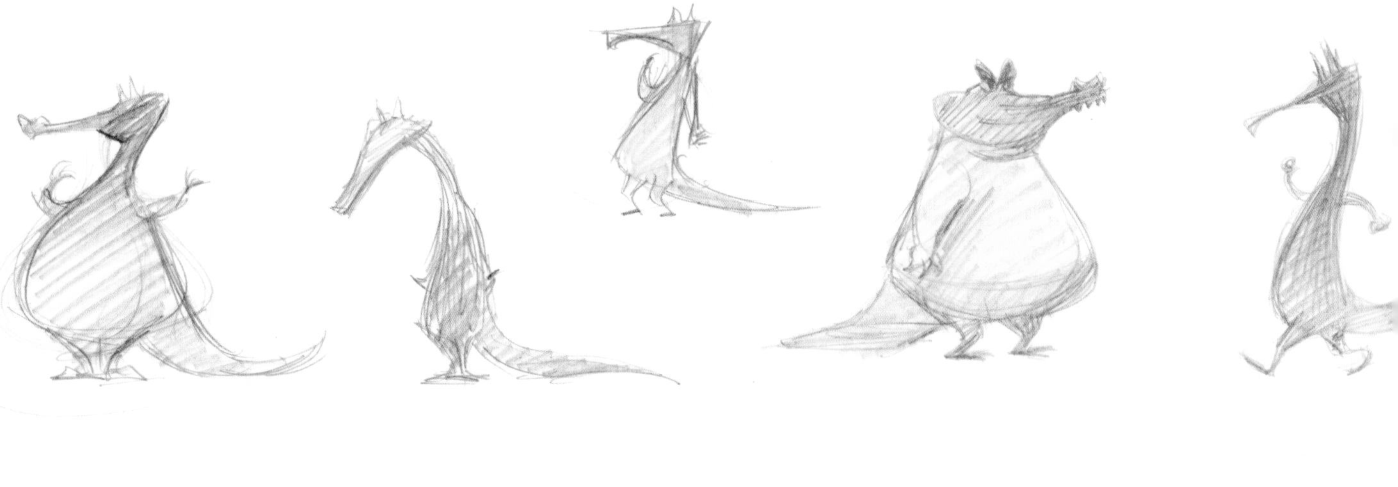

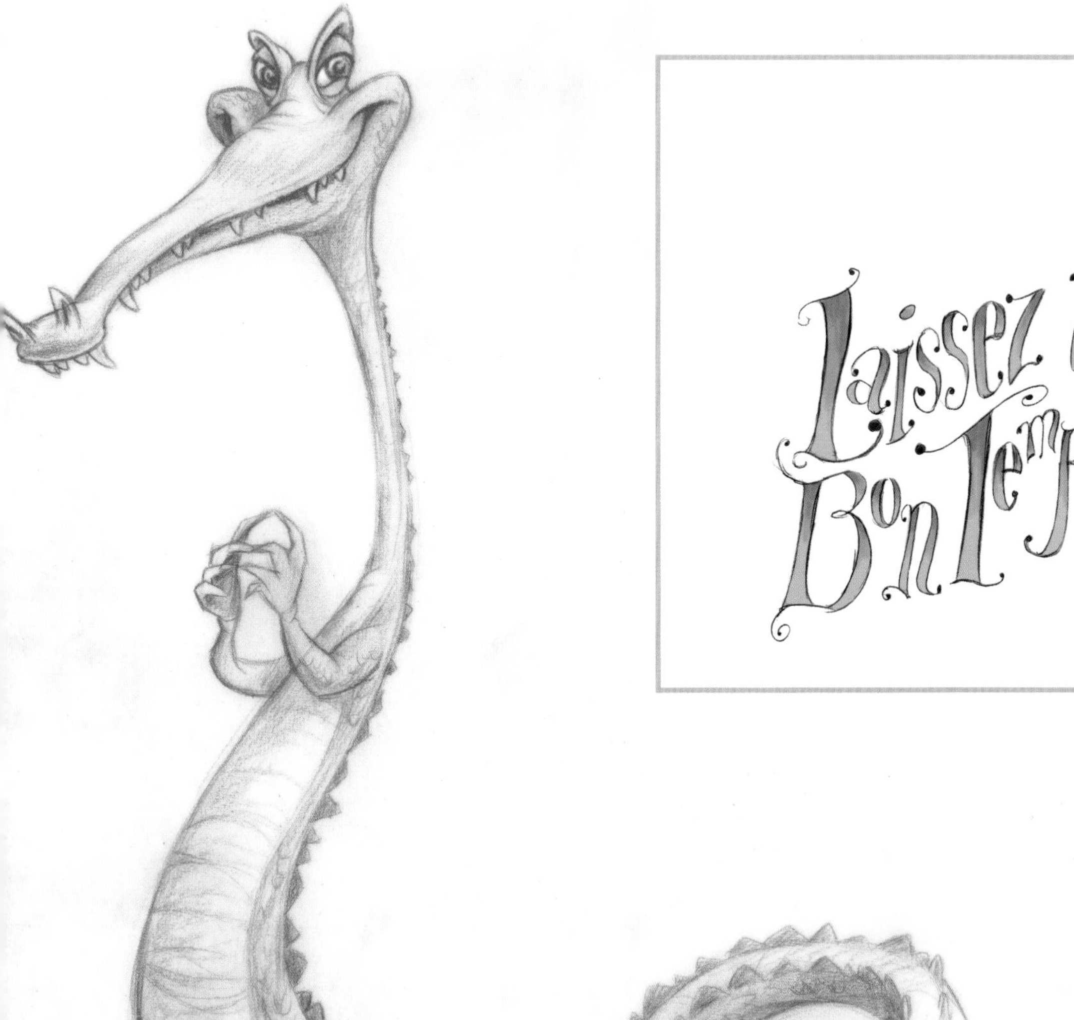

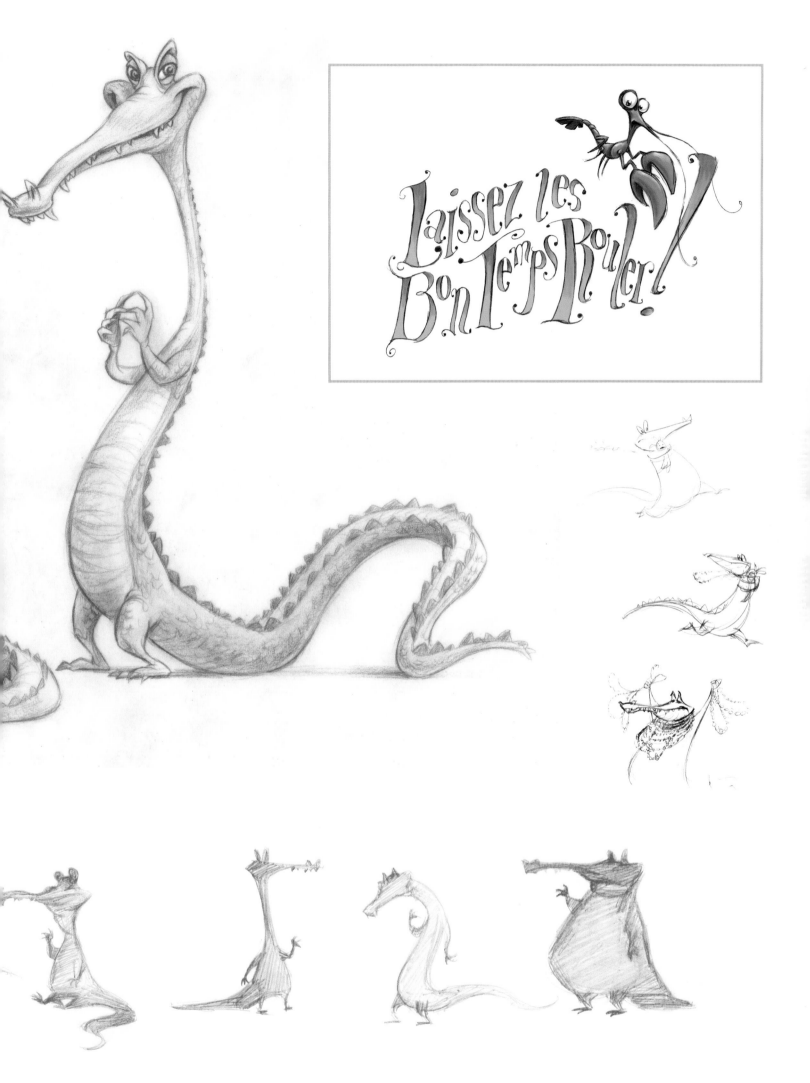

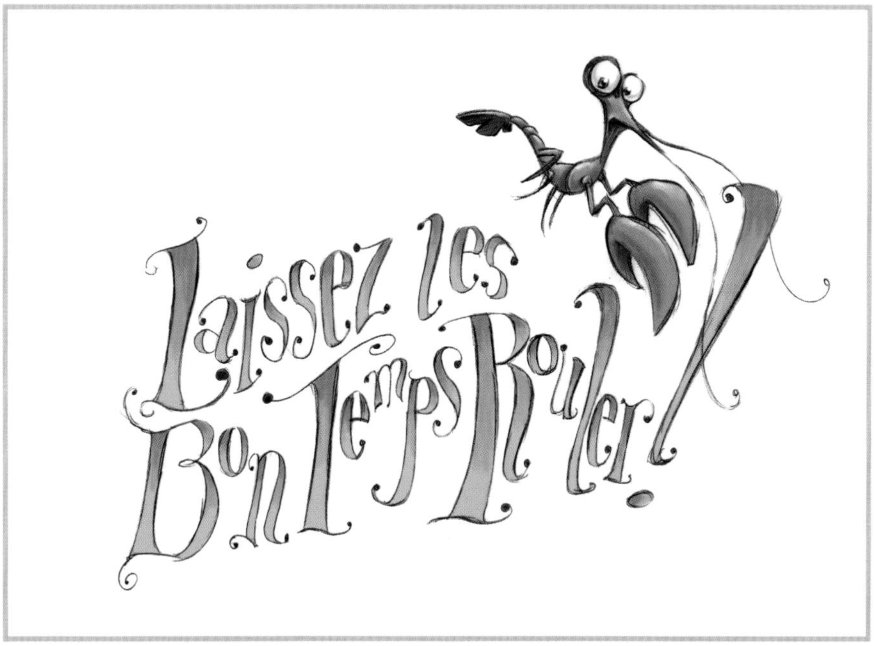
Laissez les
Bon Temps Rouler!

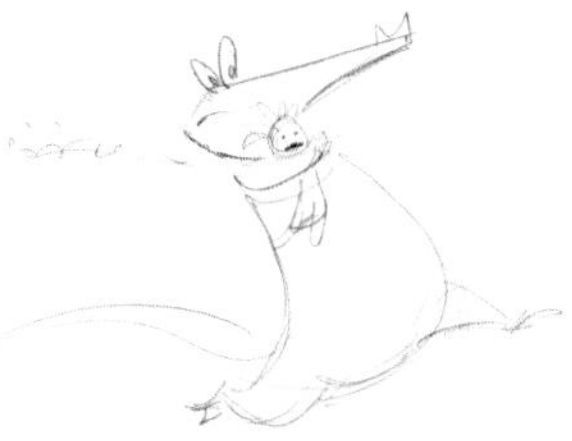

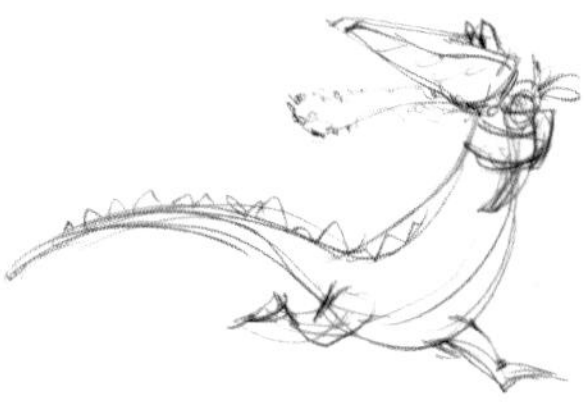

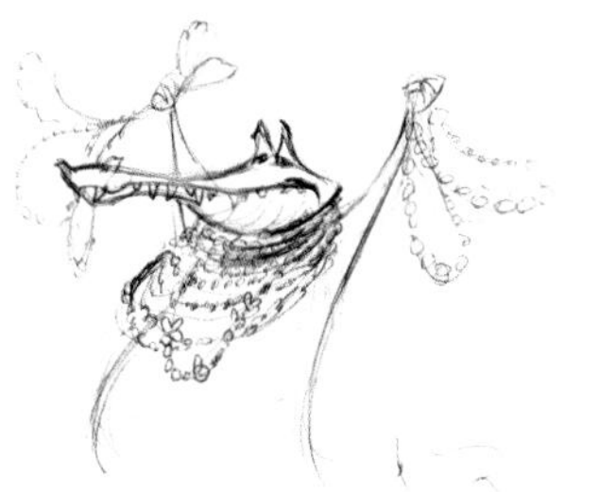

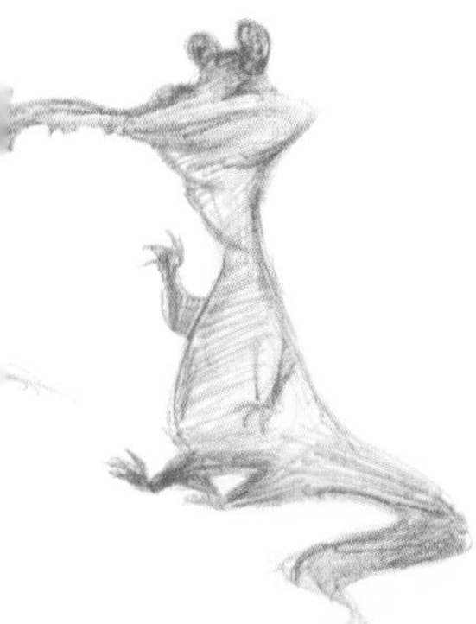

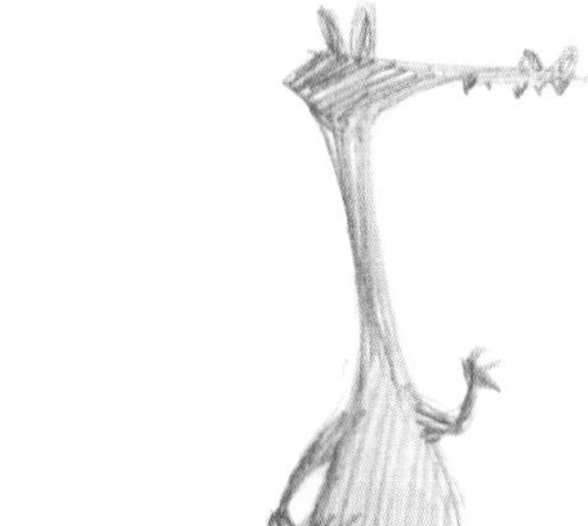

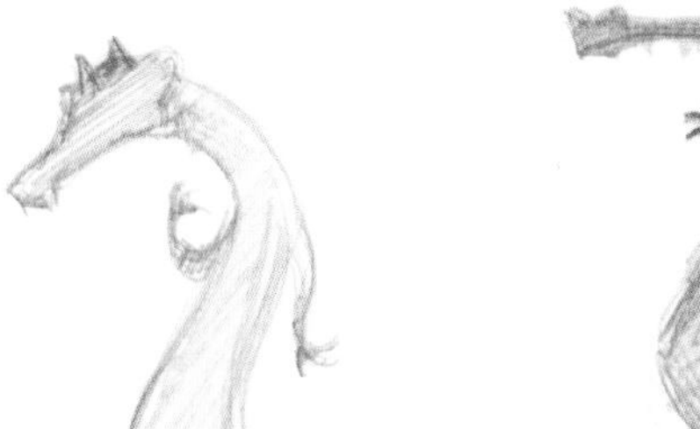

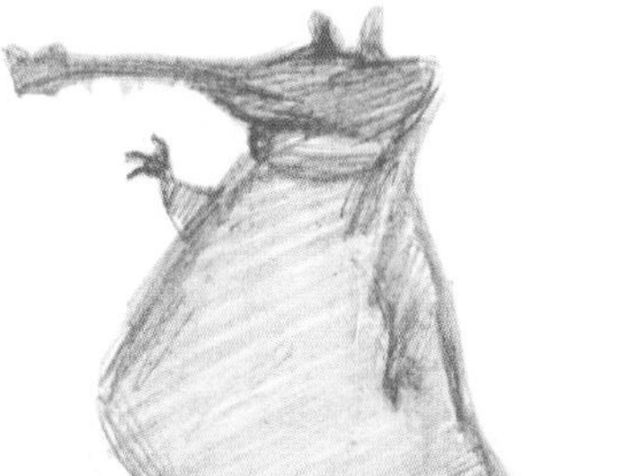

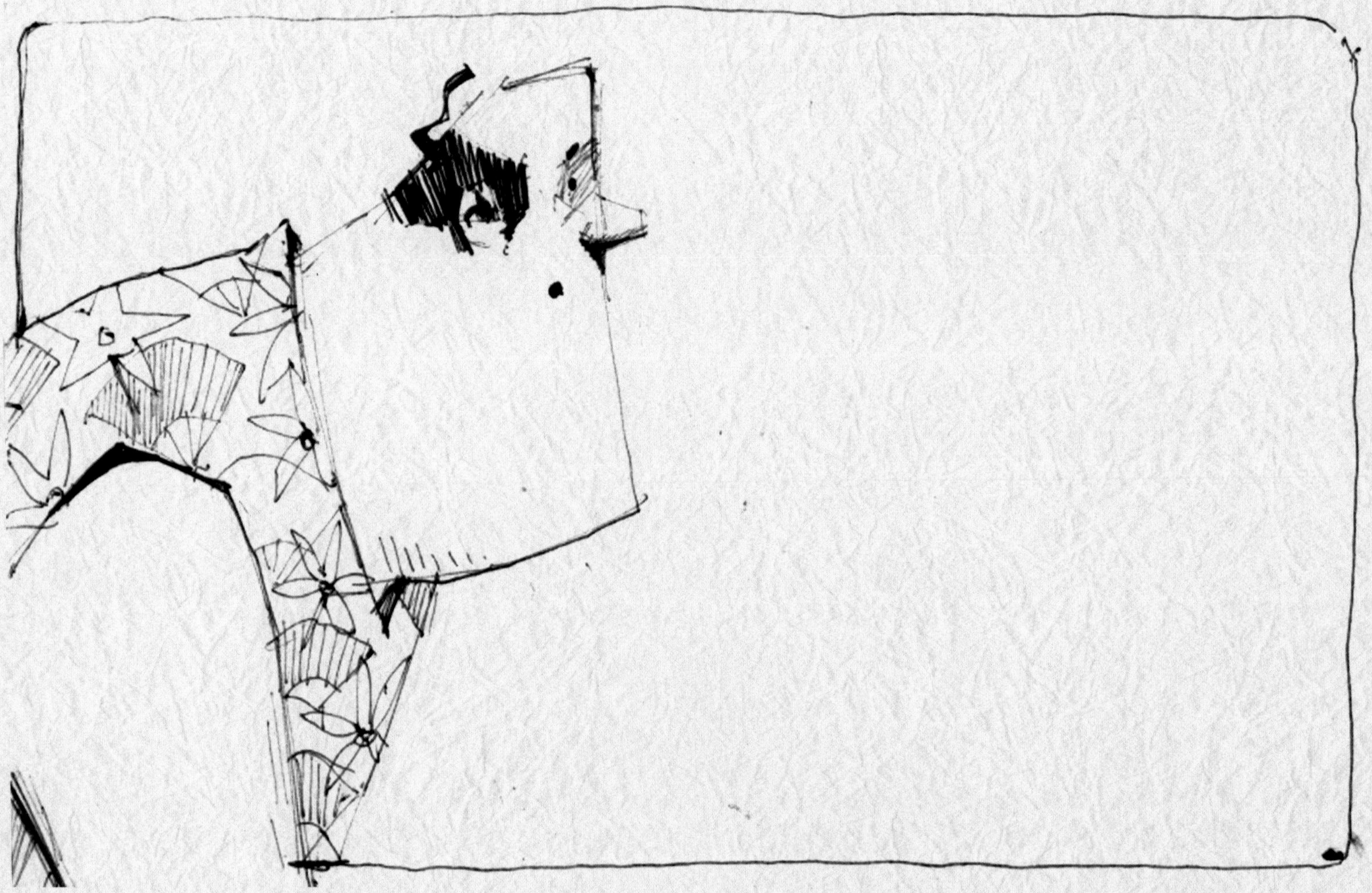

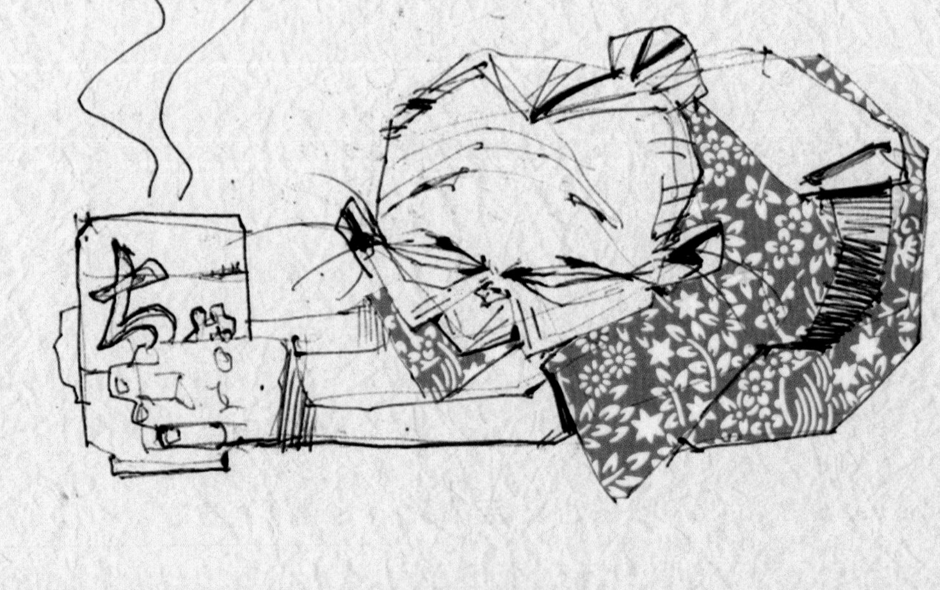
茶ぁいる・けぇ?

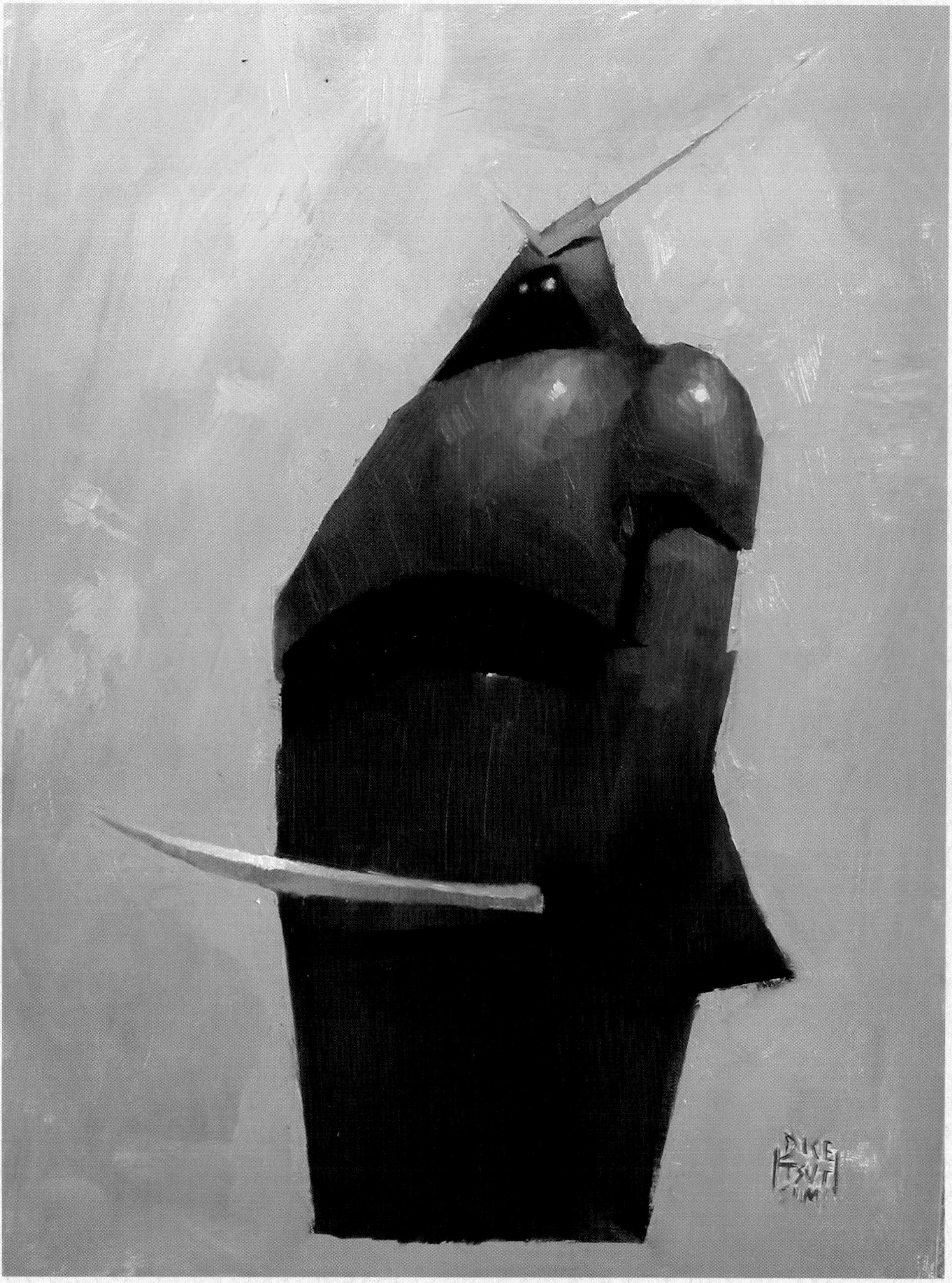

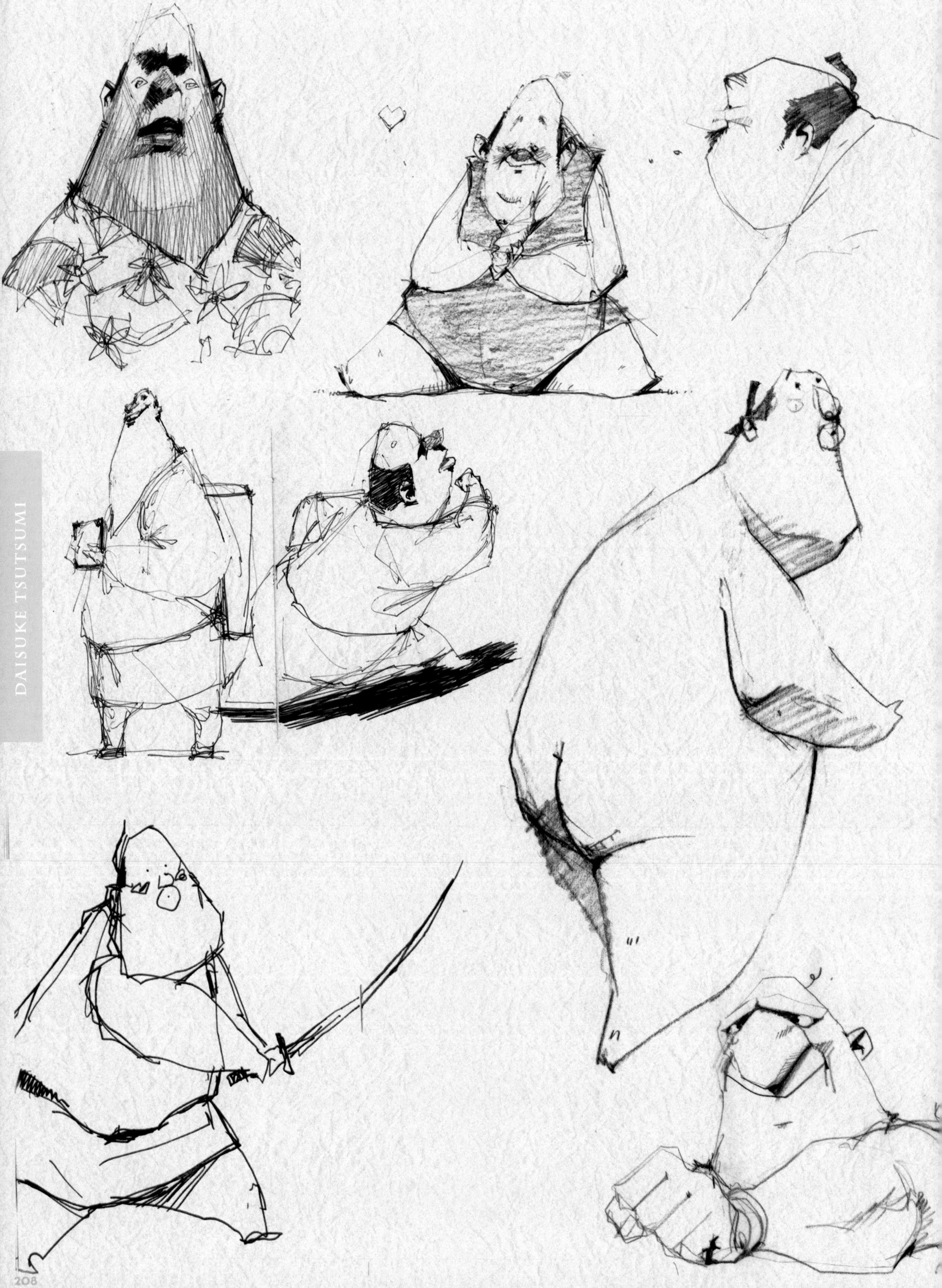

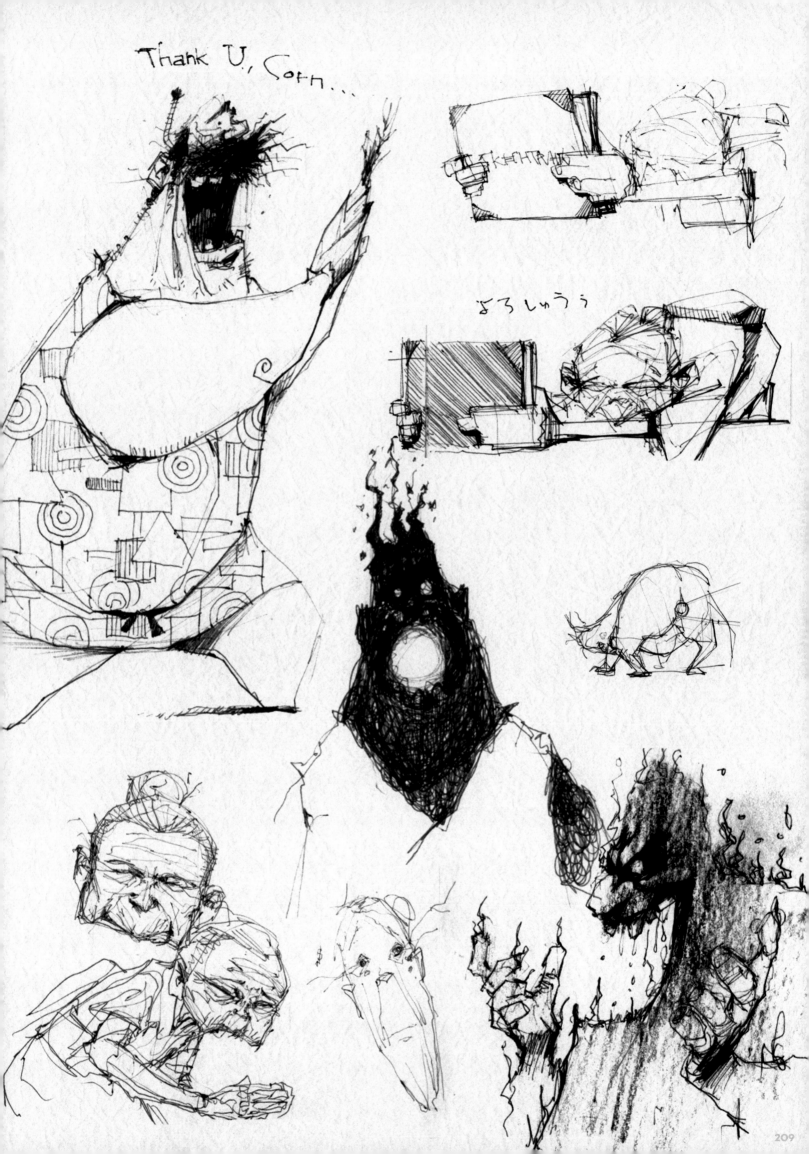

Thank U, Corn...

KEHTRAN

よろしゅうう

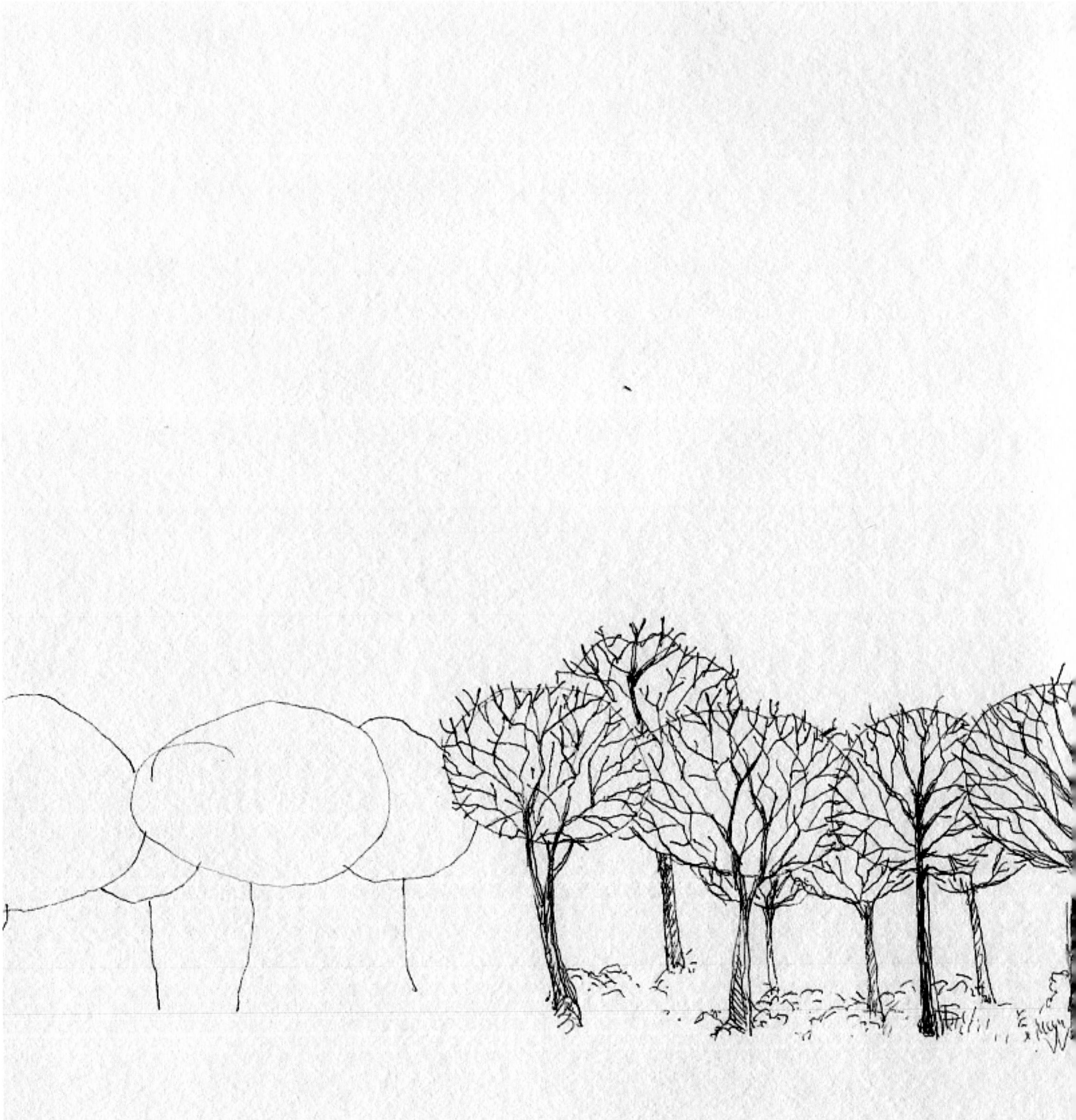

VINCENT NGUYEN

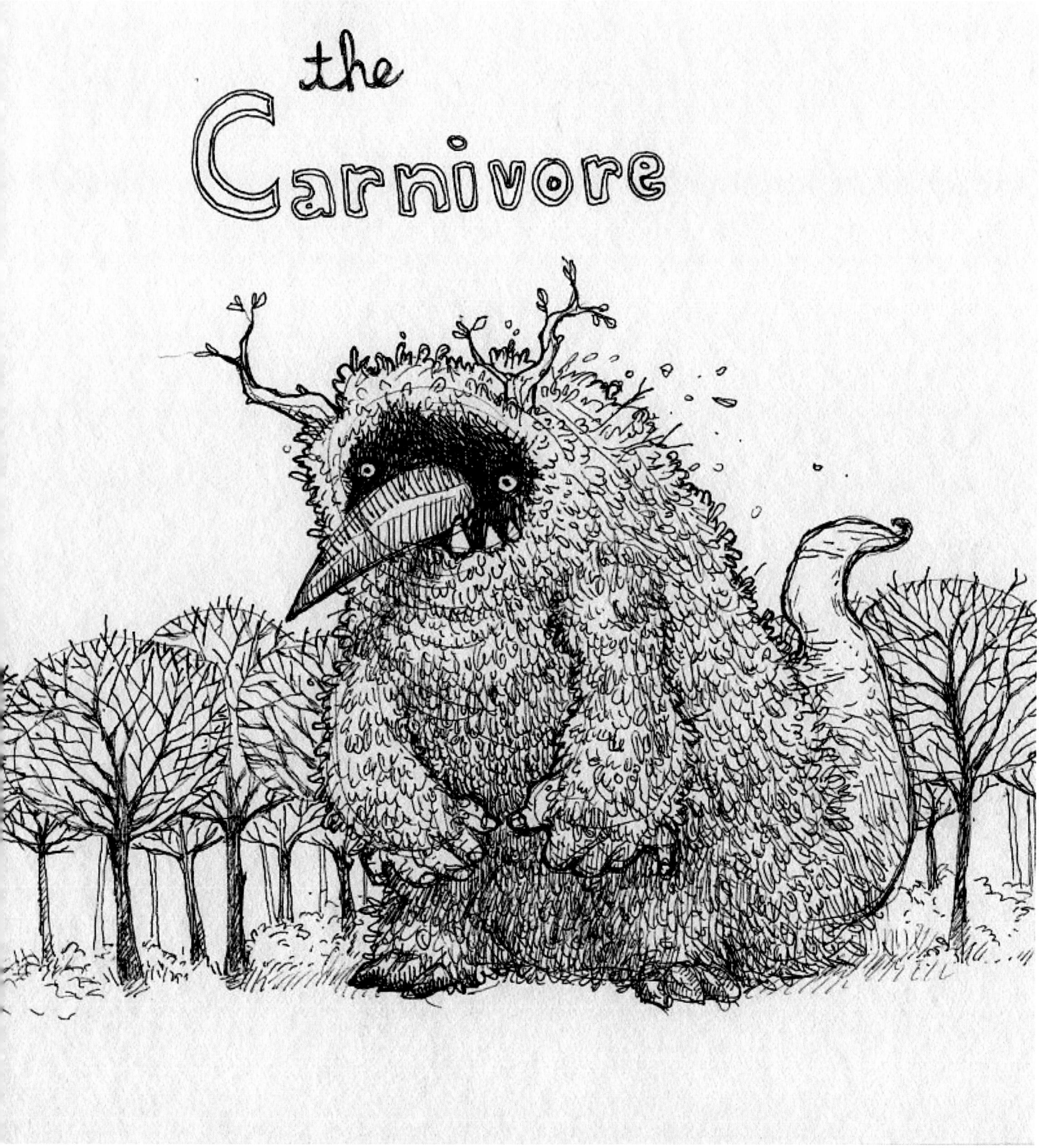
the
Carnivore

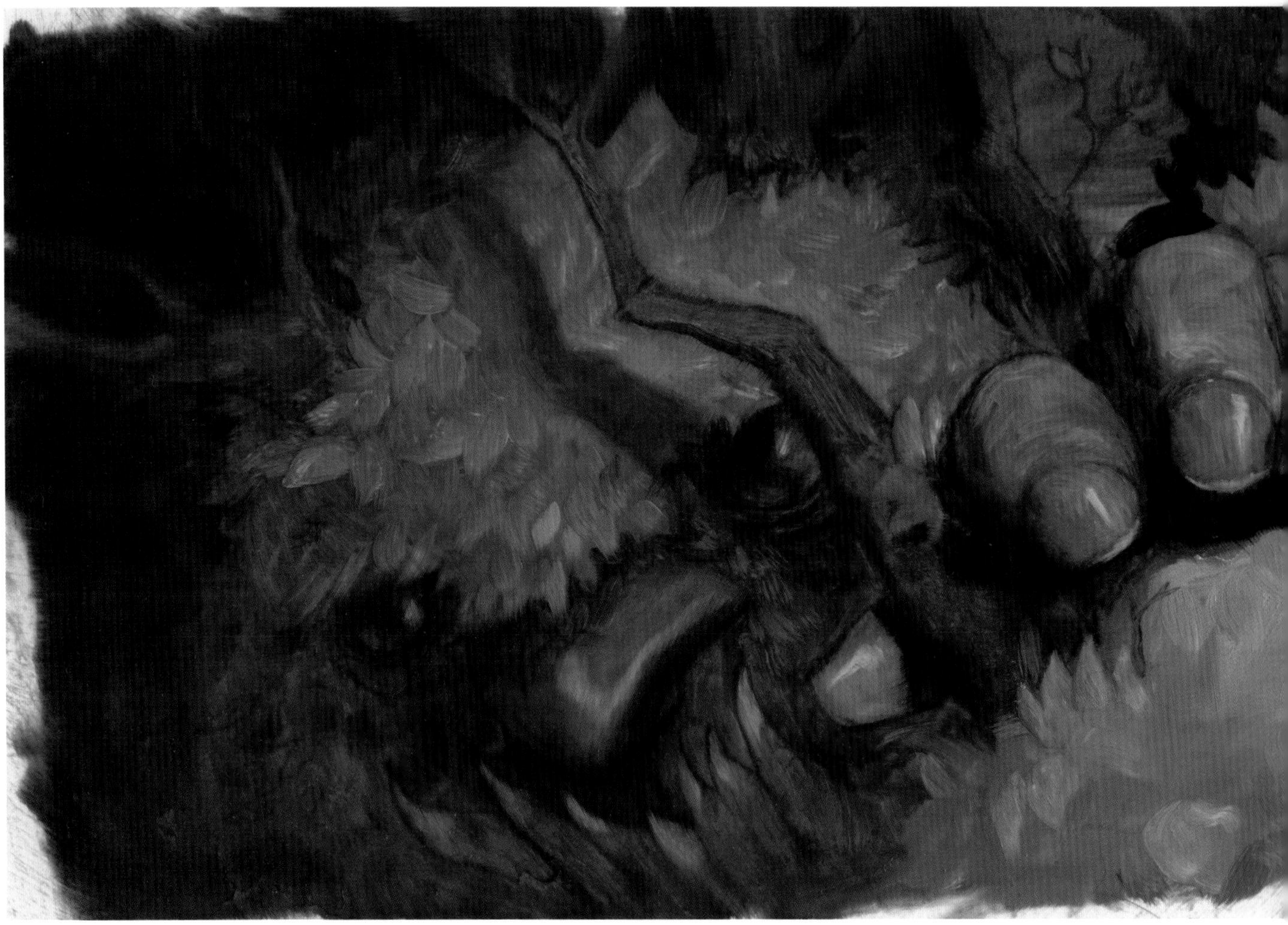

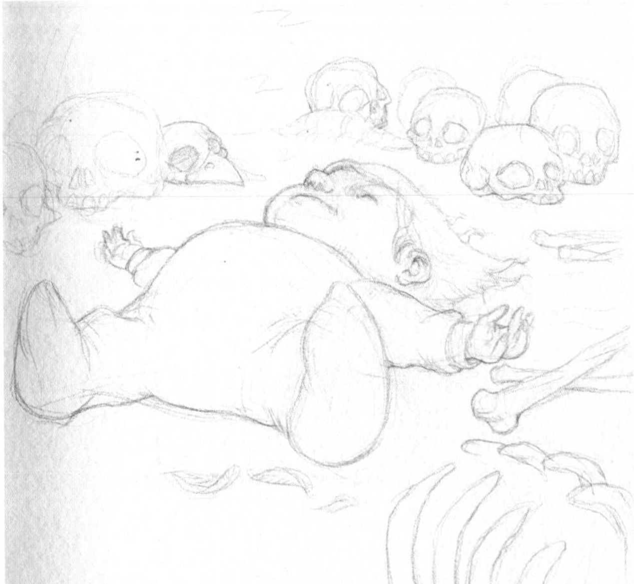

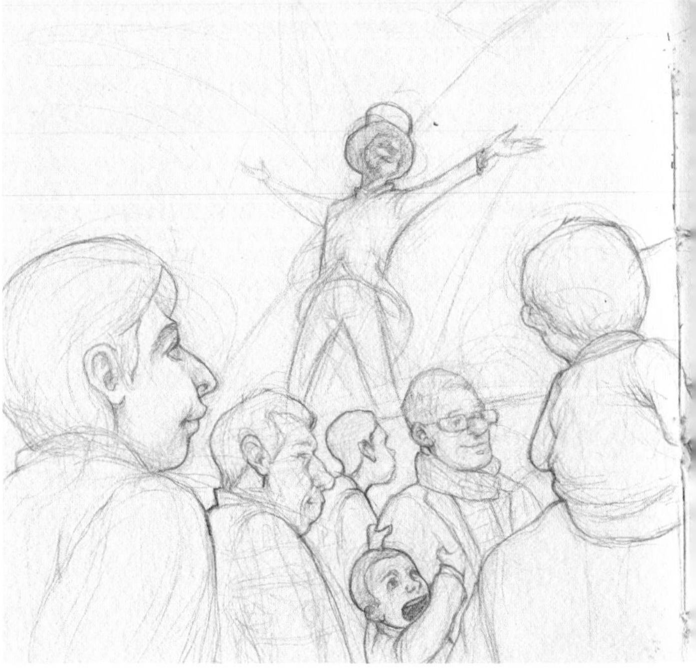

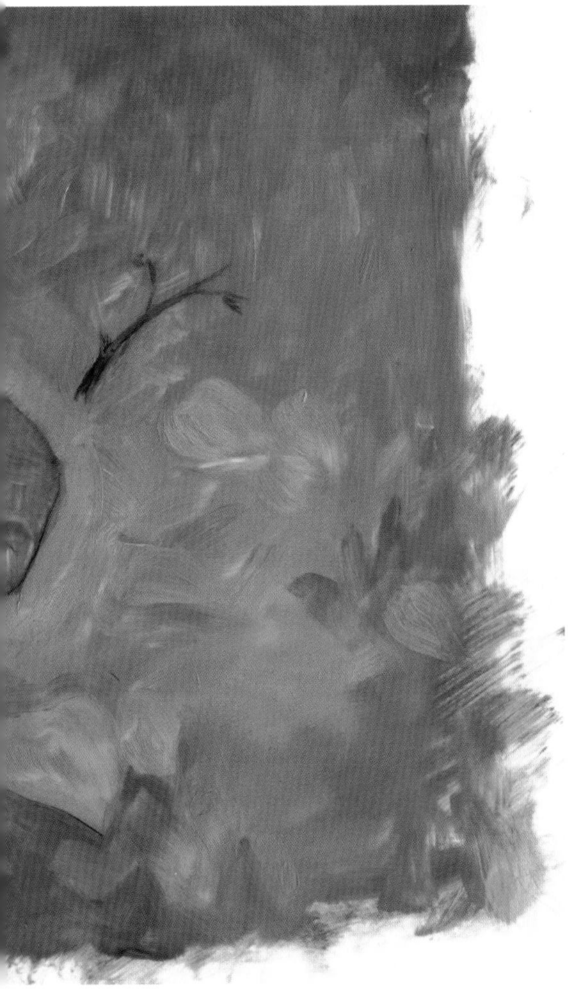

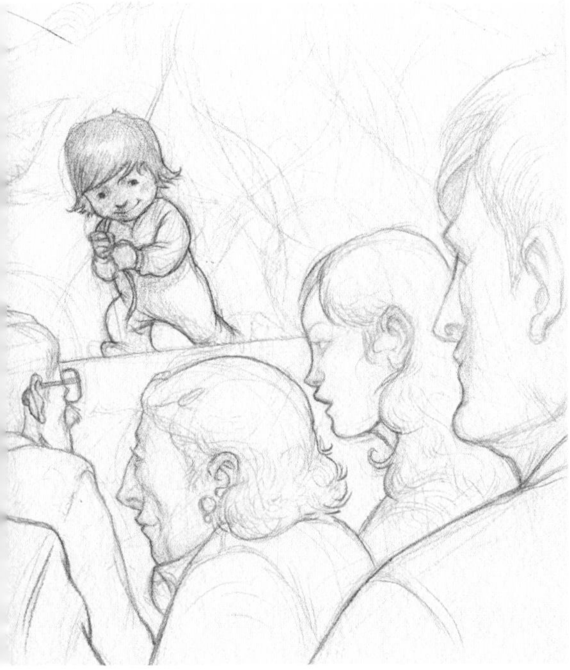

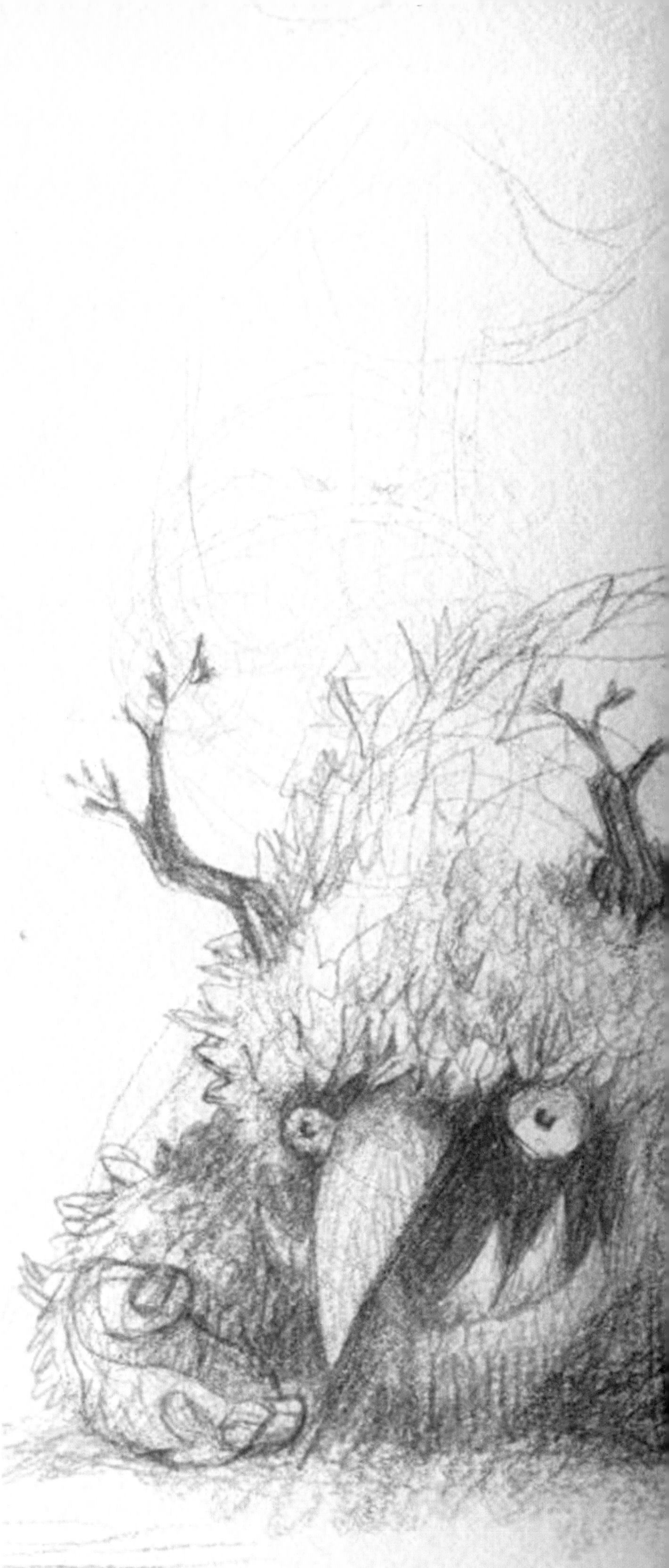

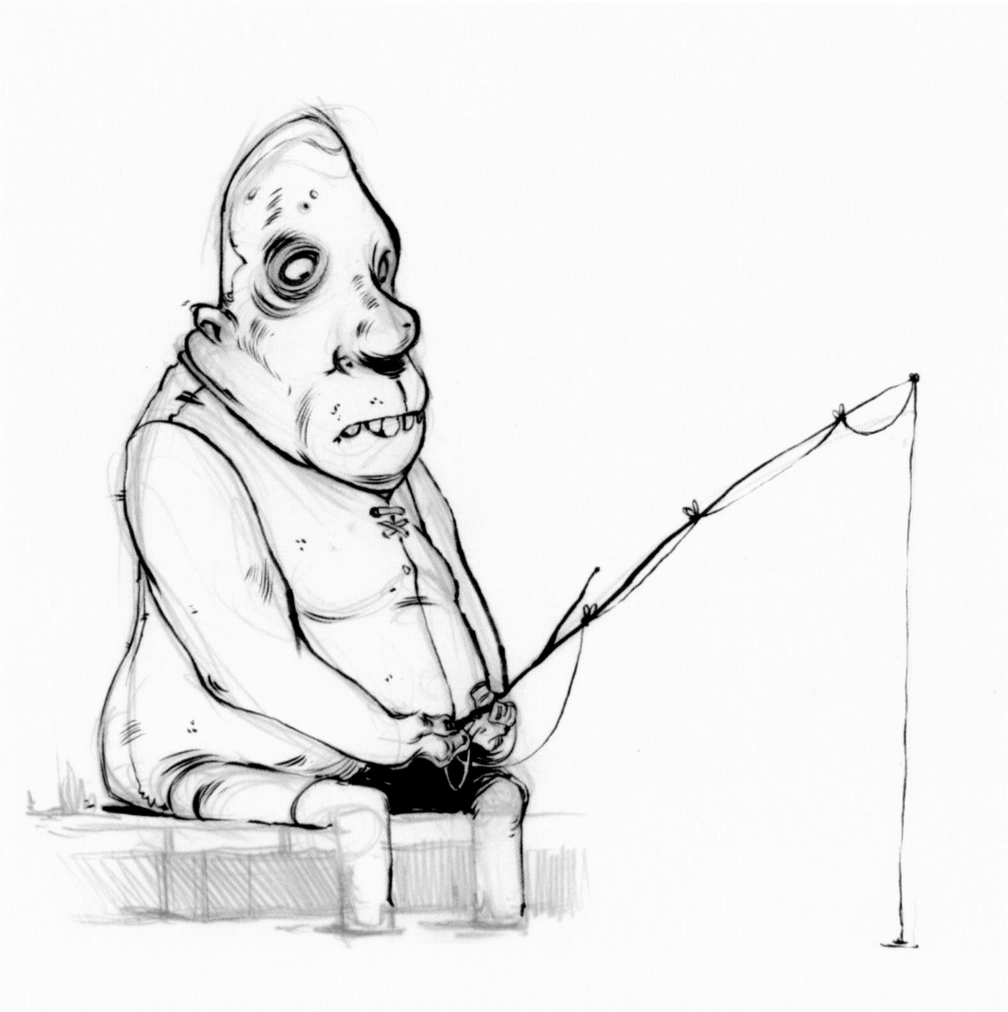

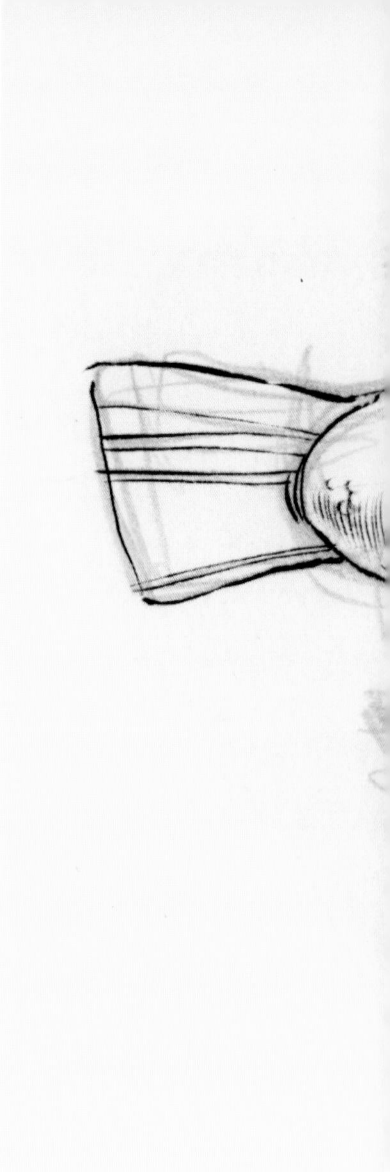

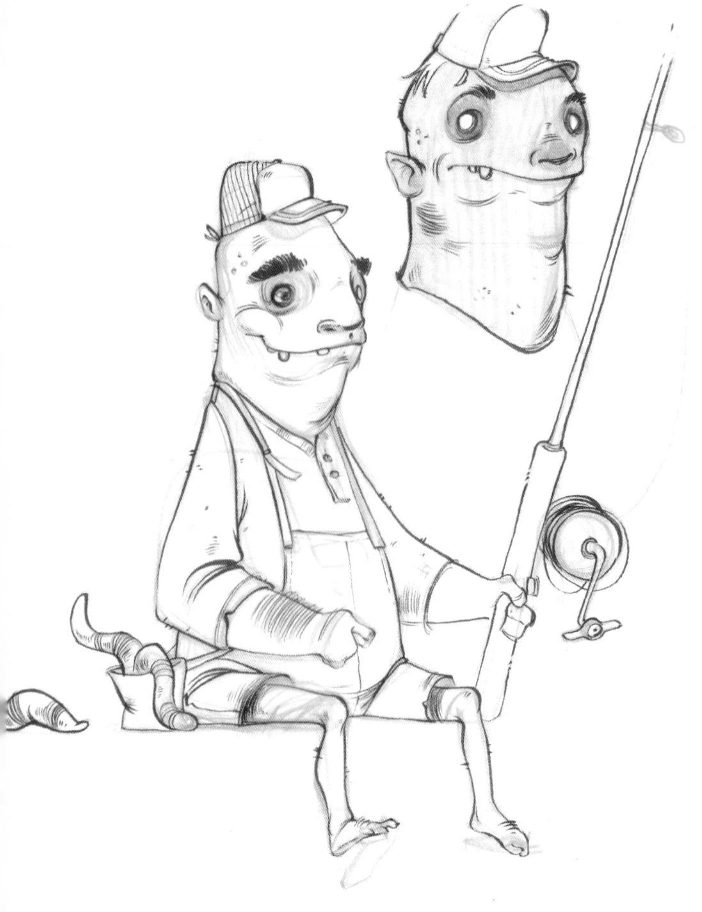

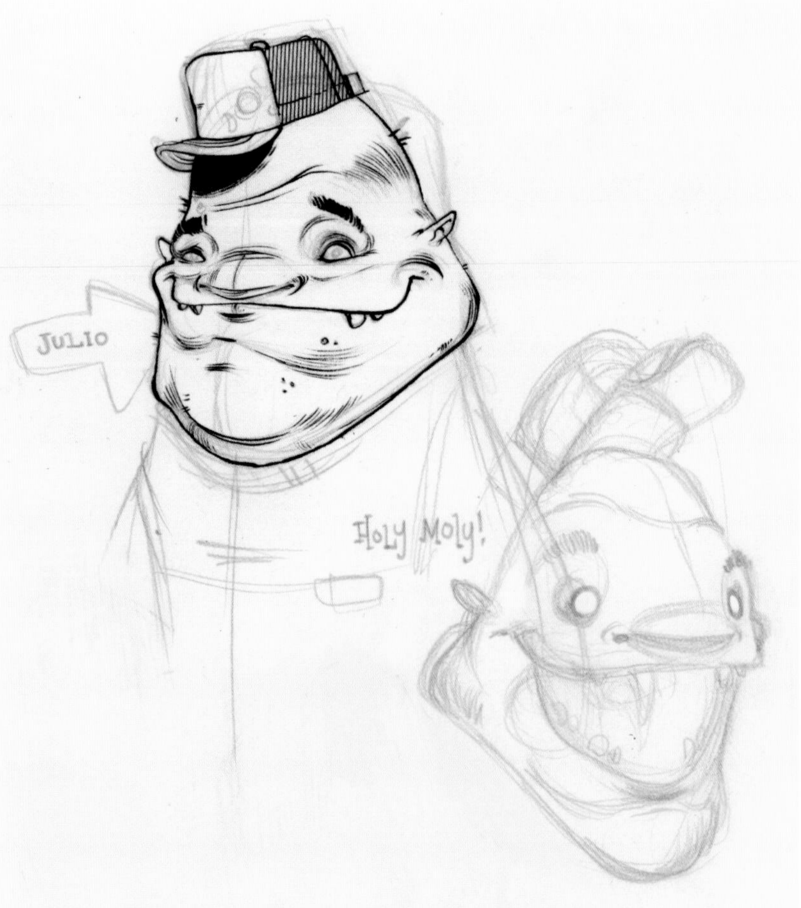
JULIO
Holy Moly!

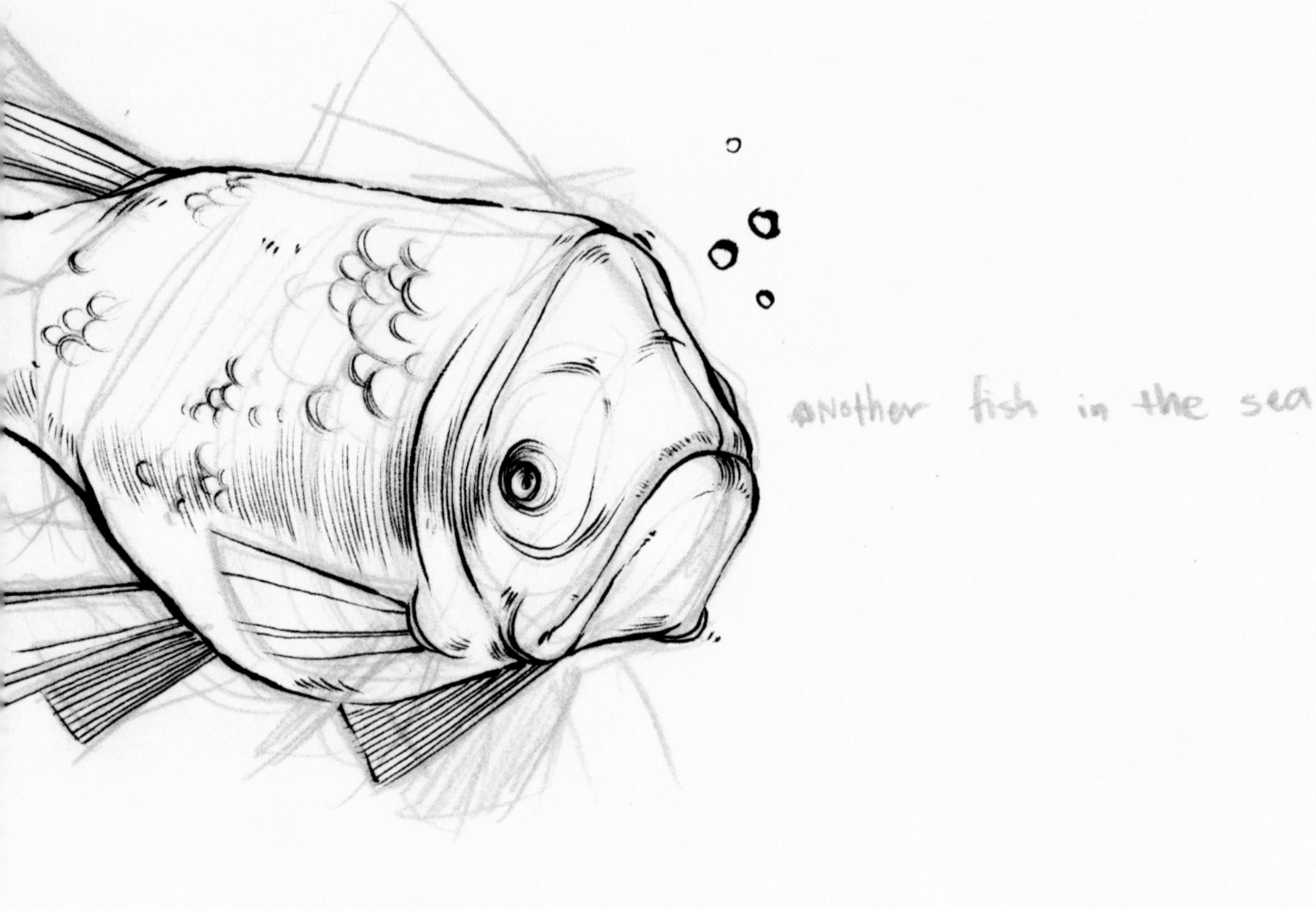
another fish in the sea

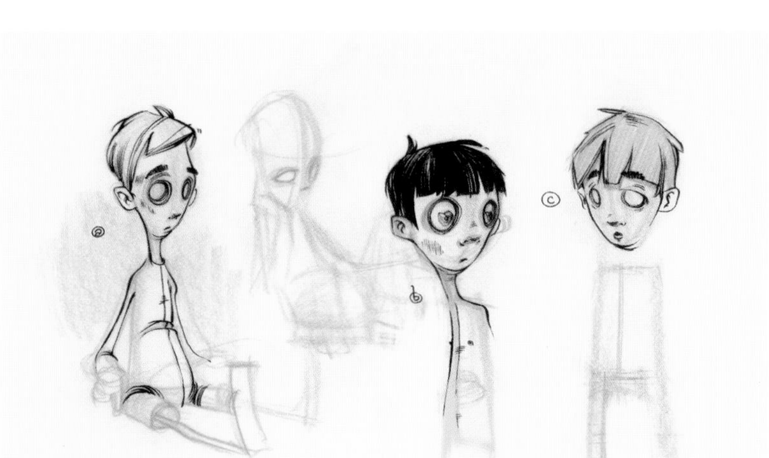

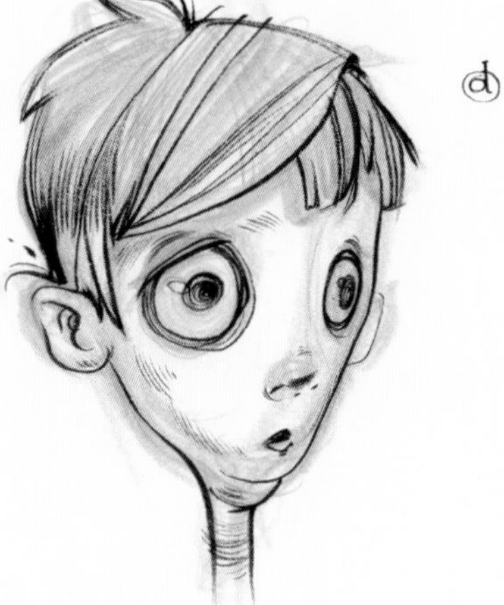

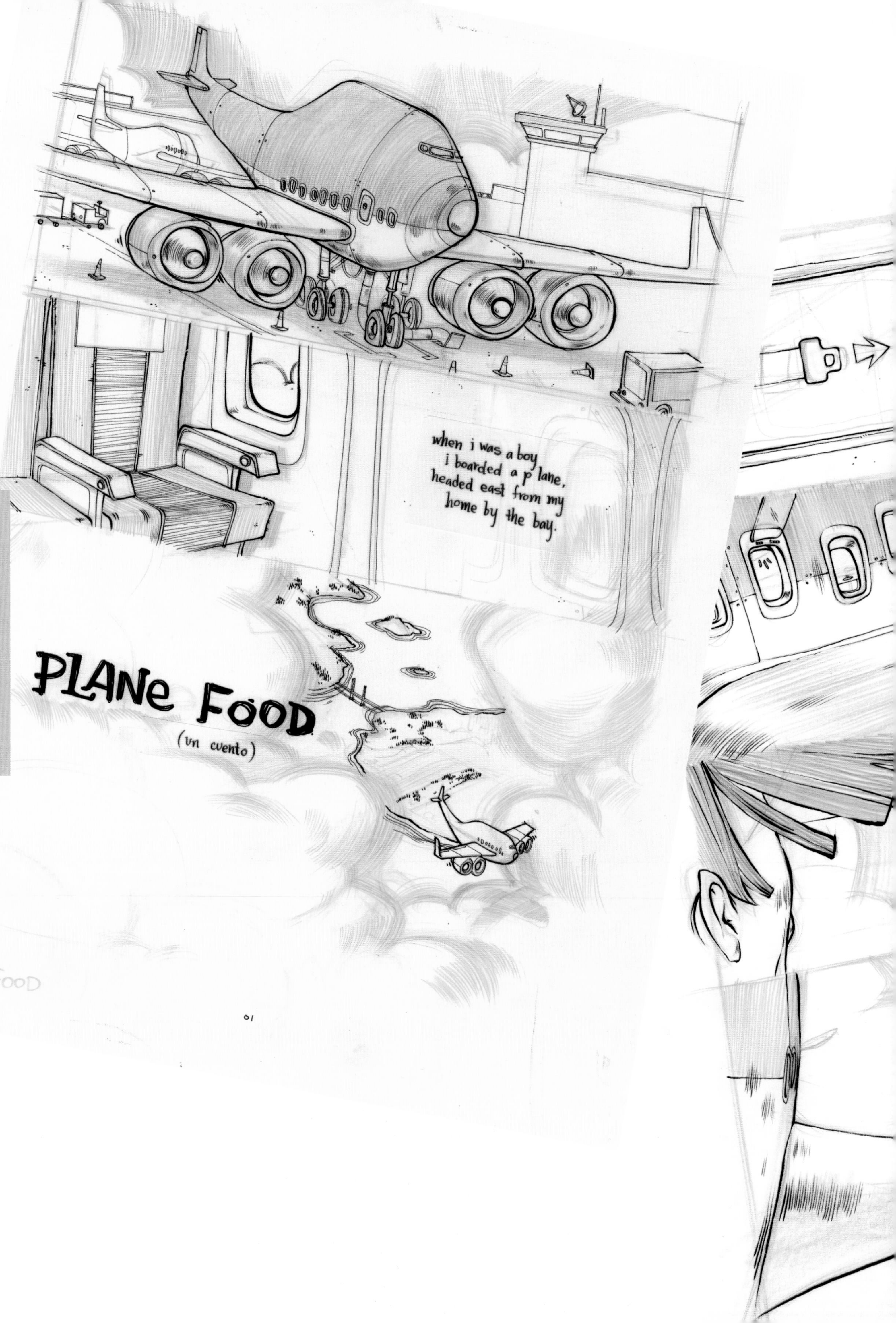

when i was a boy
i boarded a p lane,
headed east from my
home by the bay.
PLANE FOOD
(un cuento)
FOOD
01

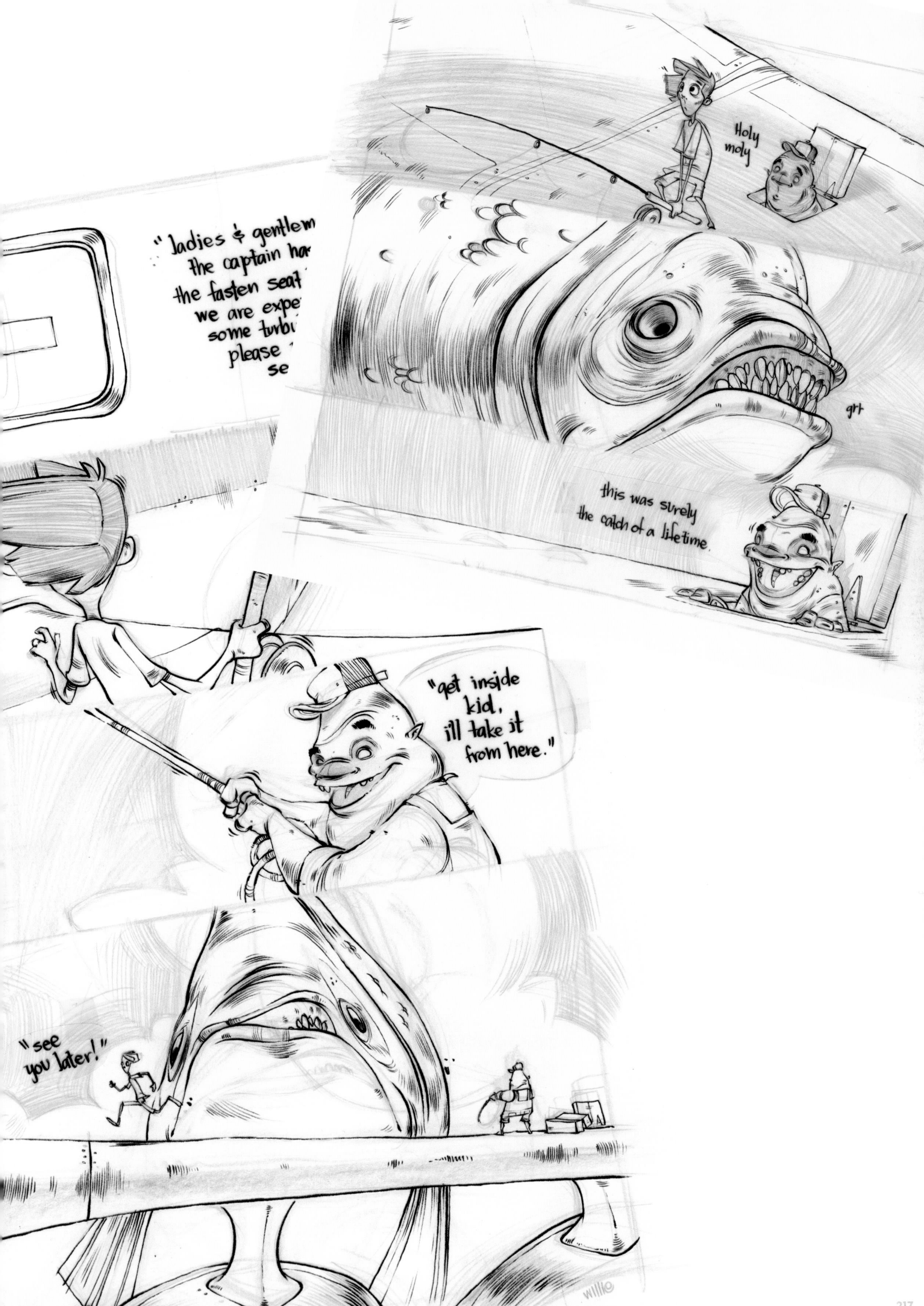
"ladies & gentlem
the captain ha
the fasten seat
we are expe
some turbu
please
se
Holy
moly
grr
this was surely
the catch of a lifetime.
"get inside
kid,
i'll take it
from here."
"see
you later!"

the Rupture

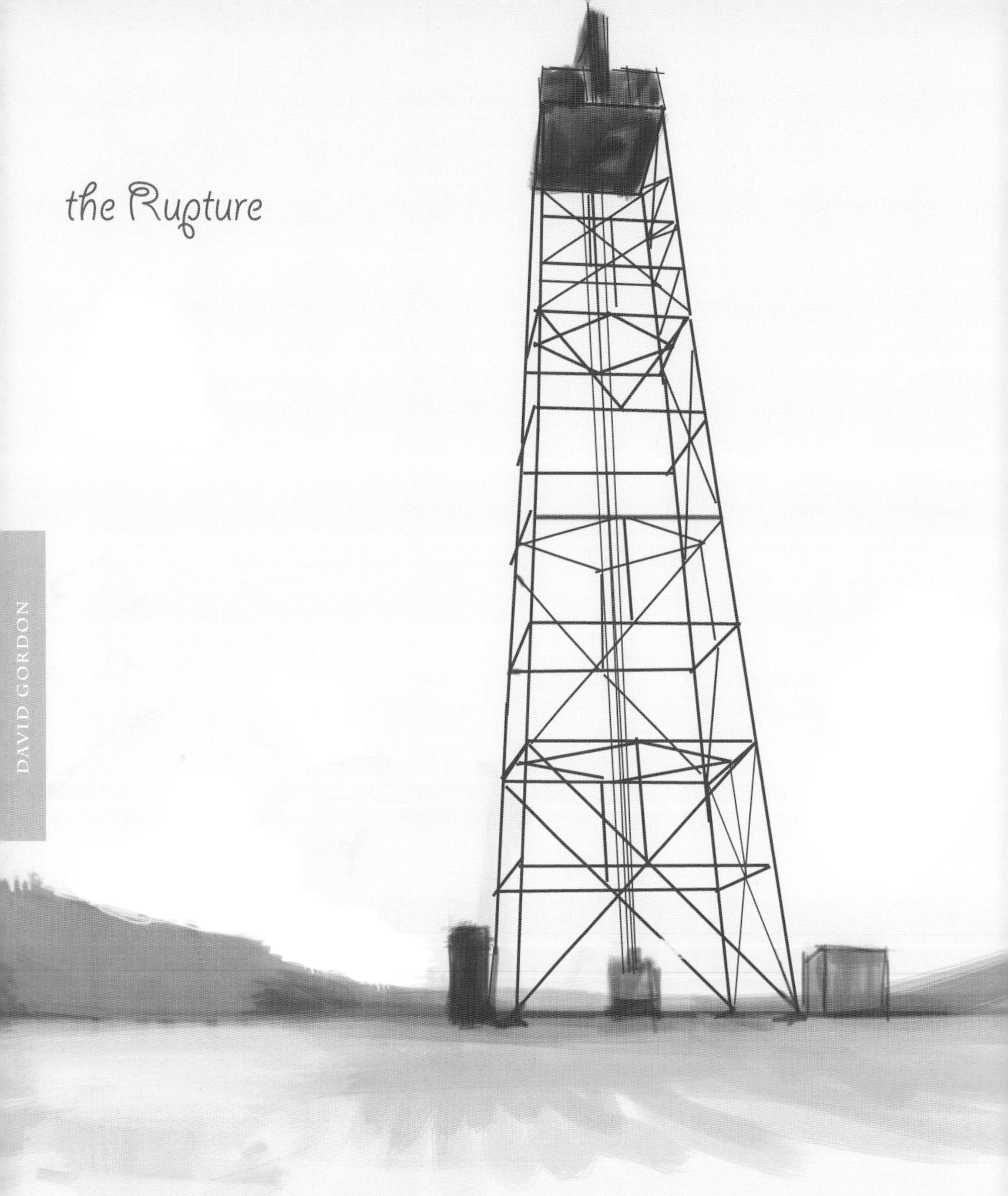

CHAPTER 1:: TRINITY

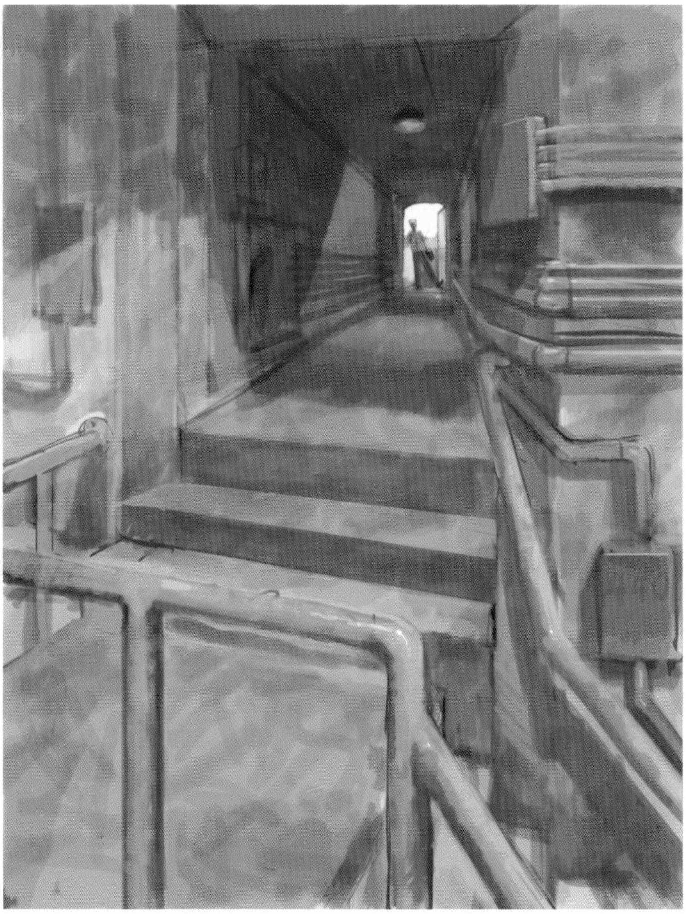

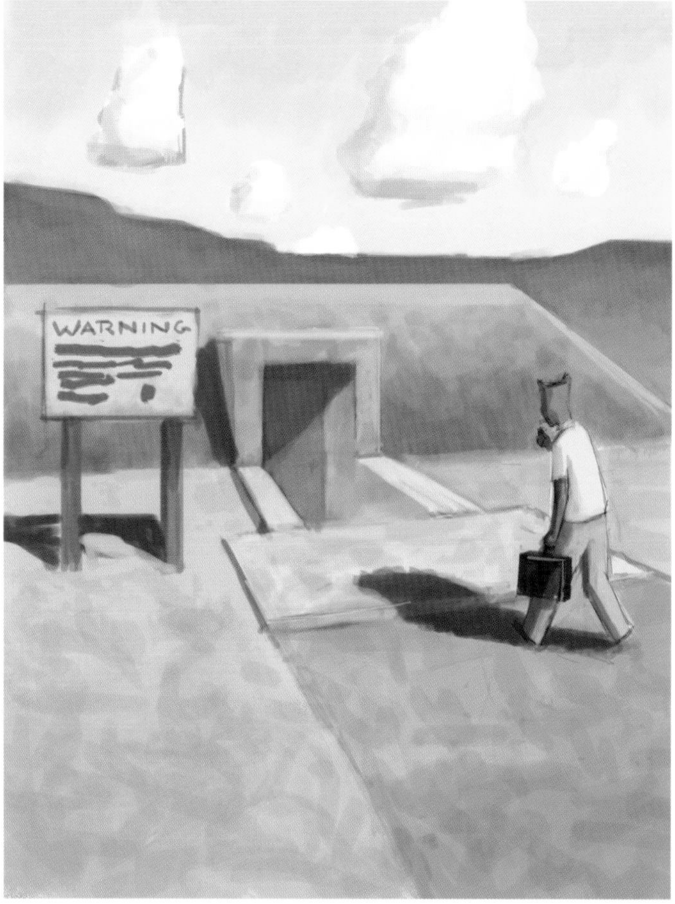
WARNING

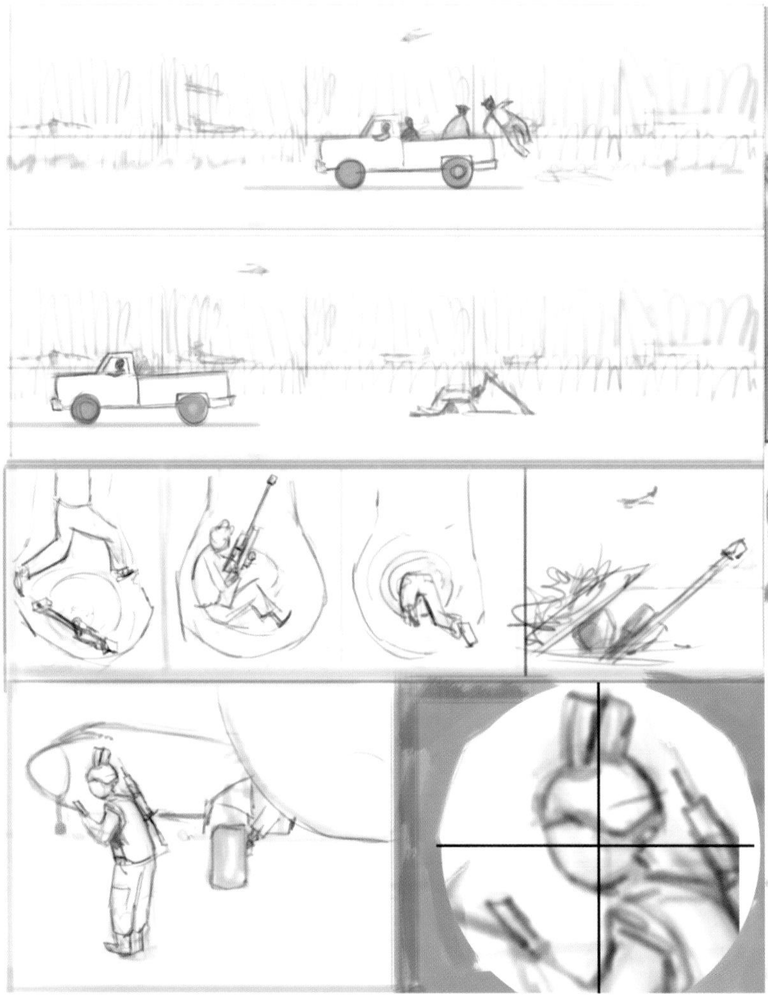

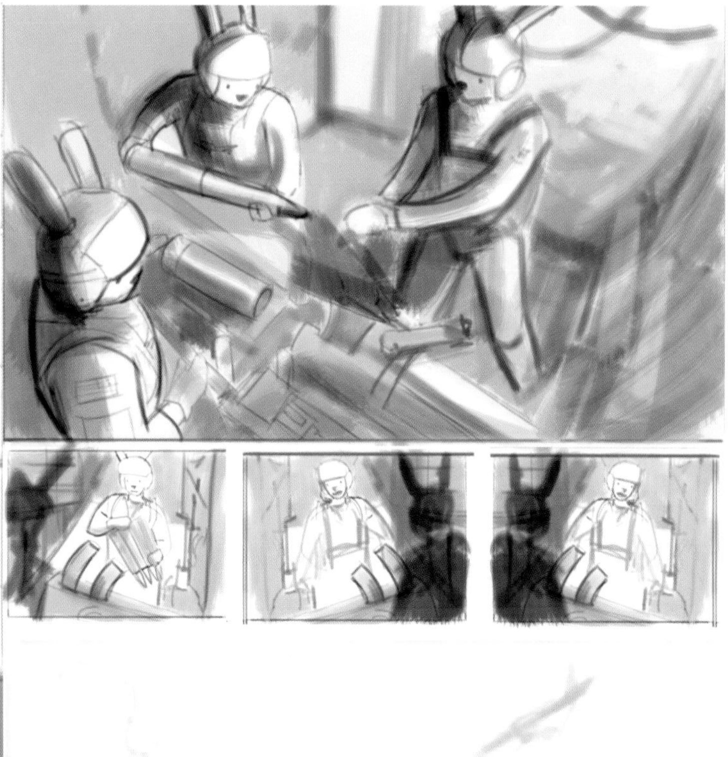

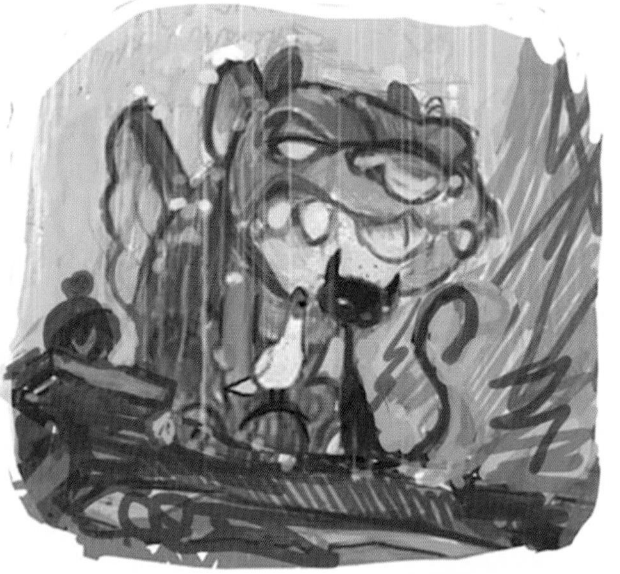

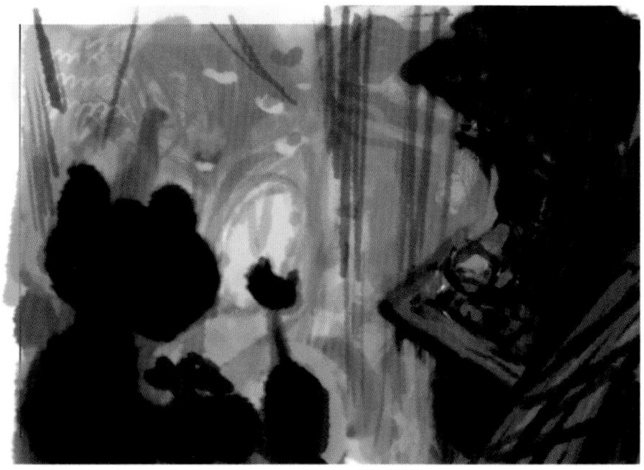

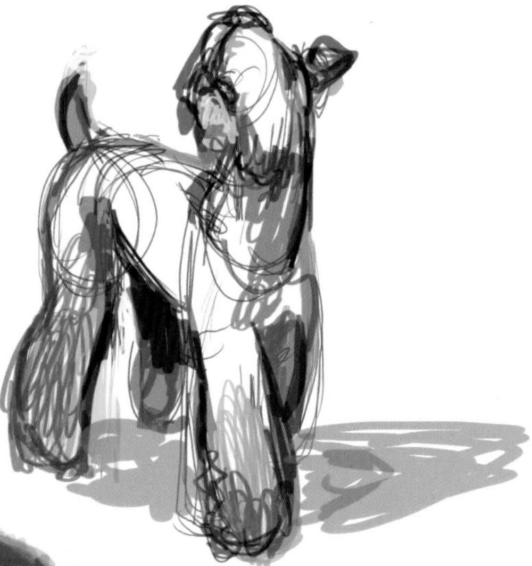

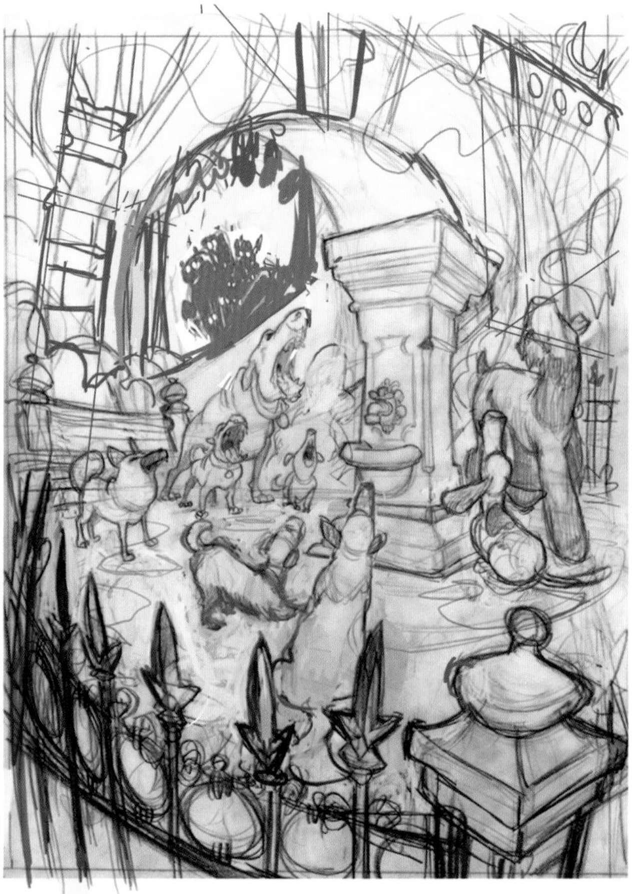

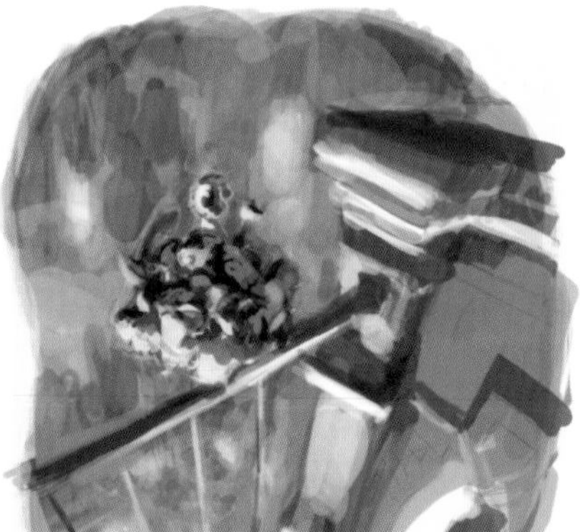

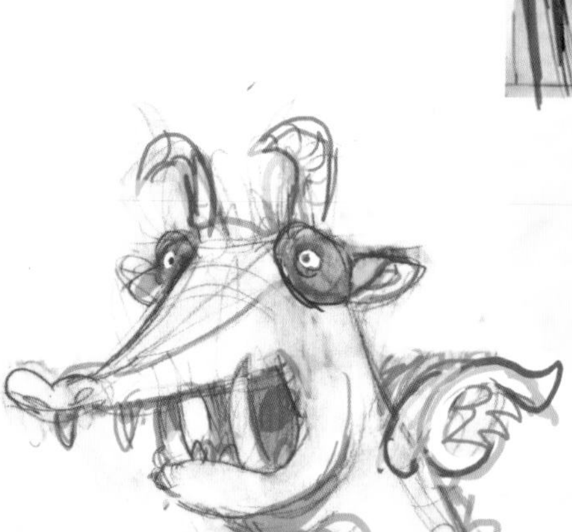

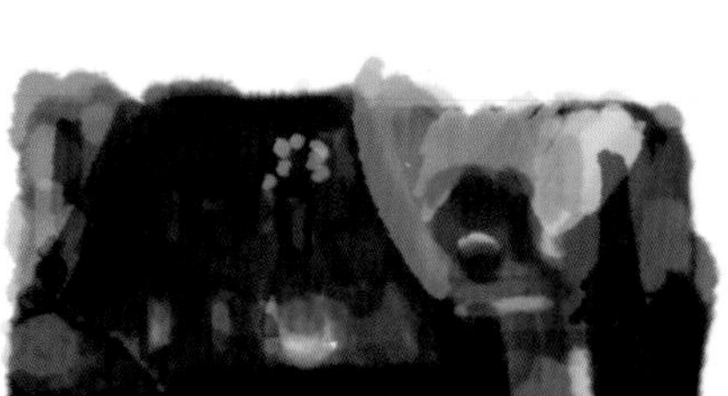

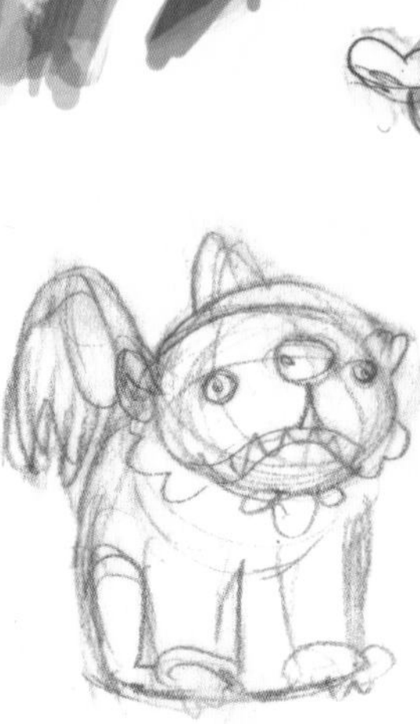

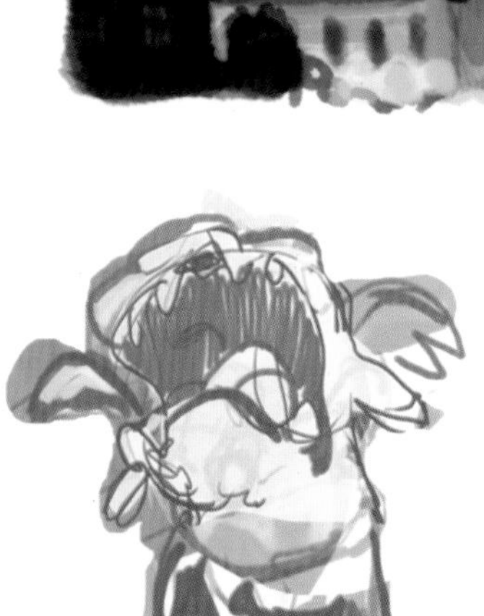

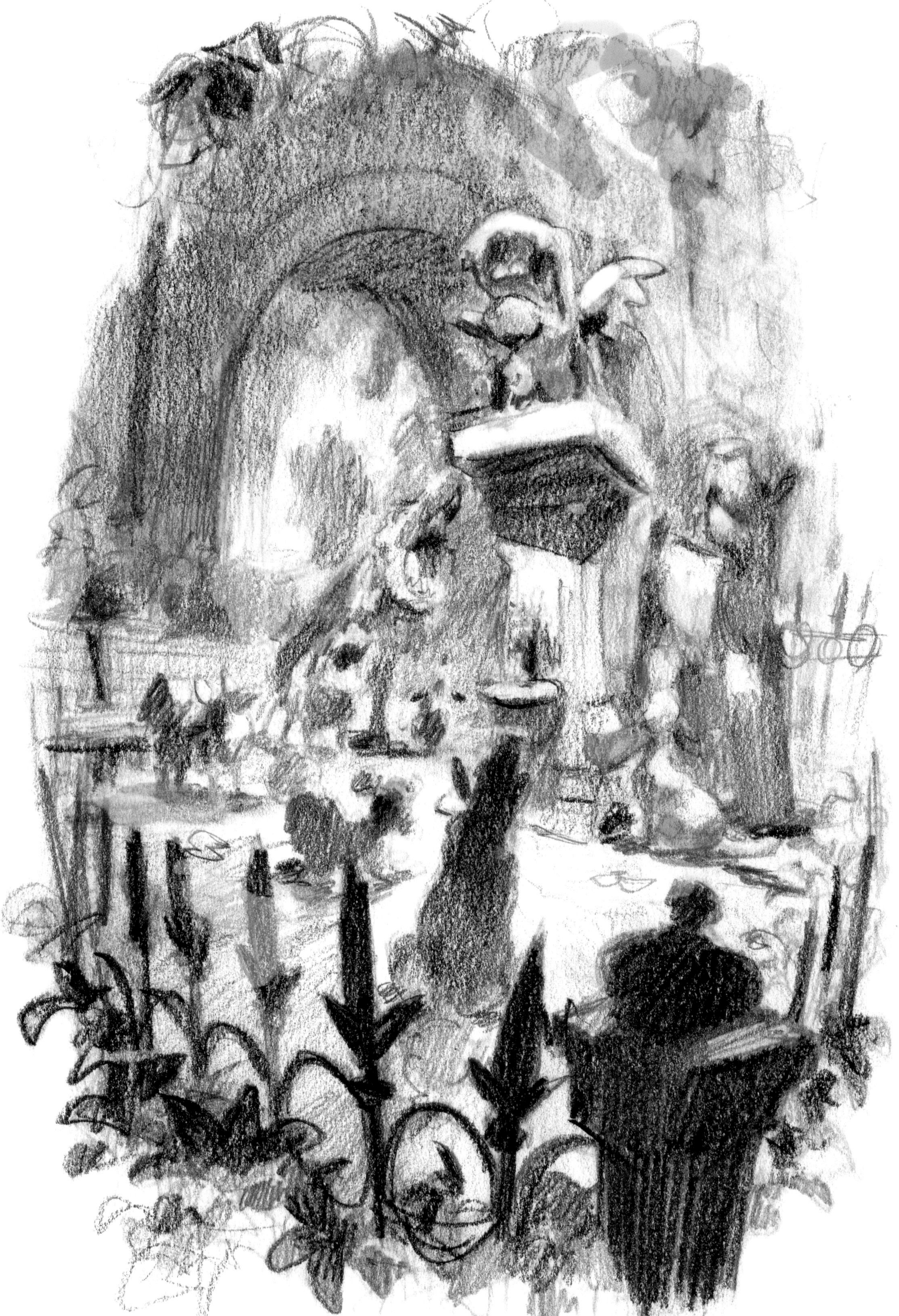

NASH DUNNIGAN

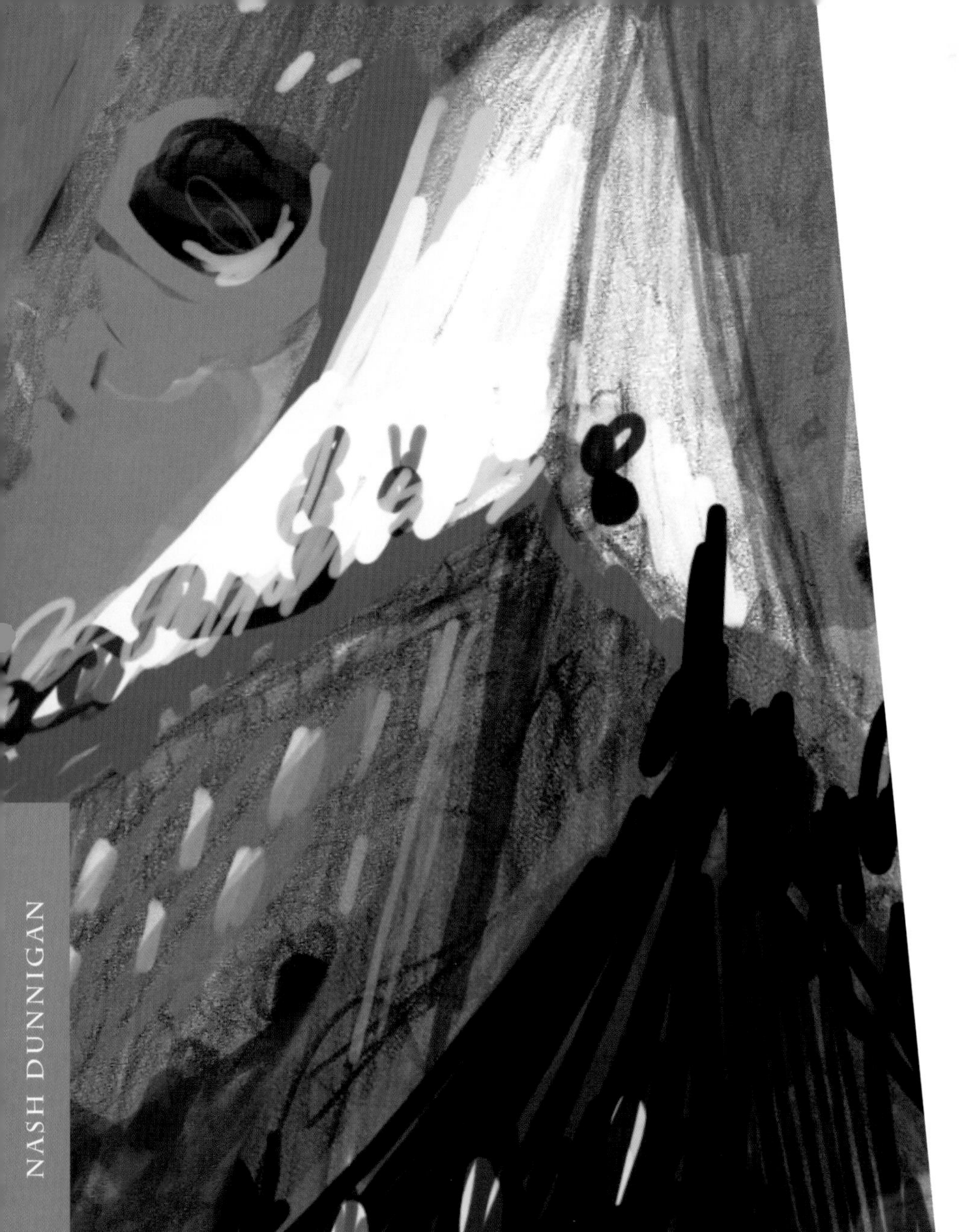

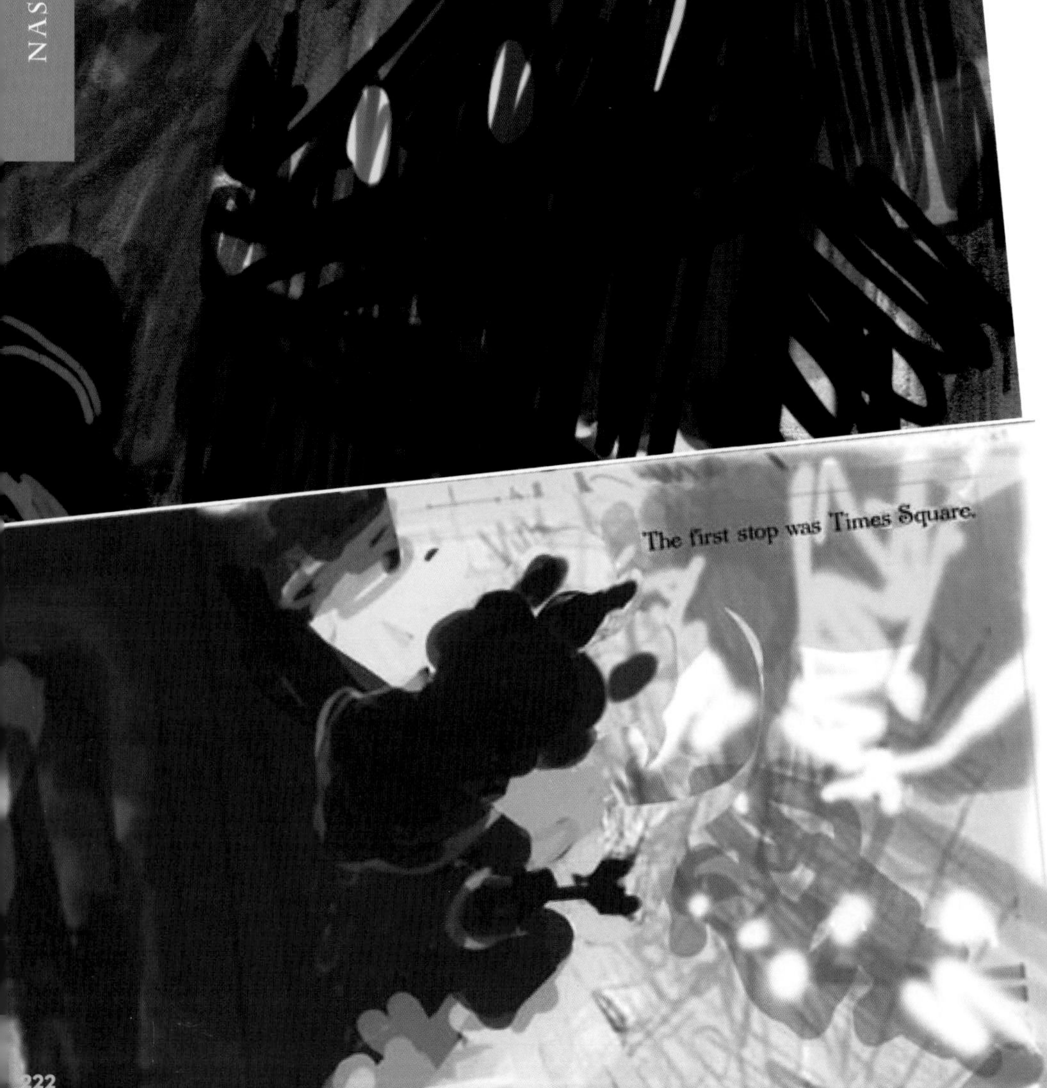

The first stop was Times Square.

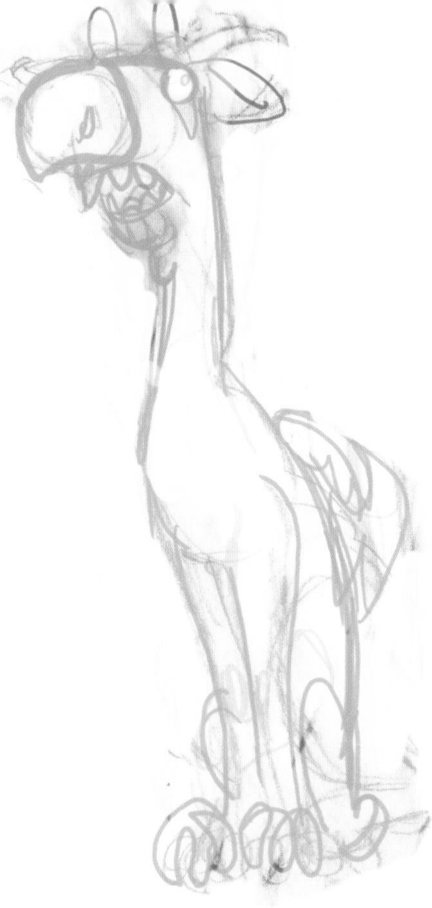

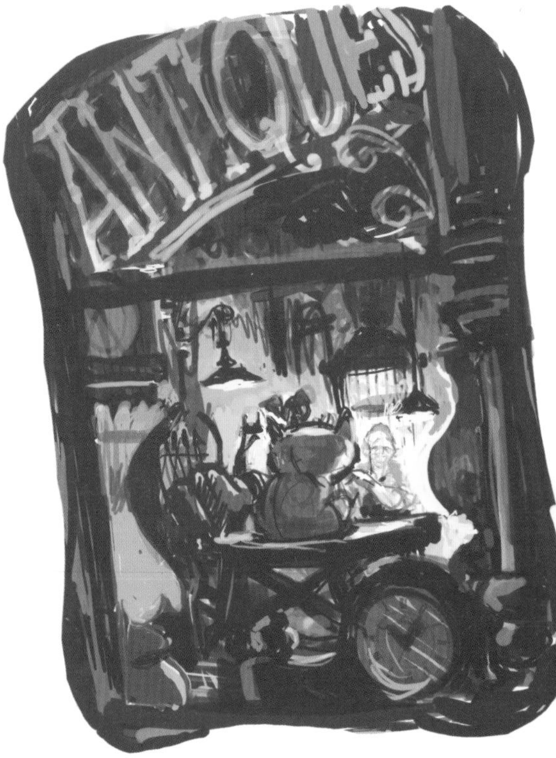

ANTIQUES

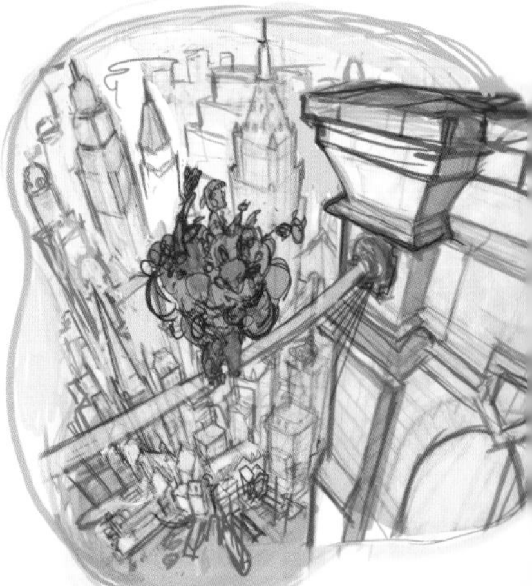

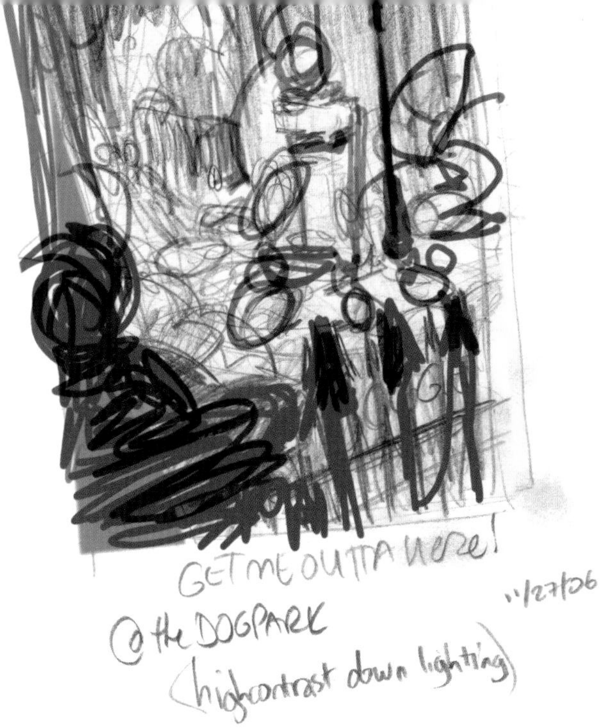
GET ME OUTTA HERE!
11/27/06
@ the DOGPARK
(highcontrast down lighting)

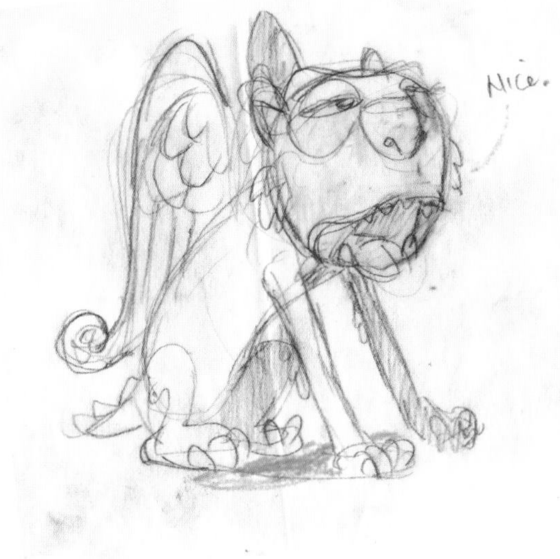
Nice.

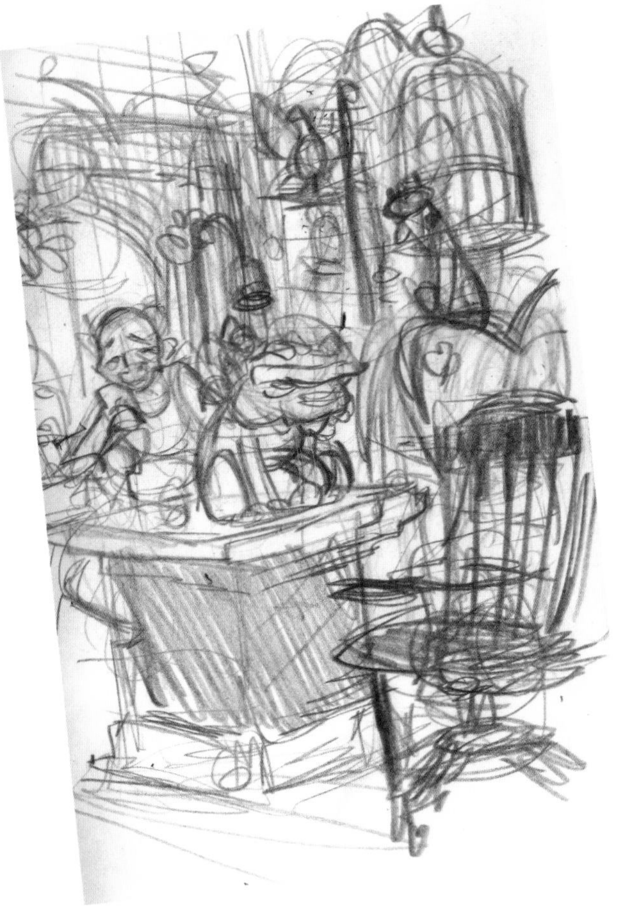

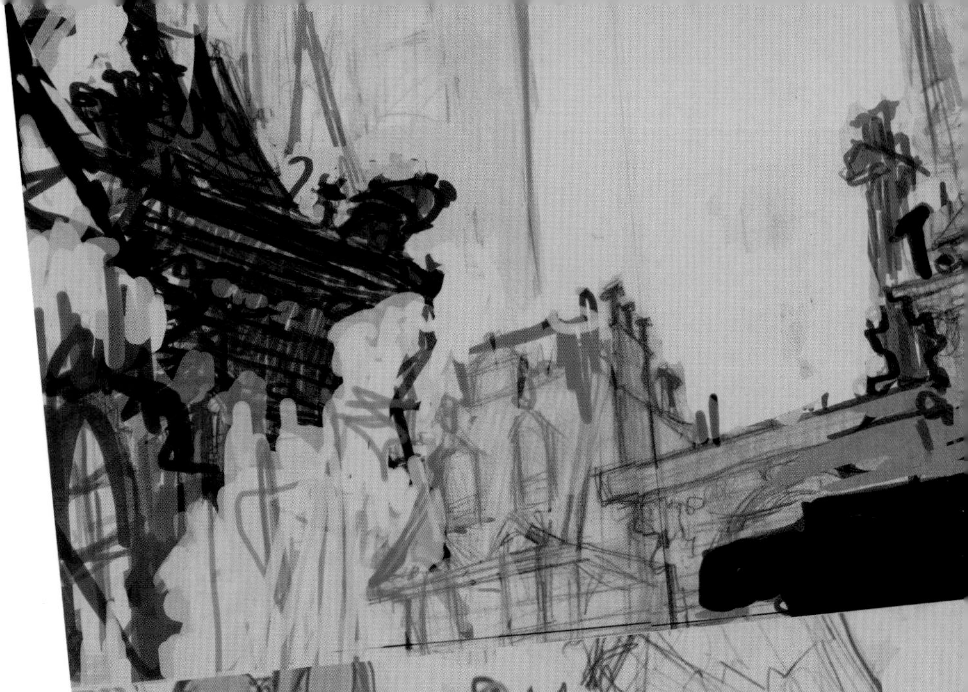

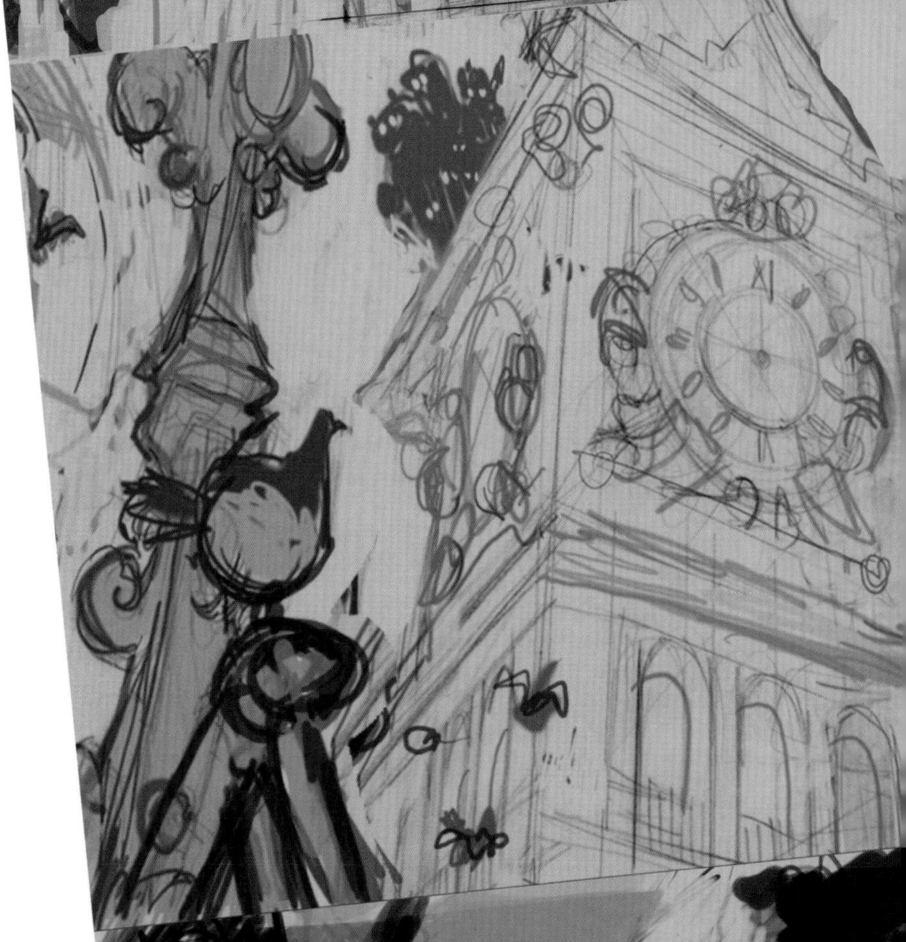

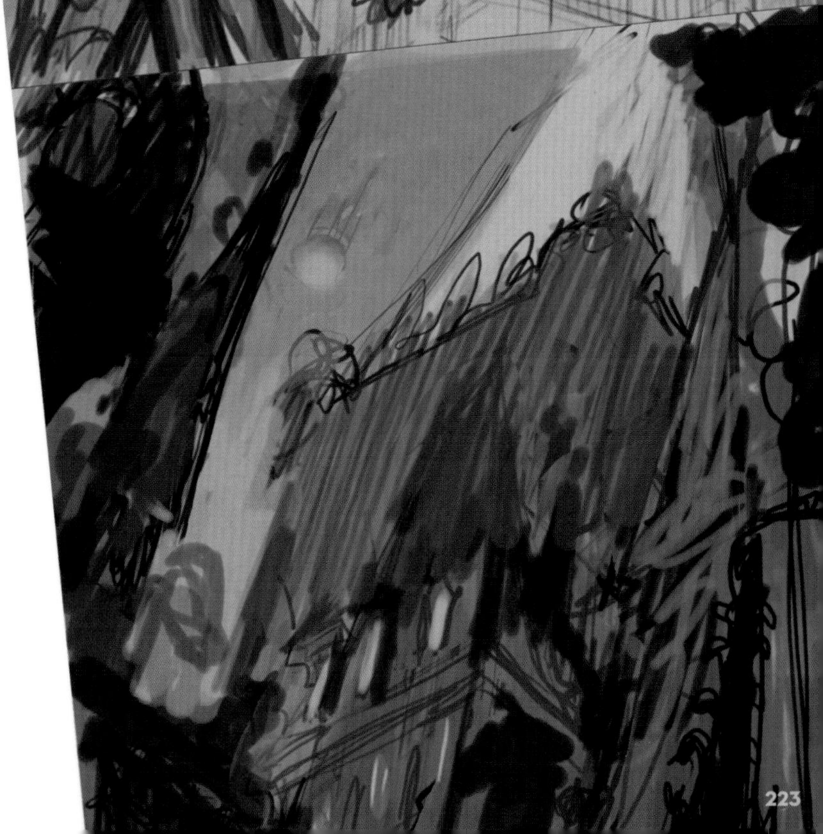

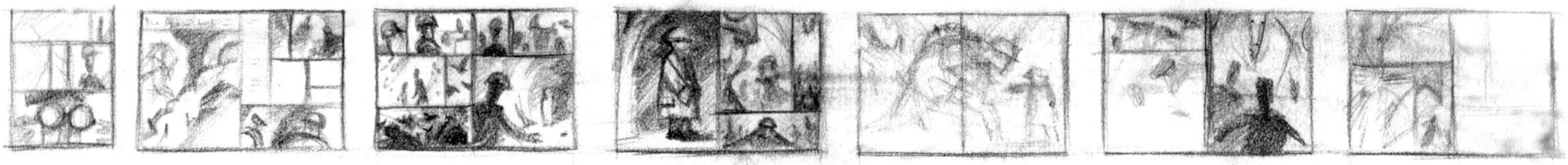

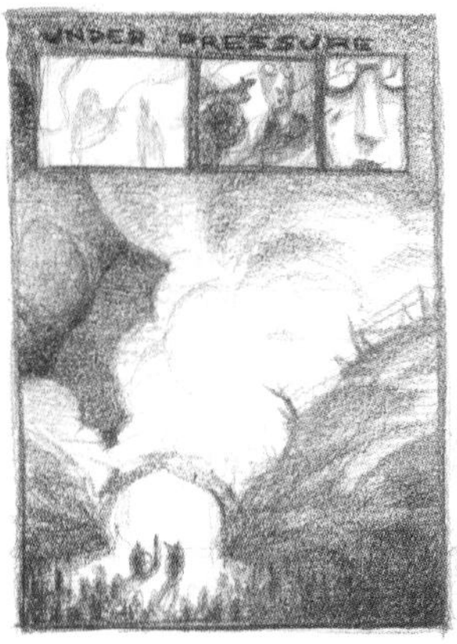
UNDER PRESSURE

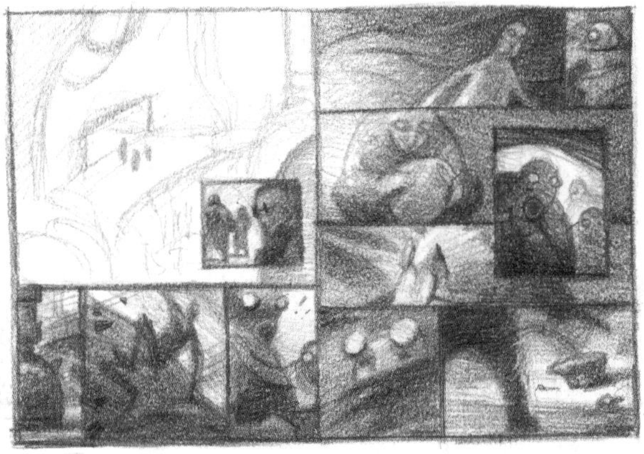

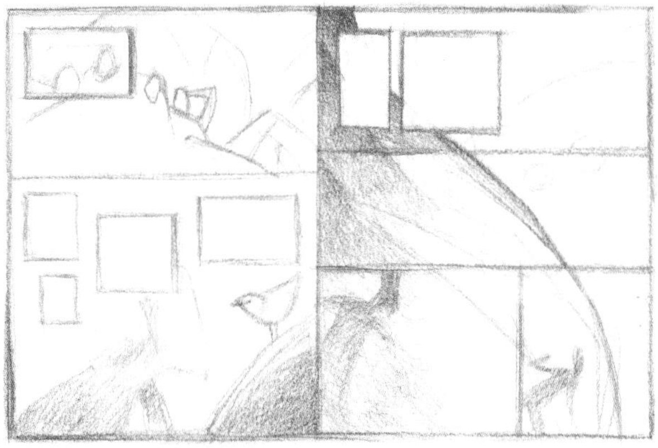

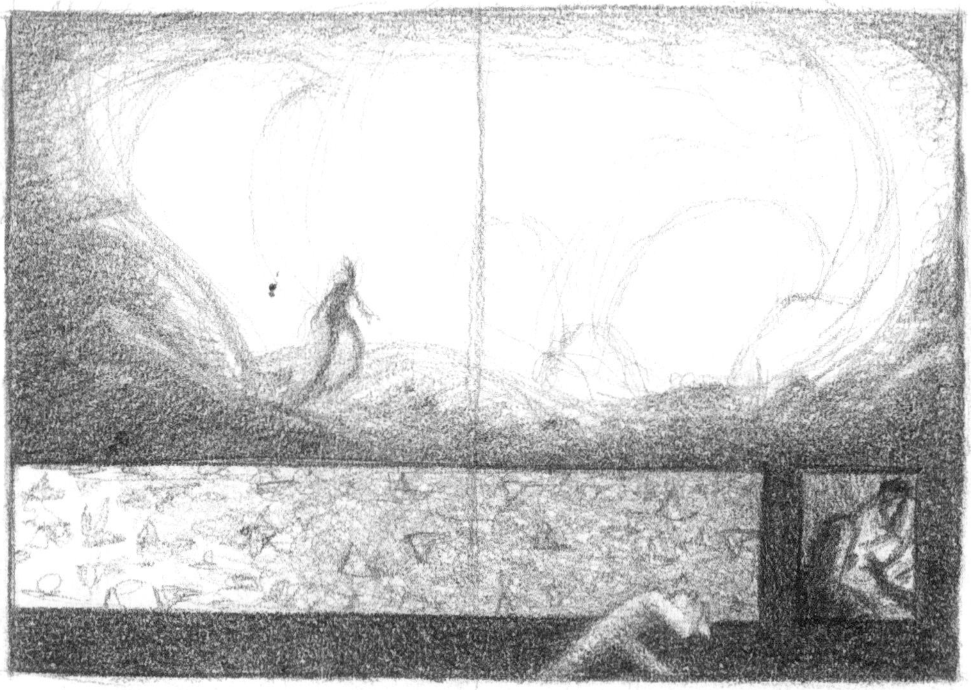

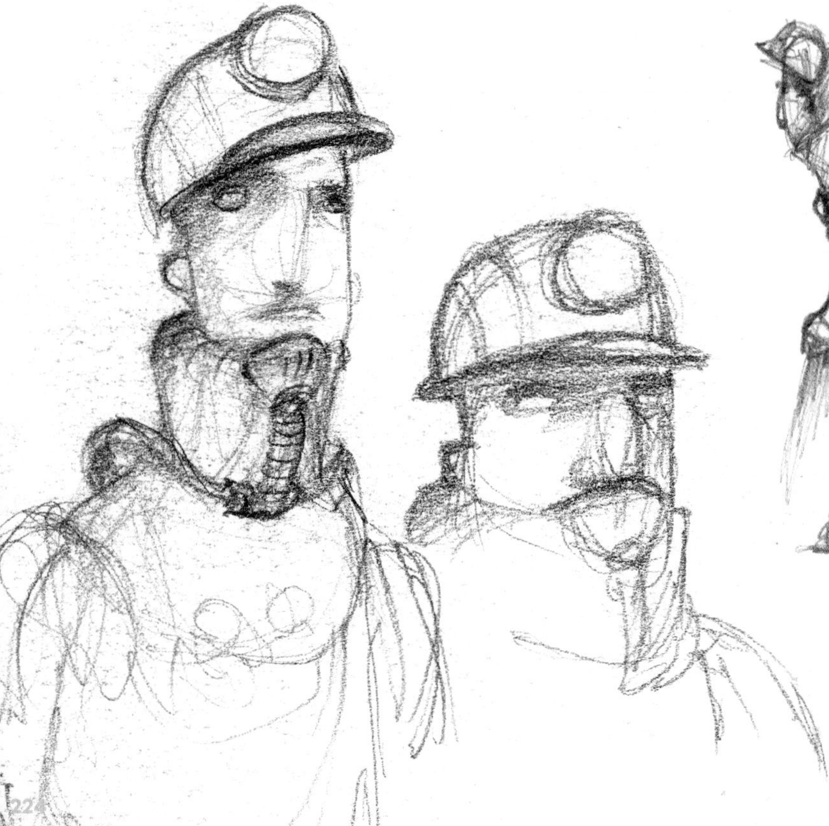

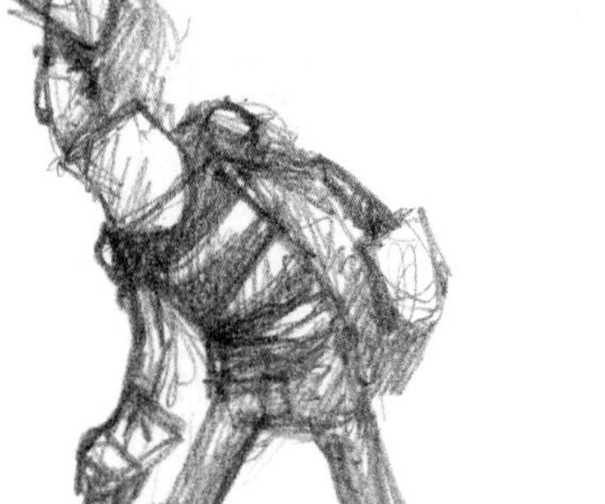

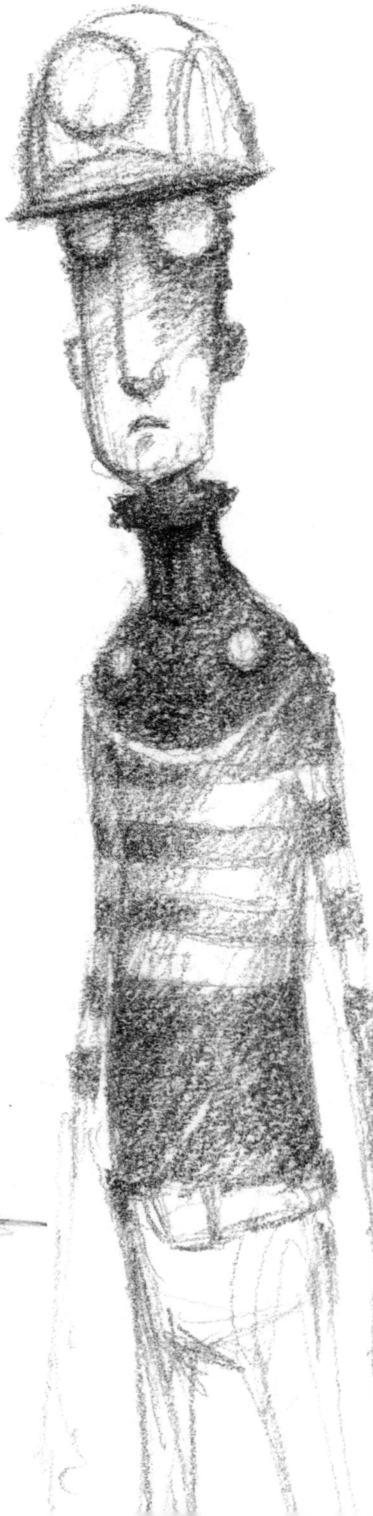

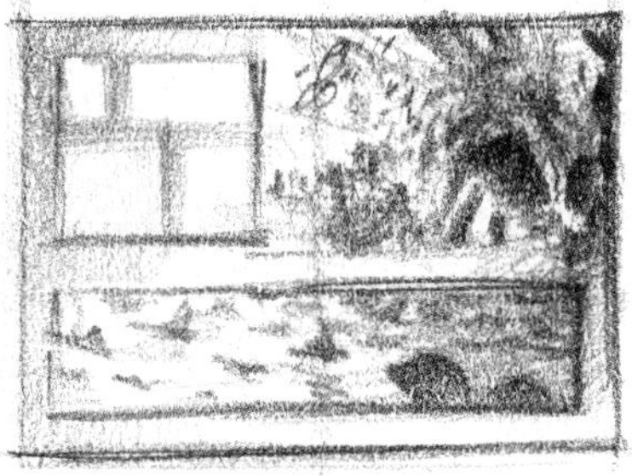

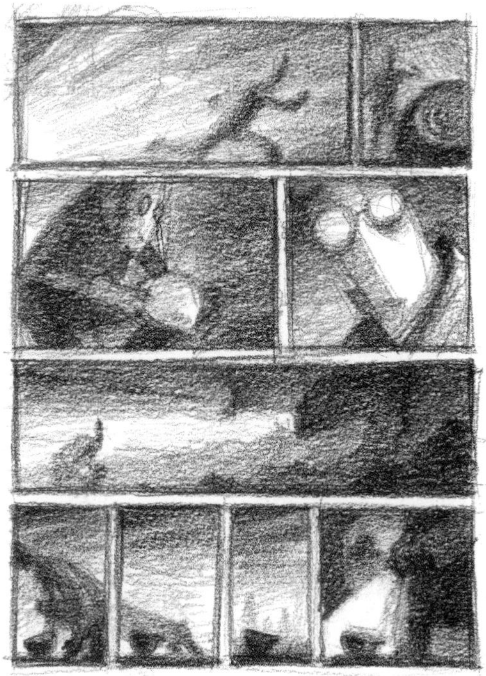

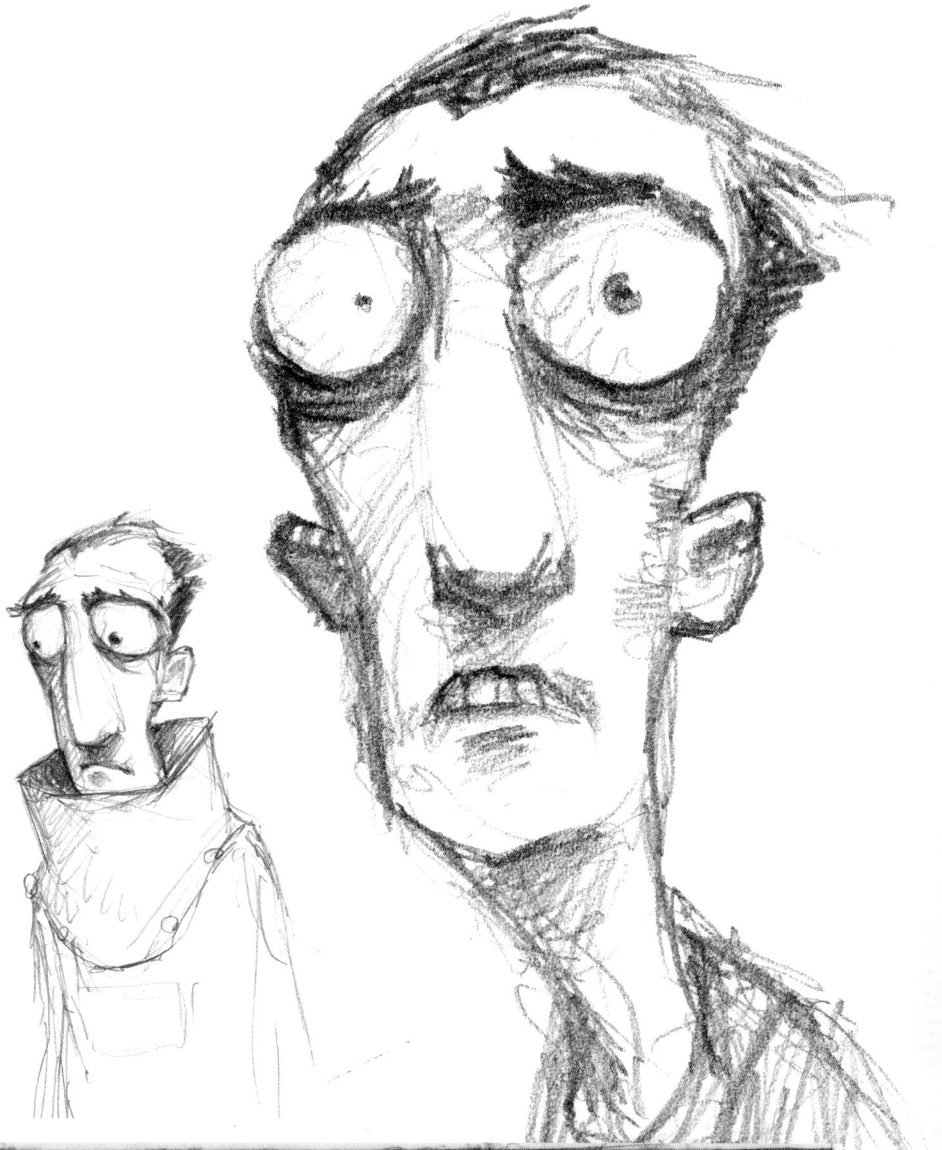

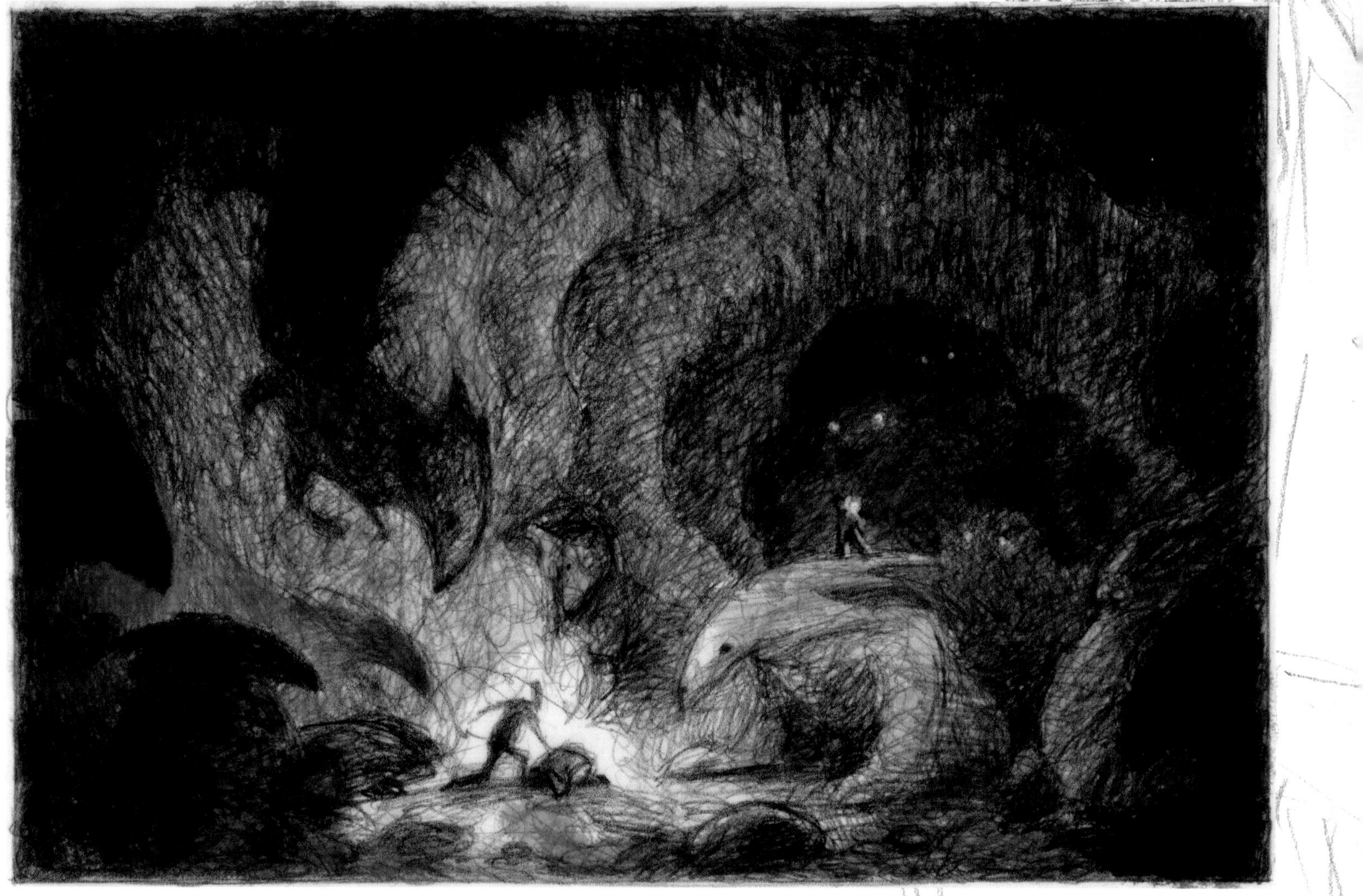

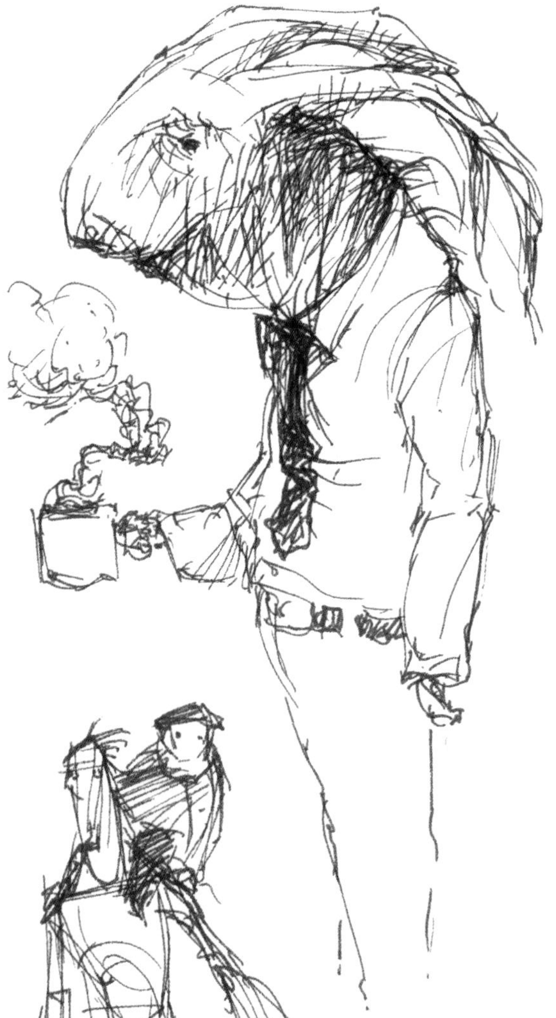

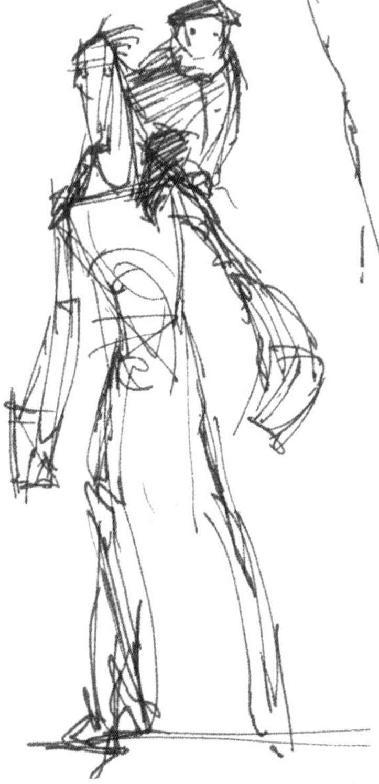

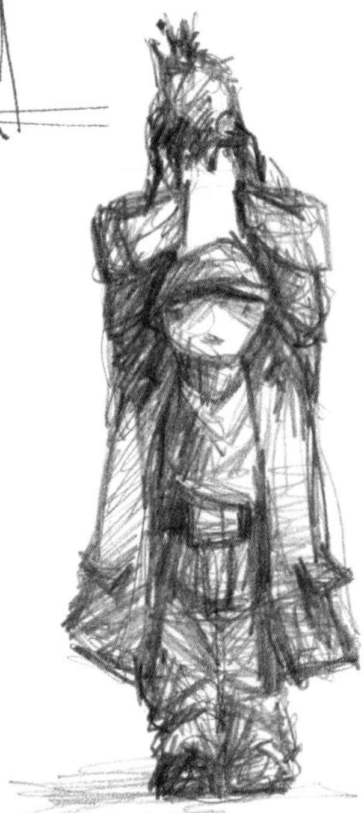

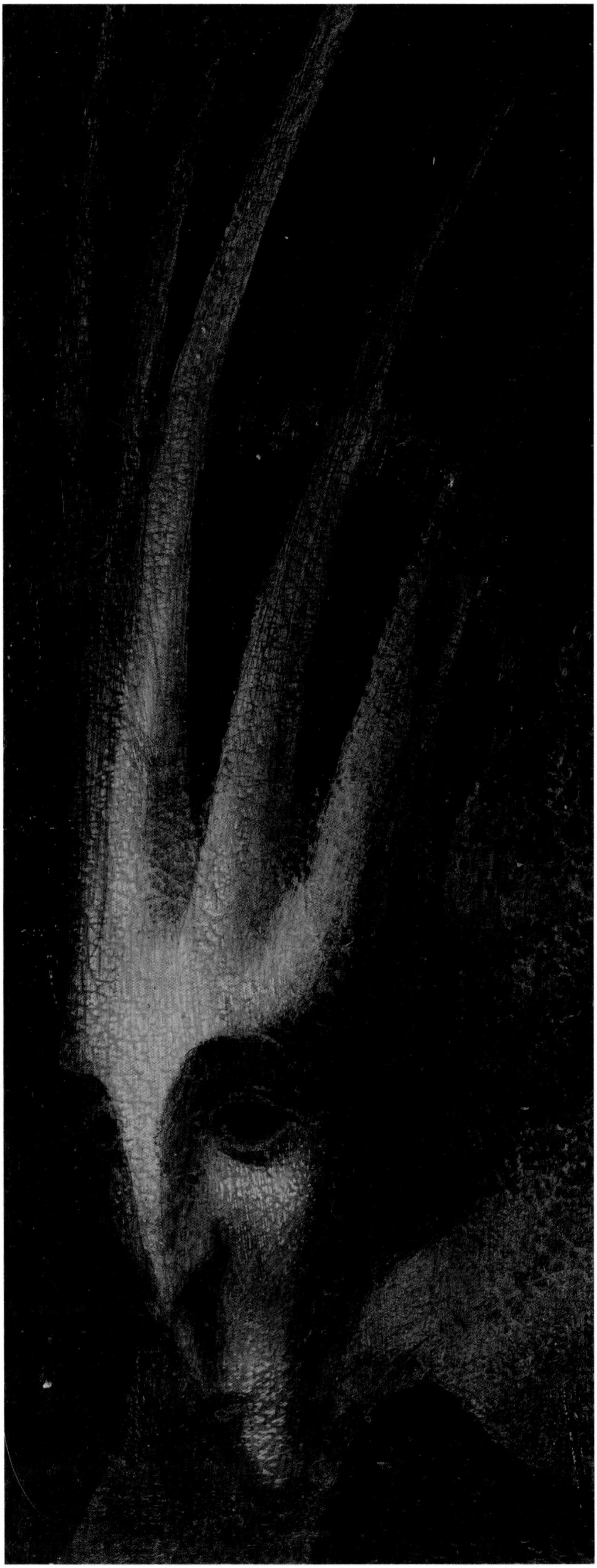

"Burrower" study - 1995

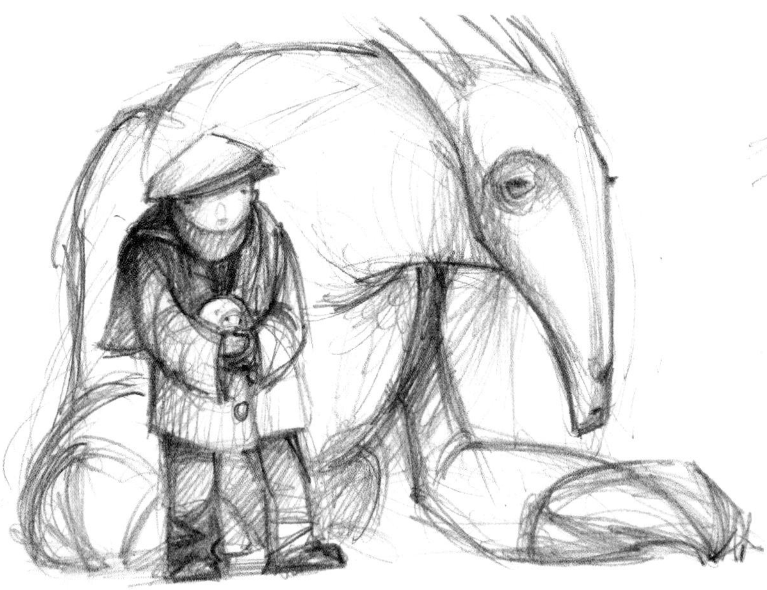
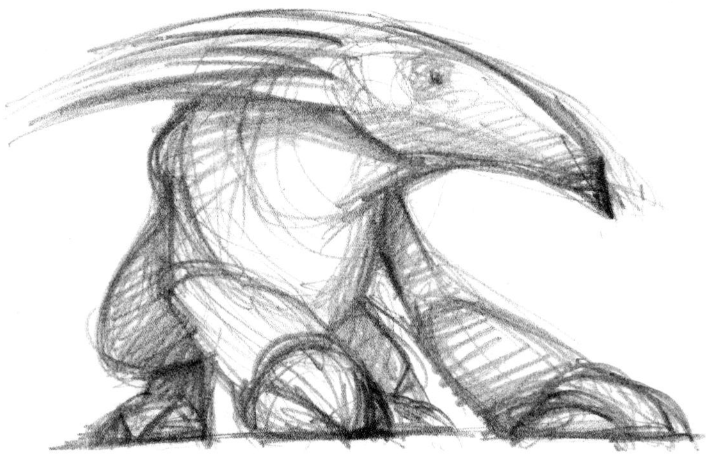
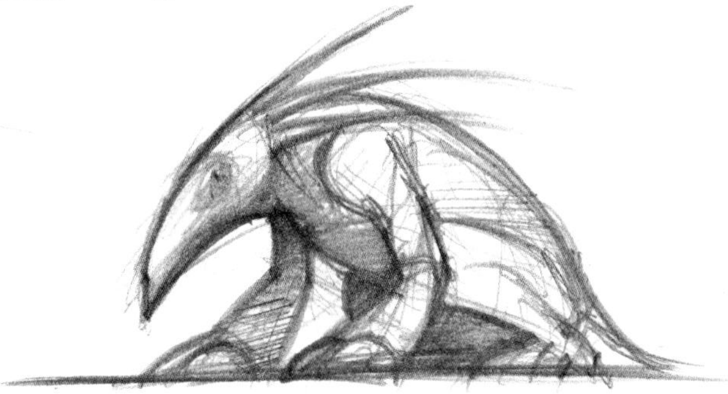
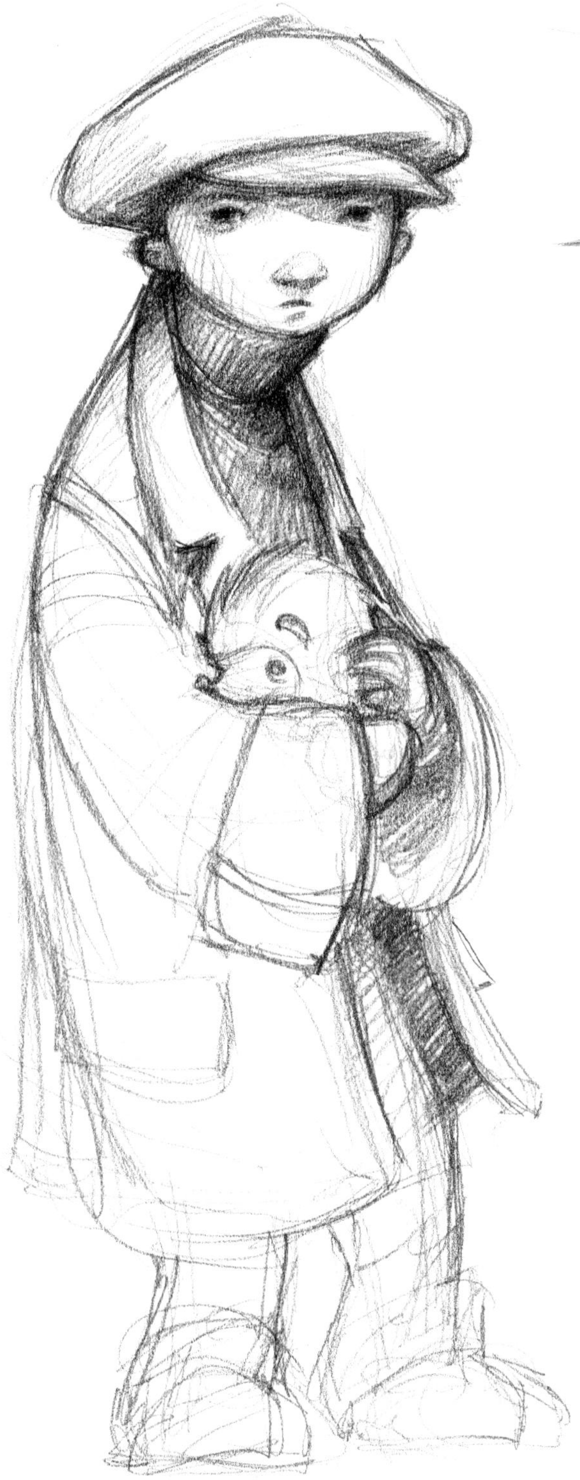
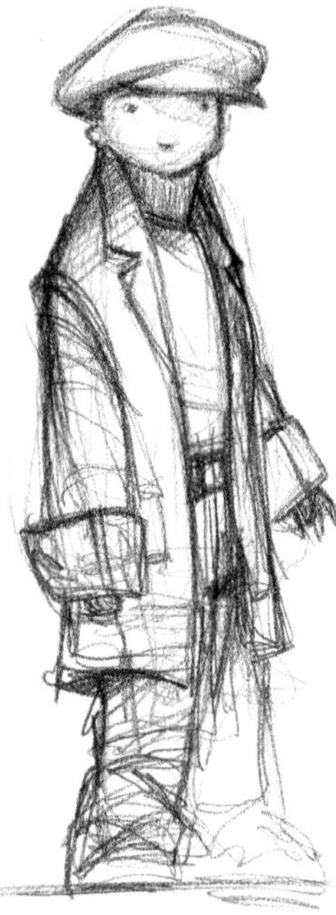
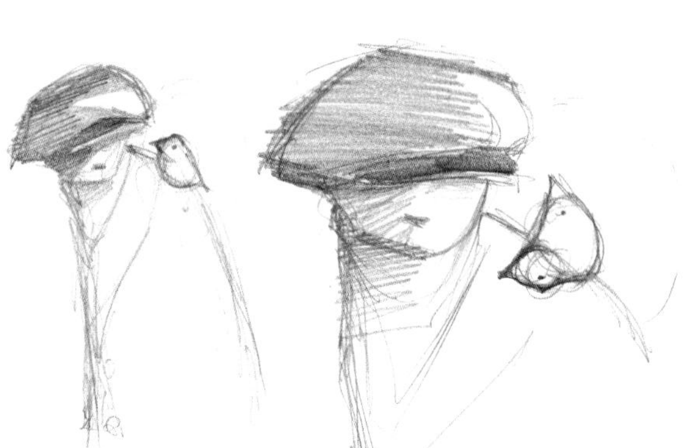
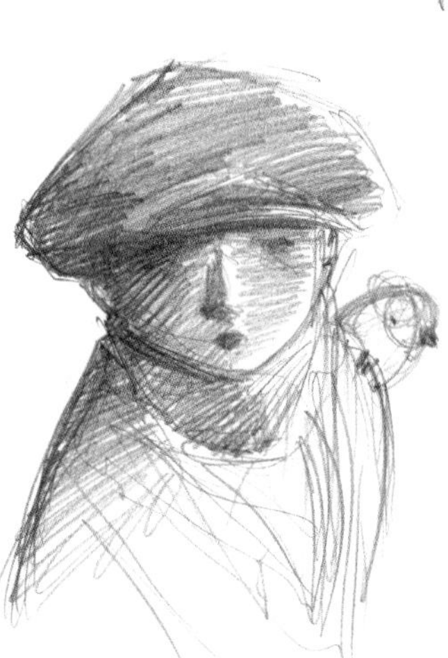

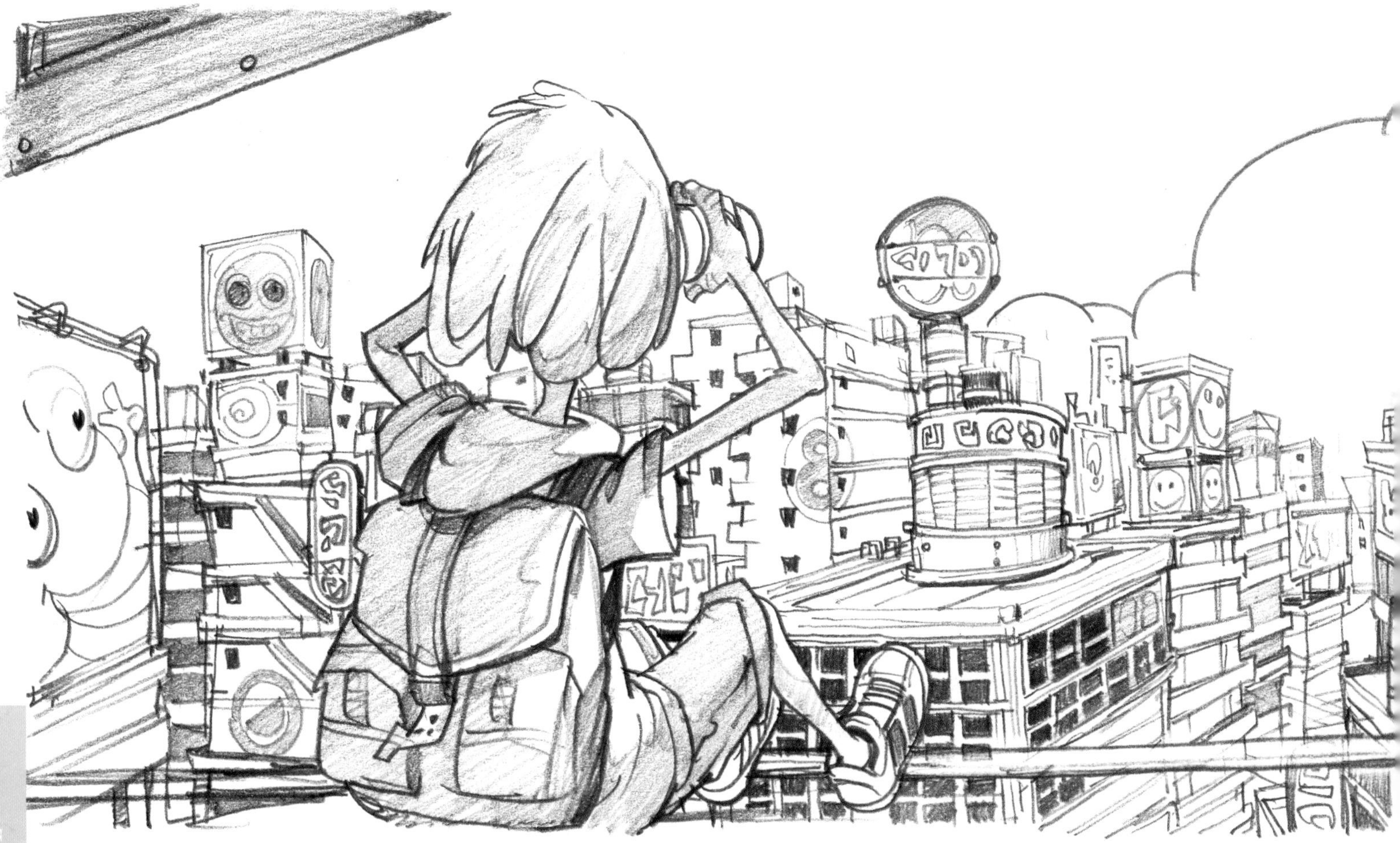

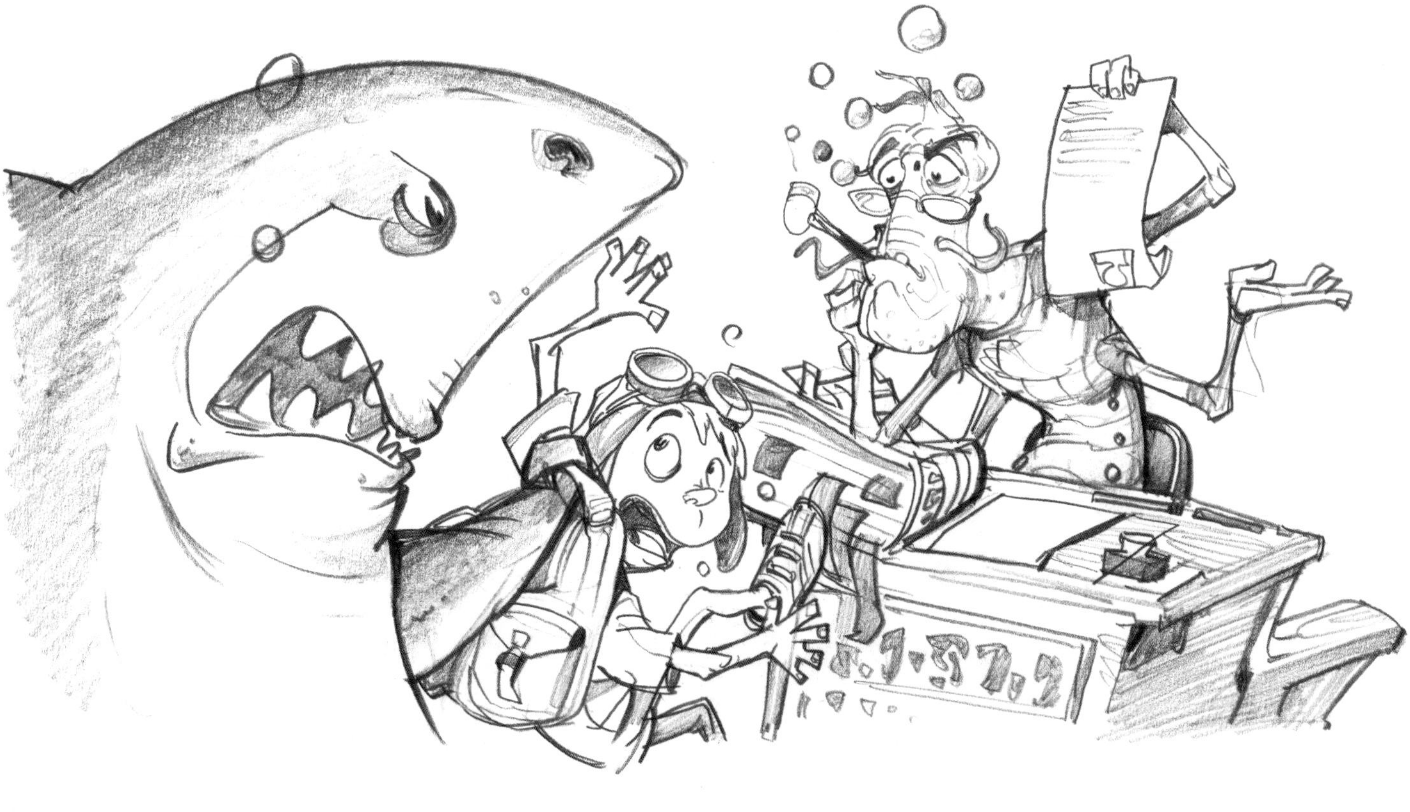

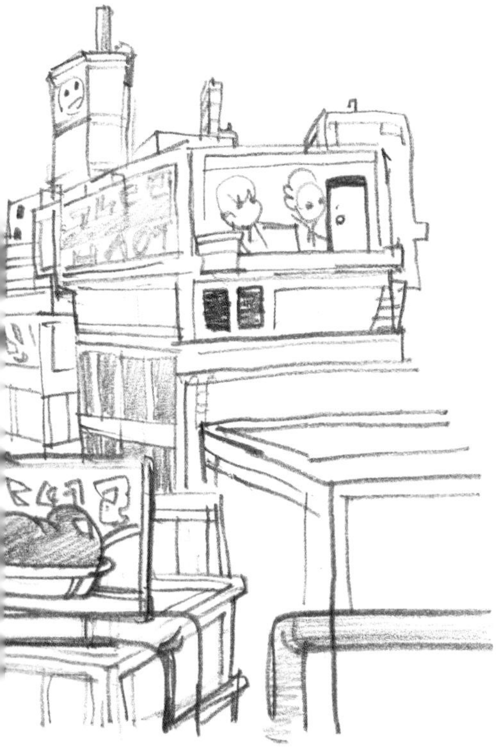

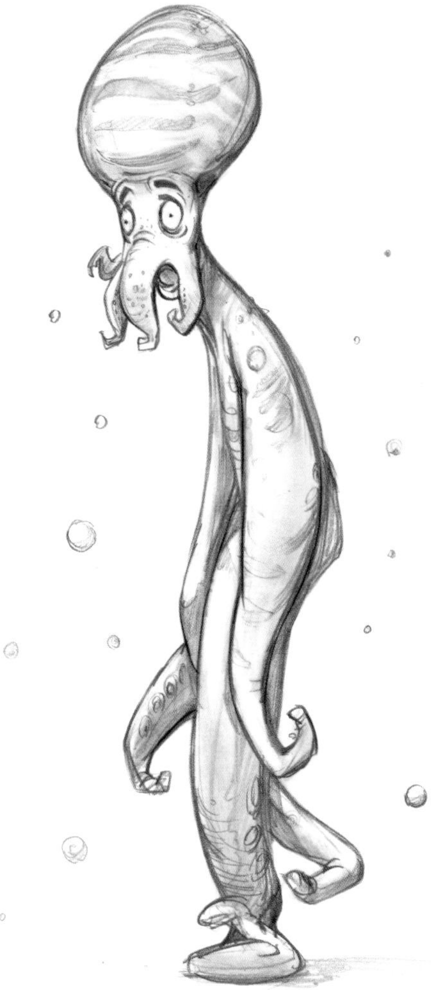

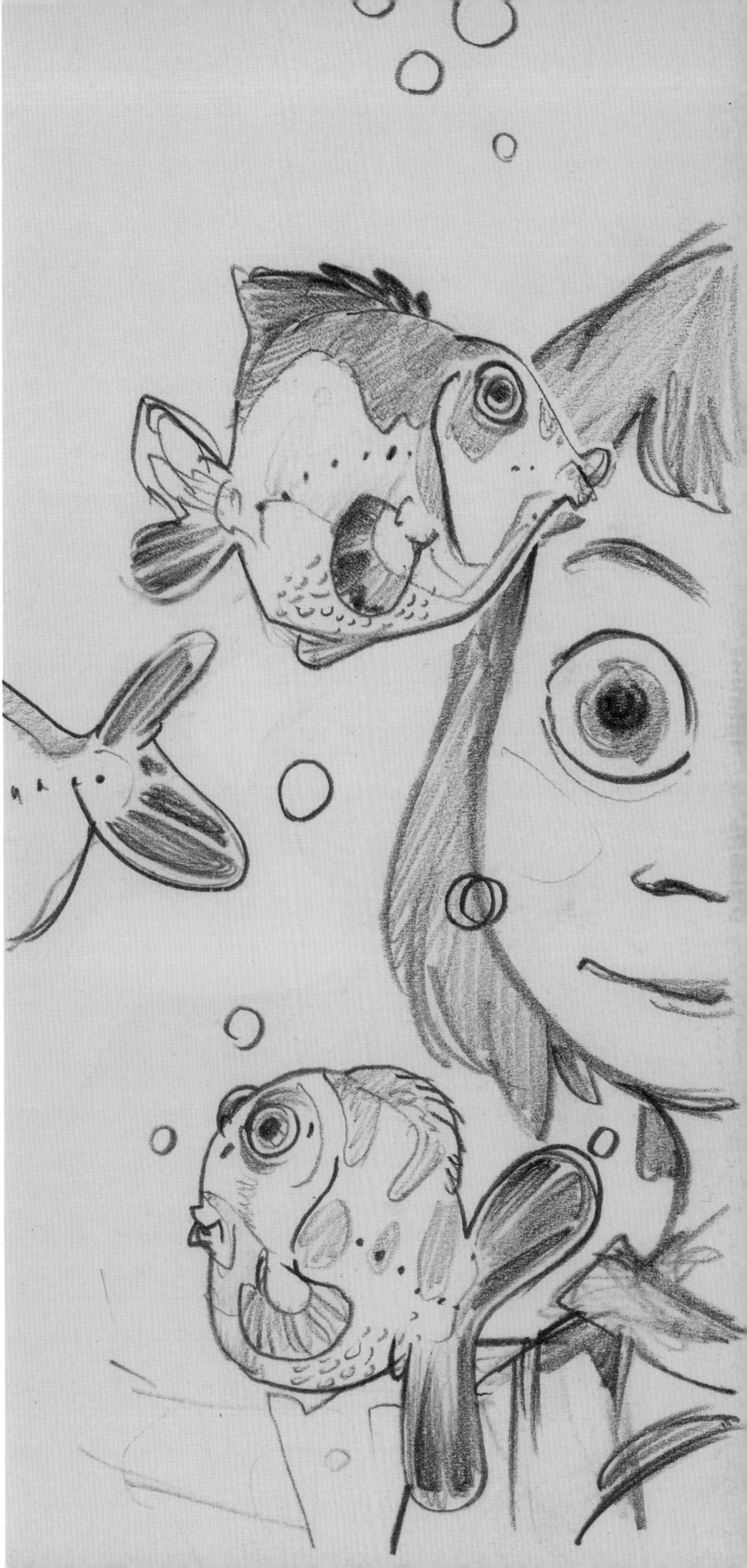

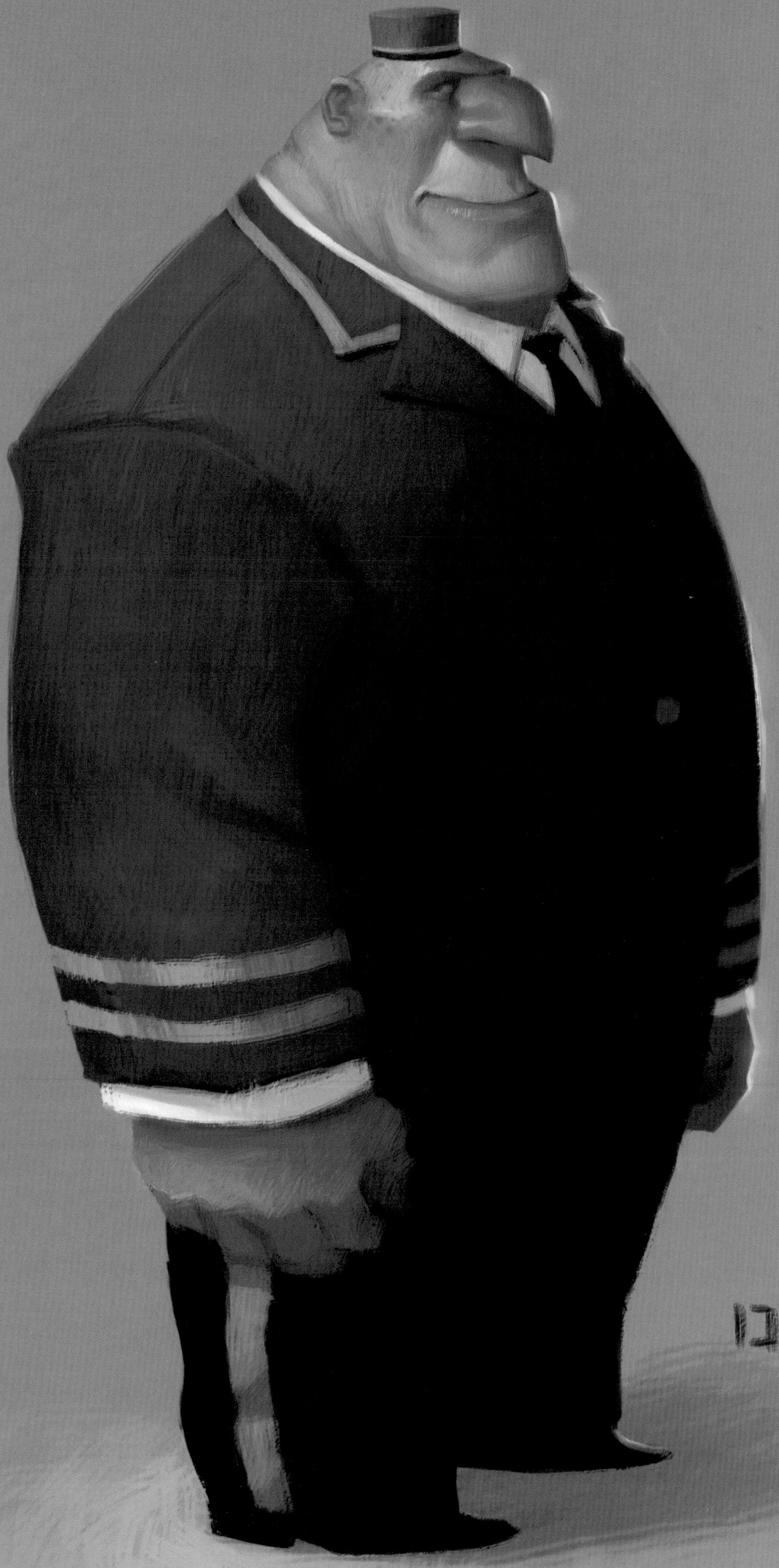

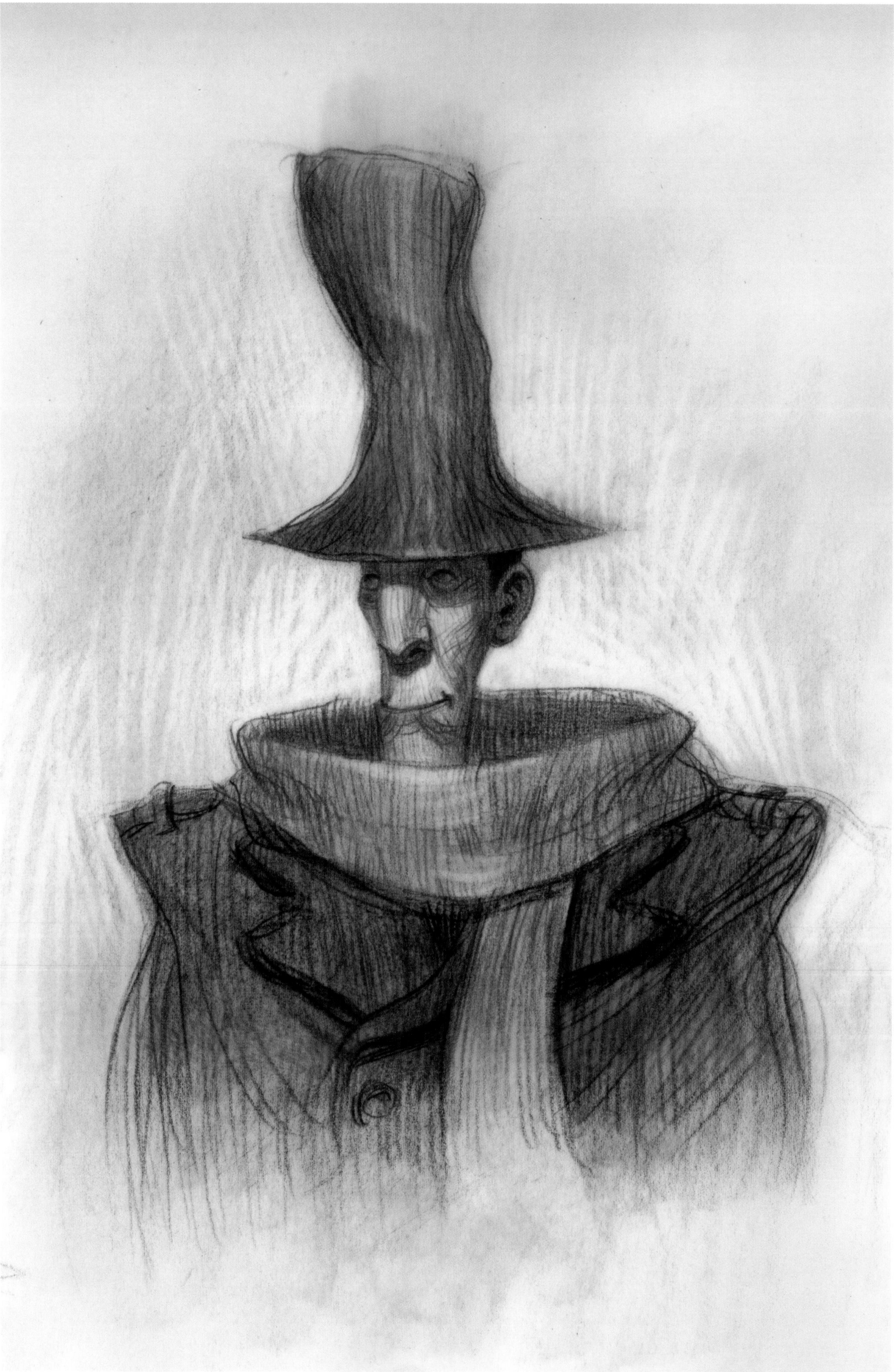

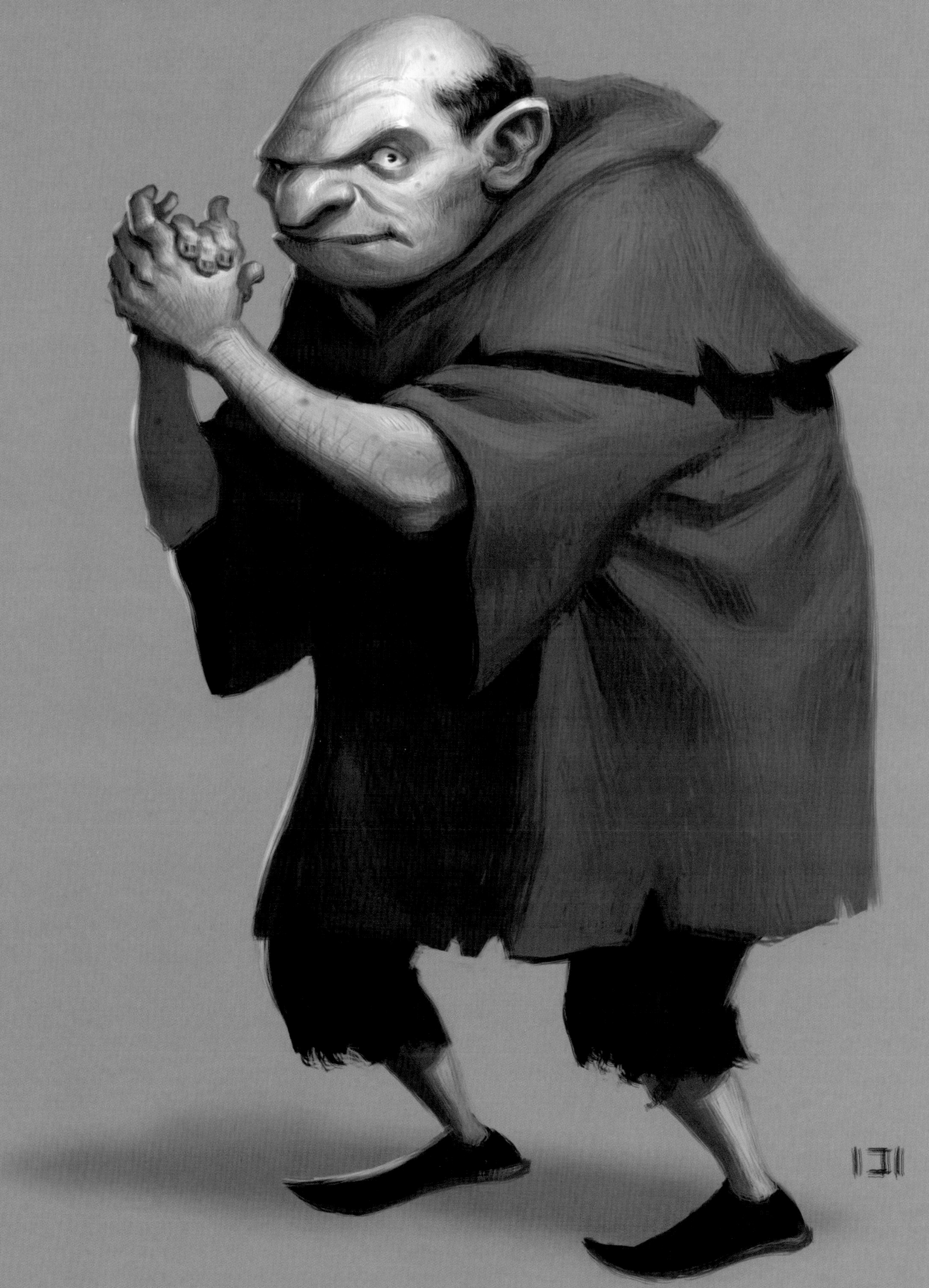

BIOGRAPHIES

ANDREA BLASICH

Milanese sculptor and handyman Andrea Blasich has worked in layout and sculpting for Warner Bros., DreamWorks, and Blue Sky. He always manages to ride a bicycle to work and he builds his own furniture. See a crib and an outdoor table on his blog—he can beat Pottery Barn prices by 500%. Andrea now lives on a beautiful hilltop in San Anselmo, California, with his wife, Alexandra, and daughter, Vanessa.

andreablasich.blogspot.com

NASH DUNNIGAN

Since the nineties, Nash has designed, storyboarded, and drawn on lots of animated shows on the isle of Manhattan. For the past four years, though, he has been at Blue Sky Studios as a production designer and layout artist on such films as *Robots*, *Ice Age: The Meltdown*, and *Horton Hears a Who!* Nash still wants to be a kids' book author and illustrator when he grows up. As his friends can attest, he is full of … stories. Lots of 'em.

Luckily, his day job pays the bills. Nash also makes a mean batch of scones.

www.nash-dunnigan-art.blogspot.com

DAVID GORDON

Dave Gordon is a children's book author and illustrator who has a passion for airplanes, trucks, tractors, construction equipment, and other cool heavy machinery. He was born and raised in Colorado and later moved to the big city to attend Parsons School of Design in New York. After graduating, Dave moved out to northern California, where he created concept art for many of Pixar's films. He also worked on the acclaimed animated television series *SpongeBob SquarePants* and Blue Sky's *Robots*.

Dave has authored and illustrated three vehicle fairy tales for HarperCollins: *The Ugly Truckling*, *The Three Little Rigs*, and *Hansel and Diesel*. Dave now lives in New York City with his lovely girlfriend, Susan, and their dog, Subway.

www.illustrationranch.com

MICHAEL KNAPP

Michael Knapp is an avowed workaholic who occasionally dabbles in laziness. For years he teetered between a dismal career playing in rock bands and a sporadically paid career as an illustrator. Through some strange twist of fate, he now pursues neither while working at Blue Sky Studios as the art director on the third *Ice Age* movie. Somehow, working at Blue Sky led to drawing comics. Go figure…

He previously worked as a designer on the animated films *Robots*, *Ice Age: The Meltdown*, and *Horton Hears a Who!* and spent a few months art directing the Academy Award–nominated short *No Time for Nuts*. His work can be found in *Spectrum* 12 and 13, as well as the Society of Illustrators annuals 48 and 49.

www.michaelknapp.com

SANG JUN LEE

Sang Jun Lee was born and raised in South Korea. He received a degree in illustration at the school now known as Academy of Art University in San Francisco. After graduating, he worked for various entertainment companies such as ILM (Industrial Light & Magic), Sony Computer Entertainment, Electronic Arts, and Lucasfilm.

Lee specializes in illustrating and creating characters, costumes, and creature design for movies and games. Exploring depths, cultures, and fascinating new worlds never before imagined plays an important role while creating content for these projects.

His film credits include *Star Wars: Episode III*, *Men in Black II*, *Hulk*, *Peter Pan*, *Pirates of the Caribbean*, and *War of the Worlds*.

Lee is currently working as a character designer at Blue Sky Studios in New York.

BENOIT LE PENNEC

Born in France in 1962, Benoit was raised mostly on comic books. After studying graphic art in Paris, he gained experience working for both publicity agencies and TV animation studios. He then moved to London to work on the movie *Balto* (a 2D animated feature) for Amblimation. When that company dissolved into Dreamworks California, he moved along with many of his colleagues to the United States, where he had the chance to work on all of Dreamworks 2D movies (from *The Prince of Egypt* to *Sinbad*) as a layout artist. He recently had the opportunity to work at Blue Sky Studios on *Robots* and got to meet the great talents of that neat east coast studio. He currently works for Disney.

KYLE MacNAUGHTON

Kyle MacNaughton grew up in Toronto (the Little Apple), Ontario. Being one of the only Canadians who could not skate, he was forced to refine his real passion—scribbling.

Kyle graduated from Sheridan College's Classical Animation Program in 1999. Since then, he has worked for various studios, including Disney and Blue Sky Studios. His main interest is visual development. He currently resides in the Big Apple, New York City, with his lovely wife, Anaolga.

PETER NGUYEN

Peter Nguyen was born in the city of Philadelphia. At an early age, his family relocated to Houston, Texas, where he would spend his next years drawing every single day. Inspired by the work of Jack Kirby and Alex Toth, he wanted to pursue a career in comic books. Somehow things didn't work out and Peter ended up in animation instead.

Drawings by Robert Mackenzie

Residing in New York for the past four years, Peter now works at Blue Sky Studios along with the most talented group of people he's ever known. His comic-book dream was fulfilled when he was invited to do a short story for something called *Out of Picture*.

saigonradio.blogspot.com

VINCENT NGUYEN

Vincent Nguyen grew up in Houston, Texas, where he began his art career drawing cowboys, monsters, and superheroes. Frustrated by his inability to draw Aquaman riding a six-headed sea horse, he decided to attend the School of Visual Arts in New York, where he earned his BFA in illustration.

A longtime fan of comics and graphic novels, Vincent has always wanted to create sequential art to tell a story of his own. He illustrated children's books for three years before joining the art department at Blue Sky Studios. This book gave him the opportunity to draw and paint all the cool stuff he's always wanted, with the exception of Aquaman riding a six-headed sea horse.

www.vincentdi.com

GUILLERMO "WILLIE" REAL

"Can I have two fish tacos, please? Along with some salsa verde…nothing too spicy, and do you have horchata?" Willie was born in 1979 in San Francisco, California, where shortly after, he started scribbling on anything within reach. While his older sister ate snails and his oldest sister hairsprayed her bangs, Willie managed to capture his fifth grade teacher's "likeness" in his drawings. He was suspended from school. In 1997 Willie's high school English teacher was also aware of his ability to not pay attention in class. Instead of suspending him she encouraged him to join an after-school program called "Student Illustrators," where Willie illustrated book reports, hand-lettered banners, and even got paid with books and art supplies! "I could do this for a living!" he thought. After spending way too many years in college, Willie finally graduated in 2005 from the Academy of Art University in San Francisco. He now resides in New York City, where he gets to throw objects at the super-talented artists he works with. Willie's a pretty lucky guy…besides doing what he loves to do for a living, Willie finally gets to enjoy his tacos.

williereal.blogspot.com

JAKE PARKER

Jake Parker was born in Mesa, Arizona, and began drawing shortly thereafter. He drew his first comic at the age of four. These days he still draws comics, some of which can be found in the *Flight* anthologies. Jake currently works at Blue Sky Studios. He lives in Connecticut with his long-suffering wife and three spirited children.

www.agent44.com

JASON SADLER

Jason Sadler grew up in Raymond, Wisconsin. He was trained as an industrial designer and studied animation at Sheridan College in Ontario. In 1994 he moved to San Francisco and worked in the animation industry there for eleven years. He now is a concept artist/designer at Blue Sky Studios and lives in White Plains, New York, with his wife, Deborah, and their daughter, Elise.

www.sadlerish.com

DAISUKE TSUTSUMI

Born and raised in the beautiful country of anime and karaoke, Daisuke "Dice" Tsutsumi was determined at an early age to become a baseball player. When faced with the reality that he wasn't actually that good, he immigrated to America to look for something else to do.

After receiving irresponsible compliments from his nice old retired classmates in his first painting class in a small community college in New York, he decided to define his American dream as making a living painting pretty pictures. Once he graduated from the School of Visual Arts in New York, his pursuit of painting pretty pictures continued.

He has been a concept artist for Lucas Learning LTD and Blue Sky Studios and recently joined Pixar Animation Studios as an art director. Many years later, he still innocently believes in his old retired classmates' compliments.

www.simplestroke.com

LIZETTE VEGA

Born in California in 1980, Lizette grew up in the suburbs of the beautiful San Francisco Bay area. She spent most of her childhood yearning to be like Wonder Woman and She-Ra: Princess of Power. Somehow, amidst her rigorous superhero training regimen, Lizette found a passion for sketching in her spare time. Eventually that passion grew and Lizette sketched her way through the Animation and Illustration Program at San Jose State University. With a BFA in hand, she gained professional experience in various creative fields through freelance work. Companies that she has worked for include Hallmark Cards Inc., EA Games, and LeapFrog. Lizette currently lives in New York, working as a designer for Blue Sky Studios.

WILLIAM JOYCE

William Joyce has written and illustrated a number of award-winning children's books and does occasional covers for *The New Yorker*. He has won four medals from the Society of Illustrators, three Emmys, two Annie Awards, and was nominated as a producer of the year for the animated feature *Robots*. His most recent work as a production designer and producer was on the feature film *Meet the Robinsons*, based on his book *A Day with Wilbur Robinson*.

Thank YOU.

To Chris, Erich, and the rest of the crew at Villard/
Random House—we are SO lucky to be working
with all of you on this! Thank you for everything.
You rock.

Thank you, Judy! Where would we be without you?

Many thanks to the legendary Daniel López Muñoz
and Robert Mackenzie for their contributions to
OOP 2. We're so happy we could sneak you guys in!

Huge thanks to Tim Mak, who helped pave the way
for this book to get made!

To Kazu—thank you so much for helping us out at
Comic-Con and for all the great advice, insight, and
inspiration!

A big thank you goes to our good friend William
Joyce. Thanks, Bill!

We would all like to express a HUGE thank you to
Chris Wedge, who played quite a large role in bring-
ing all of us together.

Also, many thanks go out to our friends and co-
workers for their encouragement and interest in
this book. They helped keep us motivated while we
worked on it for such a long time.

Special thanks to Angela, who puts up with so much
of our nonsense.

And finally, a thank you of epic proportions to our
dearest friends in Paris: the legendary Gerald and
Sophie, and the inimitable Diane and Jean-Jacques
of Galerie Arludik—we simply can't thank you
enough for all you've done for us! What did we do
to deserve such generous and kind friends?

Andrea: I would like to thank my dear friend Tatiana for the beautiful bio. Thanks also to Mike for the enormous work in putting together this amazing book, and to Alexandra and Vanessa for the love that they give me every day! I love you.

Nash would like to thank his art and animation buds for their support and critiques. Big thanks to Dice and Mike for their guidance on the project. Thanks to Mom for convincing me to do this story for OOP 2. Huge thanks to Marisa Savulich for her sense of humor and patience with this "other" job. Finally, a big pat on the back goes to caffeine, without which this work certainly would not have been possible.

Dave: Thanks again, Mitten, for all love and support—Sock.

Mike: To Chris Gilligan and Ryan Sias - thank you SOOOO much for all your insight pulling this story together. Thanks to my OOP compadres for all their help and suggestions. Mucho kudos to Joel Carrol, who suggested I finally put this story down on paper, and to all my 3010 and DigMinerDig amigos, without whom this idea would have never come to light. A HUGE thanks to my partner, Dice, who keeps this ship afloat. And finally, none of this would have happened without my wife, Ellie—I love you so much.

Sang Jun: Thanks to my friends at Blue Sky Studios.

Benoit would like to thank his family and friends.

Kyle: Mucho love to my family tree, best bud Tim Kennaley, and Anaolga MacNaughton - you are my core.

Peter would like to thank Katherine Nix.

Vince would also like to thank Katherine Nix.

Willie: To the design crew at Blue Sky Studios, I try to absorb the talent that leaks from your pores. Thank you. Lisa, besides being radical, your editing skills made this story work. Thanks kid! Amy...there aren't enough words to describe my appreciation for your patience. You've been there for me since day one and you have been my home away from home. Thank you so much, chicita. A mi familia que nunca me dijeron que "no" y siempre me appollaron con mis suenos...los adoro mucho. Nos vemos pronto. Peace.

Jake Parker would like to thank the White Vampire, the Curly Ninja, and Sidekick for their inspiration, and Alison for her mostly unfailing support.

Jason would like to thank his wife, Deborah, and daughter, Elise, for their support and love. Thanks also to Robert Mackenzie, Jake Parker, Willie Real, Mike Knapp, and Dice Tsutsumi for their help and advice.

Dice Tsutsumi wants to thank Michael Knapp for being his partner in heading this huge project, and the rest of the OOP crew for creating such incredible stories. He also wants to thank Katie Nix, Alena Wooten, Everett Downing, Kyle MacNaughton, Enrico Casarosa, Motoko Wada, Ronnie Del Carmen, and Marit Brook-Kothlow.

Lizette would like to thank her parents, Eduardo and Connie Vega, and her sister, Michelle Vega, for their love and support. Thank you to San José State professors Alice Carter and Courtney Granner. Dice and Bob—thank you for your encouraging words. And a sincere thanks to Jeff Biancalana for being a constant source of creative inspiration.